HUDSONS
SUPER SOAP

W H SMITH & SON

No M 5433

JOE CROWFOOT

Branches & Byways
East Anglia

John Brodribb

OPC

Oxford Publishing Co

Contents

Front cover and endpapers:
The early morning goods starts from Bungay, ready to head westwards along the Waveney Valley line. The signal box and goods shed can just be seen beyond the bridge, but the red sky in the east does not bode well for the day's weather.
From a painting by Joe Crowfoot

Half title:
The Hadleigh branch ran alongside the main line from the point of divergence to Bentley station. On 12 April 1965, during the last week of service, No D5699 comes off Bentley Island curve.
G. R. Mortimer

Title page:
A train from Haverhill, headed by 'E4' No E2794, pulls away from Shelford in early British Railways days.
P. Ransome-Wallis

First published 2000

ISBN 0 86093 549 3

© Ian Allan Publishing Ltd 2000

Published by Oxford Publishing Co

an imprint of Ian Allan Publishing Ltd,
Terminal House, Station Approach, Shepperton, Surrey TW17 8AS.
Printed by Ian Allan Printing Ltd,
Riverdene Business Park, Molesey Road, Hersham, Surrey KT12 4RG.

Code: 0012/A3

Introduction

RAILWAYS succeed best where there are large volumes of people or goods to be carried for significant distances. By their very nature they are potentially much faster and safer than other forms of land transport, but in order to realise this superiority trains should not stop too often, and the track should have a good alignment. This means that railways are expensive to construct, because of the need to shift prodigious amounts of earth or rock, or build tunnels that burrow through the hills and bridges which soar over the valleys. Only the railways that serve the big cities can do this: the others must be more modest affairs, although it is also true that the grand trunk lines need the traffic which is fed on to them from their branches. In the earliest days of the railway age it was these great schemes that first came to fruition and fuelled still further the industrial revolution. More and more towns and villages wanted a part of this new mobility, of the new markets that were opened up, and the new freedom to visit the outside world. Within 50 years of the opening of the Stockton & Darlington Railway in the heart of the industrial north, almost nobody in rural East Anglia was more than five miles from a railway station. Fortunes had been made and lost, and the face of the countryside had been changed for ever.

This book is about the lines that arose towards the end of the era. In Britain there was no central planning, no strategy for rail communication. The big companies schemed and plotted against each other, and many minor railways make sense only when viewed as lines of defence to stop encroachment of a rival. Only the Board of Trade Inspectors, enforcing such regulations as there were, and making recommendations to improve safety about which the companies often complained bitterly, provided any sort of continuous thread of guidance. The big main line companies gradually bought out the local concerns, and the dreams of grandeur faded as the branches and byways settled down to their everyday work of bringing order and prosperity to the countryside. Railwaymen were relatively well paid, they wore uniforms and they had responsible, secure jobs. The railways became an unchanging, fixed part of the fabric of rural life: people set their clocks by them, went to school, went to war, went to get married on them. If only . . .

In this book, I have left spellings of place names and stations as they were at the time, while trying to say when they changed, so 'Wisbeach' and 'Wisbech' both appear. Britain's railways were mostly built in Imperial units, and paid for in pounds, shillings and pence. Speeds were calculated in miles per hour, and the timetable was written with the twelve-hour clock. Modern equivalents are not given in the text; if they were, a good half of it would be in brackets or appear as footnotes. For that reason, a summary of these systems is given here — readers above a certain age may skip this section!

The United Kingdom changed to decimal currency in February 1971. Before that, the pound (£) was worth 20 shillings (s), with a shilling, in turn, worth 12 pennies, or pence (d) — but never referred to as 'dee', and note that three pence (3d) was more like 'thrupp'nce', and similarly for other amounts. A penny could be divided into two halfpennies ('hayp'nce', ½d) or four farthings (¼d). Silver coins before World War 1 were made of silver: there were the threepenny bit (later to become a 12-sided brass coin), sixpence (6d), shilling (1s), two shillings or florin, and half crown (2s 6d). Crowns (5s) had all but gone by the turn of the century. The sovereign (£1) and half sovereign (10s) were gold coins, but because of the demands of wartime, started to be replaced by notes from about 1914. Coins were much bigger than they are today; at decimalisation the shilling turned into 5p, and the florin into 10p. Both have since shrunk greatly in size and value. The sixpence, which remained briefly in circulation, was worth 2½p.

It matters more what these coins would buy. It probably is not much use to say that in 1900 one could get a gallon of 10-year-old Scotch whisky for 23s 6d (often written 23/6), or that W. Drake's 'Perfect Shirt' cost 4s 6d each, or six for 26s. A railway carriage washer in 1911 earned 21s for a seven-day week. After all their other expenses had been met, 8s 1d was left over for the family's food; there was the man and his wife and three children. Eleven loaves of bread cost 2s 7d. Half a pound of butter cost 6d, a pound of jam 3d, two pounds of sugar 4d, and tin of milk 4d. They also spent 4d on cocoa, and 2d on suet. By the 1930s a very substantial new three-bedroomed semi-detached house in an East Anglian country town would cost about £400, just about within the reach of the better-paid railway grades, many of whom had housing provided by the company.

Wages and hours improved slowly. In 1891, a newly hired engine cleaner could expect to earn 5s per week, working five days of 12-hour shifts and a half day on Saturday. The top rate might be as much as 2s 6d a day, while a top-link engine driver would be getting something like 8s a day — and that was really good money. In the 1930s, a job in the jam factory at Tiptree paid about 29s 3d per week, while the railway offered 45s for permanent way men. It would take a full social history to go through all the changes in attitude and circumstances that have taken place, and it can be well worth pursuing this.

Weights and measures do not generally come into the picture quite as much. Weight in the Imperial system is

Above:
An Upwell train at Wisbech East station, headed by 'Y6' class No 0133. *SLS Collection*

generally measured in ounces (oz) and pounds (lb), with 16oz equal to 1lb. One stone is 14lb, and a hundredweight (cwt) is 112lb. There are 20cwt to the ton. In terms of metric equivalents, there are about 454 grams to the pound — the jar of jam, and a kilogram (a bag of sugar) is about 2.2lb. The Imperial ton and metric tonne are actually very similar. Length on the Imperial system was complex, especially as the railways were originally surveyed and built long before many more modern simplifications. The mile is straightforward enough, and five miles are roughly equivalent to eight kilometres. The mile could be simply divided into halves and quarters, which is what the railways showed on their lineside posts, but could also be divided into 8 furlongs, or 80 chains (so 10 chains to the furlong), or 320 rods, or 1,760 yards, or 5,280 feet. In surveying, the other relevant measurement was 100 links to the chain. In metric equivalent, a metre is just over a yard, or about 39 inches. In terms of area, the old and new units are the acre and hectare: the hectare is much larger, with 2.471 acres to the hectare, or 1 acre being 0.405 hectares.

I must now make some acknowledgements and thanks, for a book such as this cannot be written without a great deal of help from a great many people. First, all the staff at the County Record Offices in Cambridgeshire, Essex, Norfolk and Suffolk, without whose patience and forbearance the basic research simply could not have been done, and also those at the Saffron Walden Museum. The Great Eastern

Society has an astonishing depth and breadth of expertise within its membership, and its many publications form an invaluable archive. I must mention Rod Lock in particular for his help with Norfolk matters in general, and also Albert Godfrey. Many other people have helped, often unwittingly, and I am grateful to them. The many photographers — acknowledged by name wherever possible — are one of the most important sources of information, and it is self-evident that no book such as this could be compiled without their work over many years. I apologise if your favourite line or station is not in here — from wondering whether there were enough byways and branches to fill a book, it turns out that there were quite enough to fill several. There are various detailed and specialised volumes on particular branches, many unfortunately out of print, and they are usually well worth finding.

On that note, do go and seek out what remains on the ground. A good map is essential, such as the new 'Explorer' series from the Ordnance Survey, and there is much to be seen, even on Railtrack. You can savour the newly restored buildings at Braintree, or ride along the Bure Valley Railway and see Coltishall station. Walk along the Marriotts Way and sample the 'Round the World' line, or the Stour Valley path, or the Flitch Way, or many more.

Lastly I must thank my wife Wendy for her patience while this book has been researched and written; it would have been much harder work without her.

Brightlingsea Branch

THE Tendring Hundred is that area of north Essex very roughly bounded by the coast, the Stour and Colne estuaries, and a line from Wivenhoe to Manningtree. Railway development in the area started with the building of the goods branch from Colchester to the Hythe, a busy port on the Colne, and which opened in April 1847. This was later extended by the Tendring Hundred Railway, which reached Wivenhoe in May 1863 and Walton four years later.

The bill for the Wivenhoe & Brightlingsea Railway was deposited in November 1860, with J. C. Greaves and James S. Cook as the engineers. The line was proposed to make an end-on junction with the Tendring Hundred just to the east of Wivenhoe station, on the Colchester side of Colchester Road. The line was to be exactly five miles, mainly following the estuary, but curving back to the northeast to enter the town. It was to be mostly level, with a few very short lengths of 1 in 200. There was to be a bridge over Alresford Creek, about two miles from Wivenhoe, which would have two arches of 40ft span, with 20ft clearance at low water, plus another 18 arches of 20ft span and 18ft clearance.

There were considerable problems with the line, and by the time the Tendring Hundred was authorised to extend to Walton from a point a quarter of a mile along the Brightlingsea branch, nothing had been done. The THR had to take powers the following year to allow it to build this intervening section should the Brightlingsea company be in default by November of 1864, which it was. Disputes continued for many years afterwards about the costs incurred, all of which were to be borne by the W&B.

Nothing daunted, the Brightlingsea & St Osyth Railway was promoted in a bill deposited in November 1864. James S. Cook was again the engineer. The Great Eastern was authorised to subscribe, and it would use the W&B station at Brightlingsea, making an end-on junction with it. The proposed line looped round to the north so that it could get around Brightlingsea Creek, before turning southwards on a three-furlong radius curve, and was to have a total length of 3 miles 5 furlongs and 4 chains; it stopped just short of St Osyth itself. It was to be much more steeply graded than the earlier line, with about 1¼ miles at between 1 in 72½ to 1 in 78. It had been impossible to raise money for the line from Wivenhoe locally — only when the Great Eastern offered to subscribe one-third of the necessary capital could the project go ahead — and the

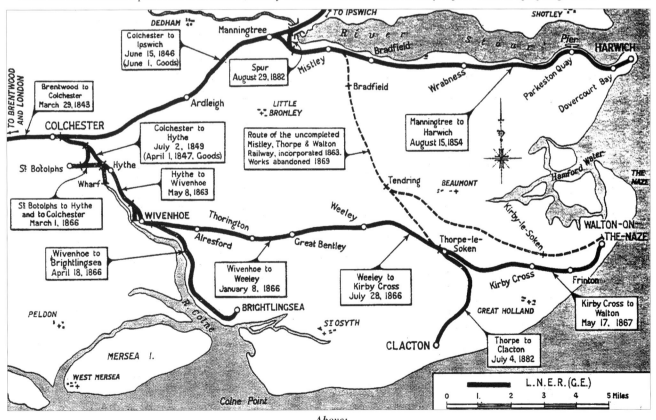

Above:
The railways in the Tendring Hundred of Essex, including the Brightlingsea branch. *The Railway Magazine*

Above:
Brightlingsea in 1937, viewed from the Wivenhoe end. This fine panorama shows the engine shed, goods yard and passenger station; the train at the platform is headed by No 8041. *W. A. Camwell (SLS Collection)*

Below:
Brightlingsea station, 1897. *Crown Copyright*

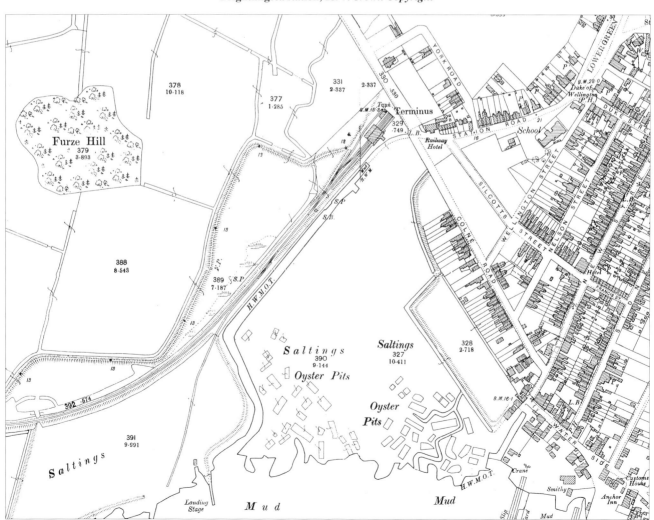

Above:
**A train for Wivenhoe stands at Brightlingsea on 17 April 1949,
in the charge of 'J15' No 65448. The coaching stock is a
mixture of ex-North Eastern (No 7624) and ex-GER
(Nos 63487 and 82003).** *W. A. Camwell (SLS Collection)*

extension to St Osyth was just too much. The line opened on
18 April 1866, with the crossing of Alresford Creek being by swing
bridge. There were no intermediate stations, and the line was
worked by the Great Eastern for 40% of receipts. The Wivenhoe &
Brightlingsea was eventually bought out by the GER in 1891.

Many branch trains operated to and from St Botolphs station in
Colchester, which was much more conveniently placed for the
town centre than North station, on the main line. This was (and is) a
single-platform terminus, reached via a triangular junction from the
Clacton and Walton line of the Tendring Hundred Railway. Hythe
station was reached a mile from St Botolphs, and handled a very
considerable quantity and variety of goods traffic. The line then ran
parallel with the River Colne to Wivenhoe, a further 2½ miles,
where there were slipways and shipbuilding yards.

Branch trains then diverged to the right on to the single-track
line, which was worked by train staff without tickets. The distance
from Wivenhoe was exactly five miles, and trains were booked
about 11-13 minutes for the journey. It was a picturesque run, with
the Colne to the right, and Mersea Island on its far bank. Passage
of the swing bridge over Alresford Creek required the use of
a pilotman until about 1927, and a slowing to 10mph. The creek
had been used at one time by barges going to sand mills and
Thorington water mill.

The original Brightlingsea station was described as draughty and
barn-like, and was destroyed by fire on New Year's Eve 1901, to
the jubilation of the local people who joined hands and sang 'Auld
Lang Syne' nearby. The replacement had a single platform with
run-round loop, which itself terminated in a fish loading dock. The
goods station was provided with three roads, and served the nearby
gas works, slipways and fish-landing causeway. The signalbox and
signals were abolished in 1922 (except for a fixed distant), with the
points thereafter being worked by ground frames released by a key

Above:
**The water column at Brightlingsea was at the end of the
platform. Here, the branch engine slakes its thirst before setting
back on to its train.** *John Brodribb collection*

Above:
Class J15 0-6-0 No 65432 arrives at Brightlingsea on 26 February 1957.
Diesel multiple-units took over the service on 4 March. *John Brodribb collection*

Below:
'J15' No 65424 takes water at the platform end at Brightlingsea. The tender cab must
have been very welcome out on the marshes in winter. *John Brodribb collection*

Above:
**An atmospheric view of Brightlingsea across the large goods yard as the
'J15' runs round its train; 26 February 1957.** *John Brodribb collection*

on the train staff and the branch being worked on the one-engine-in-steam principle.

Service levels varied considerable through the life of the branch. In 1874 there were only four return trips on weekdays, leaving Wivenhoe at 7.30am, 11.50am, 2.55pm and 6.33pm, and returning from Brightlingsea at 8am, 12.50pm, 5.5pm and 7.5pm. The first down and last up trains worked from or to Colchester, and the running time on the branch was 15 minutes. Matters were much better by summer 1922, when there were nine down and eight up services each weekday, with three return trips on Sundays. It was even better in 1937, when there were 10 down trains Mondays to Fridays, with two extra on Saturdays, the best trains giving a journey time of about 1¾ hours from London. The Sunday service had expanded to seven trains, and several worked to and from St Botolphs.

Even the wartime services from May 1942 still showed 11 down trains Mondays to Fridays, and one less on Saturdays, with a similar pattern in the other direction. The first left Brightlingsea at 6.57am, and gave a connection at Wivenhoe for London, arriving there at 8.51am. The last was at 9.1pm, to Wivenhoe only. This returned to Brightlingsea at 9.24pm, giving a connection off the 7.30pm from Liverpool Street, which required a further change at Colchester North. There were still four each way on the branch on Sundays.

Postwar traffic saw heavy loadings on Sundays and Bank Holidays, with trippers taking advantage of cheap day fares. On the latter, trains were often too long for the platforms, and it was necessary for the train engine to pull right up to the stops in order for the rear coaches to get into the platform. Another locomotive would be waiting on the goods yard, and would then back on to the train and depart. After this the first locomotive would run to the yard and await the next incoming service, and repeat the procedure. On an ordinary weekday in May 1949, there were 12 or 13 trains each way with a connection to or from Liverpool Street, and five or six on Sundays. The third class monthly return fare was 17s 1d, and first class 25s 3d. Brightlingsea was noted for its Pyfleet oysters,

Below:
A diesel multiple-unit for Brightlingsea approaches the junction at Wivenhoe. *Ian Allan Library*

Table 27 COLCHESTER, BRIGHTLINGSEA, FRINTON-ON-SEA, WALTON-ON-NAZE and CLACTON-ON-SEA

Week Days

(Detailed departure/arrival timetable — station rows including London (Liverpool St.), Colchester, St. Botolph's, Hythe, Wivenhoe, Brightlingsea, Alresford, Thorington, Great Bentley, Weeley, Thorpe-le-Soken, Kirby Cross, Frinton-on-Sea, Walton-on-Naze, Clacton-on-Sea A.)

Week Days—continued / **Sundays**

Footnotes

A Clacton-on-Sea and Holland-on-Sea
B On Saturdays departs Liverpool Street 2 15 pm

C Calls when required to set down passengers only
E or E Except Saturdays

F 3 minutes later on Saturdays
hh From Colchester, dep 5 42 pm
RC Refreshment Car

S Saturdays only
T Through Train from Liverpool Street
U 2 minutes later on Saturdays

Above and below: September 1955–June 1956 timetables. *Author's Collection*

Table 27—continued CLACTON-ON-SEA, WALTON-ON-NAZE, FRINTON-ON-SEA, BRIGHTLINGSEA and COLCHESTER

Week Days

(Detailed departure/arrival timetable — station rows including Clacton-on-Sea A, Thorpe-le-Soken, Walton-on-Naze, Frinton-on-Sea, Kirby Cross, Weeley, Great Bentley, Thorington, Alresford, Wivenhoe, Brightlingsea, Hythe, St. Botolph's, Colchester, London (Liverpool St.).)

Week Days—continued / **Sundays**

Footnotes

A Clacton-on-Sea and Holland-on-Sea
B On Saturdays runs 2 minutes *earlier*
D 4 minutes later on Saturdays

E Except Saturdays
G On Saturdays arrives 12 53 pm

H Arr 1 40 pm on Saturdays
K On Saturdays arrives 4 8 pm
RC Refreshment Car

S or S Saturdays only
T Through Train to Liverpool Street

Above:
A Wickham lightweight two-car DMU has just left Brightlingsea for Wivenhoe on 27 July 1960. *Frank Church*

Below:
ABC Railway Guide, 1949. *Author's Collection*

and it was usual for at least one fish van to be attached to almost every outgoing train. Goods traffic on the branch was usually worked by mixed trains, with the wagons being attached or detached at Wivenhoe. In season 'Sprat Specials' were worked as required. The station could handle all classes of traffic except for livestock, and had its own 1½-ton crane.

Motive power varied little. For many years ex-Great Eastern 2-4-2 tanks of Classes F3, F4, F5 and F7 handled services, with occasional help from a 'G5' class 0-4-4T. 'E4' class 2-4-0 tender engines occasionally ventured along the branch, together with 'J65'-'J69' class 0-6-0Ts. Unrebuilt 'Claud Hamiltons' were also occasional visitors. However, the ubiquitous 'J15s' seem to have taken over almost completely from about 1939 until replacement by diesel multiple-units. Coaching stock was generally Great Eastern six-wheelers until 1935 when it was replaced by bogie corridor and semi-corridor stock from both Great Eastern and North Eastern railways.

The floods of January 1953 were disastrous for the Brightlingsea branch, the line being severed from 1 February after nearly three miles of track were washed out. This led to British Railways proposing not to repair the permanent way and close the branch, which caused a storm of local protest. It was reinstated, goods traffic having been maintained by means of road transport, and the service resumed on Monday, 7 December 1953. The first train, the 6.40am from Brightlingsea,

was worked as empty stock from Colchester, and consisted of four non-corridor coaches hauled by 'J15' No 65432. It left with a good complement of passengers, and was accompanied by blasts from the locomotive's whistle and many exploding detonators. An initial speed limit of 25mph was imposed, so it was five minutes late arriving at Wivenhoe. The first down train left Colchester at 6.37am and was worked by Class 2 No 46468. The new service consisted of 11 trains each way on weekdays, with two down and three up on Sundays.

In the period following reopening, traffic levels continued to be good for some time. Throughout the 1950s and early '60s passenger levels held up at about 3,000 per week in winter and 5,000 in summer, with tickets being issued by the guards on the diesel multiple-unit trains, introduced in the mid-1950s. In 1962, Stationmaster S. E. W. Allen was in charge of Wivenhoe, Brightlingsea and Alresford with Arthur Cox, one of the clerks, at the branch terminus. He was born in the town and had then worked at the station for over 38 years — almost his entire railway career. Oysters and shipbuilding continued to provide traffic for the branch, although by the Summer 1956 timetable there were no regular booked goods workings.

The passenger figures quoted above were not nearly enough to save the branch. The Beeching report estimated the cost of a diesel multiple-unit at about 4s 0d–6s 0d per train mile, according to traffic density, the cost of stations at £2,500 per

BRIGHTLINGSEA (Essex)
Miles 62¾. Map Sq. 24.
Pop. 4,145. Clos. day Thur.
From Liverpool Street via Colchester.
1st cl.—Single 21/1, Mth. Ret. 25/8.
3rd cl.—Single 12/8, Mth. Ret. 17/1.

	Liv. St.	Bright.	Bright.	Liv. St.
	a.m.		a.m.	
	4 25	7 32	6 42r	8 51
	8 12r	10 22	7 40er	9 43
	8 24	10 55	7 40sr	9 46
	10 25r	12 42	8 40	11 5
	11 10e	2 12	11 2r	1 38
	p.m.		p.m.	
	12 38s	2 22	12 58s	3 1
	1 0er	3 22	12 58e	3 20
	1 30sr	3 22	2 31s🅰	4 54
	2 18	4 57	2 31r	5 8
	3 48k	5 52	4 15	6 52
	4 57er	6 53	5 15	8 11
	4 57s	6 53	6 .5k	9 4
	5 8sr	7 32	8 2	10 22
	5 30er	7 32	9 4	12 22
	8 44	8 50	—	—
	8 45	10 56	—	—

Sunday Trains.

	a.m.		a.m.	
	8 30	11 13	9 7	11 34
	10 0	12 42	p.m.	
	11 50	2 12	12 55	3 36
			4 35	6 40
	p.m.			
	3 55	5 57	6 52	9 25
	6 5	8 47	8 12	10 25
			9 5	12 37

🅰 3rd cl. only.
e Not Sat.   r Refresh. Car.
k Not Fri. or s Sat. only.
Sat.

WALTON, CLACTON AND BRIGHTLINGSEA TO COLCHESTER

UP

Mileage M	C	M	C	Station		K Q am	G SX am	G SX am	K SO am	G SO am	K SX am	K SX am	K SX PM
0	0			WALTON-ON-NAZE	dep 1								
1	24			Frinton-on-Sea arr	2								
				dep	3								
2	43			Kirby Cross arr	4								
				dep	5								
5	9	0	0	CLACTON-ON-SEA dep	6		7 30						
		4	50	Thorpe-le-Soken arr	7		7 40						
				dep	8								
7	20	6	61	Weeley arr	9								
				dep	10								
9	30	8	71	Great Bentley arr	11								
				dep	12								
10	50	10	11	Thorington arr	13								
				dep	14								
12	33	11	74	Alresford arr	15								
				dep	16								
				BRIGHTLINGSEA dep	17								
14	12	13	53	Wivenhoe arr	18								
				dep	19				9||10	9||32			
16	45	16	6	Hythe arr	20				9||20				
				dep	21	7 25						10 52	
		17	8	St. Botolph's arr	22								
				dep	23				8 47	9 44		10 58	12 13
				East Gate Siding arr	24	7 30							
18	42	19	30	COLCHESTER STN arr	25					9||47			
				dep	26				8 58	9 55			12 25
19	15	20	3	Colchester Goods Yard arr	27				9 11	10 3			12 33

Column notes (vertical): G (col 2) "After working £17 am from Colchester. To work 7.54 am to Walton"; SO (col 4) "Runs via Ground Frame route"; SO (col 5) "After working 5.43 am from Colchester"; SX (col 6) "Runs via Ground Frame route"; SX (col 8) "Runs via Ground Frame Route".

COLCHESTER TO BRIGHTLINGSEA, CLACTON AND WALTON

DOWN

Mileage Direct M	C	Via St. Botolph's M	C	Station		J SO am	J SX am	J SO am	J SX am	K SX am	K SO am	K SO am	K SX am	K am	K SX am
0	0	0	0	Colchester Goods Yd dep	1	5 17	5 17	5 27	5 27	5 43	5 43			6 50	7 7
0	53	0	53	COLCHESTER STN arr	2										
				dep	3	5 20	5 20	5 30	5 30	5 46	5 46			6 53	7 10
				East Gate Siding dep	4										
		2	75	St. Botolph's arr	5	5 27			5 37					7 0	
				dep	6										
2	50	3	77	Hythe arr	7					5 53	5 53				
				dep	8							7 25			
4	83	6	30	Wivenhoe arr	9							7 35			7 25
				dep	10			5 30	5 40						8 2
10	7	11	34	BRIGHTLINGSEA arr	11										
6	62	8	9	Alresford arr	12										8 12
				dep	13										8 29
7	75	9	72	Thorington arr	14										8 36
				dep	15										8 50
9	65	11	2	Great Bentley arr	16										8 56
				dep	17										9 10
11	75	13	32	Weeley arr	18			5 43	5 53						9 18
				dep	19			5 55	6 10						9 33
14	6	15	33	Thorpe-le-Soken arr	20			6 2	6 17						9 40
				dep	21			6 20	7 2			7 35	7 56		9 55
18	56	20	3	CLACTON-ON-SEA arr	22			6 33	7 15						10 8
16	52	17	59	Kirby Cross arr	23							7 43	8 4		
				dep	24							8 15	8 30		
17	71	19	18	Frinton-on-Sea arr	25							8 21	8 36		
				dep	26							8 41	9 5		
19	15	20	42	WALTON-ON-NAZE arr	27							8 47	9 11		

BRIGHTLINGSEA (Essex)
61¼ miles. Pop. 4,502. E.C. Thur.
From Liverpool Street via Wivenhoe.
2nd class 15/6, 1st class 23/3.

Liv. St.	Brightl.	Brightl.	Liv. St.
a.m.		a.m.	
4 35	7 48	6 32	8 26
7 0	9 7	7 2 e	8 35
8b 0 e	9 57	7 2 s	9b 4
8b 0 s	10 3	7 55	9b43
9b30 e	10 59	9 24 e	11b25
9b30 s	11 3	9 27 s	11b25
10b 0 e	11 57	10 5 e	11b40
10b 0 s	12 3	10 8 s	11b40
11b30 e	12 59	11 25	1b25
11b30 s	1 5	p.m.	
12b 0 e	1 57	12 5 e	1r40
12b 0 s	2 28	12 8 s	1r40
p.m.		1 25 e	3b25
1b30 s	3 17	1 28 s	3b25
2b 0 s	3 59	2 4 e	3b40
2b 0 e	4 34	3 23 s	5b25
3b30 s	5 5	4 4 s	5b40
3b30 e	5 23	5 13 s	7b25
4b 0 s	6 0	5 34 e	7b40
4 33 e	6 18	6 5 s	7b40
5b27 e	7 3	6 30 e	8b20
5b30 s	7 3	7 23	9 7
6b10 s	7 53	8 25 e	10 25
6 20 e	8 0	8 30 s	10 30
7b30 e	8 58	9 30	11 27
7b30 s	9 1	—	—
8b30	10 10	—	—

Sunday Trains.

p.m.		p.m.	
2 0	3 51	5 35	7 25
5b30	6 58	7 29	9b10

Above:
ABC Railway Guide, 1962.
Author's Collection

Left and top left:
**11 June–16 September
1956 timetable.**
Author's Collection

annum, and route maintenance and signalling costs at £3,000 per mile per annum. Even had the summer traffic figures applied all year round on the Brightlingsea branch, there would still have been a deficit of £400 per mile per annum when comparing passenger revenue with movement costs, and a loss of £2,200 per mile per annum when compared with overall costs. The latter assumed that a freight service was in operation, and although officially open for goods traffic, it was very sparse. The estimated loss with no goods services was £4,400 per mile per annum. The report concluded that if there were only a stopping passenger service, a route needed a minimum of 17,000 passengers per week to pay its way. No account was taken of the contribution of branch lines and feeder services to main line revenues, or of the social and environmental costs of such service withdrawal.

In the light of this, branch passenger services were proposed for withdrawal in the Beeching report. It had retained a Sunday service to the very end, with two return trips in the branch winter timetable, which ended on 10 May. They ran from Colchester at 3.30pm and 5.30pm, calling only at Wivenhoe, and returning at 5.50pm and 7.40pm. The branch summer timetable, introduced the following week, had seven return trains, mostly all stations to and from St Botolphs, although the 11.35am to Wivenhoe and 11.57am return were short workings. The weekday timetable showed 13 down trains Monday to Friday, with 16 on Saturdays. The up service showed 12 trains Mondays to Fridays, and 16 on Saturdays. Complete closure came about on and from Monday, 15 June 1964, the start of the full summer timetable, with the last trains running on the previous day. For a time, Brightlingsea continued to appear in the timetable with a note to say that services had been withdrawn; later a note showed that Alresford was the nearest station and that bus services were provided by Eastern National. Yet another well-used but unremunerative branch had been erased from the system.

Elsenham
and Thaxted Line

THE line to Thaxted was one of the last to be built in East Anglia and the first to be closed. It did not open until 1 April 1913, closing to passengers in 1952 and for goods in June 1953 — a total working life of 40 years. It had an exceptionally long gestation, having been first authorised in 1906 and mooted 10 years earlier.

Railway communication first reached the area in 1845, when the Eastern Counties opened to Elsenham. In due course the branches to Saffron Walden and Dunmow were built, bringing Thaxted within about seven miles of each. It had been a town of the first importance in mediaeval times, but had declined since then, especially with the absence of a direct rail connection. The 1896 Light Railways Act provided the impetus for action.

The first scheme was for a line from Elsenham, through Thaxted to Great Bardfield, a village some four miles to the east, plans for which were deposited as early as December 1896. The promoters were Sir Walter Gilbey, Thomas Bradridge of Great Bardfield, Archibald Weyland Ruggles Brise of Finchingfield, Charles Gold of Stansted, George Lee, Charles Alfred Parker of Finsbury Circus in London and George West of Thaxted. The line was planned to follow more or less the same route as the one built between Elsenham and Thaxted, and then extend via a roundabout route to Great Bardfield, giving a total length of 10 miles 6 furlongs 6 chains. The terminus would have been about half a mile north of Great Bardfield on the Finchingfield road. Trains would have run into the east side of the up platform at Elsenham, and there would

have been another line forming the other side of the triangle, again similar to the scheme as built, going to exchange sidings on the north side of the main line station. The maximum speed laid down was 20mph, and there was no need to provide second class carriages or tickets; the Great Eastern was authorised to subscribe up to £10,000 to the scheme, the total cost being estimated at just over £30,000. The steepest gradient would have been 1 in 45, and three years were allowed for its construction. Interestingly, the proposed gauge was to be 2ft 6in. Nothing came of this scheme, presumably because of lack of financial interest, possibly exacerbated by the need for transhipment of all goods at Elsenham.

Another scheme, this time only to Thaxted, was proposed in 1906. It was intended as a single-track, standard gauge line, 5 miles 66 chains in length, and terminating an inconvenient one mile from the town. The projected cost was £33,000, the Great Eastern paying half, with Treasury grants of £15,000 being given under the 1896 Act. A. P. Humphreys, of the Horham Hall Estate at Thaxted, gave land for the line, on the understanding that the railway company would construct three level crossings, 11 field gates, a stopping point and a drinking place for cattle. Other landowners also donated land — all corn grown on local farms had to be put on rail at Dunmow (6 miles) or Elsenham (6½ miles) and it was felt that the local estates would benefit from the new line.

The stopping place mentioned above was proposed for Plonks (4 miles and 5 furlongs from Elsenham), and became Cutler's Green; another was to be built at Henham. A third was proposed for Lovecots Farm, this time with a siding, and when built became 'Sibley's for Chickney & Broxted'.

Dunmow Rural District Council showed little interest in the line, which is not surprising as it would diminish the traffic via their town. By 1908, the council was in correspondence with the Great Eastern, and was sceptical about the line. A letter dated 23 January comments that 'we do not think it seems much good at present to approach them [the Great Eastern] as the railway has been projected for so long that it is sceptically regarded by all except a few of the "faithful".' For its part the GER had agreed to make a stopping place at Plonks if there were a good road, which meant the council taking over the Cutler's Green to Plonks road. The council, on the other hand, would not make up the road unless given

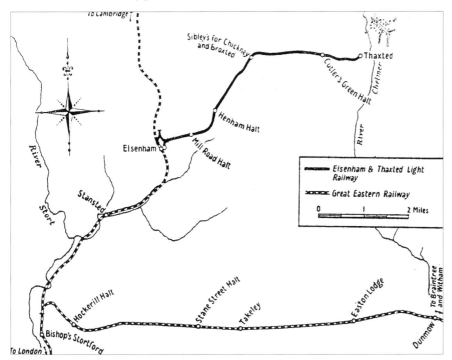

Left:
The Elsenham & Thaxted Light Railway.
The Railway Magazine

Above:
Elsenham station, seen around 1960, photographed from the up main platform, with the Thaxted train standing at the back. There was no connection between the lines at this point. *Stations UK*

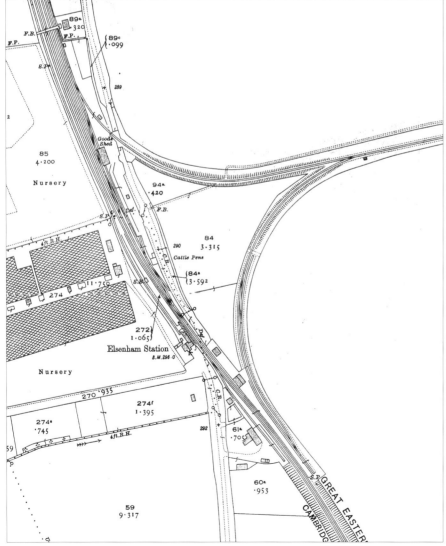

Left:
Elsenham station, 1920.
Crown Copyright

Above:
**Elsenham station, around 1950, with 'J69' 0-6-0T No 68579 having just
arrived from Thaxted. This view is looking north.** *Stations UK*

financial assistance. The cost of the stopping place here was
variously given as £65, £75 or £110.

Matters dragged on. In correspondence with A. P. Humphreys in
June 1911, the Great Eastern had reportedly said that it 'intended to
commence construction . . . at once', although concern was being
expressed that the railway company, which had evidently acquired
the necessary land, should take steps to keep it in order. The
problem was the funding of the line, and local solicitors were
anxious about their fees!

Work eventually started, the first sod being cut by Sir Walter
Gilbey at Thaxted on 25 July 1911. Construction was not without
incident. On Monday, 1 July 1912, a platelayer was killed in an
accident on the line. The *East Anglian Daily Times* reported that a
construction gang had been ordered back to Henham to unload
ballast from trucks. Thirty men got on to the tender of an engine
and sat on the coal, with their legs dangling over the sides. The
engine set off and the driver braked when nearing the trucks, but to
no effect, and it smashed tender-first into the trucks. Charles
Clayden, of Quendon, was thrown off the tender and fell between it
and the trucks and was killed immediately. Walter Dennison
sustained a broken leg and was taken to Addenbrookes hospital,
while Neville and Palmer were seriously injured. An inquest was
held the following day at the Congregational Schoolroom,
Henham, and a verdict of 'accidental death' was returned.

The line finally opened to the public on Tuesday, 1 April 1913.
The formal ceremony had been performed the previous day by Sir
Walter Gilbey, who had returned especially for the occasion from
Brighton. He had been involved from the very start, having been a
promoter of the narrow gauge proposal soon after the passage of
the 1896 Light Railways Act. A special train was run by the Great
Eastern from Liverpool Street, which conveyed many officials
including Mr W. H. Hyde, the general manager, and Mr F. G.

Randall, superintendent of the line. A number of Cambridge
officials of the GER were also present, including the district
superintendent, Mr J. B. Fitzjohn. During the course of the usual
laudatory speeches, comparison was made with the recently
opened Kelvedon & Tollesbury line, which was said to be
producing very satisfactory results.

The length of the new line was given as 5 miles 41 chains, with
the terminal station three-quarters of a mile from the town,
because of the expense of carrying it over the 'deep valley' of the
infant River Chelmer. There were halts at Henham and Cutler's
Green, while Sibley (for Broxted & Chickney) and Thaxted were
stations. At the latter, the staff were to be a foreman and assistant,
while the whole line came under the control of Mr H. M. Butters,
Elsenham stationmaster.

The layout at Elsenham was triangular, with the main line and
up platform along the western edge. Thaxted trains had their own
face on the east side of the up platform, but made no connection
with the main line. This was done by the third side, which joined
to the up-side goods sidings although the track layout did not
permit through running to the branch from either direction.
Curving away sharply from the platform, a Thaxted train passed
over the junction with the line to the goods yard, which was
controlled by a small lever frame locked by an Annett's key
attached to the train staff. The line then ran straight to Mill Road
Halt, about a mile from Elsenham, which had a low platform
characteristic of the line and was not opened until the mid-1920s.
Henham Halt was a further three-quarters of a mile, along rather
more sinuous track, again having minimal facilities. Both had
ungated level crossings which were restricted to 10mph and
protected by steel cattle guards. The line undulated somewhat on
its course to Sibley's, at 3 miles from Elsenham, and which also
had an ungated crossing. The station boasted a goods loop and

Left:
**An early view of a Thaxted train
which has just left Elsenham.**
*Ian Allan Library/
Bucknall Collection*

loading gauge, a small station building and van body as a store on the platform, which was on the northwest side of the line.

Leaving Sibley's the line curved sharply to the right to cross the valley of a stream, and then continued more or less straight to Cutler's Green, a halt with no road access. A small footpath crossed the line here and served some local farms. A coach body on the platform provided shelter. Beyond the halt the line again curved sharply, first following the course of the Stan Brook, but then turning northwards to approach Thaxted station. The distance from the town was made worse by the fact that it was at the end of a lane at the top of a hill, from which it was necessary to descend into the valley and then climb back up again. John William Jeffrey had a coal and coke business at the station, but with a population in 1922 of only 1,672 there was never going to be heavy traffic.

The branch was worked on the one-engine-in-steam principle, with a train staff without tickets, which was round and painted green. The speed limit was 25mph, and 10mph over the ungated crossings, and some of the sharper curves were of less than 9 chains radius. Speed limit boards protected the crossings 200 yards in advance, and 'Beware of the Trains' boards were placed 50 yards from each crossing on the public roads. Curiously, the only gated crossing on the branch was over the connection to Elsenham goods yard, which was not used by passenger trains. The gates normally

had to be kept locked across the railway, and had to be operated by a competent member of the station staff. Although not normally used, tender engines were restricted to 15mph running tender first. The axle limit was 16 tons, raised from an initial 14 tons. Elsenham, Sibley's and Thaxted station platforms each had siding loops, which were fitted with Hodgeson's patent hand-bolt point locks, keys for these being attached to the train staff. There were two: one painted red and used to unlock the points in the main line, and the other painted blue for the points in the sidings. Use of a tow rope was permitted at Thaxted and Sibley's, it being carried in the branch goods brake van.

The service at the opening was five trains each way daily, but by 1922 there were seven to Thaxted on Mondays to Fridays, with an extra on Saturdays. The service was unbalanced, with one fewer in the other direction. The 1937 timetable showed a goods train at 6am from Thaxted to Elsenham, taking 20 minutes, and carrying coal empties and 'unimportant down road traffic'. Having done the station shunting at Elsenham, it returned at 7.38am with the newspapers off the 5.56am from Liverpool Street, and called at Sibley's to put out papers. The 10.40am, 12.17pm Saturdays only, 1.45pm and 6.23pm SO (6.27pm SX) were booked as mixed from Thaxted, the remainder being passenger only. The 8.15am up from Thaxted, a passenger train, was permitted to work one wagon of

Above:
**Henham Halt, the first stop on the light railway from Elsenham to Thaxted.
Typical waiting accommodation is provided.** *Stations UK*

Above:
The 11.50am from Thaxted to Elsenham calling at Sibleys, on 16 April 1949. *W. A. Camwell (SLS Collection)*

Below:
Sibleys station, 1920. *Crown Copyright*

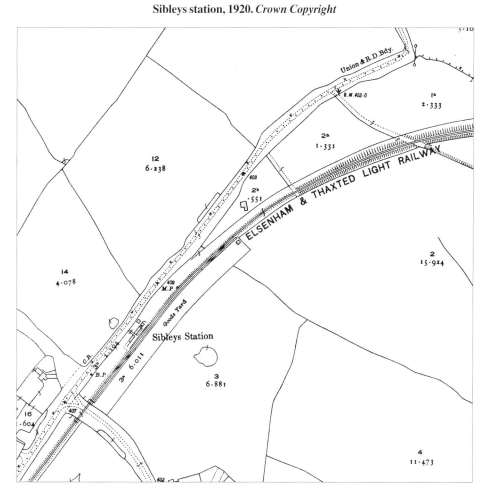

Two views of Cutlers Green Halt which make an interesting comparison. The one view is clearly brand-new, with the final preparations under way for the opening on 1 April 1913 — lamps are being fitted, the platform edge whitened, and railings are being painted. The other shows it in 1950, shortly before closure. Shelter has been provided and the nameboard has had to be moved, and only one lamp remains.
Stations UK (2)

cattle to Elsenham on Tuesdays and Thursdays. The 2.26pm SX mixed was permitted to shunt at Sibley's if necessary, in which case it arrived at Thaxted at 3.1pm instead of 2.50pm. Thaxted station could handle all classes of traffic, although no crane was provided. Sibley's handled only goods, passenger and parcels traffic.

During World War 2, the service was reduced to two trains each way on weekdays, although this rose to five and then six from Thaxted on Mondays to Fridays by 1951. Saturdays saw four and five respectively. Rolling stock was initially provided by Great Eastern conversions of six-wheeled coaches which had their internal partitions and some of the doors removed. Tramcar-type seats were fitted, and steps to the remaining doors to suit the low platforms. This meant that they were foul of the main line loading gauge, and the steps had to be removed when the coaches went to Stratford for maintenance. Early in 1948 they were replaced by GER centre-corridor bogie vehicles similar to those used on the first special train to Thaxted when the line opened.

Locomotives on the line were usually the GER 0-6-0T Classes J67, J68 or J69, with occasional forays by Class J15s. The branch engine was out-based in the corrugated iron shed at Thaxted, a sub-shed of Cambridge. Tickets for the branch were never issued at stations — not even Elsenham — and passengers had to buy them

from the guard on the train. Latterly, only singles were available, and there were no through bookings to the branch. Tickets were printed on white paper, and cancelled by bell-punch.

Traffic had been falling for some years when closure was announced. On one occasion in the early 1950s, a locomotive had derailed and all the passengers were taken onwards in a taxi. Likewise, it was felt that goods traffic could easily be handled by road vehicles. The death-knell was an application by British Transport Commission-controlled Eastern National to put on a bus service between Bishop's Stortford and Thaxted. Closure to passengers took place on and from Monday, 15 September 1952, with the last trains running on the previous Saturday. One man who had served the railway for almost its entire life — and his working life — was Mr P. Reeve, who had started as a guard on the line when it opened in 1913, and who retired on Saturday, 29 September 1951 after 51 years of railway service. Regular travellers on the line presented him with a pewter tankard on the following Monday. Goods trains were withdrawn the following year, with Thaxted and Sibley's closing on and from Monday 1 June 1953. Today there is little trace of the lightly built line, and Thaxted remains a quiet and charming country town. The light railway never did propel it into the modern age, as its promoters had hoped.

Left:
The terminus at Thaxted was a modest one, with most of the facilities apparent in this view with the branch coaches standing at the platform. The station was the best part of a mile from the town.
Stations UK

Right:
The branch loco, No 7193, on shed at Thaxted.
Adrian Vaughan collection

Left:
The branch terminus at Thaxted on 16 April 1949, with locomotive No 68609 heading coaches Nos 61471 and 62450 which will form the 11.50am to Elsenham.
*W. A. Camwell
(SLS Collection)*

Eye Branch

EYE is a small Suffolk town of considerable antiquity, and one that much of the modern world seems to have passed by. It retains many fine old buildings and a compact street layout, and was once a centre for much of the surrounding countryside. It featured in many of the very early railway schemes, and could have been on the main line from London to Norwich. In the event it had to make do with a short branch line whose passenger service closed rather early, and there are now few traces of the former railway, although one of them, a bridge at Yaxley, can be seen clearly from the nearby A140 road.

The Mellis & Eye line was authorised on 5 July 1865, with £15,000 authorised capital made up of 1,500 £10 shares. Its powers for land purchase would expire after two years, and the line had to be completed within three. There were to be no coke ovens or other manufacturing works of any description where the line passed the Yaxley Hall estate. A bridge was to be provided across the line for Patrick Robert Welch. The charges that could be levied were tightly prescribed, and a small parcel could be up to 7½lb in weight. Luggage allowances were 120lb first class, 100lb second and 60lb third. The directors were named as Sir Edward Clarence Kerrison, Rt Hon John Henniker-Major, Lord Henniker, John Major Henniker-Major, Edward Chenery, Benjamin Cotton Etheridge and Robert Chase; powers were taken for the Great Eastern to maintain, manage and work the line.

Construction of the short line went ahead without any notable difficulties, and the opening date was scheduled for Tuesday, 2 April 1867. Sir Edward Kerrison (chairman), his deputy Mr Edward Chenery and a large party of ladies and gentlemen travelled the line during the day in order to inspect the stations, sheds and sidings which were felt necessary to accommodate the large business that they confidently expected. All had been completed, and the single line was to be worked by the Great Eastern Railway for 50% of the gross receipts. Trains were scheduled to leave Eye at 6.30, 7.10 and 11.55am, 3.20, 4.10 and 7.30pm, returning from Mellis at 6.50 and 7.35am, and 12.45, and 3.45, 6.15 and 7.50pm; however, the *Ipswich Journal* reported that the service consisted of five trains each way. The journey was to take 10 minutes over the short distance of 2 miles 71 chains. The times varied a little over the years, and in 1875 the only significant difference was that the 7.10am from Eye and return had been retimed to 9.20am, returning from Mellis at 9.40am.

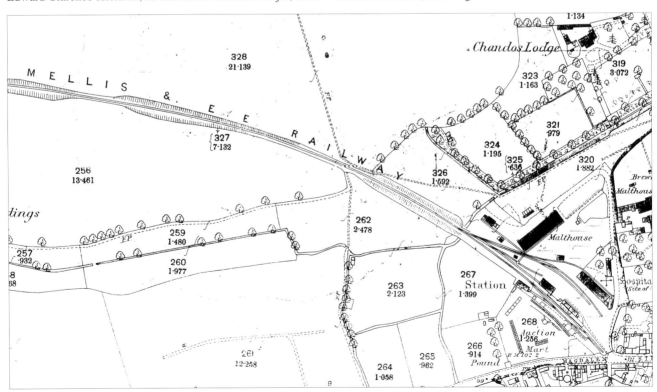

Above:
Eye station, 1886. *Crown Copyright*

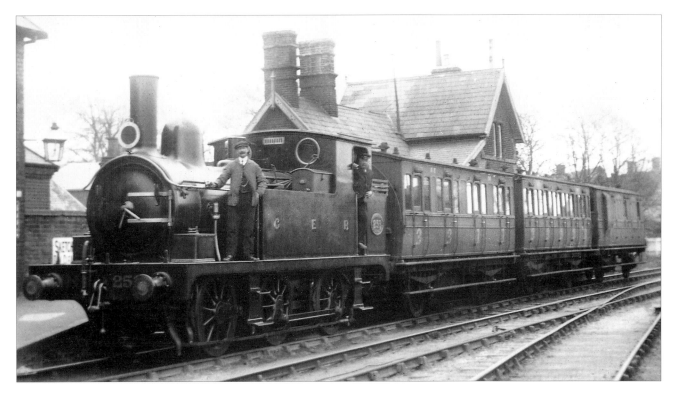

The local company remained nominally independent, holding half-yearly meetings in February and August each year, usually in the Town Hall at Eye. The 22nd such took place on Tuesday 29 February 1876, with Mr Chenery in the chair, as Sir Edward Kerrison was indisposed. The proceedings shed a useful light on the state of the company nine years after opening. Revenue for the previous half year, ending on 31 December 1875, had been adversely affected by the bad harvest. Passenger receipts were £204 15s 5d, for parcels and carriages £51 7s 9d, and for merchandise, minerals and livestock £463 9s 5d, making a total of £719 12s 7d. The shortfall was considerable, and in the corresponding period of the previous year the final item had been

£557 16s 10d. In the previous year (1875) expenditure was £359 16s 4d to the Great Eastern for working expenses, £35 15s 11d mileage proportion for compensation for accidents, £6 17s 9d for government duty, £1 10s 9d interest on outlay for sidings etc, with the balance allocated to the net revenue account for reduction of debt being £313 0s 10d. The company had borrowed £5,000 to build its line, and this was now down to £3,482 7s 3d.

Mr Henry Wells, who was Secretary of the Hartismere Highway Board, attended the meeting to call attention to the state of the level crossing over Mellis Green. The company secretary, Mr J. C. Warnes, explained that when the line was being built, the sum of £140 was awarded to common-right owners as compensation for damage

Above:
An RCTS excursion to Eye, the 'Suffolk Venturer', on 30 September 1956. The locomotive, 'J15' No 65447, had propelled the train from Mellis. *David Lawrence*

done, the money being paid to a committee formed by them. He recommended application to the land-holder Mr Frere, of Roydon, for money to repair the crossing. The newspaper report of this meeting compared the Mellis & Eye very favourably with the Bury & Thetford, which, it commented, had obtained its Act on the same day, but which had only just started running. It attributed this to a system of strict economy and rigid self-denial, with the secretary, directors and auditors working without pay, and all shareholders' earnings going to pay off debt, which was being done quickly.

Branch trains had their own platform at Mellis, using the back face of the up main platform, with the signalbox between them. There was a loop for branch trains, and two sidings accessible from both branch and main line. A short headshunt protected the up main. The branch headed almost due east from the junction, the track curving sharply away from the station, and the line was level and straight almost all the way. The Norwich to Ipswich road crossed over the line by means of a bridge at Yaxley, and having crossed this turnpike, the line then turned slightly to the south and terminated on the southeast side of the town.

The station was in Magdalen Street, with the running line very nearly reaching the road itself. The loop was relatively short, and had a short headshunt serving the loading dock. At the other end a short siding gave access to the engine shed. The platform was on the northeast side of the line, with the station buildings

Below:
Mellis, on the Great Eastern main line between Ipswich and Norwich, seen looking northwards in about 1924. The photographer is standing on the down platform, and the Eye branch train can be seen at the back of the up. *Stations UK*

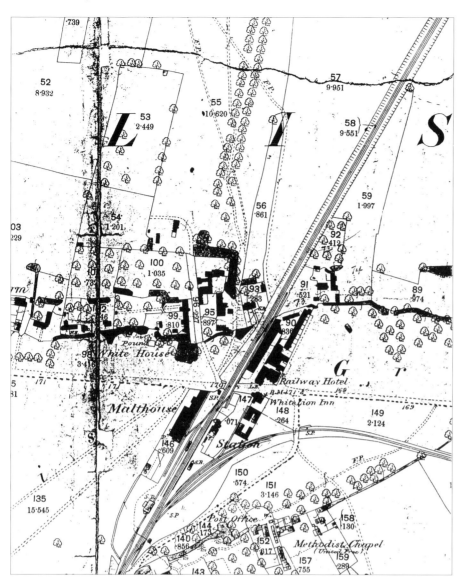

Left:
Mellis station, 1886.
Crown Copyright

Below:
An interesting view of Mellis station from the Eye branch, showing the branch platform, signalbox, goods shed and the branch starting signal.
Adrian Vaughan collection

Above:
Mellis station, looking southwards along the main line to Ipswich. The Eye branch is the line immediately to the left of the 'Beware of Trains' sign.
Adrian Vaughan collection

incorporating the station house. Passengers walked through the yard, between the sidings and the buildings, to get to the booking office, although this became disused after conductor-guard working was introduced. There was an awning for passengers at the Mellis end of the buildings, but this was partly bricked up after withdrawal of the service. It may, at one time, have housed a bookstall.

The branch was severely affected by the torrential rain and flooding of August 1912. On Monday 26th — the regular late summer Bank Holiday — nearly nine inches of rain fell within 36 hours in Norwich, and although the amounts were less towards the coast and further south, the effects were devastating over a wide area. Many roads were impassable because of floodwater in the Eye area, and in the evening of the first day the town was completely cut off. The *East Anglian Daily Times* commented that the old name of 'Ea' or 'Ey', meaning island, was singularly appropriate. A party of excursionists who had been to Yarmouth was particularly unfortunate. They could not get back on the same day, and had reached only as far as Stowmarket by 3am on Tuesday, where they had to wait; they reached Eye at 1pm on Tuesday.

By 1922, the service had shrunk to four trains each way on weekdays, with an extra on Mondays. Yaxley Halt was opened on Wednesday, 20 December of that year, and was a simple ground-level structure with a nameboard and an oil lamp. It was situated immediately to the west of Duke's Bridge, carrying the main Norwich road over the branch. At the same time, the branch passenger brake van was equipped with steps to allow passengers to access trains. It was intended to provide more comfort and convenience for local residents, and most trains were scheduled to call. Market tickets would be available to surrounding stations on market days. All this could not save the branch from being targeted in the sweeping cuts made during the years of the Great Depression. The passenger service was withdrawn on and from 2 February 1931, the last trains running on Saturday 31 January, there being no Sunday service. The Eastern Counties Road Car Company put on a replacement bus service between Eye and

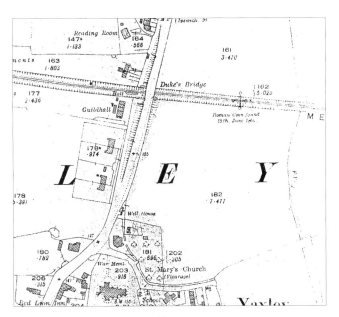

Above:
Yaxley halt, 1926. *Crown Copyright*

Mellis, and Eye and Diss. There were four return trips on weekdays on the former, most connecting with trains there. The Diss service was interworked with the Ipswich to Diss bus, and thus provided connections for Eye at Diss railway station. The *East Anglian Daily Times* headline detailing the changes shows that nothing much has changed in local journalism over the years; it said simply 'Eye-solated!'

Goods services latterly were operated as one leg of a Norwich to Stowmarket working, with the train calling at all stations to attach and detach traffic as required and carry out any shunting. In the Summer 1956 timetable, the 3.15am Class K from Norwich Thorpe

Above:
**A fine view of Mellis, looking towards Norwich in about 1950, with everything intact and as it should be.
The branch has retained its Great Eastern signals.** *Stations UK*

arrived at Mellis at 8.33am every weekday, having already called at Trowse, Swainsthorpe, Flordon, Forncett, Tivetshall, Burston and Diss, remaining at the last for nearly 1¼ hours. It would then go down the branch at 9.36am, arriving at Eye at 9.51am, and carry out the same duties there. It left for the main line at 10.35am, reaching Mellis at 10.50am, and leaving for Stowmarket at 11.1am (11.23am Saturdays only), which it reached at 12.47pm after calling at Finningham and Haughley Junction.

Traffic levels remained healthy, and in 1938 1,192 tons of grain were forwarded, together with 1,027 tons of vegetables — much of this being beet — and 165 tons of livestock. Facilities at the station were fairly extensive. In the late 1920s and early '30s all classes of traffic could be handled, and there was a 1-ton crane available. The executors of Sir Thomas Tacon had a siding at the station, which was used by a number of concerns, including the Cities Service Oil Company and F. B. Roe & Sons. A. Savill & Co, prominent local corn and feed merchants, also used the buildings next to their siding, which was on the north side of the station yard. They had

use of the granary at Mellis, which was owned by Alfred Clark. The Colchester Brewery also had its own siding at Eye. By the 1950s Savill's were still using their siding there, and M. Lewis & Co had another; only passengers could not be booked. The goods shed was relatively large, brick-built and with a hipped roof on the section at the western end, whilst the goods office was at the other end.

The branch saw the occasional enthusiasts' excursion, such as the 'Suffolk Venturer' railtour organised by the Railway Enthusiasts' Club on Sunday, 30 September 1956, which was scheduled to have a 'B12' for main line haulage and a 'J15' elsewhere, which also included the Waveney Valley, Snape and Hadleigh branches. The occasional hunt special also brought in revenue, one such running on 9 February 1957, which was hauled down the branch by a spotless Class D16/3 4-4-0 No 62615 bearing express headcode discs! This particular train was run for the Suffolk Hunt, who normally used road transport; however, petrol rationing was in force, so a special train of 10 horseboxes and two brake second passenger coaches was laid on for the journey from Bury St Edmunds. Thirteen horses and 18½ couple of hounds embarked at Bury, with a further three horses at Elmswell, with the hunt returning there after the day's chase.

The Eye branch was not one of those specifically targeted by Dr Beeching — his report did not identify freight-only lines in the same way as passenger services. Rather, he classified a number of locations by their annual freight tonnage, and both Mellis and Eye came in the 5,000 to 25,000 tons per annum category. Dr Beeching did not like traditional wagonload traffic or Class K pick-up goods trains, and saw the future in liner trains. The Eye branch did not survive, the final closure date being 13 July 1964.

WEEKDAYS					MELLIS AND EYE						
				K						K	K
DOWN				J.15 am from Norwich T.		**UP**				To Stowmarket	To Stowmarket
Mileage						Mileage					
M	C					M	C			SX	SO
		MELLIS........... arr		am 8 33						am	am
						0	0	EYE .... dep		10 35	10 35
0	0	.. .. dep		9 36		2	64	MELLIS.. .. .. .. arr		10 50	10 50
2	64	EYE .... arr		9 51							
								.... dep		11 1	11 23

Above:
1956 timetable. *Author's Collection*

Hadleigh Branch

THE railway to Hadleigh was one of those opened relatively early, seeing its first goods trains on 21 August 1847. It was promoted by a local concern, the Eastern Union & Hadleigh, with the backing of the main line company, passing into its ownership in 1848. The line was duly transferred to the Eastern Counties, Great Eastern, LNER and finally British Railways, before closing for all traffic in April 1965. It was one of the first to lose its passenger service, which was withdrawn in the sweeping cuts of the Depression, the last regular train running in February 1932. Part of the trackbed has now been incorporated into the National Cycle Network.

The Eastern Union & Hadleigh Junction Act was given the Royal Assent on 18 June 1846, the Act listing a number of directors who were also prominent in the Eastern Union Railway, owners of the main line between Colchester and Ipswich. Among these were John Chevallier Cobbold, his father John Cobbold and James Allen Ransome. The authorised capital was £75,000, made up of 7,500 £10 shares, with the first ordinary meeting to be held within eight months, and thereafter every year in August.

Above:
Hadleigh station in Great Eastern days, with a train from Bentley standing at the platform. *Lens of Sutton*

The Act specified a triangular junction with the main line at Bentley. It was to be built as a single track, but with the various structures — bridges etc — being built for double track. Three years were allowed for the purchase of lands, and the line was to be completed within four. Rates for the carriage of goods, livestock and people were tightly prescribed. For example, dung, compost and limestone were to be charged at 1d per ton per mile, plus ½d per ton per mile if carried in the company's own carriages. Coal, coke, culm (coal or anthracite dust), bricks, tiles, slates and iron were to be charged at 1½d (plus ½d for carriage in the company's own carriages), sugar, grain, timber, staves, metals other than iron at 2d (plus ¾d), with cotton, wools, drugs, manufactured goods and merchandise at 3d (plus 1d). Carriages under one ton could be carried at 6d per mile. Passengers could travel at 2d per mile (plus 1d), but at 3d (plus 1d) it was more expensive for cattle, horses and mules to travel. There was to be a minimum charge of six miles, and the company could charge what it saw fit for small parcels, although 'small' extended to 500lb in weight! There

Above:
Hadleigh station in British Railways days, showing the passenger entrance and goods shed. *Stations UK*

Above:
**The architecture of the station building at Hadleigh is shown particularly well
in this photograph, taken in 1956.** *David Lawrence*

Above:
Shunting in progress at Hadleigh in the late 1950s. Gayford's maltings are in the background. *John Brodribb collection*

Above:
Church crossing, near Bentley, with Secondman E. Browes opening the gates for the 16.10 Hadleigh to Ipswich goods on 14 April 1965, the penultimate day of service. *G. R. Mortimer*

would be no charge for luggage up to 100lb first class, 60lb second class, and 40lb third class.

Peter Bruff was the engineer for the railway, being already closely involved with the Eastern Union. The line passed through the grounds of Bentley Hall, close to the junction, and crossed the turnpike road, later the A12, at Capel, where a station was proposed and built. There were three cottages here and at Raydon Wood, which also received a station, but otherwise there was little habitation *en route*. There were few earthworks, and six level crossings, one road underbridge and one over. Most of the line was level, with about two miles at 1 in 132. The length of the line was 6 miles, 3 furlongs and 8½ chains (just under 6½ miles), with Bentley station just over half a mile south of the junction. The Act provided for a triangular junction, and it seems that this was built, although regular passenger trains appear never to have worked over the northern arm, so that Ipswich and Hadleigh did not have a direct link. The cutting lay abandoned for much of the life of the branch; perhaps the lack of track contributed to the early demise of the passenger service. It remains something of a mystery.

It was not long before extensions were proposed, and in November 1846 further plans were deposited. The new line was surveyed by Mr G. T. Cloutt, under Bruff's direction, and headed northwest from Hadleigh to Kersey and Semer, then turning west to Monks Eleigh and Brent Eleigh to Lavenham, where it would have formed a junction with the proposed extension of the Stour Valley Railway. The railway would have crossed both main streets of Hadleigh by bridges, and would have necessitated considerable demolition. It would have added about 9¾ miles to the railway.

Bentley station was located by the level crossing on the road to Tattingstone, a little over a quarter of a mile from the village, and had opened on 11 June 1846. The buildings were of wooden construction, incorporating the booking office and hall, stationmaster's office, waiting room and toilets, all being on the up platform. The goods shed was also adjacent. The main down platform, 550ft long, was opposite the up, both being to the north of the level crossing, with the Hadleigh bay forming its other face; this was rather shorter at 370ft. There were cattle pens on the up side, and two cartage sidings to the west of the Hadleigh platform; additionally, T. W. Wilson & Son's maltings were served by a siding on the down side, to the south of the level crossing. The signalbox was located on the down side, to the north of the station. The Hadleigh branch had its own rail access to the station, so that branch passenger trains leaving the bay travelled along the single line parallel to the main lines until reaching the point of divergence. This arrangement appears to have been in place from a very early stage, and there is no evidence that passenger trains worked regularly over the northern side of the triangle. Crossovers were provided to give access to the up side of the station.

There remains some doubt over the possible existence of a station at Bentley Church, this being at some distance north of the village, but immediately south of the branch and close to the junction. Climbing gently away from the junction, the line turned quite sharply to pass Bentley Hall and park to the north, and trains were limited to 15mph over this curve. Having set on its direction towards Hadleigh after about 400 yards from the junction, it then followed an almost completely straight course towards its

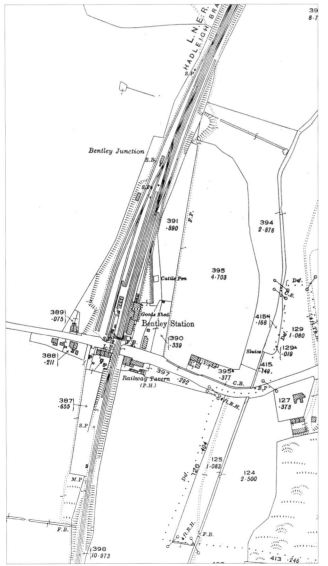

destination, curving gently northwards on the last mile. Capel station, serving the village of Capel St Mary about half a mile to the south, was situated on the east side of the Colchester to Ipswich turnpike road, later the A12, at $2\frac{1}{4}$ miles from Bentley. The station building was built in a similar style and materials to the others on the line. The single platform and buildings were on the north side of the line, with a loading dock behind the east end. There was a double-ended siding, with the signalbox opposite the platform.

Raydon Wood station (Raydon until 1 October 1895), a further $1\frac{3}{4}$ miles onwards, was also by a level crossing, this time on the minor road between Hintlesham and Raydon, the latter being about $1\frac{1}{4}$ miles to the south. The name derived from Raydon Great Wood, the railway passing through this. The single platform on the south side of the line had a two-storey building of red brick with white brick quoins. The siding, also on the south side, had access from both directions, and there was a signalbox opposite the platform controlling the level crossing, which was removed soon after withdrawal of the passenger service. There was a gate house by the level crossing, in a similar style to the main building.

The only significant earthworks lay on the final section to Hadleigh, with both cuttings and embankments, the station being situated on the hillside to the south of the town. It was extensive, having rail-served maltings on the east side, and a number of other store sheds, a large goods shed and other facilities such as cattle pens and loading docks. Hadleigh station was designed by Frederick Barnes, who was responsible for all the station buildings on the branch, which were constructed with the same red bricks as elsewhere, with whites used for quoins, reveals and so on. The station entrance was via a modest single-storey building with the usual prominent chimneys, which adjoined a lower and longer but

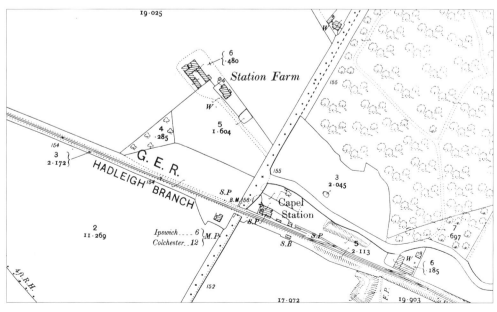

Above:
**Raydon Wood station, looking past the level crossing towards Hadleigh in 1953.
The gate hut is almost hidden by the bushes, and the yard is on the left.** *Stations UK*

Below:
Raydon Wood, looking from the level crossing towards Bentley in 1953. *Stations UK*

Above:
Raydon Wood station on 1 March 1965, with No D5636 arriving from Hadleigh. *H. N. James*

otherwise similar structure fronting the platform. An awning ran the full length of this. The wall of the building extended from the Bentley end, and a large wooden goods shed was attached to it, rail access being behind the platform. It was able to handle all classes of traffic, including livestock, horseboxes, furniture vans, carriages and portable engines, and had a 5-ton crane. Messrs T. W. Wilson also had a siding at the station. Gayford & Co were corn, poultry foods, cake, coal and seed merchants at the station, while Thomas Moy, coal merchants, had premises in Station Road. Traffic otherwise was the normal trade of a country town and its rural hinterland — coal, feedstuffs and so on. There were several

orchards in the area, and the town had a number of corn mills, as well as matting factories. Much of the originating traffic at Hadleigh was connected with the maltings, and amounted to 1,142 tons of grain in 1938, worth £926 to the LNER. In addition, 179 tons of livestock were shipped through the station, with a gross revenue of £284, mostly going to Ipswich market.

The line was worked by the Eastern Union from the outset. The initial passenger service was sparse, with the 1860 timetable showing three trains each way on Mondays to Saturdays. They left Hadleigh at 8.15am, 12.55 and 5.25pm, returning from Bentley at 10.55am, 2.10 and 6.10pm; the running time was 25 minutes.

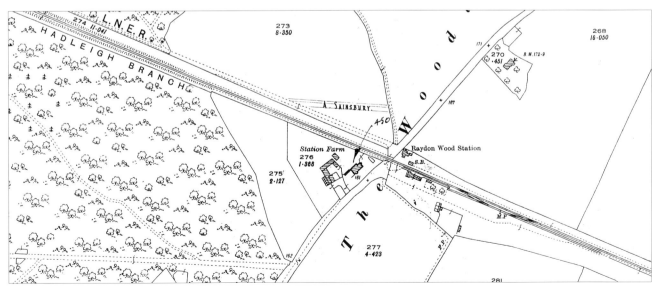

Above:
Raydon Wood station, 1926. *Crown Copyright*

DOWN	Mileage M	C		K 7.28 am from Ipswich	K 2.25 pm from Manningtree	UP	Mileage M	C		K To Manningtree	K To Ipswich
				SX	SX					SX	SX
BENTLEY .... arr				am 7 54	PM 2 41	HADLEIGH .... dep	0	0		am 10 15	PM 4 24
	0	0	dep	8 20	3 1	Raydon Wood ..	2	15		..	R
Capel	2	13		R		Capel	4	74		..	R
Raydon Wood ...	4	72		R		BENTLEY .... arr	7	7		10 50	4 56
HADLEIGH .... arr	7	7		9 5	3 35	.... dep				12 7	5 17

Above:
11 June–16 September 1956 timetable. *Author's Collection*

There was no Sunday service. The 1874 timetable showed a distinct improvement to four return journeys each weekday, with trains from Hadleigh at 8.10 and 10.10am, 1.13 and 5.23pm, returning from Bentley at 9.0 and 10.50am, and 2.0 and 6.17pm. Capel and Raydon Wood were served as required. In summer 1913 further improvements had taken place, so that the 7.53 and 9.12am up from Hadleigh ran each weekday, together with the 12.33pm and 5.35pm mixed. On Tuesdays and Saturdays there was a 7pm up, and on Tuesdays only a 2.58pm through train to Ipswich, reaching there at 3.35pm, returning at 4.17pm and arriving in Hadleigh at 4.47pm. Other down services left Bentley at 8.33am (mixed), 9.42am, 1.47 and 7.27pm, plus 6.27pm on Tuesdays and Saturdays, and the extra trains on Tuesdays were run in connection with the corn and cattle markets at Ipswich. The intermediate stations were now served by booked calls, but tickets from them were issued on the train. In summer 1922 there were five trains each way, now with a slightly shorter journey time of about 21 minutes to Hadleigh, but 19 minutes up to Bentley. The service finished on Saturday, 27 February 1932, the official withdrawal date being on and from the following Monday; the guard on the final day's service was Mr S. W. Westwood. The line remained open for goods and parcels traffic, and it was advertised that special excursion trains would be run as necessary. Passenger services were to be provided by the Eastern Counties Omnibus Company Ltd, whose route to Ipswich was much more direct than by rail.

Goods traffic was relatively light at the intermediate stations. In 1913, apart from the mixed workings, there were trains from Bentley at 7.5am on Tuesdays only when required, and 3.55pm, not Tuesdays. In the up direction they left Hadleigh at 6.35am on Tuesdays only if required, running as an express cattle train, and 2.50pm, Tuesdays excepted; Capel and Raydon Wood were served as required. This remained the case in 1937, when the 8.22am from

Above:
The end for Raydon Wood, seen here on 30 August 1965, shortly after removal of the track. *G. R. Mortimer*

Bentley started at 7am from Ipswich, and reached Hadleigh at 8.50am. The engine and brake van returned almost immediately (at 9.15am) to Bentley and then worked the 10.40am to Mistley, on the Harwich branch. They were allowed to work important traffic up the branch if necessary. Another goods working left Bentley at 3.5pm, reached Hadleigh at 3.40pm, and left again at 5.15pm; having done the necessary shunting at the terminus, this train then working back to Ipswich. The pattern in 1956 was broadly the same, with the 7.28am from Ipswich leaving Bentley at 8.20am and reaching Hadleigh at 9.5am. It left at 10.15am, reaching Bentley at 10.50 and not leaving until 12.7pm for Manningtree. In the afternoon, the train left Manningtree at 2.25pm and reached Hadleigh at 3.35pm, leaving at 4.24pm for Ipswich. Passenger trains had been generally worked by one of the smaller tank engines, although tender classes were usual on goods trains. These included 'J15s' and 'J17s', and 'E4' No 62797 turned up on an enthusiasts' excursion on at least one occasion. Latterly various types of diesel locomotive were used on the line, including what are now Classes 20 and 31. Capel closed to public traffic earlier than the others, from 13 July 1964, goods facilities at Bentley being withdrawn at the same time. Raydon Wood and Hadleigh saw their last trains on 15 April 1965, the final service being the 12.30pm from Ipswich hauled by Class 31 No D5699.

Right:
Hadleigh station, 1884. *Crown Copyright*

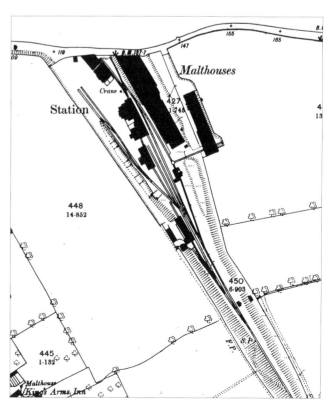

Above:

The last working from Hadleigh approaches the main line near Bentley on 15 April 1965 with No D5699 heading the train. *G. R. Mortimer*

Heacham and Wells Line

HUNSTANTON was the objective of the Lynn & Hunstanton company, incorporated in 1861, and opening its line on 3 October 1862. One aim of the line was to develop the new resort, which had been a village until the railway arrived, and to boost the development of the surrounding area. Wolferton, close to the royal residence at Sandringham, was another source of rather higher-class traffic than Hunstanton's day-trippers. Freight revenue was good, and development was rapid.

Halfway across Norfolk, Wells-next-the-Sea was the target for a number of schemes, including direct lines from Norwich. The Norfolk Railway had opened its line between Wymondham and East Dereham as early as 7 December 1846 for goods, and 15 February 1847 for passengers. An extension to Wells and Blakeney was soon sanctioned, but was completed only as far as Fakenham, this opening in March 1849. The line onwards was completed by the Wells & Fakenham, and opened on 1 December 1857.

Between them, these two lines opened up the north Norfolk coast, but left a gap of some 20 miles, and a number of towns and villages and their rural hinterland in a state of depression. There were serious agricultural problems in the area, not least cattle fever, plus the distance from ready markets now being tapped by places linked to the railway. The need for a connection between the Hunstanton and Wells lines was keenly felt. Construction of the line went ahead quite quickly after the company's Act had received the Royal Assent, Mr Valentine being the engineer. By 8 January 1866 the line had got far enough for the Prince and Princess of Wales to travel along it to Burnham in order to visit the Earl and Countess of Leicester at Holkham. In the middle of the month they then returned by the railway to Sandringham, now served by the station at Wolferton.

The line opened on 17 August 1866, having been passed fit by Capt Tyler RE, the Board of Trade's Inspector. This date was a few days earlier than stipulated in the contract, and the directors felt somewhat aggrieved that the BoT had insisted on the same arrangements for safe handling of traffic as at Clapham Junction, which they felt were superfluous. The Great Eastern was to work the line for 10 years from 16 August, and would find the rolling stock and staff, and have the use of the stations at Wells and Heacham. The GER would operate the line for 50% of earnings, although there was an 'accident clause' in the working agreement whereby, in the event of an accident anywhere on the Great Eastern system, the local company paid compensation in proportion to its mileage. The intermediate stations were at Sedgeford, Docking, Stanhoe, Burnham Market and Holkham,

Above:
Heacham station in 1959, from the north end of the down platform. Wells trains not running through to Lynn or Hunstanton used the bay on the left. The goods yard can be seen clearly. *Stations UK*

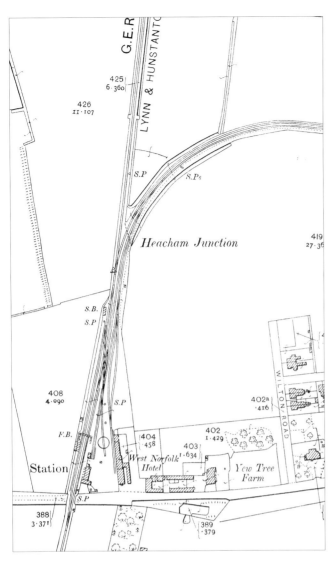

Above:
Heacham station. *Crown Copyright*

and the overall speed limit was 40mph. The total length of the new line was 18 miles 25 chains.

The line had not required extensive engineering works. Heacham boasted a substantial station north of the level crossing of one of the access roads to the beach, and had two platforms on the Hunstanton line plus a bay at the north end for Wells trains. The main buildings, goods yard and shed and turntable on the up or east side and the West Norfolk Junction line had direct access to these facilities. From the station it curved away sharply towards the east with a speed limit of 20mph, the junction being immediately to the north of the station, with the signalbox on the west side of the main line. The branch picked up the valley of the Heacham River before climbing towards Sedgeford, and there was a level crossing over the main King's Lynn to Hunstanton road, now the A149. At Sedgeford the station was about half a mile to the north of the village and three miles by rail from Heacham. The layout was simple, with a single platform and building on the north side of the line, a short goods loop to the west, and a siding serving a cattle pen running behind the passenger platform. A signalbox was provided opposite the west end of the platform, but the station was not a block post. The road to Ringstead crossed the line on the level at the east end of the station. The main building was a single-storey structure built of stone, with a fully hipped roof and a small awning.

By 1927 the points had been converted to working from a ground frame, locked by an Annett's key kept on the Docking and Heacham train staff. The line was worked on the staff-and-ticket system, but the abolition of the signalbox here meant that metal key tickets, instead of paper ones, had to be introduced, so that a train carrying a ticket could still carry a key to unlock the sidings. A crossing keeper's hut was provided. The system of metal tickets was later extended to the whole line, when a scheme for reducing maintenance costs was introduced in the 1930s. This allowed a trolley-borne gang based at Wells to cover the whole line, following the installation of a 'platelayers occupation telephone token' system, and was the precursor for other schemes on the LNER.

Docking was a further 3¼ miles, the line having climbed from Sedgeford, the station being about ¾ mile north of the main settlement. The station was altogether more substantial, with two platforms, the main buildings being on the south side of the line.

Above:
Heacham in 1947, looking north. The line to Wells diverged opposite the signalbox. *Stations UK*

There was a long siding here also, with a loading bay and 1½-ton crane at the east end of the Heacham-bound platform; the signalbox was also here. There were further sidings on the north side of the running lines, with a goods shed, cattle pens and other stores. In the 1920s, C. W. Marsters had a siding at the station, which continued after closure to passengers in the 1950s, and this was also used by Shell-Mex. Access to the station could be had from both sides of the line, the main entrance for passengers being from the south, opposite the Railway Inn. This stood right by the railway where the road from Docking to Brancaster crossed on the level. The main building, this time with two storeys, was again stone-built, although the one on the other platform was of brick, and in a quite different style. Docking generated large amounts of outward goods traffic, and in 1937 despatched 7,270 tons of vegetables, 356 tons of livestock and 1,431 tons of flour and grain, earning a healthy £4,530 for the railway.

The line left Docking on an embankment, still heading in a roughly easterly direction, and now descended towards Stanhoe, the station being about two miles from the rather scattered village. A single platform on the south side of the line sufficed, where the single-storey brick building was also located. It had a small awning, removed after passenger closure as this was a passenger-only station. The signalbox was abolished in 1920. Soon after leaving there, the railway curved to the north, crossing the Stanhoe to Burnham road on the level about a mile west of Burnham Market. The station — simply 'Burnham' until 1 June 1883 — was located immediately to the west of another level crossing, this time of the Burnham to Fakenham road, and about 3½ miles from Stanhoe.

There was a single platform on the north side of the line, and a goods shed, a loading dock at the back of the platform, a goods loop and other sidings and stores. Access was from Station Road, running parallel to the line to the north. The main buildings were located at the level crossing end of the platform, brick-built and of two storeys, plus a collection of single-storey additions housing various other functions such as the toilets. Again, because the signalbox was not at the level crossing, a hut for the crossing keeper was provided. The nameboard proclaimed 'Burnham Market for Burnham Thorpe, Nelson's Birthplace'. Outward goods traffic was mostly agricultural, and in 1937 the station forwarded 4,478 tons of vegetables and 138 tons of livestock, together worth £2,424 to the LNER.

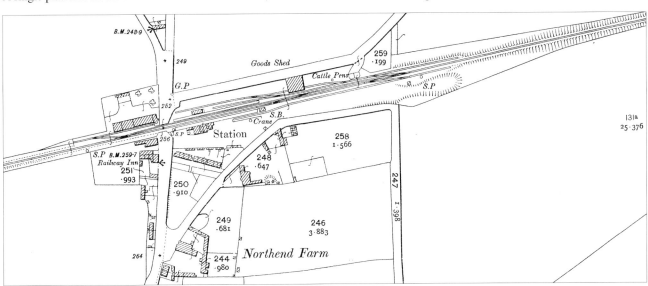

Above:
Docking station. *Crown Copyright*

The line then continued onwards, crossing the River Burn to the east of the town, and passing Peterstone siding about two miles away. This was double-ended and located immediately on the Heacham side of the level crossing of the road between Burnham Overy Town and Holkham, now the B1155. There were trap points in the siding at the level crossing end, but at the other a siding ran back into the Peterstone Brick Works, situated on the south side of the road, not far from Peterstone Farm. The points were controlled by ground frames locked by Annett's key on the Wells-Burnham train staff, and the siding was also protected by signals worked from the ground frames, which had to be placed at danger while shunting was in progress. The man in charge of the ground frame had also to ensure that any wagons were placed inside the catch points before handing the train staff back to the driver. In addition, there was a level crossing at the site, also protected by signals, and the gates had to be closed across the road when shunting was in progress. The sidings handled coal and other traffic for Holkham Hall, there being no goods facilities at Holkham station.

There were level crossings over the Burnham to Wells and Hunstanton to Wells roads, before reaching Holkham station, four miles further on. By now the railway had come very close to the coast, running parallel with it for a short distance. Holkham Hall, the seat of the Earl of Leicester, with its extensive landscaped grounds, was about a mile from the station. Holkham station had a single platform on the south side of the line. Because of its closeness to the Hall, the railway had had to agree not to provide any buildings other than the station itself, stationmaster's house and house for the lodge keeper. A special waiting room was provided for visiting royalty and nobility, as well as one for ordinary passengers. The design of the buildings, in Peterstone plain and fancy bricks, was unique; others on the line were to a standard pattern but this one had to be specially approved by the Earl of Leicester. Holkham was a passenger-only station with carriages and horses handled at Wells. The signalbox was abolished in 1920 and was later replaced by a grounded van body used as a store.

Above:
Burnham Market in 1950, looking towards Wells. *Stations UK*

Below:
Burnham Market station. *Crown Copyright*

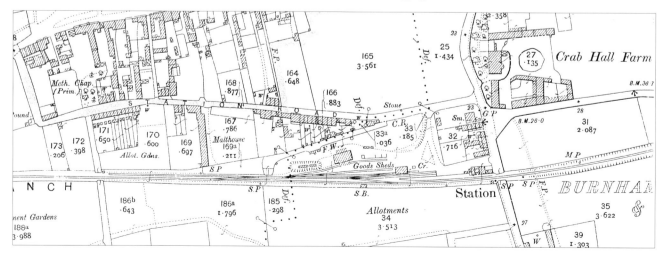

Above:
**Holkham, the first station from Wells on the Heacham
line, is seen about 1950. The van body occupies
the site of the signalbox.** *Stations UK*

Right:
Holkham station. *Crown Copyright*

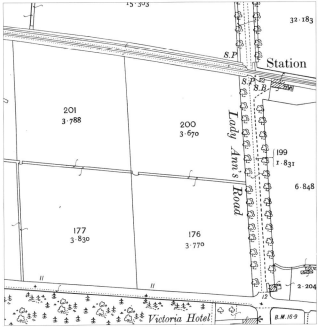

East of Holkham the line curved southeastwards, with a level
crossing of the main road into Wells, then passing to the southwest
of the town before curving very sharply, almost through 180° at the
junction with the Fakenham line; trains over this curve were limited
to 15mph, also on account of the steep gradient down towards the
station. The station was simply 'Wells' when opened, and became
Wells-on-Sea on 1 July 1923, and Wells-next-the-Sea on 1 January
1957. The signalbox was in the vee of the junction. Trains off the
West Norfolk Junction Railway thus arrived in Wells from the east!
Special provision was made for the assistance of West Norfolk
passenger trains out of the station. Seen purely as a shunting
operation, the assisting engine was allowed to push at the rear of
the train, and had to have either the stationmaster or foreman
porter on board. It also had to carry the Wells-Docking train staff if
at all possible, but was not to be block-signalled. The up starting
signal, having been passed by the train, had to be replaced at
danger and a collar put on the lever, the assisting engine then
returning to the station. Once clear of the branch, the signalman
was told verbally by the stationmaster or foreman porter,
whereupon the lever collar could be removed. Should the 'Train
out of section' signal be received from Burnham Market before the
assisting engine returned, the Wells signalman had to send
'Obstruction danger' to Burnham Market.

Wells station was a terminus, built for the line from Fakenham,
and with a curious platform arrangement so that although there
were three platform faces there were only two platform roads, one
track having two faces. In earlier days both the main platform and
the two sidings behind it were covered by adjoining and largely
similar wooden train sheds, one providing shelter for passengers
and the other forming the goods shed; later that on the passenger
side was replaced by more conventional awnings, although linked
across the centre by substantial beams. The space over the track
was then left uncovered, providing ventilation for smoke and
steam. The locomotive shed and turntable adjoined the goods shed,
while there was also the connection to the Harbour branch just
beyond the signalbox. Earthworks had also been made so that a
curve could be laid allowing direct running between Fakenham
and Heacham, avoiding Wells station, but it seems unlikely that
track was laid.

The train service was always fairly limited. Initially there were
some King's Lynn to Wells via Hunstanton workings; by 1874 the

Above:
Although the date is 1924, Wells-on-Sea shows no sign of the LNER takeover. No 544 simmers in the yard, while a passenger train waits under the overall roof. The main platform has been reconstructed, but the other is still wooden.
Stations UK

Right:
Wells-on-Sea, looking from the platform ends and past the signalbox. The turntable is to the left, and the West Norfolk Junction line to Heacham curves off to the right — the starter can be seen framed by the loading gauge.
Stations UK

Right:
This 1946 view of Wells shows the platforms and awnings to good effect. The goods yard and harbour branch are to the left.
Stations UK

Left:
Wells-next-the-Sea in 1959 when diesel multiple-units had taken over the passenger services on the route to Dereham and Norwich.
Stations UK

Below:
Wells-Next-The-Sea station.
Crown Copyright

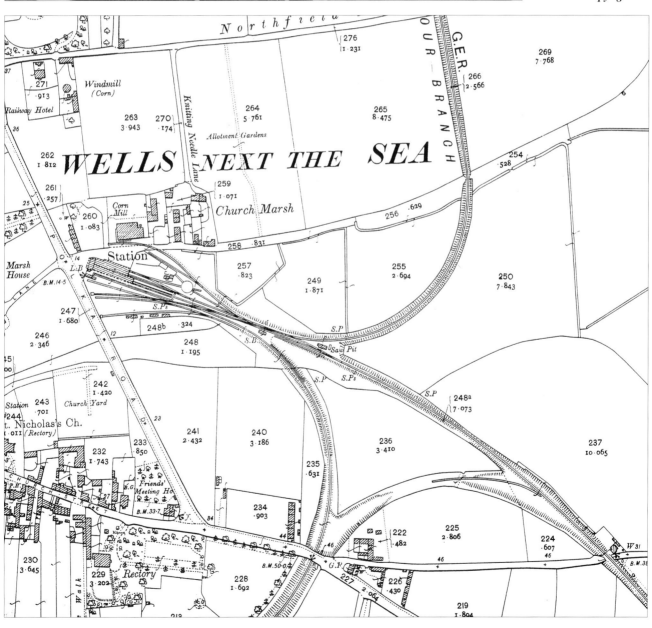

Above:
Sedgeford station, seen in freight-only days, and looking west. *Adrian Vaughan collection*

Right:
Sedgford station.
Crown Copyright

Below:
This 1947 photograph of Sedgeford station illustrates why the traffic potential of the West Norfolk Junction line was not enormous. The village was about half a mile away to the south, behind the camera. *Stations UK*

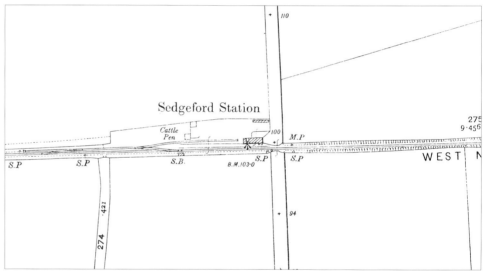

Above:
**Stanhoe station around 1950, with a short
goods train approaching from Wells, headed by
'J17' 0-6-0 No 65544.** *Stations UK*

Below:
Stanhoe station. *Crown Copyright*

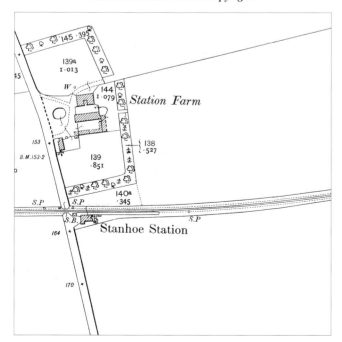

pattern had settled down to three each way Mondays to Saturdays. Sedgeford, Stanhoe and Holkham were request stops, and some mixed trains were operated. The 1874 timetable showed the first from Heacham as a mixed working which left at 7.45am and reached Wells at 9am. The second, the Parliamentary train, left Heacham at 12.58pm (12.43 Thursdays only), reaching Wells at 2.10pm, and the third — and last train of the day — left at 3.45pm, reaching Wells at 4.40pm. This last did not run on Tuesdays, and was replaced by the 6.3pm, reaching Wells at 7pm. In the other direction, the 9.30am from Wells reached Heacham at 10.25am, and the 2.45pm was mixed and reached Heacham at 3.32pm. The 5.20pm from Wells was mixed, but did not run on Tuesdays or Saturdays, being replaced on Tuesdays by the 7.15pm, and on Saturdays by the 7.45pm, both passenger trains. Connections were made at Heacham by most trains for Hunstanton and Lynn, the two lines being largely worked together. There was little enough in the way of population to support the service, although it did help stop the decline in the area. In 1891 Sedgeford had a population of 691, Docking 1,319 and Stanhoe 444; the Burnhams (Overy, Thorpe, Norton) — all served by Burnham Market station — together amassed 2,624 inhabitants, and Holkham 481. Even adding in Brancaster Staith (782), there were few people to travel on the trains.

The Summer 1913 timetable was more generous, although now the first passenger train of the day was from Wells, at 8.10am. This was followed by others at 10.18am and 2.46pm and 5.25pm (5.16 Thursdays only). An extra train ran to Hunstanton on Thursdays at 8.20pm until 11 September, with another on Saturdays only to King's Lynn, leaving Wells at 7.32pm. This last was something of

47

Table 53 HEACHAM and WELLS-ON-SEA

Week Days only

Miles	Station	a.m	p.m	p.m	p.m
—	Heacham .... dep	8 57	1220	3 45	6 25
2	Sedgeford	9 4	1227	3 52	6 32
6	Docking	9 13	1236	4 2	6 41
8	Stanhoe	9 18	1241	4 7	6 46
11	Burnham Market..	9 25	1248	4 15	6 53
15	Holkham	9 33	1256	4 23	7 1
18	Wells-on-Sea ... arr	9 40	1 3	4 30	7 8

Week Days only

Miles	Station	a.m	a.m	p.m	p.m
—	Wells-on-Sea .. dep	8 0	1015	1 35	5 15
2½	Holkham	8 6	1021	1 41	5 21
6½	Burnham Market..	8 14	1029	1 50	5 30
10	Stanhoe	8 22	1037	1 58	5 38
12	Docking	8 28	1043	2 5	5 45
15	Sedgeford	8 36	1051	2 13	5 53
18	Heacham .... arr	8 43	1058	2 20	6 1

Above:
Winter 1951-2 timetable. *Author's Collection*

Below:
ABC Railway Guide, 1949. *Author's Collection*

a marathon, being a through working from Norwich via Dereham, having left Thorpe at 5.22pm. There was no corresponding train in the other direction, either from Lynn or to Norwich. A train left Heacham for Wells at 9.16am, followed by the 11.42am and 12.40pm from Hunstanton, 3.46 and 6.41pm from Heacham, and the 9.45pm from Hunstanton, which ran on Thursdays only. All passenger trains were booked to call at Wells ticket platform for two minutes in the down direction. Goods traffic in the up direction (to Hunstanton) was covered by the 5.45am express cattle from Wells to Docking on Tuesdays only, leaving there again at 7.15am. A 2.10pm ran from Docking to Hunstanton when required, having worked out at 1pm. The 3.7pm from Wells called at all stations including Peterstone siding as required, and an engine and brake worked at 7.30pm on Tuesdays only from Wells to King's Lynn, having worked in on the 3.53pm Tuesdays-only express cattle. Booked goods trains in the other direction were the 10.47am from King's Lynn, which called at Peterstone siding as required, and an empty trucks working from King's Lynn to Docking at 5am, returning as the 6.40am express cattle. King's Lynn held markets on Tuesdays and Saturdays, the Tuesday event being the main one for cattle.

Matters were less promising by summer 1922, when there were four trains each way on weekdays, although there was still a difference between the service on Tuesdays and other days. During World War 2 the four-train service remained, although without any variation for different weekdays; in 1949 it had improved a little further, with one more train from Wells to Heacham. The fare to London for the 122-mile journey from Burnham Market was then 33s 9d third class monthly return, or 50s 5d first class. Winter 1951-2 again saw only the four trains each way. Many trains from Wells continued to Hunstanton, with the engines being turned at Heacham, where there was a 39ft 8in turntable. There was also table at Hunstanton (49ft 9in) and

Wells (44ft 8in), so locomotives almost invariably worked chimney-first. The possible exceptions to this usually came at busy bank holiday weekends when Hunstanton would be too busy to ensure that everything that needed it was turned.

Passenger services were withdrawn from the line on and from Monday 2 June 1952, the last regular trains running on the previous Saturday. Services at the end were usually worked by Class E4 2-4-0s, 'D16/3s' or 'J15s', being Norwich locomotives out-based at Wells. In the 1930s the usual passenger train had consisted of a bogie coach and two six-wheelers; by the 1950s bogie stock had completely taken over. The line remained open for goods traffic, but was severely hit by the 1953 floods. On the night of 31 January a combination of high tides and gale-force winds created havoc along the East Coast, breaching sea defences in many places. Wells station was flooded to a depth of four feet after water rushed along the line from the harbour, and the line was washed out at Holkham. Wells station was reopened on 4 February, but the line to Heacham remained permanently closed, with Holkham station quickly being demolished.

The occasional enthusiasts' special visited the line, such as that organised by the LCGB on 12 July 1959. Goods trains continued to run between Heacham and Burnham Market. Typical workings from the September 1964 timetable were at 07.26 from King's Lynn calling at all stations to Docking (Sedgeford as required), arriving at 10.37 and departing again for Lynn at 12.00. Mondays to Fridays the 11.10 from King's Lynn called at all stations as required, leaving Heacham at 13.17 and calling at all stations to Burnham Market as required. If it made it that far, it left at 14.50, again calling at all stations to Lynn as required, and running to Hunstanton if necessary. Final closure of the line came at the end of December 1964, with Docking officially going on 18 December, and Burnham and Sedgeford following on 28 December.

WELLS-ON-SEA (Norfolk)
Map Sq. 14.
Pop. 2,505. Clos. day Thur.
From Liverpool Street via Wymondham 146¾ miles.
1st cl.—Single 43/9, Mth. Ret. 53/2.
3rd cl.—Single 26/4, Mth. Ret. 35/5.

Liv. St.		Wells	Wells		Liv. St.
a.m.			a.m.		
5 50	11 53		7	2er	12 37
8 20r	2 7		7	2syr	12 45
11 50r	5 10		7	2sz	12 48
p.m.			8	10r	1 38
12 30er	6 30		10	5er	5 8
12 34sr	6 30		11	55sr	5 8
3 40r	8 28		p.m.		
6 40s¶r	10 55		12	50r	6 48
—	—		3	7	8 45
—	—		6	36e	2 30
—	—		7	15s	2 30

Sunday Trains.

p.m.			p.m.	
2 25	9 12		3 30	8 25

¶ Limited accommodation between London and Norwich. Advance reservation advisable.
e Not Sat. y Not after May 7.
r Refresh. Car. s Sat. only. z Com. May 14.

Another Route
From Liverpool Street via King's Lynn and Heacham 128¾ miles.
Same fares.

Liv. St.		Wells	Wells		Llv. St.
a.m.			a.m.		
8 20r	1 3		6 2r		10 30
11 50r	4 30		7 55er		12 37
p.m.	,		7 55sr		12 45
2 25r	7 8		10 15r		2 40
5 54mr	10 39		p.m.		
—	—		1 35r		6 48
—	—		5 15		2 30
—	—		—		—
—	—		—		—

No Sunday Trains.
e Not Sat. r Refresh. Car.
m Mon., Fri. & s Sat. only.
Sat.

Above:
There must be some possibility of a train before too long, although the Stanhoe station
cat seems unlikely to be trampled in the rush. *Stations UK*

				SX		SO	SX					SO		SO	
HUNSTANTON .. dep	1						12 51								
Burnham Mkt. .. .. dep	2	..	..	..	..	..	..	..	..	..	..	..		..	..
Stanhoe ., ...	3	..	..	..	..	..	..	..	..	..	..	..		..	..
Docking	4	..	..	..	..	..	..	..	..	..	..	..	12 00	..	..
Sedgeford	5														
Heacham.. .. .. .. arr	6	..	..	..	..	..	13 01	..	..	..	..	..	12 45	..	..
...... dep	7												13 23		
Snettisham .. .. arr	8	..	..	..	..	..	..	..	..	..	..		13 35	..	..
...... dep	9												13X46		
Dersingham .. .. arr	10	..	..	..	..	..	..	..	..	..			..	..	..
...... dep	11											Calls at Wizenhall Siding R	13R58		
Wolferton .. .. arr	12	..	..	..	..	..	..	..	..	..			..	..	..
...... dep	13												14R07		
North Wootton	14	..	..	..	..	..	..	..	..	..	..		..	..	..
KING'S LYNN ...... arr	15												14 22		

Above:
7 September 1964-13 June 1965 timetable. *Author's Collection*

Kelvedon and Tollesbury Line

THE Kelvedon & Tollesbury Light Railway was one of those eccentric byways beloved of enthusiasts, conveniently close to London, but light-years away from the bustle of the metropolis. Authorised in 1901, the line was opened on 1 October 1904, and was extended to Tollesbury Pier in the following year. Intended to tap the traffic in an area of Essex then served sparsely by rail, it performed a useful function in the carriage of goods, especially in connection with the jam factory at Tiptree, and was also the scene of operation of armoured trains during World War 2. Another claim to fame was as the home of coaching stock from the Wisbech & Upwell Tramway after that line lost its passenger service in 1928.

The Light Railways Act of 1896 had not long been on the statute book before plans for a railway to serve the rich horticultural areas of eastern Essex were brought forward. Having been missed by the main line between London and Colchester and other branches, such as those to Maldon, there was scope for development. Plans deposited on 27 May 1897 with the Light Railway Commissioners listed the following as 'undertakers' – a rather strange use of the term, more usually 'proprietors' or 'promoters': Sir William Abdy of London, Alexander McMullen JP, Mayor of Hertford, James N. Paxman JP of Stisted Hall, Braintree, John Henry Salter JP of Tolleshunt D'Arcy House, and Arthur C. Wilkin, of Tiptree Heath. The proposed line was to be 9 miles 6 furlongs 7 chains in length, and was to have a rail-over-road bridge at Tolleshunt Knights, and

three road-over-rail bridges. As was usual, the charges for passenger carriage and parcels rates were laid down, and the Great Eastern Railway was authorised to use, work, manage and maintain the line. No platforms were necessary, and mixed trains were acceptable, with continuous brakes not needed. The breakdown of estimated costs took the standard form for light railways, and was as follows:

Earthworks	£4,442 2s 0d
Bridges	£600 0s 0d
Accommodation bridges and works	£1,000 0s 0d
Culverts	£500 0s 0d
Metalling of roads at level crossings	£200 0s 0d
Gatekeepers' houses at level crossings	£3,610 0s 0d
Permanent way, including fencing (per mile £1,930)	£18,986 7s 6d
Permanent way for sidings, and cost of junctions	£1,000 0s 0d
Stations	£9,500 0s 0d
Total	£39,838 9s 6d
Contingencies (10%)	£3,983 10s 6d
Total	£43,822 0s 0d

Engineer John Wilson rounded this up to £45,000. In addition, the cost of 52 acres of land was estimated at £1,560 0s 0d.

Above:
A typical train from Tollesbury has arrived in the low-level platform at Kelvedon towards the end of the passenger service. The engine shed is beyond the locomotive, and the up main line is on the right. *Ian Allan Library/LGRP*

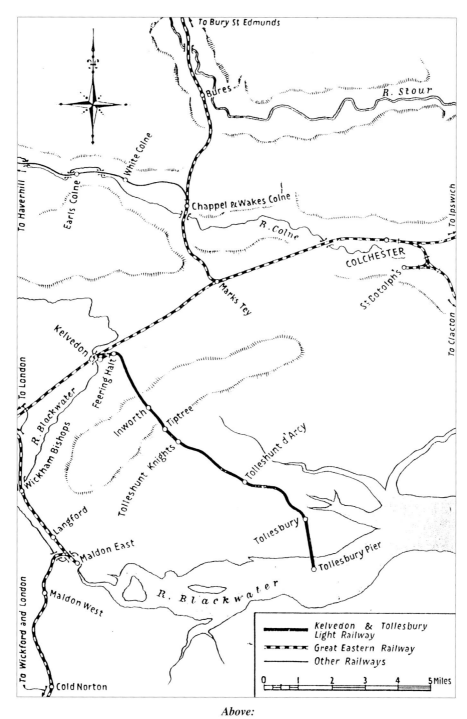

Above:
The Kelvedon & Tollesbury Light Railway. *The Railway Magazine*

The line was planned to terminate at Mill Creek on the River Blackwater, where it was hoped to tap into the burgeoning popularity of holidays and yachting on the coast, and develop coastal shipping trade. A sharp curve of one furlong radius was envisaged at Kelvedon, with frequent gradients along the line of 1 in 50, and it was to be left to the discretion of the railway company as to whether it laid single or double track. A considerable amount of the necessary land was given free of charge by Arthur Wilkin, who had extensive farming and horticultural interests in the area, and who also owned the Britannia Fruit Preserving Company Ltd. This connection ensured the continued rail service to the Tiptree factory, long after the branch had closed to passengers. Land was also given free of charge by the estate of Thomas Wallis of Tollesbury. The Light Railway Order was dated 29 January 1901, but construction did not start until early 1903. Exceptionally wet weather delayed the expected opening of the line between Kelvedon and Tollesbury

village from the summer of 1904 until 1 October, with the extension to Tollesbury Pier following early the next year.

At Kelvedon the main line runs in a southwest to northeast direction, with the main station on the London side of the River Blackwater, which it bridges together with Station Road. The light railway ran parallel for a short way and terminated below it at a low platform about a foot high, typical of those on the line. A wooden footway across the road and river bridge led from the up platform down to the low-level station, whose passenger facilities extended to no more than a small waiting shed; other business was done in the main station. The platform line extended into the corrugated-iron engine shed, and there was also a coal stage, water column and brick-built mess hut. The layout in later years was unusual in having a three-way hand-operated point in the yard. Between the up main and the low-level station a steep incline connected light railway and main line, which was normally used only

51

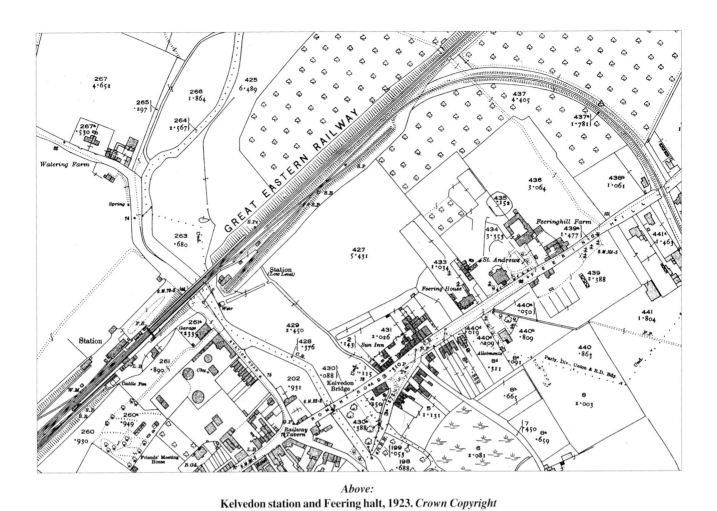

Above:
Kelvedon station and Feering halt, 1923. *Crown Copyright*

Below:
Tiptree station and Tudwick Road siding, 1922. *Crown Copyright*

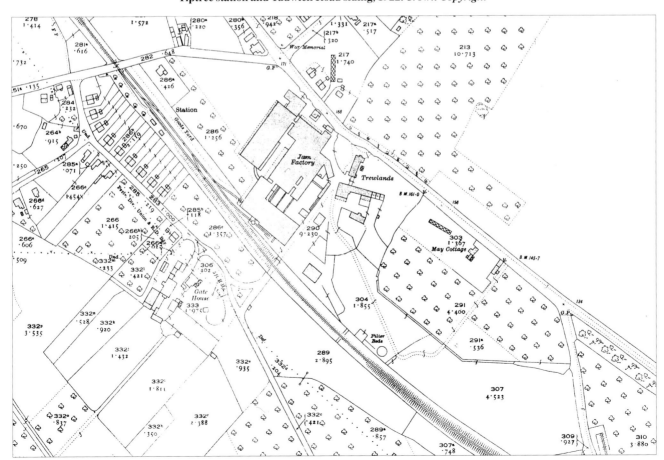

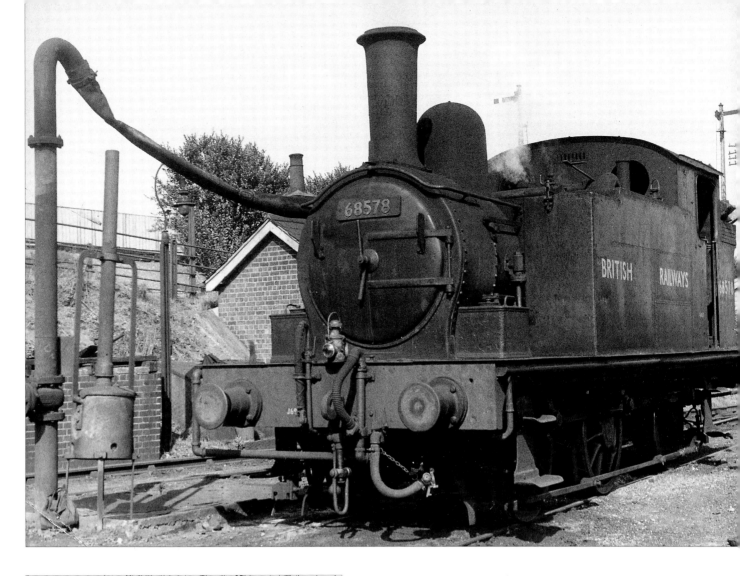

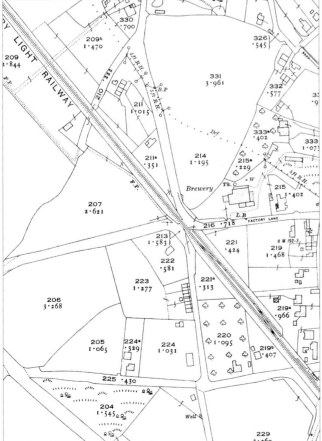

by goods trains and by the branch engine going to or from Colchester, its parent shed, for boiler washout and other maintenance at weekends.

The branch quickly turned through 90° on leaving the light railway station, rising at 1 in 63 and passing over one of many occupation crossings. The line then crossed the main London to Colchester road, later the A12, just short of Feering halt, where train crews operated the gates, and which sported a most unusual station building: an ancient motorbus body serving as waiting room and parcels office. About ¼ mile further was Brooklands private siding, followed by Heath public siding at 2 miles 62 chains, and Inworth platform a mere six chains beyond the siding. Heath siding handled general goods traffic and showed the typical double-ended Kelvedon & Tollesbury pattern with loading gauge, road access being from the Kelvedon end. When the line was being promoted, Inworth had a population of 594 (1891 census), while Tiptree itself did not exist, Tiptree Heath, the Hall and Priory being the bearers of the name. Later, Tiptree came to dominate its surroundings, outgrowing Tolleshunt and Tollesbury. Inworth had passenger accommodation provided by an old four-wheeled coach body, and handled passengers only. At the Tollesbury end of the platform was a gated level crossing, protected by the usual 10mph warning boards, followed by a half-mile run to Tiptree station, which was the main intermediate place on the line.

Tiptree had a single low platform on the southeast side of the line, on the Tollesbury side of the level crossing, here provided only with cattle guards. However, although there were no gates, barriers were provided, which had to be placed and secured across the road while shunting was in progress. Passenger provision was more extensive than elsewhere, with three buildings on the platform, all wooden with corrugated-iron roofs, and with oil lamps either on rail-built posts or fixed to the buildings. The accommodation included a waiting room, office and an oil store, and there were well-tended gardens around the buildings. Public access was by means of a path from the level crossing. Opposite the platform was the double-ended goods siding, with a headshunt running back to the crossing, and provided with a loading platform along much of its length. At the Tollesbury end it connected to two sidings which gave access to the adjacent jam factory via two wagon turntables, this providing a very important source of seasonal traffic. As with all the stations and sidings on the line, coal was important, but more specialised traffic included sugar and glass into Wilkin's factory, while fruit and vegetables, notably peas, beans and strawberries, were despatched. In the peak of the season this could mean up to 15 trucks a day of strawberries, with carts queuing outside the station to get in. Other fruits loaded included apples and pears.

The line then fell for half a mile, over the ungated crossing of Tudwick Road, with the siding of that name making a trailing connection on the north side of the line. This was a public facility, and also handled a considerable amount of traffic for the jam factory such as coal, with hay and straw from the farms going out to London, returning as manure. Spent hops from breweries also arrived for use on the farms. Tolleshunt Knights platform was only 14 chains further, and had no facilities other than for passengers, who sheltered in the usual coach body. There was an oil lamp and nameboard, and that was about it. There was a bridge over Blind Lane on the Tollesbury side of the platform, which had been built wide enough for two tracks. The nature of the countryside now changed somewhat, becoming more alluvial with grazing cattle rather than arable cultivation, and the line undulated on its way to Tollesbury.

Church public siding was about 2¼ miles from Tiptree, close to Manifold Wick farm, and had similar facilities to Heath siding. Tolleshunt D'Arcy station was a mile away, with a wooden station building similar to the largest at Tiptree, with another very small hut on the platform, and also a wooden coach body which bore the station nameboard on its roof. The goods siding was opposite the

passenger platform and took the usual form, with loading gauge. There was a gated level crossing at the Tiptree end of the station, whose working varied from that for other such crossings. The train had to be brought to a stand well clear of the gates, which were then opened by the fireman. Having pulled through, it then stopped clear on the far side, and the guard closed them, the driver being enjoined not to proceed until he had received the 'all-clear' from the guard. At Tolleshunt D'Arcy the first train of the day from Kelvedon brought a porter, who had to open and close the gates for this train, which then pulled through and left him there for the day. The person in charge had to see to the gates during the day.

Old Hall public siding was a further 1¼ miles, just beyond the 7¾ milepost, and also had an ungated level crossing, with Tollesbury reached at 8 miles 35 chains, the two miles from Tolleshunt being quite sharply curved. It was one of the few permanently staffed places on the line, with a building similar to that at Tolleshunt D'Arcy on the platform, plus an old coach body. The usual goods facilities were provided, the siding being opposite the passenger platform and reached from the road by the ungated level crossing at the east end of the station. This carried the lane from the village, which was a short distance to the south. Beyond the crossing was the run-round loop, which was the effective terminus of the line after the extension to the pier was abandoned. However, although officially closed on 17 July 1921, this remained in situ, and even in the early 1950s could still be followed by intrepid explorers prepared to pick their way through the brambles and bushes. The pier station was a further 1½ miles, at the end of an almost completely straight line, and with a wooden shelter with awning, plus two coach bodies on the far side of the track. The pier itself extended 1,770ft out into the Blackwater, although it remained a desolate spot and the hoped-for leisure traffic never materialised. The estuary was muddy, in contrast to the sandy delights of nearby Clacton and Walton, while other nearby ports such as Wivenhoe and Maldon were long-established and already rail-connected.

The only signals on the line were at Kelvedon, where there was a small signal cabin, and at Feering, site of the fixed distant for Kelvedon's home signal. The line was worked on the one-engine-in-steam principle, the train staff being round and painted green and kept in the Kelvedon stationmaster's office. Despite this, since two engines could run coupled together, shunting was permitted in emergencies at Tollesbury provided that a flagman with detonators was sent out by the person in charge to a distance of about 1,000

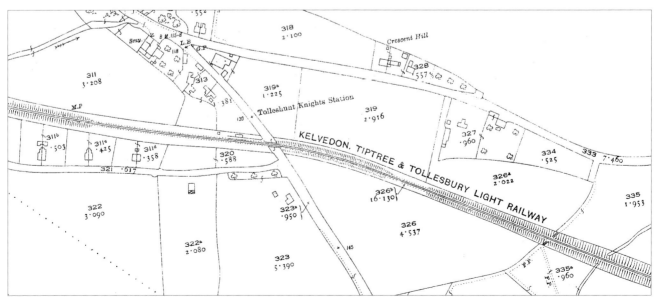

Above:
Tolleshunt Knights station, 1922. *Crown Copyright*

Above:
Tiptree station, showing the buildings on the platform from the loading dock.
The jam factory is behind the camera and to the left. *Hugh Davies*

Below:
Tolleshunt D'Arcy station in about 1950, showing the unusual
position of the station nameboard. *Stations UK*

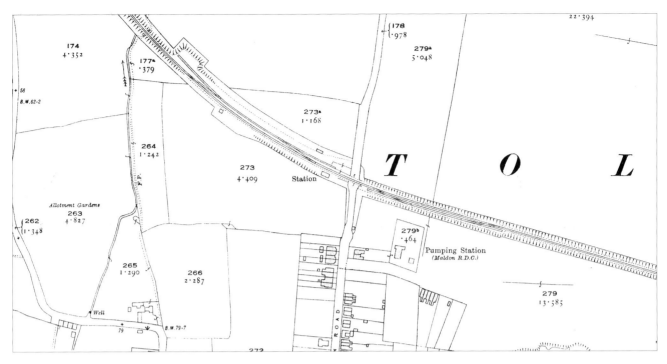

Above:
Tollesbury station, 1922. *Crown Copyright*

Above:
Tollesbury Pier, intact. The nature of the land is evident from the salt marsh
in the foreground. The line closed officially in July 1921. *Ian Allan Library/LGRP*

Below:
An altogether different view of the pier in the postwar period, with a laid-up 'Liberty' ship moored in the River
Blackwater. The Navy had blown a hole in the pier to reduce the threat of invasion. *Cyril W. Footer*

Above:
'J67' No 68608 heads a train from Tollesbury near Kelvedon.
The undulating nature of the line can easily be seen. *P. Ransome-Wallis*

yards, to prevent the train from approaching closer while the line was blocked. Tolleshunt D'Arcy had to be advised, so that the train was not allowed to leave that station for Tollesbury. As was standard on light railways, the speed limit on the line was 25mph, or 15mph if working tender-first. Level crossings were restricted to 10mph.

Locomotives on the line were usually Class J67 0-6-0Ts, although the first to work the branch was a small Great Eastern Adams 0-4-2 tank, No 25, which was scrapped in 1905. Since tickets were always issued on the trains, tram-type rolling stock was needed so that conductor-guards could get to all coaches while the train was moving, and the Great Eastern therefore converted eight six-wheeled coaches to corridor stock with vestibule connections. Steps were needed for boarding, given the low platforms, and this meant that the stock could not stray from the line, having to have the steps removed if going to Stratford for repair. Since the coaches used on the line had Westinghouse brakes, they had to travel to the works by goods train. In 1928, some of the coaches from the Wisbech & Upwell Tramway were transferred to the line, following its closure to passengers, there being both four-wheeled and bogie types. Both had end platforms with elaborate wrought-iron railings, and although strictly forbidden, riding on them when the coach was at the back of the train often happened. Because of their low frames the Wisbech & Upwell coaches had to have raised buffer beams fitted in order to bring buffers and couplings up to the

standard height. At the end, six-wheeler No 62261 and bogie No 60461 formed the train, with No 62262 as spare; it had been possible to get a train containing four, six and eight-wheeled stock in one train. This was also some of the last gas-lit stock on British Railways. Tickets were printed at Stratford works, and were punched to indicate destination; passengers travelling beyond the branch had to rebook at Kelvedon.

Services on the line reflected its rural nature and the traffic on offer. In 1913 weekdays started with the 6.50am goods from Kelvedon, which called at Tiptree, Tudwick Road and Church sidings as required, Tolleshunt D'Arcy, Old Hall siding as required and Tollesbury village, taking an hour for the journey. If necessary the locomotive then worked empty coaches to Tollesbury Pier, and the first up train started from there if required at 8.7am. If this ran, it waited at Tollesbury village from 8.13 to 8.25am, and then called at Tolleshunt D'Arcy, Tolleshunt Knights on request, Tiptree, Inworth on request and arrived at Kelvedon at 8.59am. Should there be traffic for Brooklands and Heath sidings, it was worked by special goods train from Kelvedon to Tiptree and back, hauled by the engine from the 8.7am up from Tollesbury Pier, and arranged between Kelvedon and Tiptree stations. There was then a mixed train at 10.22am from Kelvedon, which was allowed to convey horse and carriage traffic for Tollesbury, and did not serve the sidings. There were then passenger trains at 12.26, 1.58 and 5.43pm, plus one at 7.53pm on Wednesdays and Fridays only.

In the up direction, in addition to the trains already mentioned, there was a mixed at 11.9am from Tollesbury Pier, passenger at 1.12pm from Tollesbury village, empty stock from Tollesbury Pier to village at 2.43pm (this was the back working from the 1.58pm from Kelvedon), and passenger trains from the Pier at 6.28 and 8.26pm, the last on Wednesdays and Fridays only. Several trains worked to or started from the Pier only if required. In addition, there was a goods train from Tollesbury village at 3.30pm which called everywhere as required, except the platforms, reaching Kelvedon at 4.55pm. The 11.9am from the Pier was specially designated to work fruit and green peas for the north from the stations, and took 62 minutes to cover the 10 miles of the branch. In the peak of the season it was sometimes necessary to arrange for extra goods trains to work the fruit, bean and pea traffic after the normal service had finished. Coal traffic was worked into all the stations and sidings.

In the summer of 1922, the service was thinner, with only three down and four up trains, Inworth and Tolleshunt Knights being request stops. Tollesbury Pier still appeared in the timetable, even though no trains were shown and it had officially closed. Journey times were very variable, with the 3.15pm up from Tollesbury taking 65 minutes, and the 6.42pm up only 45 minutes. Feering halt had yet to be opened.

In summer 1937, the service looked more similar to that in 1913, with a few changes: a mixed at 9.30am (9.41am from 1 June)

instead of 10.22am, and the 1.48pm from Kelvedon running on Wednesdays and Saturdays only. The 8.30pm from Kelvedon, another Wednesdays and Saturdays only, worked back at 9.17pm empty stock, with the guard putting out the lights at the stations. The 3.15pm continued to call at the sidings to take up important traffic, which otherwise had to wait until the following day. The 8.30am and 6.42pm were still authorised to convey horse and carriage traffic from Tollesbury, reflecting the nature of the area. An extra allowance still had to be made for shunting on the mixed workings, and this fact did not go unnoticed by passengers, especially when there was no goods traffic, and the bus was quicker and more direct. There were two goods brake vans in use on the line, one branded 'Kelvedon' and the other 'Tollesbury'. In its heyday, a typical mixed train would consist of the locomotive, two coaches and around 10 trucks, although this could vary considerably.

The line was initially maintained by four gangs of men based at Kelvedon, Tiptree, Tolleshunt D'Arcy and Tollesbury, with four men per gang. Economy measures saw the introduction of motor trolleys, after which the number of men was reduced to seven to cover the whole line, although the track was still walked every day. The pay for railway work was considered to be good — better than in the jam factory — although there was almost always the need for week-end working. There were the usual complaints from local people about excessive smoke and fires, but there was little or no vandalism.

Wartime saw the passenger service reduced to the 10.12am and

Below:
Tollesbury station in LNER days, with the train ready to return. The level crossing is protected only by the cattle guards, while the run-round loop is behind the camera. *Ian Allan Library/LGRP*

Above:
Illustrating the connection between the light railway and the main line, this photograph shows an REC special returning to the main line on 6 April 1957. The low-level station is long gone. *Austin Attewell*

TIPTREE (Essex)
Miles 45¾. Map Sq 24. Clos. day Wed.
From Liverpool Street via Chelmsford
and Kelvedon.
No through fares.
Served by trains to Tollesbury, 21 min.
shorter journey.
Bus facilities. From Maldon, Bus Stn.,
approx. hourly (except Sun. a.m.),
30 min. journey, also from Colchester, Bus Park, approx. hourly
(except Sun. a.m.), 30 min. journey.

Left and right:
ABC Railway Guide,
1949. *Author's Collection*

TOLLESBURY (Essex)
Miles 50¾. Map Sq. 24.
Pop. 1,694. Clos. day Wed.
From Liverpool Street via Chelmsford
and Kelvedon.
No through fares.

Liv. St	Tolles	Tolles.	Liv. St.
a.m.		a.m.	
8 24	10 50	8 30	10 40
p.m.		p.m.	
4 12	6 25	12 50e	3 20
—	—	12 50s	3 33
—	—	6 37	9 4
—	—	—	—
—	—	—	—
—	—	—	—
—	—	—	—
—	—	—	—

No Sunday Trains.
❸ 3rd cl. only.
e Not Sat.   s Sat. only.

5.46pm from Kelvedon, and 8.30am and 12.50 and 6.35pm from Tollesbury, but now booked to call at all stations and platforms, and still involving some mixed workings. For a time the disused portion of the line saw use by four rail-mounted 8in naval guns, but the experiment did not last for long, although the line still had to be patrolled by the Home Guard at night. The pier was breached as a security measure against invasion. Summer 1946 saw very little change to the times, nor had they by 1949, when a departure from Liverpool Street at 8.24am could get an arrival in Tollesbury at 10.50am — 2 hours 26 minutes for just over 50 miles.

Bus competition had eroded most of the passenger traffic on the branch, helped by fares perceived as high and the slowness of the trains. At the end there was one season ticket holder on the line, a Mr Lewis, who was a boot repairer and had a wooden booth at Tiptree station, to which he travelled from Tollesbury every day. There were several people who worked at Wilkin's jam factory at Tiptree who used the train, and others who likewise used it to get to the Anchor Press at Tollesbury. The last passenger trains ran on Saturday 5 May 1951, with the last train containing both the ex-Stoke Ferry branch coaches, which had been transferred to the line some time after the withdrawal of the passenger services on that branch. This meant the closure of the platforms (Inworth and Tolleshunt Knights) and Feering halt, but the line remained open for goods and other passenger-rated traffic such as parcels. A substitute bus service connected Tollesbury, Tiptree, Kelvedon and Witham. The *Essex Chronicle* reported on the death of the 'Crab & Winkle': it should have been the 'Jam & Oyster', but the 'Crab & Winkle' tag was stuck to many branches as well as

Above:
**The last day of the Kelvedon & Tollesbury saw the locomotive decorated with wreaths and chalked
slogans proclaiming 'RIP Born 1904 Died 1951'. Here, a mixed train leaves Kelvedon Low Level,
and contains stock from both the Stoke Ferry and Wisbech & Upwell lines.** *Stations UK*

the Brightlingsea, its proper home. Driver Tom Gardener chalked 'Born 1904 — Died 1951 R.I.P.' on the smokebox door of the locomotive, as well as adorning both tank sides, and wreaths of tulips and daffodils were hung from the tanks and smokebox. Hundreds of passengers crammed into the three coaches, some riding on the platforms despite the time-stained notices forbidding it. Detonators were placed at the stations and villagers turned out to wave and cheer from the platforms and the sagging, converted carriage waiting rooms. The 'Crab & Winkle' steamed into history, killed off by Osborne's buses.

However, the section beyond Tiptree did not last long, and Church siding, Tolleshunt D'Arcy, Old Hall siding and Tollesbury closed on 29 October 1951, leaving Tudwick Road as the limit of operations. Track in the low-level station at Kelvedon was eventually lifted, although the sidings there still housed the Wisbech & Upwell coaches early in 1952, and the branch simply trailed into the up main at Kelvedon via the incline. Much of the line remaining was relaid. In 1952 the outward goods working left Kelvedon at noon and was booked to return from Tiptree at 5pm, while the Summer 1956 timetable showed the workings as a Class K goods from Kelvedon to Tiptree at 8.30am (8.40am Saturdays only), calling at Heath siding and Tudwick Road as required, and arriving at Tiptree at 9am. The train then returned from Tiptree (or Tudwick Road) at 10.30am, reaching Kelvedon at 10.45am. These trains were often worked by 'J15s'. The rise of road transport was inexorable, and although visited by the inevitable enthusiasts' excursions, where the participants rode in open trucks and entrained or detrained by means of ladders, the line finally closed from 1 October 1962, and little trace now remains. Tiptree station has vanished beneath a car park, and much of the land has gone back to the farmers. The passenger on the main line will now be hard pushed to figure out where the branch diverged.

Saffron Walden Railway

SAFFRON Walden is an important town of considerable antiquity in northwest Essex which had shrunk from a population of over 5,000 after it was bypassed by the Northern & Eastern Railway, whose line from London to Cambridge went through Audley End, opened as Wenden in 1845. In the 1860s, when the Saffron Walden Railway was proposed, the population had decreased to about 4,700, but it was still one of the largest towns in the area, and over twice the size of nearby Thaxted. The Gibsons were a prominent local family involved in banking — Gibson, Tuke & Gibson — and were instrumental in promoting the new line. Two of the family became directors, with one — Wyatt George Gibson — becoming the first company chairman. The Saffron Walden Railway obtained its Act on 22 July 1861 for a line connecting the town with Audley End; a second was needed, obtained on 22 June 1863, for the extension to Bartlow on the proposed line between Shelford and Haverhill. The new railway was seen locally as a feeder to the Eastern Counties main line, and working by that company for 50% of receipts was considered fair. The extension of the Colne Valley & Halstead line to Saffron Walden was also under consideration as a further boost to prosperity, and assurances were sought about costs and guarantees. Saffron Walden grew considerably with the coming of its railway, and had increased its population to 6,104 by 1891.

The authorised capital of the railway was initially £95,000, but this was rapidly increased to £150,000 by 1869, which was far higher than could be sustained by a local concern. As was often the case, it was worked from the start by the Great Eastern, in this instance under a provisional agreement, which was made permanent from 30 March 1869. The GER worked it as a country branch line, and although there were initially nine trips daily when the first section opened on 23 November 1865, this had been reduced to five by 1868 (with an extra on Mondays), when extended to Bartlow. The extension was opened on 22 November 1866, and by 1868 was seeing only one through train daily, with another on Saturdays.

The financial situation continued to be difficult, and half-yearly reports showed disappointing results, although for the year ended 30 June 1869 the gross receipts were £1,337 14s 3d, which represented an increase of £84 0s 9d over the previous six months. The directors at this time were George Stacey Gibson (chairman), John Stephenson Robson (vice-chairman), the Marquis of Salisbury, George Wodehouse Currie and Thomas Shirley, and the company hoped that better working arrangements to Bartlow could be made. The railway was kept going only by loans from the Gibsons' bank, and at one point its secretary, W. B. Freeland, filed a petition against it for bankruptcy. Various schemes of arrangement were proposed,

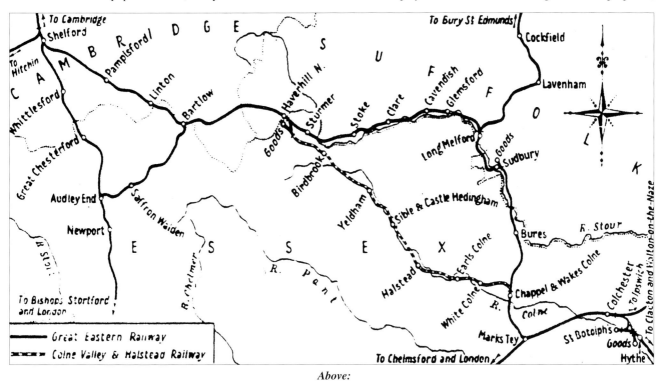

Above:
The Eastern Region lines between Marks Tey and Shelford, showing pre-Grouping ownership. *The Railway Magazine*

Above:
The Saffron Walden push-pull train is ready to leave from the branch platform at Audley End on
30 May 1953. Class G5 0-4-4T No 67269 has been unofficially named 'Lucy Belle'. *R. E. Vincent*

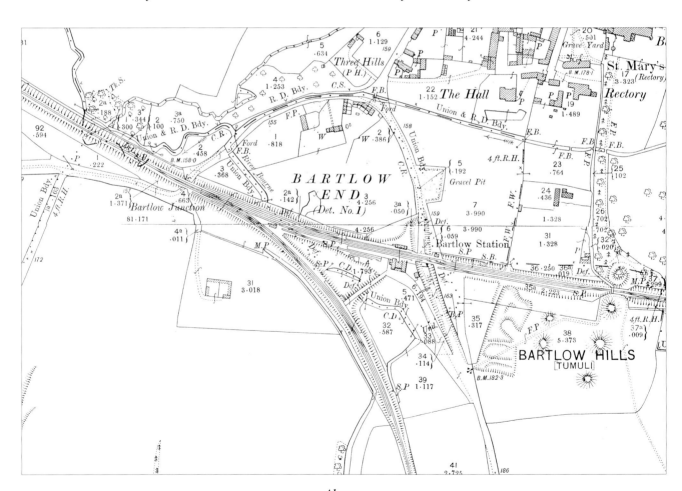

Above:
Bartlow station, 1903. *Crown Copyright*

Above:
**Class N7 0-6-2T No 69690 stands in the branch platform at Bartlow with a Saffron Walden
train on 14 June 1958, shortly before railbuses were introduced.** *G. R. Mortimer*

and there were also thoughts of liquidation. The company was capitalised at £159,000, but in 1874 the capital situation was that £82,490-worth of ordinary shares had been issued, with a further £12,510 unissued; £25,000 preference shares had not been issued, and the debenture stock was £30,985 issued and £8,015 unissued. The Great Eastern, which had subscribed to the original scheme, purchased the line for £70,750 with effect from 1 January 1877, which was authorised by its Act of June of that year. The financial situation at last became much more manageable.

There seem to have been no major problems with construction. The railway was built with the aid of a small Manning, Wardle locomotive, builder's number 143, which was delivered in January 1865 and named *Little Eastern*. The railway had its own platform on the up side of Audley End station, and curved away to the east. It crossed the Bishop's Stortford to Cambridge road, later the A11, and the River Cam in quick succession, crossing the valley on an embankment. There was then a long cutting, a further embankment over the stream, and then another cutting before passing under the road to Newport about two miles from Audley End. Saffron Walden is in a valley, and the railway did not descend and go through the centre, but approached from the southwest along the valley side and passed through the southern edge of the town. It crossed far below the Debden road, which climbs steeply out of the town, and emerged into the station, the area for which had been excavated out of the hillside, with Station Road to the north running parallel to the line and along the contour. West Road, to the south, was at a considerably greater elevation. Beyond the station South Road also crossed the line by a bridge, but the line then emerged on to an embankment, crossing over the Thaxted and Radwinter roads by bridges. It then turned more northerly in direction, crossing the road to Ashdon near the future Acrow halt, with about a mile in open country before a further succession of cuttings brought it to Ashdon halt, about 5¼ miles from Audley End. This was much

nearer Church End, at about ½ mile, than Ashdon, a mile away. The railway then followed a northerly course for a further two miles to Bartlow, crossing the River Bourne about ¾ mile south of the village. The junction faced Shelford, although trains did not generally run through from Audley End.

The Saffron Walden Railway had its own platform at Bartlow station, oil-lit to the very end, and linked to the Stour Valley line by means of a footpath carried on a bank which emerged at the back of the main station building on the Cambridge-bound platform of the main line. A run-round was provided on the Saffron Walden platform, and an extension of this loop joined that from the other platform, together forming a headshunt for both. The branch platform had a somewhat ramshackle appearance, certainly from the rail side, as the front wall consisted of sleepers, with the coping made from split timbers, although the overhang had to be supported by extra pieces of wood. A simple flat-roofed wooden shelter sufficed here.

Tickets could be issued from Audley End, Saffron Walden and Bartlow to Ashdon halt, which consisted of a simple, single platform, the line being somewhat sinuous at this point. Also oil-lit until the end, some of the standards were made of old rail with the lamp housings bolted on the top. An old coach body provided shelter. Although all trains called, tickets were not issued to passengers joining here, guards being instructed to take a record of them and inform staff at Saffron Walden or Bartlow. Those wishing to travel beyond the branch had to rebook.

Acrow halt was an austere-looking concrete structure built from prefabricated sections and serving the factory of that company. It was backed by a modern steel post and rail fence and with a concrete shelter, and the nameboard was in the company's characteristic trademark style. An elevated path led from the side of the shelter to the factory. It was opened on 25 March 1957 in a ceremony attended by the Mayor of Saffron Walden, and the driver

Above:
A railbus stands at Bartlow with a Saffron Walden working. The path to the main station is opposite, while the sum total of the passenger facilities on this platform can be seen.
David Lawrence

Left:
The railbus for Saffron Walden waits at Bartlow. The lamps provide a splendid period piece.
Hugh Davies

Left:
The view forward from the interior of a four-wheel railbus, shortly after arrival at Bartlow.
Hugh Davies

Left:
The more traditional Ashdon halt, between Saffron Walden and Bartlow, sporting the usual oil lamps and old coach body. The lineside is kept very tidy.
Stations UK

and fireman of the first train to call, hauled by 'N7' 0-6-2T No 69651, were each presented with a bottle of champagne. There was no mention of the halt in the public timetables.

Saffron Walden station, as befitted one serving an important town, was built on a large scale, even though having only a single platform and a relatively short passing loop. The main station buildings and platform were on the town or north side of the line, and in white brick with red relief on mullions, quoins and so on. It essentially had two two-storey blocks at each end, joined by a central section which housed the main entrance and booking hall. The awning spanned the length of thc main building. At the east end were a number of single-storey buildings used as stores, toilets and so on. Further along again was a covered open-fronted structure which could be used to store bicycles and the like, with a lamp hut and oil store at the platform end. Immediately past Debden Road bridge a turnout led to the sidings on the north side of the running line, and two wagon turntables located close to the road embankment gave access to two short sidings at right-angles to the line. There was a substantial goods shed and cattle pens, this siding running right up to a loading bay at the west end of the main building. On the south side of the loop a long loading dock served

an iron and brass foundry, and in the 19th century, a cement works. The site of the latter was turned over to allotment gardens during World War 1. This siding continued as far as the bridge at the east end of the layout, where there was a sawmill. South Road crossed the line here, and a headshunt from the loop continued under it and served a corn mill and a further small yard in Farmadine Road. The line, still on a double-track formation, continued on an embankment, across Thaxted Road, with the long headshunt stopping short of this point. The station could handle all classes of traffic, and had a 1½-ton crane available. In later years a number of light industries grew up in the town, including Acrow (Engineering) Ltd's Coronation Works (for which the halt was built), plastics, printing and nurseries. The last generated boxes of carnations which were sent out daily by rail all over the country. In 1938, the main freight traffic had been in hay, straw and livestock, which amounted to just over 450 tons for the year. In 1962 the total tonnage received was 7,451 and 4,945 forwarded.

The very earliest services have already been mentioned. By 1880 there were seven trains each weekday from Audley End, with four of these going through to Bartlow. There were eight in the other direction, again with four serving Bartlow, the first leaving Saffron

Left:
Acrow halt, built to serve the factory near Saffron Walden.
Stations UK

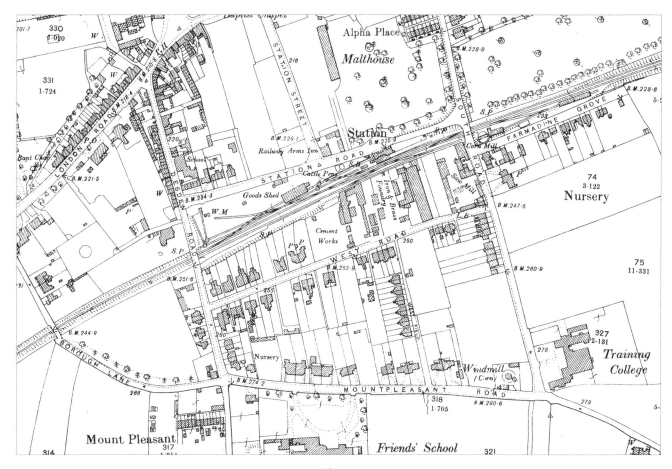

Above:
Saffron Walden station, 1897. *Crown Copyright*

Below:
A general view of Saffron Walden station from the east, taken in 1964, showing the passenger
platform and buildings, factories on the left, and goods shed in the distance. *Stations UK*

Walden at 7.30am and taking seven minutes for the journey. The 9.20am was extended to Bishop's Stortford, where it was advertised as catching the quick train and arriving in Liverpool Street at 11.10am, and St Pancras at 11.14am. The length of the branch could be travelled in about 20 minutes. Three years later matters had improved considerably, and there were now 12 trains each way on weekdays from Audley End to Saffron Walden, again with four extended to or from Bartlow. The first down was designated as 'Parliamentary', and duly took about five minutes longer to reach Bartlow. By 1911 there were more changes, with 11 trains on weekdays from Saffron Walden to Audley End, the first two going through to London, but now with only three trains from Bartlow. There were nine down trains on weekdays, but one was extended to and from Bartlow on Tuesdays only. At this time a third class ticket from Saffron Walden to Cambridge cost 1s 4d.

In the interwar period the timetable improved greatly, and by 1937 there were 18 trains daily from Audley End to Saffron Walden, seven going through to Bartlow. There was one return working daily to and from Bishop's Stortford, which left Saffron Walden at 3.35pm, arrived at Stortford at 4.5pm and returned from there at 5.13pm. There were three extra on Saturdays. Goods trains ran from Audley End at 6.35am and 2.5pm (Saturdays excepted, 2.55pm Saturdays only), with the 8.42am from Saffron Walden being a mixed train to Bartlow. In the event of the goods from London missing the 6.35am, the 9.14am was authorised to run as a mixed train, and was then allowed an extra four minutes. In the other direction there were goods trains up from Saffron Walden at 6am, 1.15pm (Saturdays excepted, 2.10pm Saturdays only), and 7.20pm Saturdays excepted. There were no scheduled goods workings from Bartlow, although the 7.55pm to Saffron Walden was allowed to convey three piped wagons of goods or cattle if

necessary. A goods engine was allocated to shunting at Saffron Walden at 9.30am on weekdays. Passenger train speeds in the mid-1920s were 40mph between Audley End and Saffron Walden, and 30mph onwards to Bartlow, while goods trains were restricted to 25mph throughout. There were additional restrictions at Audley End, where down trains running on to the branch were restricted to 15mph through the platform, and up trains to a mere 5mph when going onto the up loop from the single line. When the branch opened for traffic there had been an intention to provide another platform here, but nothing came of it.

Branch trains were worked by a variety of motive power. In the 1930s it was common for ex-Great Northern Class C12 4-4-2Ts to be seen on the line, perhaps stepping up from pilot duties at Cambridge. Ex-North Eastern 0-4-4T 'G5s' also appeared on passenger services, one running in 1953 with the unofficial name *Lucy Belle* chalked on the smokebox door. As 'N7s' were displaced by electrification from London suburban services, they migrated out into the country and became regular performers on the branch prior to dieselisation. Wartime had not seen much of a cut in services, and the May 1942 timetables still showed 15 trains from Audley End, with three going on the Bartlow. In addition, there were three Saffron Walden-Bartlow workings, and a Saturday extra. With the return of peacetime the service expanded again, with 21 trains from Audley End on Monday to Friday, five going through to Bartlow, and one early train at 7.9am from Saffron Walden to Bartlow. There were slight variations on Saturdays, and it was similar in the other direction.

The branch was one of the lines which was chosen for the 1955 traffic census, and fared badly. During the week ending 27 March it recorded 932 train miles and a load factor of just 8%. This gave it a movement costs to revenue ratio of 858%. Matters appeared to

Below:
**Saffron Walden seen from the west, photographed from Debden Road bridge in 1936.
The yard is completely full of wagons, as is the goods shed. The Railway Arms can be seen to the left
of the goods shed, with the main buildings and signalbox to the right.** *Stations UK*

have improved slightly in the second survey in the week ending 3 September, when the average throughout load was given as 10 passengers, still with a load factor of 8%, but a reduction in the costs to revenue ratio to a mere 800%. Only the Mildenhall branch had worse economics. Some lines had been converted in the interim to diesel railcar operation, with considerable improvements in both loadings and operating costs, but the Saffron Walden branch was not among them.

A memorable event on the line occurred on Sunday, 22 June 1957 when a bridge was renewed at Great Chesterford on the main line. Services between London and Cambridge were diverted via the Saffron Walden branch, Bartlow and Linton. The loop at Saffron Walden proved to be too short for passing of trains there, and the only crossing point that could be used was at Linton. The branch was then worked by staff and ticket, a supply of the latter being kept in a locked box in the stationmaster's office on the branch platform at Audley End. Because workings on this particular day were unbalanced, a Cambridge Class B1 was kept occupied taking the staff to where it was next needed. Most trains went through with a ticket, and the light engine then took the staff

through the section. Pilots had to be provided for London crews, but the Cambridge men generally knew the road. Only the evening train from Colchester to Cambridge was seriously delayed, by some 40 minutes, because of waiting at Linton for other traffic to clear the section to Shelford.

The branch duly received modern rolling stock in the form of the four-wheeled German railbuses, with ticket sales boosted by the numbers of visitors to the town's many attractions, including the ancient turf maze and ruined castle. In 1961, 86,659 tickets were collected at Saffron Walden, with 54,162 issued, which generated a revenue of £20,370. A relatively healthy parcels traffic saw 16,544 despatched and 54,875 received during the year, with a resultant revenue of £3,485.

The end was not far away, however, and the branch was proposed for closure in the Beeching Report. Passenger services were duly withdrawn in September, the last trains running on Sunday 6th, the last working being formed by railbus No E79963. Goods traffic lingered a little longer, and finished from 28 December of the same year, the last train running on Christmas Eve.

Above:
A four-wheel diesel railbus leaves Saffron Walden for Audley End on 28 May 1961.
The goods yard can just be seen through the bridge. *J. C. Beckett*

Above:
The branch platform at Audley End, looking towards Saffron Walden in 1955. Ex-Great Northern 'C12' No 67375 works the 12.46pm from Saffron Walden, the stock being ex-Great Central coaches Nos 5866 and 63525. *W. A. Camwell (SLS Collection)*

Table 41 — AUDLEY END, SAFFRON WALDEN, and BARTLOW

Week Days only

Miles		am	am	am	am	a.m	a.m	p.m	a.m	p.m	p.m	p.m	pm	pm	pm	p.m	pm	pm	p.m	p.m	p.m	pm	pm	p.m	p.m
4	London(L'poolSt)dp	..	550	..	656	820	..	10 0	..	1150	1227	1255	1 16	295	..	336	3 42	..	436	5 05	518	5 51	555	637	7 20	8 22
—	Audley End......dep	..	738	813	849	941	1015	1120	1217	1 6	502	412	534	422	5 7 5	11	535	555	617	639	7 3	338	6 8	339	9 56
1½	Saffron Walden { arr	..	742	817	853	945	1019	1124	1221	1 10	2 0	452	57	349	426	5115	1539	559	621	643	7 7	37	510	337	10 0
	{ dep	7 9	..	..	..	..	1126	..	1V14	..	..	4 0	..	515	5 18	..	..	..	7V10	..	..	..	..	..	..
5½	Ashdon Halt......	718	..	..	..	..	1135	..	1V23	..	..	4 9	..	524	5 27	..	..	..	7V19	..	..	..	..	..	..
7½	Bartlow........arr	724	..	..	..	..	1140	..	1V28	..	..	414	..	529	532	..	..	..	7V24	..	..	..	..	..	..

Week Days only

Miles		am	am	am	a.m	a.m	a.m	a.m	p.m	p.m	pm	pm	pm	pm	pm	p.m	pm	pm	pm	pm	p.m	pm	p.m
—	Bartlow..........dep	..	810	..	..	..	1150	..	2 12	1	..	422	422	..	..	..	546	..	..	..	..	8 5	..
2	Ashdon Halt.........	..	816	..	..	..	1156	..	2 7	2 7	..	428	428	..	..	..	552	..	..	..	..	811	..
5½	Saffron Walden... { arr	..	824	..	..	..	12 4	..	215	215	..	436	436	..	6 3	..	..	..	..	..	..	819	..
	{ dep	7 6	755	832	9 17	10 0	11	512 5	1246	40	225	237	317	5 4	450	455	5 20	530	547	6 6	649	722	750	8 15	8 26
7½	Audley End........arr	710	759	836	9 21	10 4	11	912 9	1250	44	229	241	321	4 9	454	459	5 24	534	551	610	653	726	754	8 19	9 30
49	4 London (L'poolSt) arr	848	924	956	10 34	11 30	12 37	1V58	233	..	..	5 05	558	..	642	6 45	..	..	8 3	..	843	..	..	1117

E or Ɇ Except Saturdays
ɪ 2 minutes later on Saturdays

S or S Saturdays only
ᴍ Arr. 2 29 p.m. on Saturdays

V or Ⅴ 7 minutes later on Saturdays
Y Arr. 1 55 p.m. on Saturdays
Z 9 minutes later on Saturdays

SAFFRON WALDEN
(Essex)
Miles 43¼. Map Sq. 19.
Pop. 5,930. Clos. day Thur.
From Liverpool Street via Bishop's
Stortford and Audley End
1st cl.—Single 15/3, Mtn. Ret. 18/5.
3rd cl.—Single 9/1, Mtn. Ret. 12/3.

Liv. St.	Saff. W.	Saff. W.	Liv. St.
a.m.		a.m.	
5 50	7 42	7 6	8 48
6 56	8 53	7 6	9 23
8 20r	9 45	8 32	9 54
10 0	11 25	9 17r	10 30
11 50er	1 10	10 0	11 36
11 50sr	1 16	11 5er	12 37
p.m.		11 5sr	12 45
12 30s	2 0	12 0	1 55
12 55e	2 45	p.m.	
1 16s	2 57	12 46s	2 34
2 25r	3 49	12 46r	2 40
3 35e	5 11	3 17e	5 0
3 42s	5 15	3 17s	5 3
4 36e	6 0	4 5r	6 0
5 0sr	6 28	4 55sr	6 48
5 15e	6 43	5 20er	6 48
5 54er	7 11	6 10	8 3
5 54sr	7 14	7 22	8 45
5 57e	7 37	9 28	11 19
6 38	8 10	—	—
7 20r	8 38	—	—
8 22	10 0	—	—
—	—	—	—

No Sunday Trains.

e Not Sat. **s** Sat. only.
r Refresh. Car.
Bus facilities from Bishop's Stortford,
E. National Bus Office, approx. two-
hourly (except Sun. a.m.), 50 min.
journey.

Above:
Winter 1951-2 timetable. *Author's Collection*

Left:
ABC Railway Guide, December 1949.
Author's Collection

Right:
ABC Railway Guide, December 1962.
Author's Collection

Below:
7 September 1964-13 June 1965 timetable.
Author's Collection

BARTLOW (Cambs)
49 miles.
From Liverpool Street via Audley End
2nd class 12/3.
Via Shelford.
2nd class 15/6, 1st class 23/3.
Via Cambridge.
2nd class 17/-, 1st class 25/6.

Liv. St.	Bart.	Bart.	Liv. St.
a.m.		a.m.	
6 32	8‡46	7 25 e	8•52
8b36	9 50	7 25 s	8 58
9b36 e	11‡18	10 38	11b58
9 36 s	11‡18	p.m.	
10b38	11 50	12 38	1b58
p.m.		2 38	3b58
12b36	1 50	4 28	5b58
2b36	4 18	5 57 e	7 46
4b36	5 48	5 57 s	7b58
6b38	7 56	8 20	10 16
—	—	—	—

K58 WEEKDAYS — BISHOP'S STORTFORD AND BRAINTREE

			8-17	8-17	8-17					8-17		8-17		8-17
DOWN			Easton Lodge arr. 8.45 dep. 9.15	Easton Lodge arr. 8.45 dep. 9.15	Easton Lodge 'R'		**UP**							
Mileage				SO	SX	SX	Mileage					SO		SX	SX
M C							M C							PM
0 0	BISHOP'S STORTFORD......dep		8 25	8 25	13 30	0 0	BRAINTREE ......dep		..	10 45		16 00
5 21	Takeley .. .. .. arr		..	..		2 14	Rayne .. .. .. arr					
	.. .. .. dep		..	..			.. .. .. dep					
9 27	Dunmow ...... arr		9 25	9 25	14 20	6 8	Felsted .. .. .. arr		..	11 06		16 21
	...... dep		9 35	9 35	14 35		.. .. .. dep		10 30	11 21		16 31
11 67	Felsted .. .. arr		9 47	9 47	14 47	8 48	Dunmow .. .. .. arr		10 42	11 33		16 43
	.. .. dep		..	9 57	15 02		.. .. .. dep		11 00	12 17		16 53
15 61	Rayne .. .. arr		..	..		12 54	Takeley .. .. .. arr					
	.. .. dep		..	..			.. .. .. dep					R
17 75	BRAINTREE .. .. arr		..	10 18	15 23	17 75	BISHOP'S STORTFORD .. arr		11 25	12 45		17 20

Swaffham to Thetford and Bury St Edmunds

RAILWAY building progressed rapidly throughout the 19th century, the main lines soon linking the major towns and ports. Frequently the main flows of traffic were towards London, and often routes were dictated by geography, so that the smaller settlements — and some of the larger ones — were not always linked to each other by rail, or to the system at all. Thetford and Bury St Edmunds were two such places, and there were many other towns and villages in Suffolk and Norfolk in a similar

Above:
The railways between Swaffham, Thetford and Bury St Edmunds. *The Railway Magazine*

position, Watton and Swaffham among them. The railway from Norwich had reached Thetford in 1845, giving it a link to London. Bury was reached the following year, from Ipswich, although the railway was not extended westwards to Newmarket and Cambridge until 1854. Swaffham had been connected to King's Lynn since August 1847, the Lynn & Dereham being opened throughout in September 1848. It was felt in the area that there was a need for better north-south rail communication, as the existing lines were almost entirely east-west orientated, and there was also an element of feeling against the Eastern Counties Railway.

There were many schemes to fill this void in rural railway communication in East Anglia. A bill for a London & Norwich Direct Railway was deposited in 1845, which would have run from Elsenham through Bury to Thetford. There it would have joined the existing main line of the Norwich & Brandon Railway, and one branch would have gone to Swaffham. The bill was eventually rejected on the grounds that the areas through which the line would have passed were too thinly populated to provide sufficient traffic. The Chelmsford & Bury Railway included in its 1846 bill proposals for an extension to Thetford, but this was also turned down. The Bury & Thetford bill was deposited in 1846, with Robert Stephenson and George Bidder as engineers, but was likewise unsuccessful. Little progress had been made thus far.

Another Bury & Thetford Railway bill was deposited in 1864, with Peter Bruff as its engineer, and this was passed on 5 July 1865. The proposed line joined the Norwich to Ely railway at Thetford, to the east of the station, with another short line forming a triangular junction. At the Bury end, the new line was shown passing over the line to Ipswich east of the station, to make a junction with the line to Long Melford. A new curve would have allowed trains from Thetford into the existing station at Bury St Edmunds.

Meanwhile, the Thetford & Watton Railway bill was deposited in November 1865, with John S. Valentine as its engineer, for a line just under nine miles in length. Its Act was passed on 16 July 1866, and allowed it to make working arrangements with the Great Eastern, which had superseded the East Anglian and Eastern Counties Railways in August 1862. Construction of this line went ahead well, and it opened for freight on 28 January 1869, initially worked by a contractor, and on 18 October for passengers. There were intermediate stations at Wretham & Hockham and Stow Bedon. The basic initial service was four trains each way between Roudham Junction and Watton, with an additional early morning working on Mondays and Saturdays. The Thetford & Watton worked its own line, having been unable to come to an agreement with the GER.

Another bill, deposited in 1868, proposed a Watton & Swaffham line, making a junction at the latter with the existing GER line, which had formerly been part of the East Anglian Railway. John S. Valentine was also the engineer of this line, which was proposed to have a length of 9 miles 2 furlongs and 8 chains, and a maximum

THETFORD AND WATTON RAILWAY.
OPENING
Of the WATTON and SWAFFHAM, and THETFORD and WATTON EXTENSION RAILWAY.
NEW ROUTE BETWEEN LYNN AND THETFORD, VIA SWAFFHAM.

On MONDAY next, the 15th day of NOVEMBER, 1875, Trains will run as under:

TIME TABLE.

DOWN TRAINS.

STATIONS.		WEEK DAYS.								
		1	2	3	4	5	6	7	8	9
					Parly.	Exp.				Exp.
		Morn.	Morn.	Morn.	Morn.	Morn.	Morn.	Morn.	Even.	
London (Liverpool) St. .. dep.			..	..	7 30	9 10	10 45	11 40	..	4 5 5 0
„ (St. Pancras) .. „	Mondays only	..	..	7 35	9 15	10 40	11 32	..	..	4 53
Cambridge .. .. .. „		..	..	10 25	10 50	1 5	1 27	..	6 50
Ely .. .. .. „		..	..	11 20		1 55		..	7 20
Brandon .. .. .. „		..	..	11 59		2 24		..	7 55
Thetford .. .. .. „		..	..	12 15		2 39		..	8 10
Roudham Junction .. .. arr.		..	..	12 26		2 49		..	8 19
Thetford (Bridge Station) dep.		..	9 15	..	12 5		2 45		..	8 0
Roudham Junction .. .. arr.		..	9 30	..	12 20		2 58		..	8 15
„ „ .. .. dep.	7 35	9 31	9 50	12 30		3 0	5 8	8 22
Wretham .. „ .. arr.	7 45	9 38	9 57	12 38		3 8	5 15	8 29
Stow Bedon .. „ „	8 0	9 48	10 7	12 48			5 25	8 37
Watton .. .. .. arr.	8 10	9 56	10 18	12 56		3 23	5 35	8 45
„ .. .. .. dep.	8 20	10 0	..	1 0		3 28		8 50
Holme Hale .. .. „	8 35	10 15	..	1 15				9 8
Swaffham .. .. .. „	8 40	10 25	..	1 25		3 50		9 15
Swaffham .. .. .. dep.	8 58	10 33	..	2 3		4 55		..
Narborough .. .. arr.	9 25	10 45	..	2 15		5 7		..
Lynn .. .. .. „	10 5	11 5	..	2 37		5 30		..
Swaffham .. .. .. dep.	9 29	1 17	..			6 49		..
Dunham .. .. arr.	9 39	1 27	..			6 59		..
Derham .. .. „	10 0	1 50	..			7 20		..
Norwich .. .. .. „	11 10	..	..			8 30		..
Roudham Junction .. .. dep.	..	..	..	12 26		2 49		8 19
Harling Road .. .. „	..	..	..	12 36		2 59		8 30
Eccles Road .. .. „	..	..	..	12 44				8 38
Attleborough .. .. „	..	..	..	12 53		3 15		8 47
Wymondham .. .. „	..	..	..	1 5		3 27		8 58
Norwich .. .. .. „	..	..	..	1 40		4 2		9 17
Yarmouth .. .. .. „	..	..	..	2 50		5 7		..
Lowestoft .. .. „	..	..	..	3 10		5 25		..

UP TRAINS.

Miles from Swaffham.	STATIONS.		WEEK DAYS.							SUNDAYS.	
			1	2	3	4	5	6	7	8	9
					Exp.		Parly.				
			Morn.	Morn.	Morn.	Morn.	Even.	Even.		Even.	
	Lowestoft .. .. .. dep.		..	..	9 10		12 42	..		..	
	Yarmouth .. .. „		..	..	9 25		12 57	..		..	
	Norwich .. .. „		6 20	..	10 40		4 0	..		..	
	Wymondham .. .. „		6 47	..	11 8		4 28	..			
	Attleborough .. .. „		7 0	..	11 20		4 41	..			
	Eccles Road .. „		7 9	..			4 50	..			
	Harling Road .. .. „		7 16	..	11 35		4 57	..			
	Roudham Junction .. .. arr.		7 24	..	11 44		5 4	..			
	Norwich .. .. .. dep.		..	..	8 50		12 15	3 15			
	Derham .. .. „		..	..	10 2		1 30	4 20			
	Dunham .. .. „		..	..	10 23		1 53	4 44			
	Swaffham .. .. .. arr.		..	..	10 33		2 5	4 55			
	Lynn .. .. .. dep.	Mondays only.	..	8 55	12 40		..	6 15			
	Narborough .. .. „		..	9 17	1 3		..	6 37			
	Swaffham .. .. .. arr.		..	9 29	1 17		..	6 49			
9½	Swaffham .. .. .. dep.		6 30	..	10 40	1 30	4 0	7 0			
	Holme Hale .. .. „		..	..	10 40	..	4 10	7 10			
12½	Watton .. .. .. arr.		6 53	..	11 5	1 50	4 25	7 30			
16	„ .. .. .. dep.		6 55	9 15	11 10	1 55	4 30	7 40			
18½	Stow Bedon .. .. „		7 2	9 23	11 18	2 3	4 39	7 48			
	Wretham .. .. „		7 12	9 33	11 23	2 13	4 49	8 0			
22½	Roudham Junction .. .. arr.		7 18	9 40	11 35	2 20	4 57	8 10			
	Thetford (Bridge Station) dep.		..	..	11 33	2 25	5 0	8 15			
	„ arr.		..	..	11 53	2 40	5 15	8 30			
	Roudham Junction .. .. dep.		7 24	..	11 44		5 4	..			
	Thetford .. .. arr.		7 36	..	11 55		5 17	11 8			
	Brandon .. .. „		7 55	..	12 10		5 36	11 25			
	Ely .. .. „		8 30	..	12 35		6 10	12 5			
	Cambridge .. .. „		9 15	..	1 10		6 47	1 10			
	London (St. Pancras) .. „		11 10	..	3 2 3 40		9 15	..			
	„ (Liverpool Street) „		11 10	..	3 0 3 43		9 10	3 45			

Above:
Norfolk Chronicle, November 1875. *Author's Collection*

gradient of about 1 in 105. The bill provided for cooperation with the Thetford & Watton and for vesting in that company. The Great Eastern was to forward traffic, and the company's trains would be allowed to run over GER metals into Swaffham station and use the facilities there.

However, all was not well with the Bury & Thetford scheme. In March 1867 the fourth ordinary meeting of the company heard that arrangements were to have been made with Messrs Sharpe to build the line, but that nothing had been heard until 12 December 1866, and then nothing more until February. The directors agreed to subscribe to have at least a part of the line built, and more shares needed to be taken up. In 1869 a further bill was deposited to permit deviations and allow more time. Nearly two miles of route were to be altered near Barnham, and a similar amount near Bury. Beyond the Fornham to Barton road at 1 mile 7 furlongs from Bury the deposited plans showed the line as 'fenced and formed under the Act of 1865' with cuttings, embankments and bridges marked. The 'intended station' was shown at Ingham near to the Griffin Inn. A bridge at 3 miles 5 furlongs was in the course of erection but beyond this nothing had been done. An intended station was shown at Melford Bridge, about a mile from Thetford, and the curve into Bury was to be abandoned. The problem was the continued inability to raise capital, and work was done only by the expedient of letting small contracts for cash. In August 1871 negotiations for the completion of the line fell through, although the following year a contract was successfully concluded, and optimistic noises were made by the directors about the prospects for the line.

The Bury & Thetford was helped when, for the 1873 session, the Thetford & Watton deposited a further bill which allowed for new lines around Roudham Junction. This station, about four miles towards Norwich on the main line, had platforms on either side of the Great Eastern's Norwich to Ely line, with a double junction connecting the Thetford & Watton's single line to it; there was also a single line from the T&W going to the back of the down platform.

The new bill proposed extending this parallel to the GER main line, rising and crossing over it, and then making a junction with the Bury & Thetford line near Melford Bridge, close to where it joined the Norwich to Ely line. This scheme would have allowed the formation of a through route between Swaffham and Bury without the need for reversal, but was not built. The Thetford & Watton sought authorisation in the Bill to contribute to the Watton & Swaffham line. It also proposed working agreements with the Great Eastern and with the other two local concerns which would have allowed them to be worked as a single entity. All of these lines had had problems with the raising of capital, and it was not until Monday 20 September 1875 that the Watton & Swaffham finally opened for goods traffic. Extra time had been needed for the completion of the line, and it appears that the Board of Trade was becoming more particular about safety measures. Passenger services began on Monday 15 November under the direction of the manager, C. F. Ward.

Work was still needed on the Bury & Thetford Railway. It was inspected on Thursday, 30 December 1875 by Capt Tyler of the Board of Trade, and was substantially passed, with only a few alterations being needed. He was met at Bury by several GER officials, including Mr Robertson, traffic manager, Mr Langley, engineer, and Mr Sach, telegraph superintendent. The Thetford & Watton was represented by its traffic manager Mr Ward, and its locomotive superintendent; the Bury & Thetford by Mr Edward Greene MP, chairman, its solicitor Mr J. S. Greene, its engineer Mr Bruff and the contractors' engineer, Mr Barham. An engine and two carriages were supplied by the Thetford & Watton. Capt Tyler first visited the new signalbox at Bury Junction and spent at least 1½ hours in there, giving his approval only on condition that certain alterations were made. He then walked over the whole line accompanied by Mr Edward Greene, and made a minute inspection of every bridge, having the train run over each several times to test the vibration. Capt Tyler did not finish until late, but was able to

Above:
Bury Free Press, 4 March 1876. *Author's Collection*

inspect the loop line at Thetford before dark. After this had been done he told Mr Greene that he was the first company chairman to have walked the whole line with him. The return journey to Bury was made by train and took about half an hour. The inspector then left for Colchester by special train, but before doing so revisited the signalbox to check that the alterations ordered in the morning had been made. He said that he would report to the Board of Trade that the line was fit to open, and could do so on receipt of the certificate. It was then expected that it would open to passengers on the following Monday.

The secretary of the Bury & Thetford, Mr J. W. Ion, received the Board of Trade certificate on Tuesday 18 January 1876, although a date still could not be fixed for the opening. The Great Eastern had yet to erect a signal, and the Thetford & Watton did not have the necessary rolling stock available. The *Bury Free Press* wondered if 1 February was possible, but opined that '. . . after so many disappointments, any positive announcement would be received with incredulity.'

At long last the line was finally opened for all traffic on Wednesday 1 March 1876. The intermediate stations were at Ingham and Barnham, and the *Ipswich Journal* stated that 'The

traffic must be limited, the district being purely agricultural; but the cost of construction has also been kept within moderate bounds.' Initially, four trains each weekday were run between Bury and Swaffham, and the opening was celebrated by a dinner in Bury presided over by Mr E. Greene MP and attended by the Marquis of Bristol, Mr Hunter Rodwell MP, Lord F. Hervey MP and Mr T. Thornhill MP.

Through trains used the east curve at Thetford, calling at Thetford Bridge, and did not go into the main station. The *Bury Free Press* reported that the directors had advanced nearly half the capital themselves and commended their sacrifice, but said that the cost was not excessive, at £7,500 per mile. The paper had little doubt that the new line would pay a 'very satisfactory dividend'. Bury people could now spend a long day in Lynn and get home the same evening, whilst in the summer excursionists could get to Lowestoft in 1 hour 20 minutes less than the first Great Eastern train of the day. A reduction of fares to many places in Norfolk was likely, because of the more direct routes.

This optimism soon proved to be misplaced, and receipts were low. In February 1878 the Bury & Thetford agreed provisionally to sell its line to the Great Eastern for £108,300, formally authorised

Above:
Ingham station after passenger closure, although there is still an oil lamp on the wall. *Andrew Muckley*

by the Great Eastern Act of 1878, as a result of which the other concerns — the Thetford & Watton and Watton & Swaffham — also reached agreement with the GER, confirmed by the Great Eastern Railway Act of 1879, for the lease of their lines. They were finally bought out under the GER Act of 1897. The Great Eastern no longer worked the lines as a through route, and all Swaffham to Thetford and Bury St Edmunds trains went into Thetford station. The east curve was removed, although the name 'Thetford West Junction' — to the east of the station — remained. Connections for local trains were arranged at Thetford and Bury, and also Swaffham, but it became difficult to use it as a through route.

The branch diverged from the main line to the east of Bury station and headed northwards, with a number of cuttings and embankments on the way. The overall speed limit was 45mph, although on the curve at Bury it was as low as 15mph. The line was worked by staff and ticket, with the only intermediate block post in later years being Barnham. Prior to 1915, no tickets were used, and all trains had to be in possession of the staff. The line undulated, but rose gently from Bury to Ingham, although there were sharper sections at 1 in 55 and 1 in 78. Ingham station was approached from the south through a deep cutting, and there were extensive woods to the east. It had a single platform on the west side of the line, with a loading dock at the north end. The signalbox closed in 1935. The station buildings here were essentially of an 'L' shape, with the

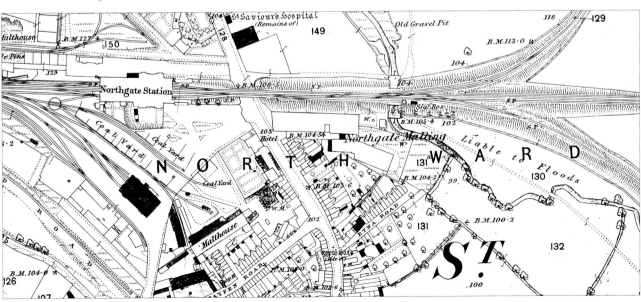

Above:
Northgate station, Bury St Edmunds, and junctions, 1886. *Crown Copyright*

accommodation for the stationmaster and his family forming a two-storey structure at right-angles to the platform, with the single-storey booking office parallel. A further single-storey building was at the other end. As elsewhere in the area, it was a flint-walled structure, with quoins, lintels and the like of brick. This pattern was repeated at many other stations on the line to Swaffham, and in the area generally. The station was never particularly busy, but handled some livestock and rabbit skins, together with local produce, and could handle most classes of traffic, although it did not have separate facilities for livestock. It saw more activity in World War 1 when there was an army camp at Ingham and a military hospital at Ampton Hall.

There was wooded countryside to the north of Ingham. The line crossed the main road to Thetford (later the A134) by a brick-built bridge, ascending at gradients varying between 1 in 529 and 1 in 126 until milepost 5, after which it dropped for half a mile at 1 in 300. Seven Hills siding — the name probably derived from a group of tumuli in the vicinity — was a short distance further, about two miles from Ingham, and had been in use since the 19th century. A halt was opened there, with an earth and cinder platform, in December 1922, while at the same time the signalbox was abolished and replaced by a ground frame.

The line curved gently to the west after leaving Seven Hills, running through heathland and rising for about half a mile at 1 in 130, level for a distance, then curving back slightly eastwards before dropping sharply at 1 in 70 for over a mile towards Barnham. Extensive sidings were installed by the Air Ministry at Little Heath during World War 2. Barnham was 9¼ miles from Bury and 5¼ miles from Ingham, and was a staff station after 1915. It had a single platform on the east side of the line and south of the level crossing over the minor road between the village and Elveden. There was a large goods yard served by a long siding, and a loading dock at the back of the platform; there was also a short goods loop to the south of the station, plus a siding on the west side of the line. Further sidings were installed during World War 2.

Leaving Barnham and continuing in a northeasterly direction, the line passed under the main road from Bury, soon crossed the

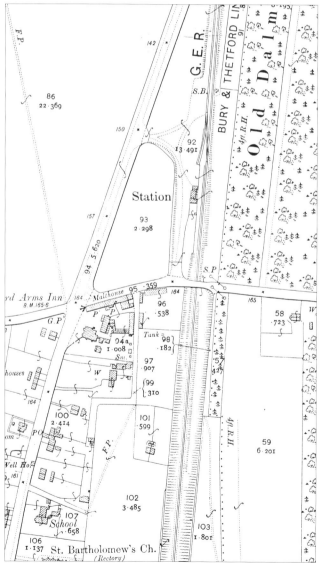

Above:
Ingham station, 1904. *Crown Copyright*

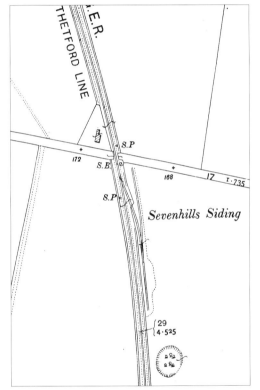

Above:
**Barnham station,
looking towards Thetford.**
Andrew Muckley

Left:
Seven Hills siding, 1904.
Crown Copyright

Right:
Barnham station, 1905.
Crown Copyright

Below:
**The exterior of Barnham
station, near Thetford.**
Andrew Muckley

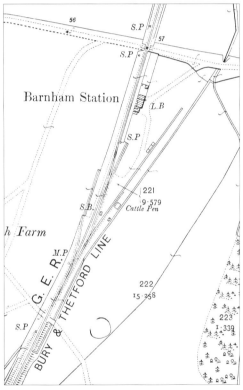

Above:
Roudham Junction in about 1924, looking towards Norwich.
The station was open to passengers, although used only as an interchange. The railway cottages can be seen
beyond the signalbox, while the Swaffham line diverges to the left via a double junction. *Stations UK*

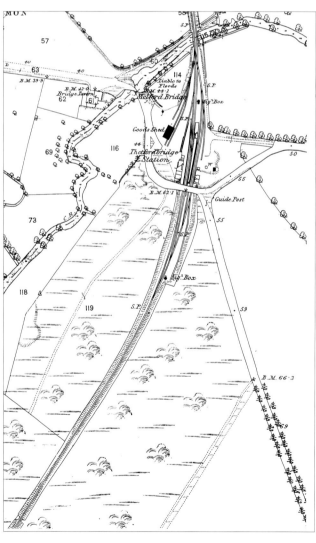

Above:
Thetford Bridge station. *Crown Copyright*

Little Ouse River, and traversed some marshy land while running along the valley floor, this section being level. Thetford Bridge station was a very substantial affair where the line became double track, it having two platforms with several sidings on both sides of the line, a signalbox (originally one each end of the layout) and a goods shed and yard on the west side. The station was at Melford Bridge on the east side of the town, where the roads from Yarmouth and Stowmarket met and crossed the River Thet, and was slightly further from the town centre than the Great Eastern's station, which was to the north. On leaving Thetford Bridge the line curved quite sharply to the west, having passed the site of the junction with the east curve, and joined the main line at Thetford West Junction. There were catch points in the down line (towards Thetford), the line rising at 1 in 88 as it climbed out of the valley of the river. Trains from Bury ran into the up (to Ely) platform at Thetford, which was about a mile away. Trains running via the east curve would also have had a run of about a further mile to get to the main line, with a tighter curve.

Leaving Thetford from the down side, Swaffham trains ran as far as Roudham Junction on the main line, before diverging to the left on to the branch. Roudham Junction ceased to be advertised as a station after May 1932, and main line trains no longer called after March 1920. The platforms remained, and it was still possible to buy a ticket and get off on request from branch trains. Its main function seems to have been for railwaymen, and although there were latterly no buildings at all, the signalbox and a hut were at the north end of the layout. There were sidings on the north side of the down (to Norwich) platform which was an island, and there were others on the up side, with the capacity for wagon storage here being considerable. There were railway houses on the north side of the line, in the junction, and they had no other access than the railway. Goods traffic was never handled here, and the passenger service officially finished on 1 May 1932.

The branch curved away from the main line, through wooded heathland, after about a mile running very close to the ancient Peddars Way. The gradients were gently upwards, with a stretch of 1 in 100 on this section. Wretham & Hockham station was located immediately south of the level crossing over the road

Above:
On 24 October 1958, the 1.44pm train from Swaffham comes off the branch at Roudham Junction and crosses
to the up main to continue to Thetford. The 12.37pm Watton-Thetford-Bury St Edmunds freight waits on the back road.
Note the change of signalbox and that the old Great Eastern bracket signal is about to be replaced. *Hugh Davies*

between Wretham and Great Hockham, and was about 6¾ miles from Thetford and just under 2¼ miles from Roudham Junction. It had a single platform, and sidings on both sides of the line, together with a 1-ton crane. Although there was a signalbox, it was not a block post. The main building was of knapped flint with a slate roof, set at right-angles to the line, while a single-storey structure at right-angles had an open front which was used as a sheltered waiting area, with a store at the far end. Another building beyond that was also a store.

The line beyond Wretham went across heath and woodland, and entered a long cutting about three-quarters of a mile from the station where it started to curve gently towards the northeast, away from the Peddars Way. North and south of Wretham & Hockham station, on both sides of the line, there were areas where the risk of lineside fires was particularly high, and special care had to be taken; fires had to be reported on the appropriate form. Throwing of hot ashes from engines was banned, and brick arches and baffle plates on locomotives had to be kept in good condition. This was

Above:
Wretham & Hockham station was the first on the branch from Thetford,
seen here with a Swaffham train arriving in 1964. *Stations UK*

Above:
**The goods leaves Wretham & Hockham for Watton on a very
chilly winter's day in 1955.** *Stations UK*

Below:
**The signalman hurries towards a diesel multiple-unit as it
passes his box, one day in 1964.** *Stations UK*

Above:
Stow Bedon station in 1924. It retains its nameboard mounted on posts, and the wooden
paling fence is still in place. This view is looking towards Watton. *Stations UK*

Below:
Thirty years on, the fence and nameboards have changed, and the gardens on the opposite side of the track look immaculate.
The station has otherwise been altered little. The goods yard can be seen to the left of the platform. *Stations UK*

Above:
Easily the most important intermediate station on the line, Watton sported two staggered platforms
and extensive facilities. This early postcard view is looking towards Swaffham from the up platform,
and clearly shows the goods shed, loading dock and crane. *SLS Collection*

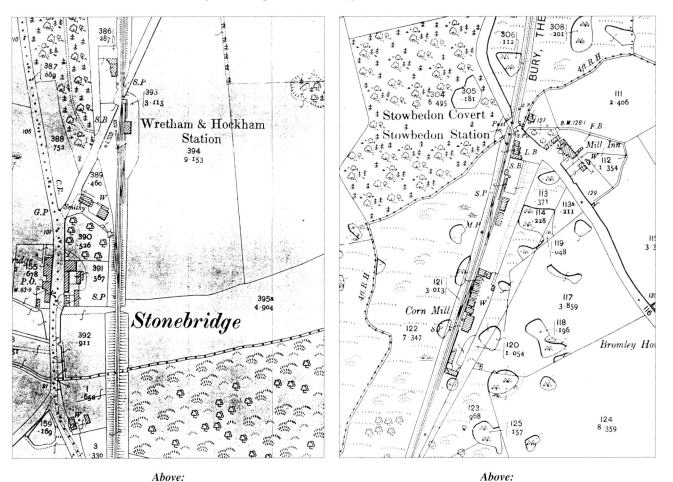

Above:
Wretham & Hockham station. *Crown Copyright*

Above:
Stowbedon station. *Crown Copyright*

Above:
Watton station from the level crossing end in 1964, looking south towards Roudham Junction. *Stations UK*

particularly important as the railway companies were liable for damage to forests, woods, orchards and plantations under the 1905 and 1923 Railway Fires Acts. Although they could, if absolutely necessary, go on to land to clear undergrowth which was a potential hazard, they were liable for any damage that might result.

With the line again rising at about 1 in 100 in places, trains reached Stow Bedon, also located immediately to the south of a level crossing, this time over the Great Hockham to Watton road, and about 2½ miles from Wretham. The stations were similar in many ways, with a single platform, although at Stow Bedon the sidings were on the east side of the line, one of them used by Littleproud & Sons, who were corn and feed merchants: there were many poultry farmers in the area. Oldman & Sons were coal merchants based at the station in the 1920s. Unlike Wretham & Hockham, which could handle all classes of traffic, Stow Bedon was only able to deal with ordinary goods, passengers and parcels. The signalbox of all-wood construction was almost in the middle of the platform, but was not a block post. Locomotives were allowed to tow up to six loaded wagons by means of a rope in the sidings.

The line continued to climb towards Watton, running close to the main road and curving back towards the north and west. There was a level crossing over the road to Griston after which the line descended towards the station, a further two miles or so, and which was the only intermediate block post. On the approach to the town there was an RAF airfield on the northeast side of the line, used extensively in World War 2 and providing much traffic for the branch. The station had two staggered platforms and extensive sidings on both sides of the line. To the west were the original general offices, locomotive and carriage sheds of the Thetford & Watton company, while the main station buildings and goods shed were near the level crossing at the north end of the layout. This carried the road to Hingham over the line, with the Railway Hotel on one side and a foundry on the other. The station handled

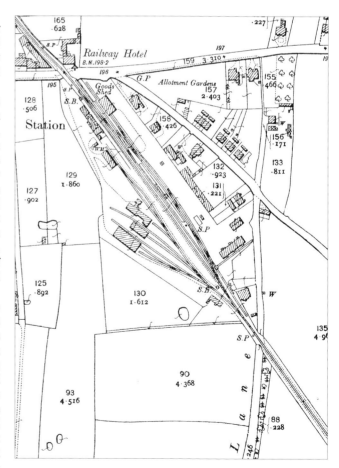

Above:
Watton station. *Crown Copyright*

Above:
**A 1924 view of Watton, looking southwards, with a wealth of passenger-rated traffic in
evidence on the platform, and a goods train standing in the up platform.** *Stations UK*

considerable tonnages of vegetables and livestock, these being 1,590 and 232 respectively in 1938 and was also responsible for Stow Bedon, which loaded 977 tons of vegetables in the same year. A 1-ton crane was available, and the station could handle all classes of traffic. T. S. Howlett & Son had a siding at the station.

The down platform (towards Swaffham) was especially notable in the 1950s for its topiary, where Mr S. Fagg had clipped the hedge into the shape of a locomotive and the words 'British Railways Watton'. In fact, in BR days, the whole line was noted for its station gardens, and they regularly won prizes. The station buildings were very similar in design and general layout to the others on the line, although here they were of brick.

Leaving Watton the line crossed the road to Shipdham, and was carried across a small valley on a long embankment. It passed Saham Toney to the west and Ovington to the east, and then started to climb again at about 1 in 100 for about two miles, before descending again and turning northwestwards. At 5 miles 42 chains from Watton the line reached Holme Hale station, similar to Stow Bedon and Wretham & Hockham, with the buildings mostly of knapped flint construction. It was about a mile from the village, although the line passed closer, but on an embankment. The extra expense of building it nearer would probably not have been justified as Holme Hale had a population of only about 400 in the 1950s. The single platform was on the north side of the line, together with the signalbox and station building. A long siding ran back towards Watton, and extended behind the platform to form a loading dock. The goods shed was on the opposite side of the line, also served by a single siding. A 1-ton crane was available, and the station could handle all classes of traffic. The level crossing at the west end of the station was over a minor road from Holme Hale to the Pickenhams. It was operated by the station staff, and was interlocked with its protecting signals. The signalbox was only switched in if the pick-up freight needed to call, to attach or detach

wagons. Holme Hale was staffed in the late 1940s and 1950s by two porter-signalmen, Fred Eagle and Frank Hewing, the latter living in the station house. Their many duties included operation of the gates and signals. They were responsible for ticket issuing, raising charges for any parcels, plus work in the goods yard such as shunting, labelling of wagons, and maintaining records of wagons received and forwarded. If there were any problems then they contacted either the goods or booking offices at Swaffham by 'phone on the local Roudham Junction to Swaffham circuit. All money collected was sent weekly to Swaffham in a sealed bag, although this could be done more frequently if business was good. Details of all tickets and cash sales were entered in a cash book, the ticket register for the station being maintained at Swaffham. After about 1936 the station came under the control of Swaffham, and the stationmaster there would visit at least once a week by car, or possibly via the twice-weekly parcels delivery van.

The main source of passenger traffic was RAF service personnel, mainly National Servicemen, from 281 Maintenance Unit at North Pickenham, which was about two miles from the station. It had been a USAAF heavy bomber airfield in the war, and was used by the RAF for the storage of bombs. The peak time for their travel was out on Friday afternoon and back on Sunday evening, which probably accounted for the late working back from Thetford at 11.19pm in the summer 1958 timetable, reaching Holme Hale at 11.52pm. This connected with the 8.24pm from Liverpool Street via Cambridge, and also from Peterborough East which reached Thetford at 11.13pm and 10.43pm respectively. In spite of the line being operated on the conductor-guard principle, many of these personnel bought Forces Leave tickets at discounted rates from the station, and some used warrants from their annual entitlement to obtain Forces Duty tickets free of charge. On such occasions a booking clerk from Swaffham would go up to Holme Hale to help with the surge of traffic. At the end of the month all warrants

Above

**Holme Hale, next station north of Watton, in about 1937, and looking towards Watton. The family likeness
of the station buildings is evident. Note the three-way point in the running line at the platform end, and the
reconstruction of the main part of the platform to raise its height and provide an overhang.** *Stations UK*

were sent to the Accountant at York, who then raised a bulk charge against the Ministry concerned. On bank holidays, personnel who could not get home and back in the two days of the normal weekend added to the numbers of people travelling. Given that there was a similar situation at Watton, the 1.45pm Swaffham to Thetford would be strengthened from its normal three coaches to six by use of the school coaches which normally stood at Thetford from 8.30am (having formed the 7.40am school train from Swaffham) to 4.15pm, when it normally worked back. They would

first be worked back on the 11.32am from Thetford and then form the 1.45pm up.

Holme Hale did not handle large amounts of goods. The main traffic inwards was coal, and sugar beet and grain out. The RAF sent bombs to Cairnryan, near Stranraer, for dumping in the Irish Sea, but these were loaded at Swaffham. Facilities at the station were very limited, both in respect of standage for wagons and of space for lorries to manoeuvre. Because of the lack of a loop, it was another of the places where locomotives were permitted to

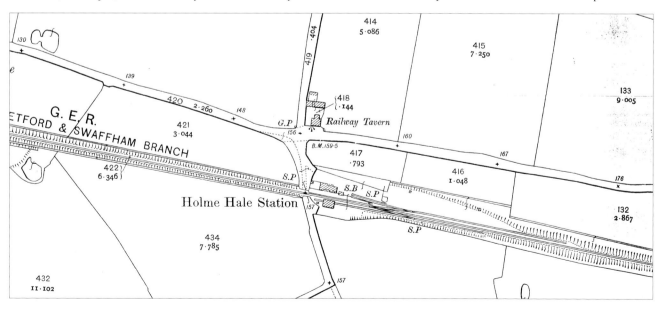

Above:

Holme Hale station. *Crown Copyright*

tow wagons by rope, up to five loaded being allowed. There was a gang of platelayers based at Holme Hale, with Ernie Green in charge in the 1950s. Some of the track towards Swaffham was laid on ash ballast, which must have made it much harder to maintain a good alignment.

The line then rose again for some two miles, crossing the River Wissey about half a mile from Holme Hale by an iron bridge. Passing North Pickenham to the south, the line turned slightly towards the north, and passed another large aerodrome to the south, also crossing the Peddars Way again here. Nearly four miles from Holme Hale, the line finally joined that from Dereham just to the east of Swaffham station, the curve being limited to 15mph. Both lines were single, but became double before reaching the junction, and there was double track through the station to just beyond the west end of the platforms.

Swaffham had an extensive layout with sidings and yards on both sides of the line. The main buildings were on the south side of the line (to King's Lynn) and were approached from Station Street. There were loading docks and stores here, and the station signalbox at the east end of this platform, with the footbridge. On the other side was the large goods shed, and to the west were refuge sidings. To the east side — back towards the junction — there were more sidings on both sides of the line, and a 45ft turntable. There were many private sidings at the station, in 1927 these being for Chamberlayne & Co, Jeffrey & Co, Kenny Co, W. Preston and Vynne & Everett. As with other stations in the area, Swaffham's buildings were mostly of knapped flint construction, although the style was very different from those on the line to Thetford.

The early problems with train services have already been recounted. It might have been possible to run through from Mark's Tey, call at Bury (East Gate) and not the main station, cross the line from Ipswich, run via Ingham to Thetford Bridge, down to Roudham Junction and via Watton to Swaffham. Quite what the demand for such a service would have been is another matter: passenger loadings between Bury and Swaffham were always low, and both branches were operated on the conductor-guard principle from October 1922. The 1874 timetable showed four trains each weekday between Roudham Junction and Watton, leaving the latter

at 11.10am, 2.0, 4.30 and 7.25pm, and taking between 25 and 38 minutes for the journey. They tended to pause for only a short time at Roudham Junction before returning. There was an additional early train from Watton to Roudham Junction and back on Mondays at 8.15am and Saturdays at 8.47am, the last being mixed. When the extension to Swaffham opened, the timetable showed trains for Swaffham starting either from Roudham Junction or Thetford Bridge, the overall journey now taking just over an hour. It is interesting to note the use of Thetford Bridge station, since the line from Bury was not yet open for traffic. A train left for Swaffham at 7.35am on Mondays only from Roudham Junction, calling at Wretham, Stow Bedon, Watton and Holme Hale, and arriving at 8.40am. The next started back from Thetford Bridge at 9.15am, and also called at all stations. On Saturdays only the 9.50am from Roudham Junction to Watton was hard on its heels. The next had interesting connections. It left Thetford Bridge at 12.5pm and reached Roudham Junction at 12.20pm. It then waited for 10 minutes, and was there overtaken by the 11.20am from Ely, due at 12.26am and going on to Norwich. The 2.45pm from Thetford Bridge followed the 1.55pm from Ely along the main line, and then called at Stow Bedon and Holme Hale only as required. There was then a train from Roudham Junction to Watton at 5.8pm, and the last down service of the day was at 8pm from Thetford Bridge. In the other direction it was fairly similar, with trains up from Swaffham at 6.30am (Mondays only), 10.40am, 1.30, 4.0 and 7pm, with a Saturdays-only 9.15am from Watton to Roudham Junction. It is difficult to see the purpose of this service and its return, since there were no connecting trains either way along the main line.

By 1913 there were four passenger trains from Bury to Thetford, at 8.57am, 11.18am, 4.35pm and 7.9pm, taking just under half an hour. Likewise, there were four trains between Thetford and Swaffham, at 9.45am, 12.8pm, 5.52pm and 8.18pm. The first two in each case had reasonable connections at Thetford, of 20 and 22 minutes respectively; the others were not so good, at 49 and 42 minutes. On Mondays there was an extra from Thetford to Watton at 8.36am, and on Wednesdays from Watton to Swaffham at 3.40pm. The journey from Thetford took just over

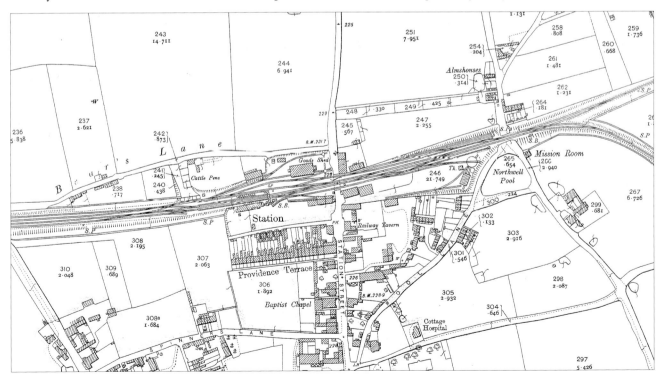

Above:
Swaffham station. *Crown Copyright*

Above:
Thetford Bridge in 1924, looking towards the main line at Thetford.
This was a large station, having been built to rival that on the main Norwich to Ely line, and
intended to be served by through Bury to Swaffham trains. *Stations UK*

three-quarters of an hour. In the other direction, there were five trains from Swaffham, at 7.35am, 8.41am (this started from Watton on Mondays), 10.52am, 4.32pm and 6.52pm, the last two being allowed to carry cattle to Bury in trucks fitted with Westinghouse pipes. An extra to Watton ran at 1.20pm on Wednesdays. From Thetford to Bury, there were trains at 9.50am. 12.20pm, 5.57pm and 8.14pm. Since these last two were also allowed to work cattle to Bury, and had connecting times of 35 and 32 minutes respectively, it is possible that the same trains actually worked through. Both branches were shown as part of the same timetable, and most trains were advertised to call at Roudham Junction.

This was no longer the case by 1922. The service from Bury remained at four trains each way, with the only connections being shown at Bury. In fact, apart from the 4.20pm which reached Thetford at 4.50pm, with a London departure at 5.29pm, they were quite good at both ends. It continued to be possible to connect between the two branches, although it was still necessary to wait some time at Thetford with some trains. There were five trains to and from Swaffham, although one of those back to Thetford started from Watton and had a connection from Swaffham which ran at a different time on Wednesdays. Roudham Junction had only one call in each direction, at 5.42pm from Thetford and 8.13am from Swaffham, and was advertised as an exchange station only, with no tickets issued to or from it.

By winter 1937, Roudham Junction had disappeared from the public timetable, although in the working timetable, all passenger trains were still shown as calling as required. Thetford to Swaffham had essentially the same weekday service, but without the complication on Wednesdays. There was now a single return working on Sundays, the better connection from London being via Norwich, although if going to the capital it was necessary to travel via Ely. The service to Bury remained at four trains each way on weekdays, always working out and back from Bury, but now with an extra on Saturdays only, from Bury at 9.40pm, arriving at Thetford at

10.10pm, and returning thence at 10.20pm, reaching Bury at 10.49pm. There were no Sunday trains.

The outbreak of war saw services reduced in many places, although on these branches they could not be cut much. The emergency service introduced on 2 October 1939 saw the Bury-Thetford line continue with its weekday service of four trains, while the line on to Swaffham was cut back to this level. When these were revised from 2 May 1942 very minor changes were made from Bury, but Thetford-Swaffham regained its fifth train, leaving Swaffham at 7.35pm and returning from Thetford at 9pm. Sundays remained without passenger services.

After the war, matters improved again. The Winter 1951-2 timetable saw the Bury line regain its Saturday evening train to and from Thetford at times similar to prewar. Between Thetford and Swaffham there were five trains each way along the whole line, with slight differences in timings on Fridays and Saturday evenings. There was now also a school train from Swaffham at 7.40am, back from Thetford at 4.13pm, plus a Thetford to Watton working at 9.50am, returning from there at 10.35am. There were also two return trains on Sundays. The first train of the day to Thetford, in 1953 the 6.10am, was handled by a Swaffham crew with an 'E4' 2-4-0, with three ex-Great Eastern corridor coaches, although Class F6 2-4-2Ts, 'J15' 0-6-0s and 'D16/3' 4-4-0s occasionally deputised. The coaches were stabled overnight in the trap siding at the King's Lynn end of the station and were drawn back into the up platform by the locomotive. Since a Thetford train had to pass over unprotected points to gain access to the branch, they had to be clipped by the station foreman.

The 7.40am to Thetford would be worked by a 'C12' 4-4-2T or a 'Claud Hamilton' 4-4-0, with a King's Lynn crew and Swaffham guard; possibly it would work from Lynn as pilot on the 6.50am to Dereham. It would go to the locomotive depot for water on arrival, but in winter would be coupled to its train, which had been stabled overnight in one of the sidings east of the platforms, to provide maximum heating before departure. This train primarily catered for students at Thetford Grammar School, but also had a very good connection to Birmingham, running on a very tight headway in front of the express from Roudham Junction. The 6.1am from Swaffham worked back as the 8.2am from Thetford and was quite well used for connections to King's Lynn, a fact canvassed by Swaffham guards. The 8.12am from Dereham preceded it into Swaffham, and would be drawn forward so that only the rear coach was still at the up platform. The Thetford train would be held outside the station, at the branch inner home signal, and would then be piloted in by the station foreman, thus making the connection.

The 11.32am passenger train from Thetford was double-headed by the locomotives off the 7.45am and 10.5am up from Swaffham, and could produce some interesting pairings, between Swaffham-based 'E4', 'J15', 'J17' and 'D16' engines and King's Lynn 'C12s' and 'D16s'. The branch locomotive would be replaced by another from Dereham once a week, or possibly more often if there had been a failure. This was most likely to happen on the 3.30pm from Thetford, which was worked by King's Lynn men unfamiliar with 'E4s'. Should this happen on a Saturday it was particularly unfortunate, as bus replacements were then hard to come by. If

possible, it was much quicker to do this than wait for an engine from Dereham to come to the rescue. Should this train be seriously late it might have to leave from the down platform. It was mainly used by Hamards Grammar School boys returning home to Holme Hale and Watton.

The 7.50pm to Thetford, which loaded very lightly most weekdays, was retimed to 8.10pm on Saturdays to cater for people going to the first show at the Regal Cinema, just a few minutes' walk from the station. When it returned, as the 9.30pm from Thetford, it was generally well loaded with RAF personnel from Watton and Holme Hale. On arrival at Swaffham, the coaches were drawn forward into the trap and stabled for the night, the locomotive then retiring to the locomotive siding, where the fireman cleaned the fire before handing over to the shedman.

One event of note happened on Monday, 10 June 1950, when a violent storm during the early hours caused a landslip near Holme Hale, and about five tons of earth fell across the line. This was spotted by one of the platelayers at about 6am, and a bus service between Swaffham and Thetford was therefore instituted. The 6.11am, 7.40am and 8.40am trains from Swaffham, plus the

Below:
Class F6 No 67236 leaves Bury St Edmunds with the 1.44pm for Thetford on 25 April 1953, a few weeks before withdrawal of the service. *G. R. Mortimer*

Above:
**Thetford Bridge station looking back towards Bury in 1953, around the
time of withdrawal of passenger services.** *Stations UK*

8.40am from Thetford were cancelled. On another occasion, on 22 August 1952, 'F6' No 67222 failed at Barnham with valve trouble, fortunately while 'J15' No 65420 was in the goods yard there. Although unbraked, it was requisitioned to work the train onwards to Bury, the 'F6' working the brakes. The real glory for the Thetford & Swaffham came in the aftermath of the January 1953 floods, which resulted in the line being open continuously for a period while the direct route for freight between King's Lynn and Whitemoor via Wisbech East was closed by flooding near Magdalen Road. On one occasion an unfitted freight, hauled by a Class J19 0-6-0, became divided between Holme Hale and Swaffham, the driver being unaware until stopped by the Swaffham signalman as he was about to enter the single-line section to Narborough & Pentney.

The weather again caused problems on 24/25 February 1958 when a blizzard raged for nearly 48 hours. On Tuesday 28th, a diesel multiple-unit left Swaffham for Thetford at 6pm, but got stuck in a drift near Holme Hale. It proved impossible to send an assisting steam engine from King's Lynn as the line thence to Swaffham was already blocked in two places by drifting snow; Middleton Towers was blocked by another stuck DMU, and the 12.40pm Lowestoft to Spalding parcels was also stuck in a drift between Narborough and East Winch. The train at Holme Hale was eventually dug out at 10pm, and the boys on the train were taken back to school when it reached Swaffham.

The end was nearing for passengers on the Bury & Thetford line, however, and services were withdrawn on and from Monday 8 June 1953, the last trains running on the previous Saturday. The *Bury Free Press* reported the closure under the headline 'Old Thetford Flyer Gets the Gayest Funeral of All Time'. The last train was given a rousing send-off with pageantry, fireworks and large

INGHAM (Suffolk)
Map Sq. 19.
Pop. 209. Clos. day Wed.
From Liverpool.Street via Bury St.
Edmunds 81¾ miles.
1st cl.—Single 28/-, Mth. Ret. 34/2.
3rd cl.—Single 16/10, Mth. Ret. 22/9.

Liv. St.	Ingham	Ingham	Liv. St.
a.m.		a.m.	
5 50	10 49	8 57	12 7
10 25r	1 49	11 57r	3 37
p.m.		p.m.	
1 0r	4 32	3 37	6 52
—	—	6 57	11 19

No Sunday Trains.
*Refresh. Car.

Another Route.
From Liverpool Street via Thetford
102¼ miles. Same fares.

Liv. St.	Ingham	Ingham	Liv. St.
a.m.		a.m.	
4 20	8 57	10 49r	2 40
8 20r	11 57	p.m.	
11 50r	3 37	1 49r	6 0
p.m.		4 32	8 45
2 25r	8 57	—	—

No Sunday Trains.
r Refresh. Car.

Above:
**ABC Railway Guide,
December 1949.**
Author's Collection

crowds at stations and crossings, and the local amateur operatic and drama society in Bury staged a procession. The driver of the last train was Mr A. E. Steward, his fireman Mr Peter Buckle and the guard, Mr J. Howard. Detonators were set off at many places along the line. At Ingham Mrs A. W. Smith, aged 84 of Home Cottage, joined the train; her father Mr Cobb, had been the first stationmaster there in 1877. Seven Hills Halt closed completely, the siding there having been out of use since 1918. Thetford Bridge, Barnham and Ingham remained open for goods traffic until 27 June 1960 when the line was closed finally.

The Thetford to Swaffham line continued rather longer, with its services seeing further improvements. The Winter 1955-6 timetable now showed six return workings over the whole line, now with one train working Thetford-Swaffham-Dereham on Mondays to Fridays. It left Thetford at 11.31am, reaching Swaffham at 12.16pm and Dereham at 12.50pm, returning at 1.2pm and reaching Thetford at 2.22pm.

The line was one of those selected for the census of costs and loadings in 1955. In the week ending 27 March 1,748 train miles were run, with an average load factor of 12%, and a movement costs to revenue ratio of 617%. The service was converted to diesel railcar operation later in the year and, with the benefit of summer loadings, then looked a little better, with average throughout loads of 16 passengers, a load factor still of 12%, and a costs to revenue ratio reduced to 594%. While one of the worst, it was not bottom of the table.

However, Dr Beeching was determined to make an example of the branch, and quoted its shortcomings at length in *The Reshaping of British Railways*, published in 1963. He quoted annual train miles of 86,000, with an average of nine passengers per train. The earnings were £3,700, movement expenses £13,200 and terminal

SWAFFHAM (Norfolk)
111¼ miles. Pop. 3,040. E.C. Thur.
From Liverpool Street via King's Lynn.
2nd class 23/-, 1st class 42/-.

Liv. St. a.m.	Swaff a.m.	Swaff. a.m.	Liv. St. a.m.
8b36	12 10	7 7	9b58
10b36	2 10	8 29	11b58
p.m.		p.m.	
12b36	4 38	12 12 ws	3b58
2b36	5 51	1 15	5b58
4b36	8 58	4 42	7b58
—	—	5 55 e	9K35
—	—	5 55 s	9K▪56
—	—	5 55	10 16
—	—	—	—
—	—	—	—
—	—	—	—
—	—	—	—

No Sunday Trains.

SWAFFHAM—continued

Another Route
From Liverpool Street via Thetford.
2nd class 29/3.

Liv.St. a.m.	Swaff. a.m.	Swaff. a.m.	Liv.St.
8b36	12 11	10 24	1b58
12b36	4 20	p.m. 2 25	5b58
3Kb 5	7 11	4 25	7b58
6b36	10 1	—	—
—	—	—	—
—	—	—	—

No Sunday Trains.

Another Route
From Liverpool Street via Norwich.
2nd class 37/-, 1st class 55/6.
Via Ely and Wymondham,
2nd class 34/6, 1st class 51/9.

Via Norwich

Liv. St. a.m.	Swaff. a.m.	Swaff. a.m.	Liv. St. a.m.
9b30	1 15	8 26	11b40
11b30	3 13	9 29	1r40
p.m.		p.m.	
1b30	4 42	12 13	3b40
3b30	6 53	2 13	5b40
5b30 s	8 50	3 48	7b40
—	—	4 43	9 7
—	—	—	—
—	—	—	—

No Sunday Trains.

Via Ely

Liv. St.	Swaff.	Swaff. p.m.	Liv. St.
—	—	8 58 e	2 20
—	—	8 58 s	2 33

No Sunday Trains.

Above:
ABC Railway Guide, December 1962. *Author's Collection*

expenses a further £3,900. This gave a shortfall of £13,400, in addition to which he estimated that track and signalling expenses which could be saved by withdrawal of the service were £17,200, increasing the shortfall to £30,600. On the other hand, Thetford-Swaffham passengers contributed £16,000 to other services where they started or finished their journey on the local line. Dr Beeching estimated the maximum loss of revenue here to be £1,700, making a gross revenue loss of £5,400 were the service to be withdrawn. The improvement in the financial position overall from withdrawal of the service would be about £29,000, equivalent to over four-fifths of total direct expenses. Given all of this, the branch was never going to survive, and the passenger service was duly withdrawn on Monday 15 June 1964, the start of the summer timetable. There were now no Sunday services, so the last train ran on Saturday 13 June. This was the 9.21pm DMU from Thetford with Driver David Grant and Guard Len Woodhouse, both of Dereham, in charge. At Holme Hale, 25 members of the Fireside Club boarded the train, and returned from Swaffham by coach. Stow Bedon and Wretham & Hockham closed completely on that day.

Goods traffic had always been healthier than passenger, with cattle a prominent feature. In 1913 an engine and brake left Bury on Wednesdays at 7.23am for Thetford, returning with the 8.10am Class B express cattle train for Bury, arriving at 8.55am. Goods trains left Bury at 12.55pm (Wednesdays excepted, 1.25pm Wednesdays only) calling at all stations (and Seven Hills siding as required). The 7.9pm passenger train from Bury was allowed to work up to three wagons to Thetford provided that they were fitted with Westinghouse brake pipes.

In the other direction, the 9.58am Class B goods from King's Lynn called at East Winch and Narborough on its way to Swaffham, leaving there at 11.30am and calling all stations to

Above:
Long after closure of the line to Thetford, the 11.36 King's Lynn to Norwich approaches Swaffham on 3 September 1968.
Much of the track has gone, but there are still several passengers. *G. R. Mortimer*

Above:
Thetford Bridge station on 24 October 1958, with J17 No 65561 heading the 12.37pm goods from Watton.
Track rationalisation has taken place following passenger closure some five years earlier. *Hugh Davies*

Roudham Junction whence it returned at 3.35pm, reaching King's Lynn at 7.30pm. Southbound from Thetford the service was provided by the 3.15pm (3.25pm Wednesdays), which called at the stations but missed Seven Hills and arrived at Bury at 4.25pm.

The 1937 timetable showed a similar pattern of working to and from King's Lynn, out from there at 7.42am, reaching Swaffham at 10.20am and Roudham Junction at 1.25 pm. It left again at 2.15pm and arrived at Swaffham at 5.45pm (3.35pm on Saturdays, since it did not then shunt at Watton). The first up passenger train on Wednesdays was allowed to work up to four piped wagons of cattle from Swaffham and Watton to Bury, this traffic having to be advised by Watton the previous day. The 4.15pm passenger from Swaffham was allowed to work piped wagons of cattle for Bury from Swaffham to Thetford, and on Wednesdays from Watton, in which case this traffic could not be loaded from Swaffham. Similarly the 7.15pm from Swaffham could also work up to three piped wagons of cattle from Watton to Thetford. This traffic was conveyed onwards from Thetford on similar terms by the 8.41am or 6.2pm, which were permitted up to four piped wagons of cattle. In the reverse direction, the 4.20pm from Bury could work three wagons to Thetford. Ordinary goods services were provided by the 12.15pm from Bury to Thetford, which could be extended to Roudham Junction when required to pick up 'up road' and Bury branch traffic from the King's Lynn train. It returned from Thetford at 4.20pm. and reached Bury at 5.50pm. It is worth noting at this point that Bury generated huge quantities of goods traffic from the sugar factory there (28,072 tons forwarded in 1938), as well as pulp, molasses, etc, while 1,407 tons of livestock were despatched

during that year, as well as grain, seed, machinery and iron. Thetford on the other hand forwarded 1,199 tons of grain, but also a grand total of 5,388 tons of manure.

After World War 2, the pattern of goods workings remained much the same, if slightly retimed, the first leaving King's Lynn at 7.15am, returning from Roudham Junction at 2.45pm (1.30pm Saturdays only). The train was worked by a Class J17 0-6-0 running tender-first in the up direction (towards Thetford). It terminated at Roudham Junction because there were run-round facilities there as well as stabling sidings for empty wagons for the Middleton Towers sand traffic, detached from Norwich-line trains. These would be attached behind the engine, with more from Swaffham often being added. Goods loaded at Watton would be marshalled just in front of the brake van, and on leaving Swaffham it could load up to 60 wagons.

After the withdrawal of passenger traffic, the section between Roudham Junction and Watton closed completely, and Holme Hale and Watton were served by a working from King's Lynn on Mondays, Wednesdays and Fridays. This left at 8.15 and called at East Winch, Narborough & Pentney and Swaffham before going down the branch, calling at Holme Hale at 12.51 and reaching Watton at 13.12. The return working left Watton at 14.00, called at Holme Hale as required and reached King's Lynn at 16.54. On other days of the week (except Sundays) the trip was from King's Lynn to Dereham via Swaffham and back, leaving and returning at the same times. This service did not last for long, and Holme Hale closed on 28 December, with Watton hanging on until 19 April 1965.

Wisbech & Upwell Tramway

AT the start of the 19th century Wisbeach — the 'Capital of the Fens' — was a port on the River Nene with aspirations to take over from King's Lynn as the most important of the Fenland ports. Large amounts of timber from the Baltic were being shipped in, and the corporation made considerable improvements to both the harbour facilities and the river approaches. The first rail connection arrived from March, opened on 3 March 1847 by the Eastern Counties Railway, and was closely followed by the connection to Watlington (later Magdalen Road and now Watlington again) by the East Anglian Railway, opened on 1 February 1848. It was not possible to extend the line on from the original Eastern Counties station, so it was turned over to goods use, and the ECR and EAR lines used the latter's station, both railways later being incorporated into the Great Eastern. Later, in June 1866, a connection arrived from Peterborough in the form of the Peterborough, Wisbeach & Sutton Bridge, later becoming part of the Midland & Great Northern Joint. The spelling 'Wisbeach' was used for the earlier railway bills and acts, and later changed to the modern version: the Great Eastern station was amended to 'Wisbech' in 1877.

The surrounding area was rich fenland country, and with the rapidly growing demands of the burgeoning conurbations such as London there was much potential business for the local farmers and for the Great Eastern; after all, it did not have the guaranteed long-haul coal traffic that was the staple of other railways. Given the topography, the area lent itself to the use of tramways which could easily connect with the existing railways for onward shipment of goods but also penetrate deep into the surrounding villages and countryside at minimal cost.

The Great Eastern already had an interest in building tramways in Wisbech, since it needed to connect the harbour with its main line; its Additional Powers bill of 1866 contained such provisions.

There were a number of proposals for lines to link Wisbech with Upwell and Outwell. A bill deposited for the 1872-3 session for the Upwell, Outwell and Wisbech Railway had George B. Bruce and C. Knightly Orlebar as its engineers, and allowed for working by and incorporation in the Great Eastern. It was proposed to start 72 yards from the end of Wisbech station's passenger platform, and would have been all-but-level for all of its course. (The maximum

Below:
A fine view of a passenger train on the Wisbech & Upwell Tramway, in Great Eastern days. *Ian Allan Library/Bucknall Collection*

gradient was actually 1 in 610, with much at 1 in 5,610.) Its length would have been 6 miles 2 furlongs and 98 yards, and it would have stayed mostly in Cambridgeshire, crossing into Norfolk at the county and parish boundary between Outwell and Upwell. It was proposed to terminate near Three Holes Bridge at Popham's Eau; no on-street running was proposed, but there would have been 15 level crossings. The bill was passed, but the powers were allowed to lapse.

The Great Eastern came back in the 1881-2 session for more powers to build a tramway between Wisbech and Upwell via Outwell, the Act being passed on 24 July 1882. In all, five tramways were proposed, No 4 starting close to Wisbech station, running alongside the line to Lynn for a short distance and then turning southwards to pass along the west bank of the Wisbech Canal; this is where it started to run on the road. It then crossed the canal by an existing bridge and swung east, away from the canal at the Duke of Wellington and Blacksmith's Arms pubs in the parish of Elm. It generally kept close to the canal, leaving it when the road did so, and rejoining it at Boyce's Bridge. Passing places were provided at fairly frequent intervals. Approaching Outwell it left the road and stayed with the canal, crossing it soon after.

The tramway continued to Outwell Sluice, where it was on the south side. Here the canal continued southwards and the Old Welney River to the west. The tramway crossed this near where they joined, following the east bank of the canal for a short way and then headed across country to Upwell. The total distance was just under six miles. For the 1882 session, the GER came back with further proposals for tramways in the Wisbech area, this time for three on-street sections within the town, and a further route from the already authorised Upwell line to Elm and Friday Bridge. The populations of the settlements almost ensured that the newer line was not built: Elm had a population of 1,779 but was also close to the Wisbech & Upwell, while Friday Bridge boasted only 94 people in 1891. Outwell, on the other hand, had a population of 1,233 and Upwell 3,494. The line to Outwell Basin opened on Monday, 20 August 1883. Four coaches were brought into use on the day, and it was reported that 960 passengers had paid their fares for a ride. Several trucks of coal and merchandise were also carried.

On Monday 8 September 1884 the extension to Upwell opened for traffic. It had been inspected the previous Wednesday by Maj-Gen Hutchinson RE of the Board of Trade, who passed it fit for traffic without further alteration. The new service consisted of six trains each way on weekdays, and there were again many passengers on the opening day. The only casualty was a cow that got on to the track and broke its leg. It was confidently expected that, should the new line be successful, it would be extended to Welney via Lakesend. This would have taken it a further five miles or so to the Old Bedford River, but serving a small population, with Welney (1,079 in 1891) only 2½ miles from Manea station on the Ely to March line. Nothing more came of the proposal.

The Wisbech & Upwell was built at a cost of around £2,300 per mile, well before the Light Railways Act of 1896 which was designed to promote the building of railways in rural areas as a means of alleviating economic depression. It was often quoted as an example of a line which was having a beneficial effect on its local community, developing both passenger and goods traffic. Being a tramway running along the public highway, the regulations originally decreed that speeds should not exceed 10mph, with locomotives being fitted with governors which shut off steam and applied the brakes should it be exceeded. The normal limit for everyday use was to be 8mph, 4mph over pointwork, and trains had

Right:
Wisbech & Upwell Tramway. *The Railway Magazine*

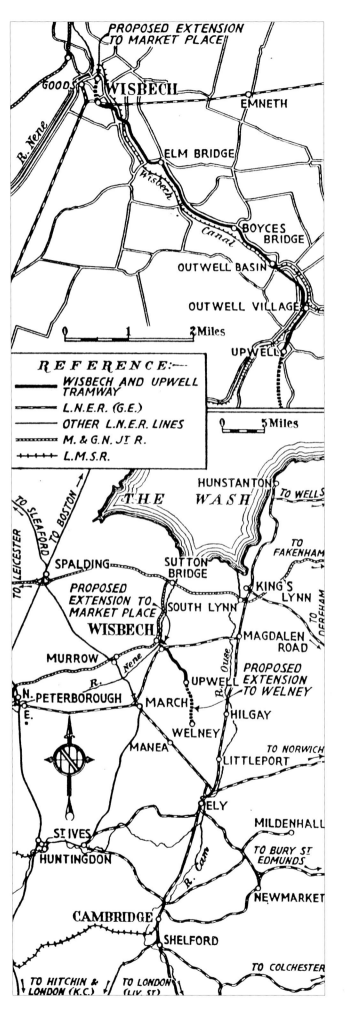

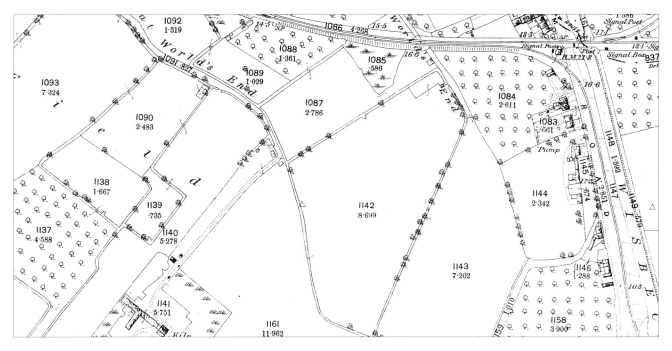

Above:
Wisbech station, 1886. *Crown Copyright*

Below right:
Upwell station, 1902. *Crown Copyright*

Below:
Outwell Village and Outwell Basin stations. *Crown Copyright*

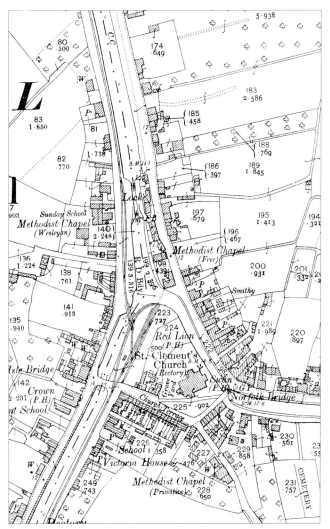

to come to a stand before crossing the road near the Duke of Wellington's inn. Engines had to carry a bell, to be sounded as a warning if necessary, and to have fenders to sweep aside any obstructions on the track. Since everything above four inches from rail level was enclosed, safety was also ensured. Noise had to be kept to a minimum, the blast having to be silent and the machinery free from audible clatter. The fire had to be concealed, and smoke was not to be emitted. Entrance to and exit from the coaches was by the rear, or conductor's, platform.

The route as constructed was much as described in the Act. The tramway ran from the western end of Wisbech station, there being a low platform of a suitable height for the tram coaches. Tram engines ran along the main line as far as the goods station. There was a locomotive depot to the south of the passenger platform with coaling stage, water column, a two-road running shed and sidings. The tramway then ran from the eastern end of the main station parallel to the single line to Magdalen Road for a short distance before diverging to the south just before the main line crossed Elm Road and the Wisbech Canal. The tramway crossed Elm Road and ran along its east side, west of the canal, then crossing the canal about ¼ mile further on at New Common Bridge, now running along the east side of Elm High Road, the main road to Ely and Downham Market. The old brick bridge was replaced in the mid-1930s by a new concrete structure which eliminated the sharp

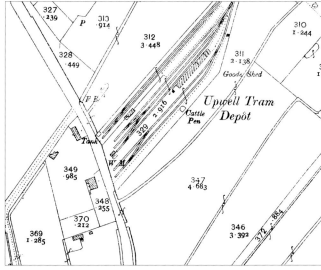

Above:
Upwell in about 1910, with a passenger train arriving. *Stations UK*

curves and steeply sloped approaches. The line then continued along the road to the Duke of Wellington, where it crossed to the west side and soon reached Elm Bridge depot, 1 mile 53 chains from Wisbech. There was a siding and loop here, together with a small office.

The route onwards to Boyce's Bridge, 3 miles 25 chains from Wisbech, was notable for the archway over the line formed by large trees growing by the roadside. The depot was very similar in provision to Elm Bridge, and retained its passenger waiting room long after withdrawal of the service. Shortly after Boyce's Bridge the tramway parted company with the road and continued on its own formation to Outwell Basin, so called because of provision on the canal, and which had the usual tramway facilities of siding, loop and office. Passenger shelter was at one time provided by an old coach body, later used as a store. Immediately to the south of the basin the tramway crossed the canal by an iron bridge, the approaches on both sides being inclined at 1 in 30. It then continued in a straight line until reaching a minor road to Outwell, following the east side of this until reaching Outwell village, again with a passing loop, later used as a coal siding. The village itself straggled

along both sides of the canal, which at its southern end joined Well Creek, leading eastwards to Popham's Eau and the Great Ouse river, and the old course of the River Nene. The tramway then crossed the Nene on another iron bridge, and passed Outwell village depot in the angle between Well Creek and the river, with sidings and goods office.

Crossing Church Terrace south of the depot, the tramway then continued along the west side of the road, on the east side of the river, leaving it for a short distance *en route* for Upwell. It crossed a small drain and a by-road, finally reaching the terminus at a total distance of 5 miles 72 chains from Wisbech, a considerable distance short of the original destination of Three Holes Bridge. The depot was extensive, with seven sidings separated by loading grounds, goods shed and passenger station.

In 1913, the original six-train service remained in operation on Mondays to Fridays, with services leaving Wisbech at 7.30, 9.45 and 11.45am, and 2.36, 5.20 and 8.10pm. Journeys were scheduled to take 39 minutes, and trains would stop additionally at Elm Road crossing, New Common Bridge, Rose Cottage, Duke of Wellington Junction, Inglethorpe Hall, Collett's Bridge, Dial House, Horn's

Above:
Upwell depot in about 1937, with various items for despatch, and large numbers of vans awaiting loading or unloading. *LGRP*

Above:
Elm Bridge depot, with a train approaching in 1966. *Stations UK*

Below:
No 68217 on shed at Wisbech in 1950, by the water tank. *Adrian Vaughan collection*

Above:
No 68225 heads a long train of vans for Wisbech at Boyce's Bridge depot in 1951. *Stations UK*

Corner, Goodman's Crossing and Small Lode. Two through trucks could be worked in rear of any of the tramcar trains, although coal and 'dead buffer' trucks were prohibited; they had to be worked by special trip. Of the above trains, the 2.36 and 8.10pm did not run on Saturdays, although there was then a later working at 8.30pm. There was also a 3pm on that day.

From Upwell, passenger trains ran back to Wisbech at 8.26 and 10.49am, and 1.11, 3.21, 6.16 and 8.35pm, the last running at 9.l5pm on Saturdays and the 3.21 running at 4.6pm on Saturdays. Loadings on the passenger trains could not exceed nine vehicles, and on mixed workings 10, with a maximum of four goods wagons. Boyce's Bridge was the most usual crossing place. In addition to these mixed trains, goods traffic was carried on four return trips on Mondays to Fridays and two on Saturdays. These started from Wisbech at 6.45 and 10.25am, with others at 12.30 and 2.10pm, Saturdays excepted. On the return they left Upwell at 8.40am, and 12.40, 3.30 and 4pm. The afternoon workings did not run on Saturdays (there was a single trip at 1.50pm) and while the 3.30pm did not call at Outwell Village, the 4pm did, but missed out Outwell Basin and Elm Bridge. Special trips were run at night to convey coal traffic as required, which had to be arranged by the stationmaster at Wisbech. Coal trains were permitted four loaded trucks in winter and five in summer.

With time, the original restrictions were slightly relaxed, so that the governors on the engines were set at 14mph. Four-coupled engines had to have brake blocks acting on each coupled wheel, but a six-coupled was required to have them on only four. The engines had to be conspicuously numbered and, as part of the regulations protecting the safety of passengers, the coaches were double-coupled. The railway company was liable to a penalty of £10 for every offence against these Board of Trade regulations, and a further £5 for every day that the offence continued. Engines had to carry a special warning bell, and after dusk, in foggy weather or in falling snow were required to carry one red and one white light on the front, with one red light on the rear of the train. There were loops at Elm Bridge depot, Outwell Village and Outwell Basin and the only crossing stations were at Boyce's depot and Upwell, with the man in charge of Boyce's depot being responsible for unlocking

and locking the points when trains required to pass. Telephones were provided along the tramway at the main stopping places.

The passenger service, hampered by the slow speeds and bus competition, was withdrawn on 1 January 1928, at least some of the coaches later being transferred to the Kelvedon & Tollesbury Light Railway. No 8 survived at least until 1957, when it was photographed restored to its original teak livery at Stratford Works. In spite of its cheap construction and operation, the line had not stemmed the drop in population, with Outwell being down to 1,022 in 1931 and Upwell plummeting to 1,918. The passing loops then became used as sidings, often for coal, and goods traffic continued to be healthy. In 1937, there were three return workings Mondays to Fridays, out from Wisbech at 9am, 12.45 and 2.10pm, and on Saturdays at 6.30 and 11.25am, which were allowed between 60 and 75 minutes for the journey, calling at the intermediate points as required. Passenger-rated parcels and livestock continued to be carried, as on most goods-only lines. They left Upwell on Mondays to Fridays at 11am, 3.20 and 4.15pm, and on Saturdays at 9.15am and 12.30pm.

Locomotives used on the tramway had to comply with the regulations and be light enough for the track. Immediately after the closure to passengers at the start of 1928, tram engines working the line included Nos 7131-6. In 1937, LNER Class Y6 0-4-0s Nos 07125, 07126, 7133 and 7134 were based at Wisbech, these having a 6ft 6in wheelbase, weight in working order of 21¼ tons, and tractive effort of 5,837lb. The last two survived into World War 2, and No 7133 had had the honour of taking part in the centenary procession for the Stockton & Darlington Railway in 1925. There were also 0-6-0 Class J70 engines, Nos 7125, 7126, 7129, 7130, 7135, 7136, 7137, 7138 and 7139. In 1930, the LNER had bought two Sentinel four-wheeled geared 200hp double-cab locomotives, numbered 8403 and 8404, but they were later transferred to Yarmouth to work on the tramways there.

Traffic was heavy during World War 2, with Nos 7137 and 7138 seen hauling successive trains of over 20 wagons leaving Upwell, which both carried blue-painted vans with the lettering 'LNER Fruit Traffic Office Van'. The regulations on maximum lengths of train had clearly been relaxed by this time. Traffic on the tramway

Above:
Outwell Basin in about 1951 with No 68225 passing the former waiting room. *Stations UK*

Below:
One of the 0-6-0 diesels heads a short train along the road at Collett's Bridge in 1966. *Stations UK*

Above:
A tram crossing the river at Outwell Basin. Although this view is not quite sharp, it gives a good indication of the locality. The train consists of a horsebox and box van. *Adrian Vaughan collection*

was heaviest in the soft fruit season, although it continued around the year, and in 1952 diesel-mechanical locomotives were introduced on the line. There were a number of other places where they were used including Eastern and North Eastern Region docks lines, and orders were placed with the Drewry Car Company Ltd for 204bhp 0-6-0 shunters. Four of these, built by Vulcan Foundry, were equipped as tram engines with side valences and cowcatchers. Nos 11102 and 11103 were allocated to March for use on the Wisbech & Upwell, while No 11100 went to Ipswich and No 11101 to Yarmouth Vauxhall. They were fitted with over-speed governors designed to put the final drive out of mesh and apply the air brakes if speed exceeded 12mph, the apparatus being located in a cabinet in the cab. Unlike the steam locomotives, where the governor had to be such that the driver could not tamper with it, these could be overridden when the locomotive was in use other than on the tramway; the top speed was then 30mph. The locomotives had a 9ft wheelbase and 21ft frame length, with a Gardner 8L3 engine providing the power. Tractive effort at the lowest gear step was 14,550lb, with a maximum speed then of 4mph. The new engines were introduced on the Wisbech & Upwell on 4 June 1952. No 11101 worked a special train of three brake vans along the line for the Railway Club on 9 July 1955, and No 11102 another for the RCTS on 9 September 1956. After renumbering in the series starting D2200, they continued to work the line into the 1960s when there remained a booked daily working along the length of the line. This typically left Wisbech at 1.30pm and reached Upwell at 2.15, calling at Elm Bridge depot as required, and returning at 3.30, reaching Wisbech at 4.15pm. On Saturdays this was a 'Q' working — as needed — out at 11am and back at 12 noon.

Closure came in stages. Boyce's Bridge closed on 5 November 1962, Outwell Basin on 5 October 1964 and Elm Bridge on 28 December, with Upwell and Outwell Village the last to go, on and from 23 May 1966. The tramway had survived almost as long as the former Great Eastern harbour branch, which closed on 12 September, and even the passenger service from March survived only another three years, being withdrawn from 9 September 1968.

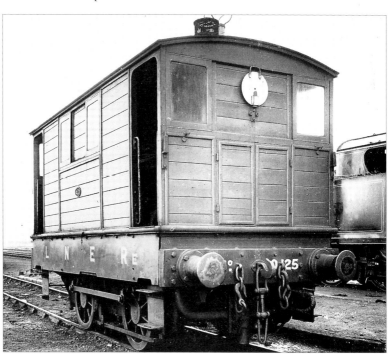

Above:
LNER Class Y6 No 0125 (GER Class G15 No 125) on shed at Wisbech. *SLS collection*

Bishop's Stortford
to Braintree

DUNMOW was one of those towns left behind by the early growth of the railway network: had things been different it could have been on a Great Northern line between London and York. The Northern & Eastern line was one of those actually built through Bishop's Stortford, opening thence in 1842, and was soon incorporated into the Eastern Counties Railway. With the Witham to Braintree line opening in 1848, Dunmow, noted for its flitches of bacon, felt its isolation from the growing network. Plans for the Bishop's Stortford, Dunmow & Braintree Railway were deposited by a local company of that name for the 1860-1 session of Parliament, with the engineers being Robert Sinclair and W. P. Gale. Powers were included to make working arrangements with the Eastern Counties Railway, and for that company to subscribe. In the event, the ECR authorised subscription of one-third of the capital, the total being £120,000.

By the middle of 1863, Thomas Brassey had been awarded the contract to build the line, having submitted the lowest tender and agreed to take £40,000 in shares. Work had started by the end of November. Uptake of shares had been very small locally, and only about £6,000 was subscribed, which was far short of what was expected. The scheme was soon in trouble, and in April 1865 the Great Eastern Railway agreed to promote a bill to authorise the absorption of the line, and to raise £80,000 share capital.

The plans showed the main line making a junction with the Eastern Counties' Braintree branch near Courtaulds silk mills,

although it was not intended to be end-on, as it subsequently became. The new line was to join the old just to the south of Braintree station before curving quite sharply to the west. At Dunmow, provision was made for a connection with the projected extension of the Epping Railway Company's line from Ongar, which would have crossed the new east-west route and terminated just to the north of it. The connection would have allowed through running via a new curve in the direction Ongar to Bishop's Stortford. The length of the new railway was given as 17 miles, 6 furlongs 5 chains and 85 links — just over 17¾ miles.

On 11 September 1866, the secretary of the Bishop's Stortford, Dunmow & Braintree Railway requested an inspection by the Board of Trade, which was followed by another on 13 November. In Col Yolland's report, dated 20 November, he noted that the over-bridges were built for a second track. There were 14 over- and 18 underbridges, made of cast or wrought-iron, all of which he found strong enough for their purpose. The line required lifting here and there, and a signalbox was needed at the eastern end of Dunmow station. Braintree's original station was still in passenger use, but the company had told him that this was to be discontinued. Col Yolland required the sharp curve at Bishop's Stortford to be check-railed, and noted that recent heavy rain had caused embankments to subside. He also identified slight settlement in the western end of the viaduct over the Chelmer at Dunmow, and concluded that the line could not be opened without danger to the public.

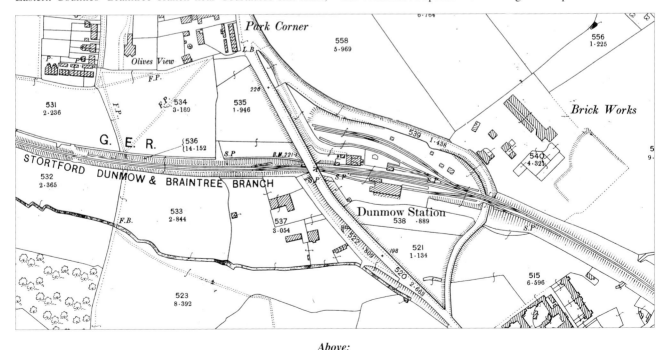

Above:
Dunmow station, 1897. *Crown Copyright*

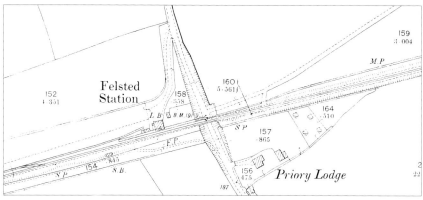

A further inspection was carried out on 27 January 1869. The report noted that Bishop's Stortford station was being enlarged, having been much too small for the traffic. A turntable would be provided there, as well as one at Braintree. Unnecessary and objectionable curves should be taken out at both ends of Takeley station, while most of the platforms at the stations required filling up. Part of the locking at Dunmow was not in order, and permission to open the line was again, not surprisingly, withheld.

After being reinspected again on 18 February, permission was at last given for opening, the new line being worked on the train staff system, with Dunmow the only intermediate staff station. It opened on 22 February 1869, although the branch to Ongar and Epping had not been built. Dunmow experienced a brief rise in population, which then continued its decline towards the turn of the century. When the railway opened, the old Braintree station was turned over to goods use, and a new one brought into use (on the present site) about half a mile west of the junction, served by all passenger trains. It had two platforms linked by a footbridge, with the main station buildings being on the north side. A small turntable was provided, and there was a siding into the brick and tile works, also to the north of the station. This siding crossed the station approach road. A long headshunt extended towards Dunmow. The goods station had cattle pens and substantial coal yards, and the engine shed remained on this site. The gas works was adjacent, as were malthouses and the local brewery.

Leaving Braintree, the line needed considerable earthworks to make its way westwards, crossing Pods Brook about a mile from the station, and reaching Rayne about a mile further on. Here there was a single platform on the north side of the line, and a level crossing at the west end. The sidings and goods facilities were on the north side of the line, with one running behind the passenger platform and another back towards Braintree. Since the line was on quite a steep gradient, rising at 1 in 66 towards Dunmow, special instructions were issued regarding shunting of goods trains. On arrival from Braintree they had to pull up clear of the points, which had then to be set for the sidings before the train was divided or any wagons were detached. No wagons were allowed to be left on the main line at any time, all shunting having to take place within the sidings.

The railway continued westward, with Stane Street, the Roman road which has here become the A120, parallel and slightly to the north. The line passed under the Great Saling to Felsted road, with Bannister Green Halt, opened in December 1922, on the east side of the bridge. The village was about ¾ mile to the south, with Watch House Green at about half the distance. Felsted station was just under two miles further, and became an important place for goods traffic with the opening of the beet sugar factory. Incidentally, the railways called it 'Felstead' for much of its life, although altered in the timetables to 'Felsted' in June 1950. In 1926 the LNER built a loop here, capable of holding 50 wagons, together with a spur, to aid the shunting of traffic in the sugar factory. Prior to this the station had consisted simply of a single platform on the north side of the line and immediately to the west of the bridge over the road from Little Dunmow to Felsted, the latter being a mile to the southeast of the station. A single siding, which could be accessed from either direction, ran up behind the platform. The sugar factory was to the south of the station, and had extensive sidings, and provided much of the traffic on the line; in 1938, over 1,300 tons of oilcake originated here.

After Felsted the line dropped briefly into the Chelmer Valley, crossing the river to the southeast of Dunmow before entering the station. Speeds were limited to 35mph on this section. The station was situated to the south of the town, by the main road to Chelmsford. The railway was already climbing out of the river valley on an embankment, although the station was on an area that had been excavated and levelled to provide a suitable site. It had two platforms, the goods shed adjoining that on the south side (to Bishop's Stortford), with a siding running through it and having its own road access. The main station buildings were on the other side, together with the goods yard. A crane of 1½ tons capacity was provided. Dunmow generated large amounts of freight, and in 1938 this included nearly 1,400 tons of grain and flour, 687 tons of bacon — the famous Dunmow flitches, 189 tons of seeds, and 166 tons of livestock. The Dunmow Flitch Bacon Company had its own siding at the station.

A mile and a half to the west was Easton Lodge. Again, this was a single platform station, but with no goods facilities. It had been specially provided to serve the home of the Earl and Countess of Warwick, whose home was about two miles to the north. The railway continued for a further 2½ miles in an almost dead straight line to Takeley, where the station platform was on the north side

of the line, with the road to Hatfield Broad Oak crossing over at the west end. Goods facilities were limited to horseboxes and general traffic. A mile further was Stane Street, a halt opened in December 1922. Similar to Bannister Green, it had a platform only 9in high and 34ft long, and necessitated the use of a special brake-third carriage with retractable steps, operated by a lever in the guard's van. Hockerill halt was a further 2½ miles away and located just to the east of the bridge taking the main road from Dunmow into Bishop's Stortford. It served, among others, the nearby teacher training college. After the National Cold Stores siding was opened at Hockerill it was permissible to propel up to 10 wagons to it from Bishop's Stortford. The line then swung in a northwesterly direction, before curving round sharply to join the main line from Cambridge about half a mile north of Bishop's Stortford station. Branch trains were limited to 15mph on this last mile of their journey.

Services were fairly sparse throughout the life of the line. The GER timetable for May 1883 showed five trains from Bishop's Stortford to Braintree, at 8.48 and 10.25am, and 1.0, 3.35 and 6.12pm, the first two calling at Felstead as required, but otherwise booked to stop. In the other direction, trains left Braintree at 7.45, 9.34 and 11.10am, and 1.55, 4.25 and 6.5pm, the first two booked to call at Felstead, but otherwise as required. Rayne was served by all trains on an 'as required' basis. Journey times were about 45 minutes each way, and Easton Lodge was not shown. A feature of the Summer 1913 timetable was that most passenger trains worked through between Bishop's Stortford and Witham, although there was sometimes a fairly lengthy wait at Braintree. The Summer 1922 timetable showed five passenger workings each way on Mondays to Fridays, with an extra return train on Wednesdays, Thursdays and Saturdays. Perhaps surprisingly, the service was not enhanced for Dunmow's market day, which was a Tuesday. During World War 2 there were five trains each way on Mondays to Saturdays, although times varied slightly at the weekend. End-to-end times varied, but were usually just over 40 minutes, although

Above:
Dunmow station from the western end, showing the water tank, main buildings and the substantial goods shed, taken in 1955 during the goods-only period. Note the station is still fully signalled. *Stations UK*

Above:
Rayne station, seen here in 1952, just after closure to passengers. It retains seats, lamps and notice boards. *Stations UK*

Below:
Rayne station in 1955, looking towards Bishop's Stortford, still appearing neat and tidy. Although the signalbox
was retained to control the level crossing, it was not a block post. *Stations UK*

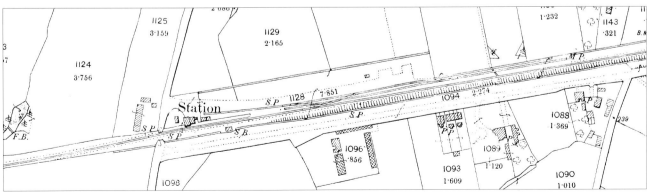

Above:
Rayne station, 1897. *Crown Copyright*

Table 29 — BISHOP'S STORTFORD, DUNMOW, and BRAINTREE AND BOCKING

Miles		Week Days only									Miles		Week Days only							
		mrn	mrn	mrn	aft	aft E	aft S	aft E	aft S					mrn	mrn	mrn	aft	aft E	aft S	aft
—	4 London (L'poolSt)dep	656	8 20	1150	2 20	4 40	4 55	6 30	7 15			Braintree & Bocking dep	7 30	..	10 50	2 0	4 30	4 50	6 35	6 38
—	Bishop's Stortford. dep	830	9 50	1245	3 26	5 40	5 49	7 30	8 10		2¼	Rayne	7 36	..	10 56	2 6	436	456	641	6 44
1½	Hockerill Halt	834	9 54	1249	3 30	5 44	5 53	7 34	8 14		4¼	Bannister Green Halt	7 40	..	11 0	2 10	440	5 0	645	6 48
5	Stane Street Halt	840	10 0	1255	3 26	5 50	5 59	7 40	8 20		6¾	Felstead for Little Dun	7 45	..	11 6	2 15	446	5 6	650	6 53
5¼	Takeley	844	10 4	1255	3 40	5 54	6 3	7 44	8 24		8¼	Dunmow [mow	7 53	9 5	11 14	2 22	454	514	657	7 0
7¼	Easton Lodge	849	10 9	1	4 3	45	5 59	6 8	7 49	8 29	10¼	Easton Lodge	7 59	9 11	11 20	2 28	5 0	520	7 3	7 6
9¼	Dunmow [mow	852	1015	1 10	3 50	6 7	6 14	7 56	8 36		12¾	Takeley	8 4	9 16	11 23	2 33	5 5	525	7 8	7 11
11¾	Felstead for Little Dun	..	1022	1 16	3 56	6 13	6 20	3 3	8 43		14	Stane Street Halt	8 7	9 19	11 28	236.5	8 528	711	7 14
13½	Bannister Green Halt	..	1027	1 20	4 1	6 18	6 25	8 8	8 48		16¼	Hockerill Halt	8 13	9 25	11 34	242	514	534	717	..
15¼	Rayne	..	1033	1 26	4 7	6 24	6 31	8 14	8 54		18	Bishop's Stortford. arr	8 16	9 28	11 37	245	517	537	720	7 21
18	Braintree & Bocking arr	..	1038	1 31	4 12	6 29	6 36	8 20	9 0		48½	4 London(L'poolSt arr	9 23	1036	12M37	5 H5	6 48	6 48	8 50	8 50

E Except Saturdays.   H Arr 5 10 aft on Sats.   N Arr 12 43 aft on Sats.   **S** Saturdays only.

Tickets from the Halts and Easton Lodge issued on train   Passengers to or from Stane Street and Bannister Green Halts must travel in special car provided.

Table 38 — BISHOP'S STORTFORD, DUNMOW, and BRAINTREE AND BOCKING

Miles		Week Days only										Miles		Week Days only							
		am	a.m	a.m	pm	p.m E	pm S	p.m E	p.m S	p.m				am	am	a.m	p.m	pm	p.m E	p.m E	p.m S
—	4 London (L'poolSt)dep	7 6	8 20	1150	225	4 36	5 0	5 21	6 36	7 20		Braintree & Bocking dep	650	730	10 51	2 0	326	4 20	4 50	6 35
—	Bishop's Stortford dep	855	9 50	1245	326	5 35	5516	31	7 35	8 15		Rayne	656	736	10 57	2 6	332	4 26	456	6 41
1½	Hockerill Halt	859	9 54	1249	330	5 39	5556	35	7 39	8 19		Bannister Green Halt	7 0	740	11 1	2 10	336	4 30	5 0	645
4	Stane Street Halt	9 9	10 0	1255	336	5 45	6 1	6 41	7 45	8 25		Felsted	7 5	745	11 6	2 15	342	4 35	5 6	650
5¼	Takeley	9 9	10 4	1259	340	5 49	6 5	6 45	7 49	8 29		Dunmow	711	752	11 14	2 22	351	4 42	514	657
7¼	Easton Lodge	914	10 9	1 4	345	5 54	610	6 50	7 54	8 34		Easton Lodge	717	758	11 20	2 28	357	4 48	5 20	7 d3
9¼	Dunmow	920	1015	1 10	350	1 6	156	6 58	8 1	8 41		Takeley	722	8 3	11 25	2 33	4 2	4 53	5 25	7 d8
11¾	Felsted	926	1022	1 16	356	6 7	621	7 4	8 7	8 47		Stane Street Halt	725	8 6	11 28	2 36	4 5	4 56	5 28	7d11
13¾	Bannister Green Halt	931	1027	1 20	4 1	6 12	626	7 9	8 12	8 52		Hockerill Halt	731	812	11 34	2 42	411	5 2	5 34	7E17
15¼	Rayne	937	1033	1 26	4 7	6 18	632	7 15	8 18	8 58		Bishop's Stortford. arr	734	815	11 37	2 45	414	5 5	5 37	7U20
18	Braintree & Bocking arr	942	1038	1 31	4 12	6 23	637	7 20	8 24	9 d		4 London (L'poolSt) arr	848	916	12 37	5 0	..	5 58	6 42	8 43

d 3 minutes later on Saturdays   **S** Saturdays only
E or E Except Saturdays   **U** Arr. 7 21 p.m. on Saturdays

Tickets from the Halts and Easton Lodge issued on train. Passengers to and from Stane Street and Bannister Green Halts must travel in special car provided

Top: **Summer 1946 timetable.** *Author's Collection*

Above: **Winter 1951-2 timetable.** *Author's Collection*

Bowmer was able to brake before the impact and escaped injury, although his fireman sprained his arm after jumping off the engine and falling down the embankment. Guard Bradley sustained cuts over his eye, and most passengers suffered some bruising. Trains were delayed for some two hours.

The line closed to passenger services on and from Monday, 3 March 1952, the last trains running on Saturday 1 March. The halts closed at this time, but goods traffic continued to be handled elsewhere. Easton Lodge reopened on 1 March 1962 as a private siding to the nearby works, lasting exactly 10 years to the day in

this capacity. Traffic was mostly beet and coal, with some general goods. Felsted closed from 4 May 1964, although the sugar beet factory continued to be served. Rayne closed on 7 December, and on 18 December 1966 the Felsted to Dunmow section and Takeley closed completely. Easton Lodge to Dunmow went on 1 April 1969, Braintree to Felsted on 20 June 1970, and Bishop's Stortford to Easton Lodge on 1 March 1972. Much of the trackbed has now been taken over by the Flitch Way, a recreational path, although the Dunmow bypass uses some of the alignment. It is also severed by the M11.

Above:
They don't come much more basic than this — Bannister Green halt, between Felsted and Rayne. Passengers had to travel in a coach provided with steps. This photograph was taken in 1955, hence the lack of nameboard and lamp. *Stations UK*

Ely to St Ives

THE Ely, Haddenham & Sutton Railway was first proposed in a bill deposited in November 1863, the company being incorporated the following June. There were many schemes to extend to Somersham or St Ives, but they were long in coming to fruition, and the line did not open throughout until 1878.

The railway, as initially envisaged left the Cambridge-Ely main line at Sutton Branch Junction, about half a mile south of Ely Dock Junction. Having diverged, it went westwards in a straight line, passing quite close to Haddenham and turning north to Sutton, where the station was close to the village. Before this was open, schemes were afoot for extension. Plans deposited for the 1865 session envisaged a new line via Earith, Bluntisham and Holywell-cum-Needingworth to St Ives. The Great Eastern was authorised to contribute, and the name of the concern was changed to the Ely & St Ives Railway. Already the station at Sutton was seen as unsuitably situated, and the new line had to join the old to the south, curving away sharply westwards, with a replacement passenger station on the new line. The engineer for this concern was John S. Valentine.

By 1869, plans had been deposited for a Sutton, Mepal & Somersham Railway. Mepal is about 1½ miles to the north of Sutton, and this route would have allowed an end-on junction at

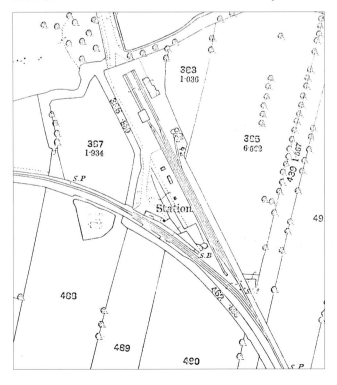

Above:
Sutton station, 1886. *Crown Copyright*

Sutton, although the plans still showed it bypassing the station. The line then swung westwards to join the March-St Ives railway at Somersham. The engineer was D. Oldfield. Meanwhile, the original line between Ely, Stretham, Wilburton, Haddenham and Sutton had been opened on 16 April 1866 by the Great Eastern, that company having subscribed one-third of the £36,000 capital cost. It was hit by serious flooding in November 1875, and was severed between Haddenham and Sutton for several days, reopening before the end of the month.

In 1876, the Company came back again for another attempt at extending its line. Plans were very similar to those deposited for the 1865 session, except for the junction arrangements at St Ives. In 1865 the proposed line approached St Ives from the east, making a junction with the Cambridge line a short distance from the station. The 1876 proposals showed the new line making a junction to the north of St Ives, with the line to Somersham and March, and would have meant that trains from Ely would have entered St Ives station from the west. Further new connections would have bypassed this curve, so that both March and Ely trains approached from the north instead of swinging round in a sweeping curve, before turning sharply right to enter the station from the east. Another chord would have allowed them to proceed directly towards Cambridge. Although the main line was built substantially in this form, the extra connections were not. The new line was to be just under 8½ miles long, and was also to be leased to the Great Eastern. The engineer was again John S. Valentine.

The line finally opened on 10 May 1878, leased to and operated by the Great Eastern. The old station at Sutton was replaced on this day by the new one on the extension, the old being relegated to goods use. The places served were all of small population, although the area comprised mostly rich fenland which grew much produce. At the turn of the 19th century, Haddenham was the largest intermediate station served, with a population of just 1,719. Stretham had 1,055, Wilburton only 452, Sutton just under 1,500, Earith Bridge 76 and Bluntisham 1,065. Other settlements added little more, with Mepal, once a target for the railway builders, having only 390 inhabitants. To put this in context, Ely and St Ives had respectively 8,017 and 3,005 people. As might be expected, passenger services were sparse, the 1922 timetable showing an unbalanced weekday service of four trains from Ely to St Ives and five the other way, with one fewer on Mondays from St Ives. Both Haddenham and Wilburton loaded substantial quantities of potatoes: in 1938, the traffic amounted to 1,133 and 1,330 tons respectively at each. Sutton loaded 1,957 tons, plus a further 2,631 tons of other vegetables. There were numbers of private sidings, with two at Haddenham (Isle of Ely Brick Works Ltd and J. Porter), and another between there and Sutton (F. Jewsons). All stations offered passenger, parcels and general goods facilities, although Earith Bridge was the only one to have its own crane, of

Right:
The 'new' station at Sutton, opened with the extension onwards to St Ives. This view is looking towards Ely. *LGRP*

Above:
Stretham station, the first from Ely on the line to Needingworth Junction. Given that it lost its passenger services in the 1930s, it is remarkably intact in this 1961 view. *Stations UK*

Below:
Stretham station, 1886. *Crown Copyright*

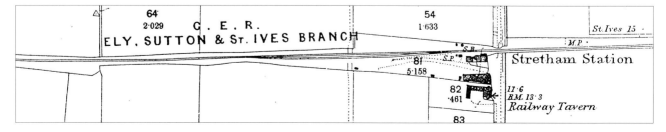

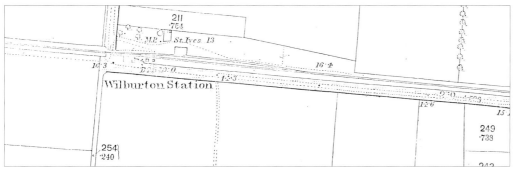

10cwt capacity, by virtue of the wharf on the River Great Ouse. Bluntisham, Sutton and Haddenham could handle all classes of traffic; others were more restricted.

The line diverged from the Cambridge to Ely route at Sutton Branch Junction, through running to Ely being possible. It swung away to the west, and more or less straight for Haddenham. The first station, Stretham, was only 2¾ miles from Ely, and initially had only a simple passing loop. There was a level crossing immediately to the east of the station, where the line crossed the Stretham to Witchford road, and the Railway Tavern was on hand for thirsty travellers. Wilburton station, two miles further, had a similar layout initially, also with a single platform located on the up side of the line, and a goods loop opposite. The level crossing was at the west end. Headshunts were later added at each end of the loop, which had a large goods shed adjacent. There was a signalbox at the Ely end of the platform, which was abolished soon after withdrawal of the passenger service. The station was over a mile from the village, with Haddenham almost as near.

Haddesham station was a little more conveniently placed for its village, which was somewhat sprawling around the junction of the Newmarket to Huntingdon main road, and that from Sutton. The layout was rather more extensive, with the platform and buildings being on the south side of the line next to the bridge carrying the Sutton road over the line. The goods yard was quite extensive, with two sidings converging on the goods shed, a cattle dock and the siding into the brick and tile works. The local gas works was also sited here, which must have made a stay at the Railway Hotel an interesting olfactory experience!

Past Haddenham, the line curved sharply to the north to head for Sutton, terminus for some years before the extension to St Ives came into being. The old station was turned over to goods use, and boasted four parallel roads organised as two loops. The new passenger station was on the extension, with the buildings being in the vee of the junction. The new line curved away to the southwest, approaching Earith Bridge, about 4½ miles from Sutton, almost parallel with the New Bedford River, also called the Hundred Foot Drain. At Earith Bridge both Old and New Bedford rivers joined the Great Ouse, the railway crossing this a short distance after the level crossing of the Haddenham road, the station being between these. Its single platform and station buildings were on the north side of the line, with goods loop opposite, this extending towards the wharf on the river. Earith itself was about half a mile away to the west, and had a good coal, timber and building materials trade by virtue of its position on the inland waterway system. The fens here often froze in the winter, and special trains would be run from Cambridge bringing skaters.

Less than a mile further on the line again crossed the river, and shortly afterwards reached Bluntisham. The layout here was again simple, with the platform and buildings on the north side of the line. The cattle dock and pens were served by a short siding from the goods loop, which was to the east of the passenger station. The signalbox was on the south side of the line, part way along the loop, and the Stretham to St Ives road was carried over the line by a bridge at the western end of the station. The surrounding farmland grew wheat, barley and beans, and the area was noted for its large orchards and gooseberry gardens. The stationmaster in 1914 was Tom E. Tagg. The railway had not brought great prosperity, though, the population had fallen in 1911 to 1,022. Needingworth Junction, 14 miles 2 chains from Ely, marked the end of the Ely & St Ives line: the single track became double just short of the junction, with the signalbox opposite the point of divergence. The line was worked on the train staff-and-ticket system, with the staff stations being Needingworth Junction, Bluntisham, Sutton and Sutton Branch Junction.

Above:
Haddenham, on the line between Ely and Sutton, with Class J15 No 65477 busy shunting.
David Lawrence

Right:
Haddenham station, 1887.
Crown Copyright

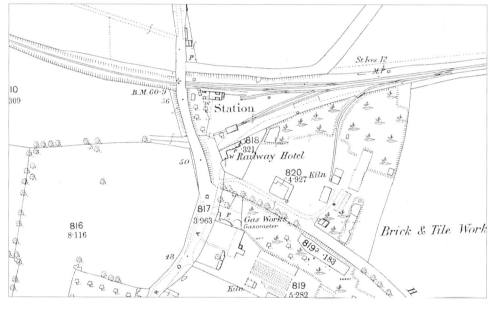

Below:
Earith Bridge station, 1886.
Crown Copyright

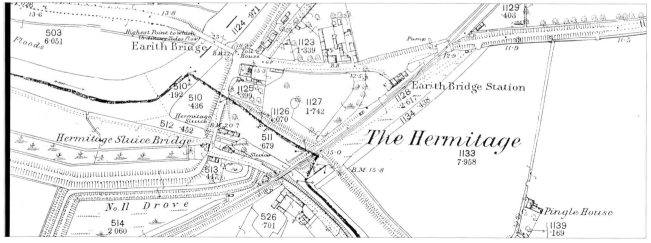

Above:
Earith Bridge was a little way from the village, seen here with Class J15 No 65477 shunting. *David Lawrence*

Below:
A view over the level crossing at Earith Bridge with 'J17' No 65565 arriving from Sutton.
It illustrates well the nature of the surrounding countryside. *Stations UK*

Above:
Class J15 No 65477 shunts at Bluntisham, probably in the early 1960s. *David Lawrence*

Below:
A splendid view of Bluntisham in about 1930, not long before closure to passengers. *Stations UK*

Early services were limited. The May 1883 GER timetable showed four up trains (from Ely) each weekday, generally calling at Stretham, Wilburton and Earith Bridge as required, and taking between 45 and 95 minutes, the slower times being for mixed trains which were booked to call everywhere. Trains left Ely at 6.5am, 9.20am Mondays only, 9.30am Mondays excepted — this was mixed and very slow, 2.5pm Mondays and Thursdays only, 4.40 and 7.10pm. In the other direction trains left St Ives at 7.30am, 11.30am (not Mondays and Thursdays), 12.47pm Mondays and Thursdays only, 3pm Mondays and Thursdays only, and 5.30pm. In summer 1913, there were slightly more trains: up passenger, now booked to call at all stations, from Ely at 9.25am, and 2.12, 4.19 and 7.10pm, and down at 7.30 and 11.35am and 12.53, 3.15 and 5.18pm. Running times had remained largely unchanged, and some, notably the 2.12 and 7.10pm from Ely, could work cattle to St Ives if in Westinghouse-piped trucks. There was a light engine working on Mondays from St Ives to Ely at 7.40am, and this was also allowed to work cattle if required. Goods traffic was covered by the 10.30am up from Ely to Ramsey via Sutton, the 2.18pm Ely to Peterborough via St Ives (not Saturdays), and the 6am express cattle on Mondays only, which deserved the 'express' title because it did not call at Wilburton and Earith Bridge. In the down direction a goods train left St Ives at 6.15pm, having started from Ramsey at 3.23pm.

The passenger service lasted only until 31 January 1931 when the last regular trains ran. Goods, parcels and perishable traffic continued to be handled, but bus services replaced the trains. Outwardly the stations remained unaltered long after closure to passengers. Excursion traffic continued to be handled on an occasional basis; for example, on 27 August 1932, the six inter-mediate stations on the line were reopened to local people to join an excursion to Hunstanton. Half-day excursions to London continued until the outbreak of World War 2. After that, two annual excursions continued to operate, to Hunstanton and Yarmouth Vauxhall, for Yarmouth races. Goods services in 1937 were typified by the 7.18am all-stations milk and parcels train from St Ives to Ely, with an all-stations goods at 4.10pm. A conditional goods left Sutton for Ely at 6.10pm, calling at Haddenham.

Closure came about in stages, with Earith Bridge closing completely on 6 October 1958. This left goods services to be operated in two sections, from St Ives to Bluntisham and from Ely to Sutton, with some of the track being lifted. For a time, the line between Sutton and Earith Bridge was used to store empty wagons. Ely to Sutton closed on 13 July 1964, while St Ives to Bluntisham succumbed on 5 October 1964.

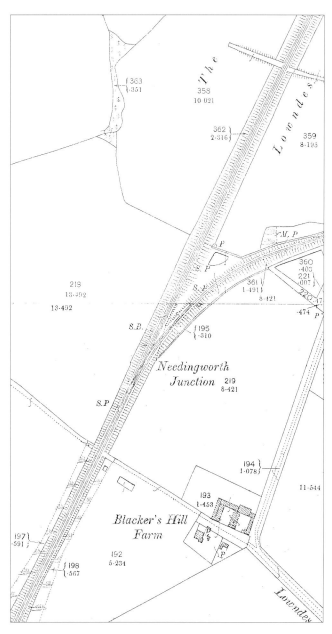

Above:
Needingworth Junction station, 1900. *Crown Copyright*

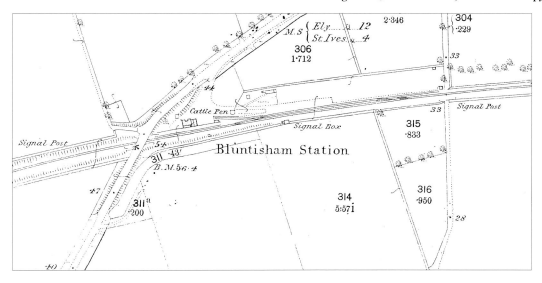

Above:
Bluntisham station, 1886. *Crown Copyright*

Benwick Branch

THE Benwick branch was one of the few in East Anglia that never operated any scheduled passenger services, having been built by the Great Eastern to tap the agricultural traffic of the Fens, and which it did very successfully for many years. It is perhaps surprising that it was not built under the provisions of the Light Railways Act, but the conception and authorisation of the branch slightly predated this piece of legislation.

Authorisation to construct the line was obtained in the Great Eastern General Powers Act of 1895. It was to run from a junction facing Peterborough at Three Horseshoes, and turn sharply to the south, passing to the west of Floods Ferry after about a mile, where it crossed Whittlesey Dyke, and where there was a wharf or quay. It was to be level all the way, except where it had to rise at 1 in 100 to cross Whittlesey Dyke, and would have a length of 4 miles 3 furlongs 2.70 chains. The line opened in two stages, to Burnt House on 1 September 1897 and Benwick on 2 August 1898. Three Horseshoes, probably named after the nearby farm and public house, had no passenger facilities, but was provided with sidings and loops, and had a level crossing at the west end of the layout. There was also a goods shed and cattle pens on the north side of the

main line, with two sidings being provided to the south of the branch as it trailed into the down (towards Peterborough) main line. One of these could be used as a loop, being double-ended. The branch diverged about ¼ mile to the east of the junction, with the first siding at Quaker's Drove 73 chains away. The layout took the standard form for intermediate stops on the branch, with a double-ended siding and short headshunts. Quaker's Drove itself — 'droves' are roads across the fens — was on the west side of the railway, and where it crossed the line became Hake's Drove.

West Fen Drove was 1 mile 42 chains from the junction, with a very similar layout, but this time with the siding on the east side of the line. Burnt House Drove, at 2 miles 3 chains, was on the west side, followed by Jones' Drove at 2 miles 62 chains, on the east side. The siding here was to the south of the bridge over the old course of the River Nene. White Fen, at 3 miles 40 chains, was on the west side, and completed the pattern of sidings on alternate sides of the line. Each also had a nearly square brick building, with a fully hipped slate roof, which could function as an office. The terminus at Benwick at 4 miles 41 chains, was somewhat different, and was located on the bank of the former course of the River

Below:
Quaker's Drove, the first siding along the branch from the junction at Three Horseshoes with shunting in progress. *Stations UK*

Above:
**Burnt House, illustrating the
levels of traffic available
on the branch.** *Stations UK*

Left:
**White Fen, showing the layout
of the depot, which was
similar at all locations except
Benwick. There was a double-
ended siding and square brick-
built hut, with access from a
drove.** *Stations UK*

Below:
**Three Horseshoes junction,
1900.** *Crown Copyright*

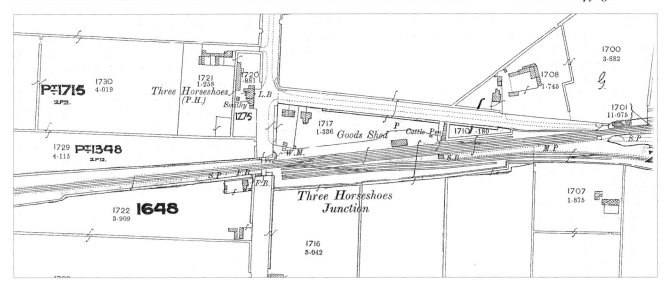

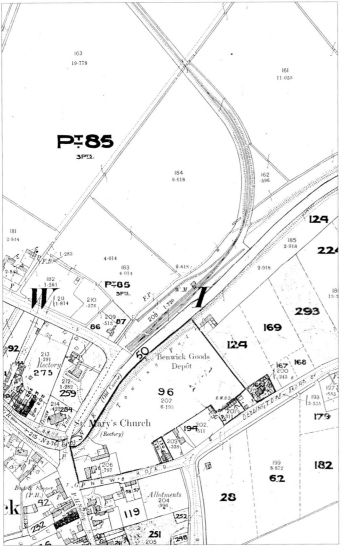

Above:
The terminus at Benwick, seen from the road. There was a fan of sidings, plus one to serve the wharf, and a loading dock on the left.
Stations UK

Left:
Benwick station, 1900.
Crown Copyright

Above:
The Benwick branch served a rich farming area, and generated a good amount of traffic for the Great Eastern. Class J19 No 64671 shunts at Jones' Drove in 1953. *Stations UK*

Nene. There was a loop about 600ft long on the approach to the station, the line arriving from a northwesterly direction and having to turn through 90° to come parallel to the river. The loop occupied almost all of this curve, and sidings fanned out at the station end. One, on the north side terminated short of the station entrance in a loading dock, while the four others between them provided for shunting, wagon storage and general loading and unloading. Another ran back parallel to the river and served the wharf. The goods depot (all the sidings on the branch were officially so designated) was conveniently placed close to the village centre near the river bridge, with the entrance being controlled by a typical large railway gate. Traffic was what might be expected from a farming community: a variety of vegetables such as potatoes, carrots, swedes, turnips and later, sugar beet, with coal, manure and seed potatoes inwards. In later years the sidings were served on an 'as required' basis,

The branch was worked on the one-engine-in-steam principle, with the staff being green and round, and lettered 'Three Horse Shoes and Benwick'. Tickets were not used, and the staff, when not on the branch, was kept in the signalbox at the junction, where the signalman was the only authorised person able to deal with it. At the same time that the staff was collected by the driver, the guard had to collect the key used to lock the points at the sidings, and it

was his responsibility to ensure that they were correctly set and locked when work was finished. The overall speed limit was 15mph, reduced to 8mph when passing over the points at the sidings. The branch was used on occasion for the stowage of trucks, and when this happened any class of engine could be used to work them on or off the line. Typically, Great Eastern 0-6-0 tender engines such as 'J19s' handled the traffic.

There were two trains each way on weekdays when the line opened, but this soon went down to one. In 1913 this was a working from Peterborough, which left at 12.30pm, called at Whittlesea between 12.45 and 1.10pm, and reaching Three Horse Shoes (the exact form of the name seems to have varied) at 1.20pm. It left at 1.25pm, having had to set back from the up to the down line to get on to the branch, and then called at all depots to Benwick, where arrival was at 3.15pm, thus allowing nearly two hours for working along the branch. Departure from Benwick was at 5.30pm (4.50pm Saturdays only), with White Fen and Jones' Drove not served on the return, and Three Horse Shoes served only on Saturdays.

Traffic on the branch fell gradually as the motor lorry encroached, and although it saw the occasional excursion for enthusiasts, who clambered into open trucks for the journey, closure came about on and from 13 July 1964.

Forncett to Wymondham

THE Forncett to Wymondham line turned out to be a minor rail byway, but had been envisaged as a significant part of the main line system dealing with heavy traffic at high speeds. Its construction took place at a time of optimistic expansion, and whilst it very occasionally came into its own, the hopes were never fulfilled and it lost its passenger services early on. It had an ignominious end as the last repository of condemned rolling stock.

The line was promoted in the Great Eastern Railway Act of 1876, and the contract awarded to W. Bell & Sons for £3,026. It is possible that the construction of this line, and that of the Dereham avoiding curve, were ploys to counter the incursions of the Eastern & Midlands line into GER territory, although the ostensible reason for its construction was concern about congestion in the Norwich area.

The line opened without any ceremony on Monday 2 May 1881, it having earlier been intended to do so on 1 March. The *Norwich Mercury* reported that this short loop line, 6¾ miles long, would prove to be of great advantage to the district. Previously communication between the north and south of Norfolk had been via Norwich, most traffic having to connect between Thorpe and Victoria stations. The line between Wells and Wymondham had no connection with the direct line to London, and a roundabout and

tedious journey through the city was necessary for both goods and passenger traffic. The new and direct route via Ipswich for north and central Norfolk to London was several miles shorter than via Cambridge. The new line branched from the main line at Forncett, running parallel with it for about a quarter of a mile before diverging to the left. There was a station at Ashwellthorpe, and it was then a short run to Wymondham. The line was built double throughout, and it was felt that it would also be very valuable as a means of relieving the ever-increasing traffic on the Cambridge line. This would become even more important when the Great Eastern opened its new joint line with the GNR to the coalfields of the North of England. The paper felt that the passenger and goods traffic of central and north Norfolk would speedily gravitate to this new, shortest route. The sidings on the new line (presumably at Ashwellthorpe) were incomplete at the time of opening, and through carriages from all parts were not provided on all trains.

Before the advent of the new line, travellers from Ipswich to the market at East Dereham had had a journey of five or six hours each way, much of this taken up with delays at Norwich. The new line offered times of under two hours, with a special fast train from Ipswich to Dereham on Fridays (market day), and a through express train every evening in connection with the 5pm down from

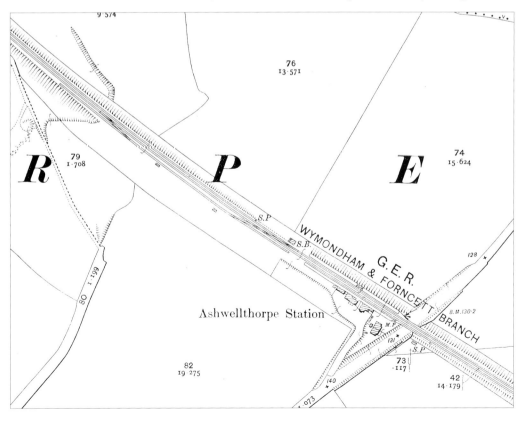

Left:
Ashwellthorpe station.
Crown Copyright

Above:
Forncett station, on the main line from Ipswich, looking towards Norwich in about 1924. The junction for Wymondham was a little way to the north of the station. *Stations UK*

Left:
Ashwellthorpe in around 1939, looking towards Wymondham. Built on a grand scale, traffic did not develop to any significant extent. *Stations UK*

Below left:
The north end of Ashwellthorpe station, showing the signalbox and the interesting signal just past it. At first looking like an ordinary bracket signal, the two posts in fact carry the down starter and up home arms. *Stations UK*

Liverpool Street, leaving Ipswich at 6.40pm and reaching Dereham at 8.19pm and Wells at 9.15pm. At the same time, the Great Eastern was also proposing to double the line between Wymondham and Dereham, doubtless in anticipation of the great increase in through traffic from London via Forncett.

The route was easily graded and curved, and built to main line standards. Forncett had only the usual two side platforms, and mostly single-storey wooden buildings. Leaving the main line, the branch crossed over a minor road between Tasburgh and Ashwell-thorpe, and then a minor tributary of the River Tas. Although running through gently undulating countryside, it used many embankments or cuttings to ease its path, and reached Ashwellthorpe station, 2 miles 77 chains from Forncett. The station was located to the west of what is now the B1113 Tacolneston to Norwich road, which passed under the line at the east end. Being double track there were two side platforms, each 400ft long, with the main buildings on the down (to Wymondham) side. These were not in a standard Great Eastern style, and may have been designed by the contractors. The two-storey stationmaster's house had a fully hipped roof, with the booking office and other facilities housed in single-storey structures on the Wymondham end. A small canopy was provided in front of the booking office, and a simple open-fronted brick shelter and awning sufficed on the other side. There was a single siding beyond the west end of the passenger station, which could be reached by a trailing connection from the up line, near the signalbox, which crossed the down. There was also a trailing connection from the down line at the other end of the siding, which

had headshunts at each end. There was no goods shed or crane, and the station could handle only passenger, parcel and ordinary goods traffic. Wymondham was 6 miles 64 chains from Forncett, the line approaching along an embankment and curving gently round to the junction. The station had two platforms, the up side (to Ely) being an island, although the outer face was not normally used by passenger trains.

The branch had a brief moment of glory in the wake of the floods in August 1912, when the main line was closed near Flordon, the next station north of Forncett. Trains between Ipswich and Norwich used it, reversing at Wymondham, and it is said that relatively little time was lost because of the good alignment. The 'Norfolk Coast Express', normally nonstop between Liverpool Street and Cromer, was one such train.

The 1913 summer timetable showed that the line's promise was already sadly unfulfilled, with only five passenger trains each way on weekdays. These left Wymondham at 9.53am and 12.7, 5.10 and 6.50pm, all calling at Ashwellthorpe. In addition, there was a train at 1.58pm from Wells which called at all stations to Dereham, reached at 2.37pm, arriving at Wymondham at 3.13pm. It then ran via Ashwellthorpe, where it called if required to pick up London passengers, and reached Forncett at 3.30pm. From there they could connect with the 3.27pm London express from Norwich Thorpe, which left Forncett at 3.50pm and called at Diss, Stowmarket, Ipswich, Colchester and Ilford on its way to Liverpool Street, arriving there at 6.38pm. On Mondays there was another train from Wymondham, at 7.42am, also calling at Ashwellthorpe if required

Below:
**Wymondham station on 31 July 1955, with No 62556 arriving with the 9.51am Norwich to Dereham and Wells.
The service was dieselised about two months later. The junction from Forncett is behind the train and to the right.** *SLS Collection*

118

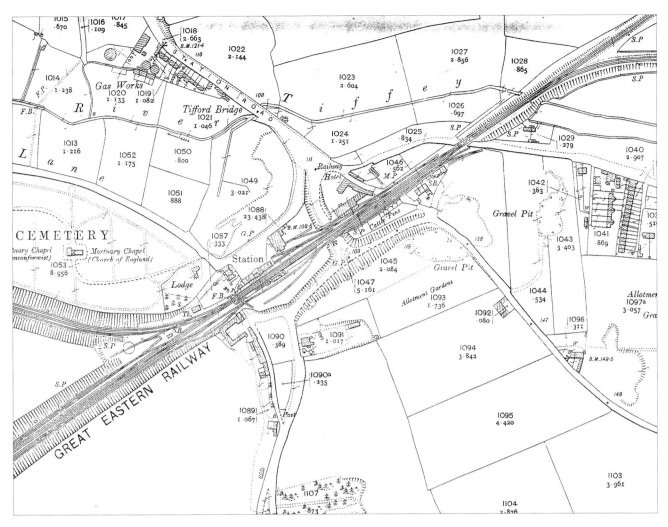

Above:
Wymondham station. *Crown Copyright*

to pick up London passengers. The corresponding down workings were at 7.36pm from Forncett, which arrived at Dereham at 8.8pm and then called all stations to Wells, reached at 9pm. This gave a good connection from the 4.55pm from Liverpool Street, which had called only at Ipswich, Stowmarket and Diss. Otherwise the service showed departures from Forncett at 7.15am on Mondays only, 8.10 and 10.33am, and 12.57 and 6.15pm. Goods services were provided by a single working each weekday from Beccles, which on Mondays to Fridays worked out from Beccles at 10.30am, left Tivetshall at 2.10pm, Forncett at 2.30pm and reached Wymondham at 3.5pm, having shunted at Ashwellthorpe. It ran 50 minutes earlier on Saturdays, despite leaving Beccles at the same time, spending the extra time at Harleston on weekdays. In the other direction it left Wymondham at 4.30pm Mondays to Fridays (5.20pm Saturdays), reaching Forncett at 5pm, leaving there at 5.40pm and finally reaching Beccles at 8.45pm.

In 1922, the passenger service was slightly better, with six trains each way every weekday, but still with a small variation on Mondays. In the summer 1937 service there were still six trains each way, with the first up being a through working from Dereham

at 6.57am, and connecting into a London train at Forncett. The down train left Forncett at 7.54pm and called at all stations to Dereham, extended on Mondays only to Wells. The public timetable continued to show connections at Forncett for London and Beccles via the Waveney Valley, and at Wymondham for Dereham and Wells, and the Ely line.

With the outbreak of war in 1939 the passenger service was suspended and never reinstated. Goods traffic lasted longer, and the line remained open throughout the war for this purpose, although it is not clear how much traffic there was from Ashwellthorpe. There was one down train from Whitemoor to Norwich Victoria via Forncett, entailing reversal there, and a handful of other workings. The line was singled operationally, the up being used as a running line, and withdrawn and damaged rolling stock being stored on the down. It closed completely from 4 August 1951 and most of the track was lifted soon after, except for a section at the Wymondham end, which was used by King's of Norwich for dismantling condemned rolling stock; this company had long had a siding at Wymondham. Final lifting of this section did not take place until the early 1980s.

Maldon Branches
Maldon-Witham; Maldon-Woodham Ferrers and Witham-Braintree

THE Eastern Counties Railway Company's line from Shoreditch, built at almost ruinous cost, opened as far as Colchester for goods on 7 March 1843, and for passengers on 29 March. The prospect of rail connection to London was an enticing one for many towns and villages, and opened up great opportunities for trade, although early on, the ECR acquired a reputation for poor management and services. The Maldon, Witham & Braintree Railway was a local concern that aimed to connect both towns with each other and the capital. Its bill was deposited in November 1845 for the following session of parliament, and was approved in 1846.

The total length of the line was to be 12 miles 5 chains and 85 links. It was to be gently graded, much being at 1 in 300/350, but with one long stretch of 1 in 186. The line terminated in Maldon at the River Blackwater, on a headland in the parish of St Peters. The river and the Chelmer Navigation were crossed just outside the town, and it then passed close to Wickham and Langford Halls. At Witham the new line would have crossed the ECR's main line, so that direct running was possible between Maldon and Braintree. From the first, the projected Branch A was a curve which would have allowed a train from Maldon to run direct to Colchester, while Branch B gave direct access to Witham station. Branch C took trains from Braintree into Witham station, the only part missing from the proposals being a curve to allow direct Braintree-Colchester working. Certain alterations to the curves at Witham

were authorised on 25 February 1848, the radius of both Branches B and C being reduced, while Branch A seems to have remained unaltered. At Braintree, the station site did not allow for future extension, and became the goods station when the line to Bishop's Stortford was opened.

One of the prime reasons for the building of the railway was to tap into the traffic flowing through the port of Maldon, which handled considerable tonnages of potatoes and grain. The Eastern Counties Railway allowed the new line to cross its own on the level, so that through running was effectively prevented, and the railway became two branches, opening for goods traffic on 15 August 1848. The line was inspected on 30 September by Capt George Wynne of the Board of Trade, who reported that the direct crossing (at Witham) had not been made and that it seemed doubtful that it would ever be. The earthworks were not heavy, and the slopes stood well at 1½ to 1. Seven carriage and two occupier roads crossed over the line by bridges, and seven under, of which only two were public roads. There were six simply constructed timber viaducts over rivers and brooks, the piers and abutments being piles and the spanning timbers whole baulks. The line was laid with double track throughout, and there were four stations (according to Capt Wynne's report), at Bulford (Cressing from 1 February 1911), Braintree, Wickham Mill and Maldon, all of which had semaphore signals. Capt Wynne found the line to be in good order and free of obstructions, and

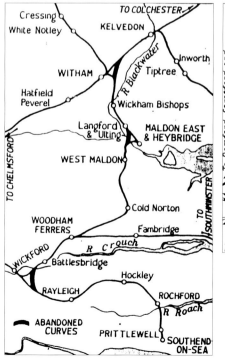

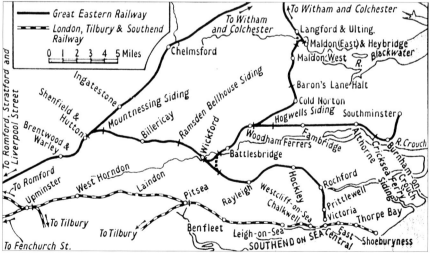

Above: **Map of the railways serving Southend, including the Maldon branches.** *The Railway Magazine*

Left: **Map showing the three abandoned curves which had allowed direct running between Southend and Colchester.** *The Railway Magazine*

Above:
The outside of Braintree's second station in Great Eastern days. The buildings remain substantially unaltered, and have recently been restored by Railtrack and First Great Eastern. *Lens of Sutton*

sanctioned its opening for passengers, which duly took place on 2 October 1848.

It was not long before the line was employing substantial numbers of people for its operation, and in associated trades. The 1851 census for Braintree and Bocking showed 15 men living there and working on the railway in a variety of jobs, including porters, clerks, stokers, labourers and enginemen. Some had travelled considerable distances, such as John Adams, 33, an engine fitter and fireman from Coventry, and James S. Smith, 18, from Holloway. At Cressing, George Aston, 30, was from Yorkshire and worked as a platelayer. Staff at Witham included William Atkinson from York, who was the stationmaster, plus two signalmen, a telegraph clerk, four porters, an inspector and two labourers. Men at Maldon included a clerk, telegraph clerk, porter, the stationmaster, Henry Clerk Francis, 28, from Bishop's Stortford, and two signalmen.

Maldon was the target of other schemes. Sir Samuel Morton Peto, the well-known entrepreneur, promoted a line during the 1850s which would have connected Pitsea, on the London, Tilbury & Southend line, with Maldon and Colchester. It was probably mostly a ploy to force more favourable terms from the Eastern Counties Railway for his other schemes, since it would have given a route independent of the ECR between London and East Anglia, but nothing came of it. Another such was the Southend & Maldon Railway of 1872, with Russel Aitken and J. W. Wilson as the engineers. The proposed line branched from the Witham to Maldon railway at Langford station, and swung to the west of Maldon. It then crossed the River Crouch at Fambridge, and went via Rochford to a junction with the London, Tilbury & Southend just to the west of the Southend terminus. Bear in mind that the Great Eastern lines to Southend and Southminster were in the future, and that the LT&S had not yet been extended to Shoeburyness. This line would have had a total length of about 16 miles. The bill sought powers to use both Southend and Maldon stations, although reversal would have been necessary to gain access to both.

Services on the lines between Maldon, Witham and Braintree were fairly limited. The 1874 timetable showed trains from Braintree at 7.13, 7.55 and 9.45am, and 2.15, 4.30 and 6.35pm, the 4.30pm not calling at White Notley or Bulford. There were return workings from Witham at 7.30, 10.23 and 11.5am, and 4.10, 6.6 and 7.28pm, and trains took between 15 and 22 minutes for the 6¼ mile journey.

Trains left Witham for Maldon at 8.28 and 10.27am, and 2.50, 5.35 and 7.27pm, and in the other direction at 7.5 and 9am, and 12.30pm, 4.25pm (3.45pm on Wednesdays only) and 6.30pm. There were two return workings on both lines on Sundays, although it is not clear whether they simply provided good connections at Witham or were through trains. Typical fares between Braintree and Witham were 1s 3d first class, 1s 0d second, 9d third and 6d parliamentary. Langford, Wickham, White Notley and Bulford were all request stops.

A bill for the Bishop's Stortford, Dunmow & Braintree line was deposited for the 1860-1 session, and this was opened for traffic on 22 February 1869. The original Braintree station was then turned over to goods use and a new station opened on the new line a little to the southwest of the first, served by all passenger trains. It had two platforms linked by a footbridge, with the main station buildings being on the north side. A small turntable was provided, and there was a siding into the brick and tile works, also to the north of the station. The old station had cattle pens and a substantial coal yard, with the engine shed remaining on this site.

During the 1880s, the Great Eastern promoted a number of new lines in Essex mainly to improve its access to Southend. Among these was the new line from Shenfield to Wickford, opened on 19 November 1888, with passenger services on the branch from Wickford to Southminster starting on 1 June 1889. The main line was extended to Southend Victoria on 1 October 1889, and at the same time the new branch between Woodham Ferris, on the Southminster line, and Maldon was opened. Curves were provided at Wickford so that trains from Southend could run direct to Maldon without reversal, and also at Maldon so that they could continue northwards without reversal at the original station, which had become Maldon East. The east curve at Witham also allowed them to continue on to Colchester without reversal at Witham, and a through service was briefly operated from 1890 to 1894. One train on Saturdays only left Southend at 10.22am and called at all stations to Maldon West, and then Colchester only. Latterly it went into Maldon East, and called at Wickham Bishops if required. This appears to have been the only booked through service, and one theory is that the curves were built at the insistence of the military, nervous about the need to move troops and materials quickly along the East Coast in the event of threats from the Continent.

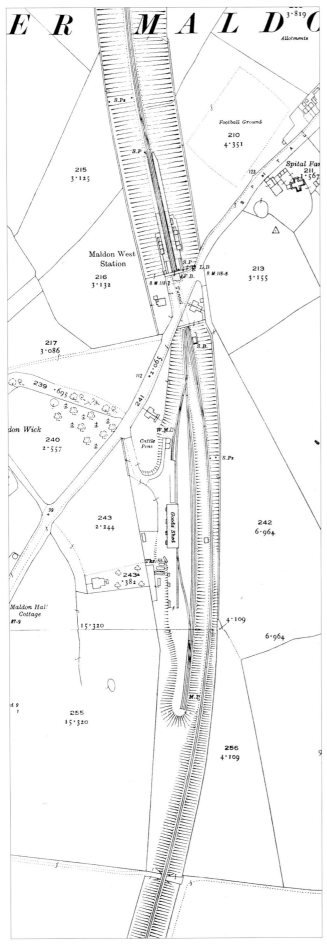

Above:
Maldon West station, 1922. *Crown Copyright*

The stations on the new line were initially at Woodham Ferris (Woodham Ferrers from 1 October 1913), Cold Norton and Maldon West, with trains continuing into Maldon East, renamed Maldon East & Heybridge from 1 October 1907. Maldon West was the only intermediate staff station, and the line was worked on the staff-and-ticket principle. It was single, apart from the sections between Maldon West and Maldon East Junction, and Langford Curve, which allowed direct running towards Witham. The total length was 8¾ miles, and there was a goods siding at Baron's Lane, which was also able to handle livestock. On 10 July 1922 the LNER opened a passenger halt there, 3¾ miles from Maldon East, and in 1928 on 24 September at Stow St Mary, 2¼ miles from Woodham Ferrers.

At Woodham Ferrers the station was provided with two platforms, the line curving slightly to head almost due east towards Fambridge. The Maldon branch diverged some way beyond the level crossing, the speed limit for the whole journey to Witham being 40mph. The line turned towards the northwest for a short distance, and then in an easterly direction to the south of Stow Maries, mostly on embankment. It then curved to the north, entering a short cutting before crossing under the road from Stow Maries at Cold Norton. The station there was a block post, but trains could not cross, and it was not a staff station. It could handle all classes of traffic, although with a population in 1911 of only 233, there was never going to be much. The signalbox had been slated for abolition in 1924, together with that at Maldon West, but this did not happen.

Maldon was approached from the southwest, largely on embankments. The West station was approached along an embankment which became a cutting, with the goods yard on the west side and at a higher level. The line became double just before entering a short tunnel (which in reality was a large, skewed road bridge) which took Spital Road over the line, the points giving access to the goods yard being in the tunnel at the south end. One siding gave access to the cattle pens and loading dock, while a branch off it ran through the goods shed. Two other sidings ran back parallel to the running line, with a crossover at the southern end allowing them to be used as a loop. The station could handle most classes of traffic except horseboxes and carriages by passenger trains. The signalbox was situated on the east side of the line at the south end of the tunnel, and was reduced to ground frame status in 1929. The passenger platforms were to the north of the tunnel, and extended almost up to it. There were buildings and canopies on both platforms, and also on the tunnel itself, this last being the booking office and other accommodation, and having the appearance of a medium-sized house. Spital Road widened out in front of it, providing an approach for vehicles and people. In passenger days the footbridge seems to have been almost a part of the tunnel portal, with steps down to each platform and direct access from the booking office. There was a crossover beyond the tunnel. The line between Maldon East and West was singled in 1924, and staff and ticket working introduced, as with the rest of the branch to Woodham Ferrers.

The line then continued to curve gently, although heading in a more or less northerly direction to Maldon East station. It crossed the Chelmer by means of a very substantial brick viaduct, the river itself being spanned by an iron bowstring bridge, and then the Blackwater, with a short section of embankment between them. At the eastern end of this was Maldon West Junction, where the line originally became double, the left-hand line (Langford curve) going to Langford Junction, and the right to Maldon East. The curve between the Maldon stations was limited to 15mph.

Maldon East & Heybridge was an impressive station. Passengers approached from Station Road, and were faced with a brick building sporting a colonnaded front, with decorated gables, chimneys and balustrades. Going through the booking office, there was a single main platform, plus a bay, the latter having cattle pens and loading docks adjacent. The line approached the station from the northwest,

Left:
Maldon West station seen in about 1910. The line passed under the road here in a short tunnel, and passengers descended flights of steps to the platforms. *Stations UK*

Below:
Class J67 No 68628 runs round its two-coach special train at Maldon West on 6 April 1957. The bricked-up entrances from the station building to the flights of steps can be seen. *David Lawrence*

Above:
The line from Woodham Ferrers crossed the river by this splendid bridge between the two Maldon stations. *Ian Allan Library/Bucknall Collection*

Above:
**The exterior of Maldon
East station, taken in the
1950s.** *David Lawrence*

Right:
**Maldon East station,
1897.** *Crown Copyright*

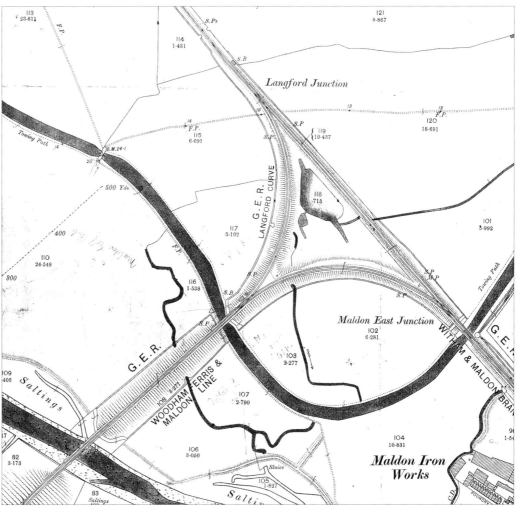

and continued through it a short distance, leading to the engine shed beyond the platforms and a 50ft turntable. A siding running back from this gave access to Dock Wharf, timber and coal yards. At the other end of the station was the large goods shed. The line crossed The Causeway/Fullbridge Road by both a bridge and level crossing, and on the Witham side of these were more sidings, with access to wharves on the Blackwater by means of a wagon turntable. There was also a large timber yard and sawmill here, which, in conjunction with the movement of timber through the port, provided much of the originating goods traffic on the branch. There was a ground frame hut at the engine shed end of the platform for controlling the yard and other pointwork there. The station could handle all classes of traffic, and had a 1½-ton crane. One of the most important originating traffics was small machinery, with 510 tons being loaded in 1937; this generated a very good revenue of £1,328 for the railway.

Trains for Witham left in a northwesterly direction, over the Blackwater by the trestle bridge, past Maldon East Junction, Langford Junction and then back on to the single line. Although built with double track, this had gone by the time of the 1897 Ordnance Survey revision, and may have been done during the Crimean War so that the surplus materials could be put to military use. Langford & Ulting halt was 1¼ miles from Maldon East, and had a single platform and shelter, and was reached by passengers down steps from the adjacent road bridge. The line passed through pleasant water meadows close to the Blackwater, then reaching Wickham Bishops, after a further two miles. The station here also had a single platform, but with no shelter at all, and with a loop passing behind it. The station building, in half-timbered style, stood on the other side of the loop, so that passengers had to cross this to get to the platform. The signalbox stood opposite the platform, but was abolished in 1932, although the building remained in existence, even retaining its redundant block instruments.

Witham was reached 2½ miles further on, about 15 minutes' journey from Maldon, the branch passing under the main

Colchester road and then curving very sharply (limited to a mere 8mph) to get into the outer face of the up platform, main line trains using the other. The former east curve had reached the main line at Witham East Junction, later simply 'Witham East', but this was in the process of being removed by 1897, soon after the through service between Colchester and Southend was withdrawn. Witham has two island platforms, with the booking office above, both platforms having waiting rooms, awnings and other facilities; Braintree branch trains had to run round using the main line, while Maldon trains had their own loop. Both had water available and there was a 42ft turntable with lengthening irons. Braintree trains left from the outer face of the down platform, and were faced with a very tight curve to the north west, limited to 10mph in both directions, to get away from the main line. There was a level crossing soon after the junction, and the line then passed under the road to Braintree, which ran very close and parallel for most of the way. On the other side of the line was the River Brain, a minor tributary of the Blackwater, which river also takes a rather more circuitous route between Witham and Braintree.

Much of the line as far as White Notley was in cutting, the station being three miles from Witham. There was a single short, low platform with a wooden building acting as a waiting room, the station being on the Braintree side of the level crossing taking the minor road between White Notley and Cressing over the line. The signalbox was on the Witham side of the crossing, with the station house on the other side of the road, but there were no facilities other than for passengers. Cressing was only a short distance further, and also had a single platform, but this time with a loop. There was a level crossing at the Braintree end of the station, controlled by a signalbox, and the station house was opposite. A small brick building on the platform housed a waiting room, office and toilet, and had a ticket window cut into the platform wall until removed prior to electrification in 1977. The building had an awning, passengers having to get on to the platform by walking up the ramp in front of the signalbox.

Below:
Wickham Bishops, with the strange arrangement whereby the single platform could be reached only by crossing the siding. *Stations UK*

Above:
**On Saturday 9 May 1953 the 2.40pm to Maldon is near London Road bridge, Witham,
headed by Class F5 242T No 67191.** *G. R. Mortimer*

Below:
Wickham Bishops pre-1956, with a 'J15' calling with a three-coach train for Maldon. *David Lawrence*

Above:
Witham station, with the 10.50 for Maldon leaving on 5 September 1964; passenger services finished the following day. Hunslet 0-6-0 diesel No D2571 has paused in its shunting while the DMU passes, with No E79290 leading. *G. R. Mortimer*

Left:
A typical view of a Maldon service in later days, with a railbus having arrived at Witham. *P. J. Sharpe*

Above:
On 15 October 1977 a BR Derby-built diesel multiple-unit arrives at Witham with the 15.13 from Braintree.
The wires are up, but the electric service has not yet started. *Brian Morrison*

On from Cressing, the line continued the final two miles to Braintree, curving sharply to the west at Braintree Goods Junction to reach the station. There was a siding into the brick and tile works, also to the north of the station, this siding crossing the station approach road. The goods station had cattle pens and substantial coal yards, and had the gas works adjacent, as well as malthouses and the local brewery. The town was noted for its silk mills, and Courtaulds was a major employer in the town. There were very many companies at the station, including in 1929, the Anglo-American Oil Co Ltd, Belsham & Sons, the Braintree & Bocking Gas Company, the Braintree & West Essex Co-operative Society, Bristowes Tarvia Ltd, Crittalls Manufacturing, Firmacrete, Johnson & Stratton, Lake & Elliott, Shell-Mex and Walford, Hasler & Co. A 5-ton crane was available. Much of the traffic was inwards — coal, oil, feedstuffs and so on — although scrap metal formed a significant outflow.

The whole line between Bishop's Stortford and Witham was still worked on the electric token system in the 1960s, long after the Stortford to Braintree section had closed to passengers, and there was an auxiliary token instrument at Braintree Goods Junction. The other intermediate token stations then were Hockerill halt (intermediate instrument), Dunmow, Felsted, Braintree and Cressing. Trains approaching from Cressing for either the goods or passenger

stations at Braintree obviously had to carry the token for the section, passenger drivers handing it in at Braintree Station signalbox, while goods train drivers had first to ensure that they had arrived at the yard complete with tail lamp, and then place the token in the auxiliary instrument. Shunting or light engine movements between the goods and passenger stations did not need to carry a token, since the whole area was track circuited. Trains originating at Braintree for Cressing and Witham picked up the token from the station signalbox or goods yard. Special provisions had been made for the working of mixed trains from Witham, and the shunting engine and shunter had to be in readiness in the goods yard. The arriving train was brought to a stand on the running line, and the guard applied the brake in his van, and also the handbrakes on several of the wagons. The goods portion was then uncoupled, after which he took the token from the driver and gave it to the shunter. He then went back to the passenger brake, and the train went forward to the passenger station. Meanwhile, the shunting engine had come on to the goods portion and taken it into the yard, after which the shunter advised the signalman the train had arrived complete and put the token into the auxiliary instrument. This procedure was forbidden after dark, in fog or falling snow.

Early train services between Maldon and Braintree have already been mentioned, and for much of the life of the branches, service

Above:
Cressing on 12 October 1963, with a two-car DMU bound for Braintree.
The station was still open for goods traffic. *J. Spencer Gilks*

Below:
White Notley station in Great Eastern days. *Lens of Sutton*

Above:
Another view of Cressing showing the station after modernisation. All that remains are the
passenger facilities, the platform much extended and raised. Electric multiple-unit
No 308153 calls with the 11.49 Sundays-only from Witham to Braintree on 7 June 1981. *John C. Baker*

Below:
White Notley in 1955, looking towards Braintree as a train for Witham approaches. *Stations UK*

provision was quite limited. When the Woodham Ferris to Maldon branch opened, it had only four trains each way on weekdays. By 1913 it showed an interesting variety of workings, and had increased to six from Maldon to Woodham Ferris on Mondays to Fridays, with one fewer on Saturdays. The service in the other direction showed trains arriving at Maldon East at 9.16am, 12.21pm, 1.50pm and 9.37pm (7pm Saturdays only), with an arrival at 6.49pm from Southminster. Economies were made, after which tickets were issued on the train from all intermediate stations between Maldon East and Woodham Ferrers. In summer 1922, the service remained at five trains, leaving Maldon East at 8.2 and 9.19am, and 12.57, 4.43 (4.56 Saturdays only) and 6.9pm, not all having connections from Witham; in fact, there were some near-misses (such as the 6.19pm arrival from Witham) which must have discouraged passengers. In the other direction trains left Woodham Ferrers at 8.46 and 10.38am, and 1.30pm (2.29pm Saturdays only), 5.15pm (5.38pm Saturdays only) and 6.50pm. The journey took about 21 minutes. In October 1931 things looked very similar, although the journey was now slightly longer because of the two new halts. However, an extra train had been put on in the evening, leaving Maldon East at 8.40pm (9.15pm Saturdays only), and returning from Woodham Ferrers at 9.20pm, or 9.57pm on Saturdays. There was not enough traffic to support the service, and it was suspended from 10 September 1939 following the outbreak of war, and never reinstated. However, Maldon West continued to be served by goods trains, and did not close completely until 31 January 1959. It also saw the occasional enthusiasts' excursion.

Following the electrification of the main line between Liverpool Street and Shenfield in 1949, much of the redundant steam coaching stock, mostly quad and quint-art sets, was taken out to the section between Woodham Ferrers and Cold Norton and stored. In the winter of 1955-6 it was decided to take this to Stratford for disposal, but as the line had been severed at the southern end, it had to come out via Maldon. Two 'J15s' were sent from Colchester to Maldon, from where one went to Cold Norton to bring a rake of coaches back. They had been severely vandalised and stripped of anything such as brass handles and other fittings, so the doors could be secured only by tying them up with string. Tree branches that had grown through windows had to be sawn off. When they reached Maldon the other 'J15' backed on and took them to Witham, where rumour had it that this stock had to be moved on Sundays to ensure that no Carriage & Wagon examiner was present to red-card them.

Services were better on the other lines, but hardly lavish. In 1913 the Braintree line saw six down (to Braintree) passenger trains each weekday, with an extra on Monday evening, plus two mixed workings. The first was at 8.20am and the last at 7.52pm, except on Mondays when there was an extra at 9.21pm. The mixed trains left Witham at 10.20am and 8.22pm. The 1.12pm from Witham, arriving at Braintree at 1.28pm was notable for being a through working from Shenfield, which it left at 12.27pm, calling at all stations. There were also three passenger trains on Sundays, as well as a mixed at 9.44am, the first down train of the day. In the up direction there were six passenger trains, the first at 7.40am being one of only two to make a booked call at Cressing. The other was the 7.12pm from Braintree, and all other trains called at Cressing and White Notley on request. The 11.17am from Braintree (11.20am Saturdays only) ran through to Shenfield, and there were

Below:
Braintree station, 1897. *Crown Copyright*

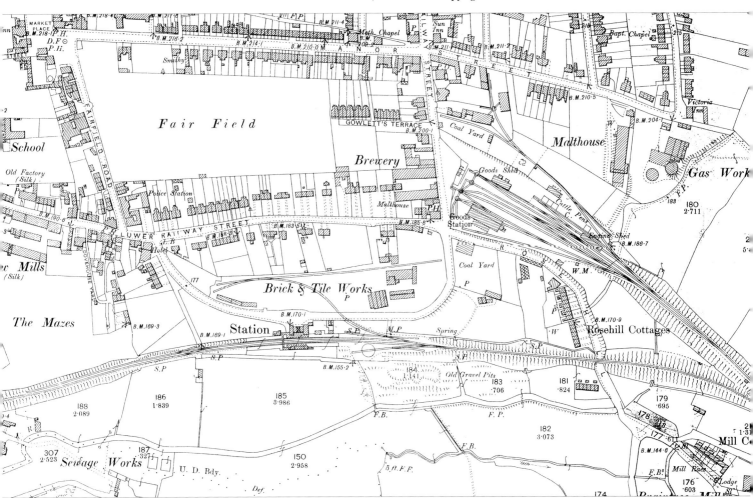

no mixed trains in this direction. The Mondays-only evening train from Witham was formed from an empty stock working from Braintree at 8.50pm. There were two booked up goods workings on weekdays, at 5.50am and 7.20pm (6.25pm Saturdays only), against one the other way. On Sundays passenger trains left Braintree at 8.48 and 10.25am and 4.17 and 6.30pm, the 4.17pm being allowed to work up to four piped wagons of cattle. There was also a path for an express cattle train at 5.20pm, run as required. Provision was also made for the branch engine to make a special trip with goods traffic between Braintree and Witham after the finish of ordinary trains for the day.

On the Maldon branch the service started with the 4.55am up goods from Maldon East to Witham, this being allowed to convey no more than 20 empty trucks; the engine then shunted at Witham. There were then seven up passenger trains, the first at 7.19am and the last at 7.6pm, although there was a later train from Maldon East to Woodham Ferris, at 8.8pm (7.15pm Saturdays only). There was an extra train on Wednesdays and Saturdays, and another on Wednesdays and Fridays. There was a similar service in the other direction, and a mixed train at 10.22am from Witham, which was not allowed to work coal trucks. As with the Braintree branch, certain passenger trains were allowed to attach specified goods traffic, such as the 7.6pm from Maldon, which was allowed to attach a van of flowers at Wickham, or the 7.54pm from Witham which could convey two Westinghouse piped wagons with Alexander's cattle from Braintree for Maldon. On Sundays there were four up passenger trains and three down, plus a down mixed.

The 1922 timetable showed a considerable improvement on the Braintree line, with 10 down and nine up trains, the first down the branch being at 6.40am from Witham, returning at 7.48am from Braintree as the first up service. At the other end of the day the 7.9pm from Braintree arrived at Witham at 7.25pm, left again at 7.55pm and reached its destination at 8.11pm. Although there were slight variations between Fridays and other weekdays, there was no chance of a late night out by train! The Sunday service continued at four trains each way. On the Maldon branch the Sunday pattern was also four trains each way, usually with about a half-hour wait at Witham after the Braintree train arrived, so that a day out could be had in Maldon. The weekday service consisted of eight trains each way, the first up from Maldon at 7.17am and the last at 7.22pm, and in the other direction starting from Witham at 7.42am and finishing with the 7.57pm. Single journey times were about 16 minutes for the 5¾-mile run.

By 1937, tickets from Langford & Ulting and Wickham Bishops were being issued on the trains on Sundays. Weekday services now extended to 10 trains each way, with slight variations on some days, and typical journey times for trains stopping at all stations were down to about 14 minutes. The first train from Maldon was at 4.55am and the last at 7.26pm (7.22pm Saturdays only), and in the other direction from Witham at 6.30am and 7.57pm. The Sunday service of four trains each way remained. On the Braintree branch there were also 10 trains each way, the first from Braintree at 7.50am and the last at 7.15pm, and from Witham at 6.22am and 7.55pm. In some cases there were good connections with Bishop's Stortford trains at Braintree, giving stations on that line a service to Witham, and most Braintree trains also had reasonable connections there, allowing passengers to reach Liverpool Street relatively

Above:
Langford & Ulting, seen from the road bridge. *Stations UK*

quickly. For example, the 10am arrival connected with the 10.11am departure (an Ipswich semi-fast), arriving in London at 11.8am. Tickets from White Notley were, by now, being issued on the train.

During World War 2 the inevitable cuts were made, with the Braintree service going down to seven up and eight down trains each weekday, still with four each way on Sundays. However, this service — introduced on 4 May 1942 — represented a considerable improvement on the emergency timetables brought in on 2 October 1939, which had seen trains reduced to a mere six up and five down. The starting and finishing times tended to remain much the same throughout. The last train having a London connection was the 7.54pm from Witham, which connected with the 6.20pm from Liverpool Street, while the earliest possible arrival in town was off the 7.51am from Braintree, giving a London arrival at 9.27am. Maldon, having been deprived of its service from Woodham Ferrers, received a service of nine trains from Witham on Mondays to Saturdays from May 1942, and the same number in the other direction, with a Sunday service of three trains each way. Again, this was an improvement on the original emergency service, which consisted of seven trains each way on weekdays.

Matters improved after the war, with the summer of 1946 seeing the Braintree branch increased to 11 trains each way, one more than the prewar service. On Sundays there were five each way — there being a huge pent-up demand for travel that could not be satisfied during hostilities. The Maldon service went back to 10 each way Mondays to Fridays, with 10 down on Saturdays and eleven up. The Sunday service also consisted of five return workings, with connections allowing people from Braintree a day in Maldon by train, as could Londoners. In 1949, when British Railways had taken over, the service was similar, and a third class monthly return from the capital cost 11s 9d, or 17s 8d first class. Freight traffic at this period was handled by the 12.25pm and 4.52pm workings from Maldon, and 6.35am and 1.15pm from Witham. The 4.52pm did not always run, with any traffic being attached to the passenger working at about 4.30pm — 4.20pm in summer 1946, 4.40pm in winter 1951-2. Later, when traffic improved, due to Kingsmere Jams, tinned fruit and vegetables from Goldhanger fruit farms (distributed to Woolworth's stores around the country), the 4.52pm ran regularly, and on one memorable occasion loaded to 56 vanfits,

Table 15 WITHAM and MALDON (East) AND HEYBRIDGE

Miles		Week Days mrn	mrn		mrn	mrn		aft S	aft	aft	aft E	aft S	aft E	aft		Sundays mrn	aft	aft
	3 London (L'poolSt.) dep	4 40	8 12	..	8B36	1120	..	1 0	2 15	4 0	4 54	4 18	6 0	6 20	..	10 0	4 0	6 8
–	Witham .... dep	7 38	9 28	..	1018	1242	..	2 18	3 40	5 11	6 4	6 48	7 8	7 54	..	11 16	5 15	7 29
2½	Wickham Bishops	7 45	9 35	..	1025	1249	..	2 25	3 47	5 18	6 11	6 55	7 15	8 1	..	11 23	5 22	7 36
4½	Langford and Ulting	7 49	9 39	..	1029	1253	..	2 29	3 51	5 22	6 15	6 59	7 19	8 5	..	11 27	5 26	7 40
5¾	Maldon (East) B .... arr	7 53	9 43	..	1033	1257	..	2 33	3 55	5 26	6 19	7 3	7 23	8 9	..	11 31	5 30	7 44

Miles		Week Days mrn	mrn	mrn	mrn	aft S	aft	aft S	aft	aft E	aft S	aft E	aft		Sundays mrn	aft	aft
–	Maldon (East) B .... dep	7 17	8 23	9 54	1040	1212	1 45	3 15	4 20	5 35	6 25	6 40	7 32	..	10 46	4 46	6 9
1½	Langford and Ulting	7 21	8 27	9 58	1044	..	1 49	3 19	4 24	5 39	6 29	6 44	7 36	..	10 50	4 50	6 13
3½	Wickham Bishops	7 25	8 31	10 2	1048	..	1 53	3 23	4 28	5 43	6 33	6 48	7 40	..	10 54	4 54	6 17
5¾	Witham .... arr	7 31	8 37	10 8	1054	1225	1 59	3 29	4 34	5 49	6 39	6 54	7 46	..	11 0	5 0	6 23
44½	3 London (L'poolSt.) arr	8 51	9 42	1121	12 7	1 35	3 38	..	5 49	7 47	7 47	8B45	9 30	..	12 37	..	7 30

B Maldon (East) and Heybridge
B Third class only between London and Witham
E Except Saturdays
S Saturdays only

On Sundays tickets from Wickham Bishops and Langford & Ulting are issued on the train

Table 15 WITHAM and MALDON (East) AND HEYBRIDGE

Miles		Week Days mrn	mrn	mrn	mrn	mrn		aft S	aft X	aft		aft	aft		aft		Sundays mrn	mrn		aft M	aft	aft	
	3 London (L'poolSt.) dep	4 25	8 12	8Y33	1030	1110	..	1 0	1 0	2 30	..	4 0	4 54	..	6 44	..	8 30	10 0	..	..	3 55	6 8	..
—	Witham .... dep	7 33	9 32	1025	1145	1245	..	2 10	2 30	3 55	..	5 14	6 15	..	8 10	..	10 0	1118	..	1240	5 15	7 39	..
2½	Wickham Bishops	7 40	9 39	1032	1152	1252	..	2 17	2 37	4 2	..	5 21	6 22	..	8 17	..	10 7	1125	..	..	5 22	7 46	..
4½	Langford and Ulting	7 44	9 43	1036	1156	1256	..	2 21	2 41	4 6	..	5 25	6 26	..	8 21	..	1011	1129	..	..	5 26	7 50	..
5¾	Maldon (East) D .... arr	7 48	9 47	1040	12 0	1 0	..	2 25	2 45	4 10	..	5 29	6 30	..	8 25	..	1015	1133	..	1253	5 30	7 54	..

Miles		Week Days mrn	mrn	mrn	mrn		aft	aft	aft	S 3	aft E	aft S		aft	aft		Sundays mrn	mrn		aft	aft	aft M	
—	Maldon (East) D .... dep	7 10	8 20	9 54	10 52	..	12 9	1 31	3 15	4 11	4 20	4 43	..	5 36	7 25	..	9 35	1046	..	4 35	6 5	7 10	..
1½	Langford and Ulting	7 14	8 24	9 58	10 56	..	1213	1 35	3 19	4 15	4 24	4 47	..	5 40	7 29	..	9 39	1050	..	4 39	6 9	7 14	..
3½	Wickham Bishops	7 18	8 28	10 2	11 0	..	1217	1 39	3 23	4 19	4 28	4 51	..	5 44	7 33	..	9 43	1054	..	4 43	6 13	7 18	..
5¾	Witham .... arr	7 24	8 34	10 8	11 6	..	1223	1 45	3 29	4 25	4 34	4 57	..	5 50	7 39	..	9 49	11 0	..	4 49	6 19	7 24	..
44½	3 London (L'poolSt.) arr	8 51	9 41	1124	12X20	..	1y35	3 Z7	4SY53	5 42	5 53	6z51	..	7 50	9 8	..	1133	1238	..	6 40	7 30	8 43	..

D Maldon (East) and Heybridge M Runs 9th June to 8th September inclusive. S or S Saturdays only
X Third class only on Sats. X Arr 12 26 aft on Sats Y Third class only between London and Whitham
y Arr 1 38 aft on Sats. Z Arr 3 23 aft Sats z Arr 6 47 aft from 6th July to 14th September inclusive
3 Third class only

On Sundays tickets from Wickham Bishops and Langford & Ulting are issued on the train

Table 24 WITHAM and MALDON (East) AND HEYBRIDGE

Miles		Week Days am	am		am	am	am		pm		pm	pm		pm	pm		Sundays						
	5 London (L'pool St) dep	4 30	6 54	..	8 36	1030	11S30	.	1K30	..	2F10	3 36	..	4 56	6 42	..	..	..	..	..	..	..	..
—	Witham .... dep	7 30	8 50	....	9 50	1135	12 50	...	2 40	....	3 53	5 10	....	6 0	8 11	....	....	....	....	....	....	....	....
2½	Wickham Bishops	7 38	8 58	..	9 58	1143	12 58	.	2 48	..	4 1	5 18	..	6 8	8 19	..	..	..	..	..	..	..	..
4½	Langford and Ulting	7 42	9 2	....	10 2	1147	1 2	...	2 52	....	4 5	5 22	....	6 12	8 23	....	....	....	....	....	....	....	....
5¾	Maldon (East) D .. arr	7 46	9 6	..	10 6	1151	1 6	.	2 56	..	4 9	5 26	..	6 16	8 27	..	..	..	..	..	..	..	..

Miles		Week Days am	am S	am E	am	am		pm	pm S	pm E	pm S	pm E	pm	pm	pm		Sundays						
—	Maldon (East) D .. dep	6 59	8 20	8 25	9 19	11 5	.	12 7	2 7	2 15	3 2	3 4	4 30	5 34	7 30	..	..	..	..	..	..	..	..
1½	Langford and Ulting	7 3	8 24	8 29	9 23	11 9	...	1211	2 11	2 19	3 6	3 8	4 34	5 38	7 34	....	....	....	....	....	....	....	....
3½	Wickham Bishops	7 7	8 28	8 33	9 27	11 13	.	1215	2 15	2 23	3 10	3 12	4 38	5 42	7 38	..	..	..	..	..	..	..	..
5¾	Witham .... arr	7 14	8 35	8 40	9 34	11 20	...	1222	2 22	2 30	3 17	3 19	4 45	5 49	7 45	....	....	....	....	....	....	....	....
44½	5 London (L'pool St) arr	8 24	9 42	9 43	1116	12B40	.	1B45	3 33	4 13	4 46	4 34	6 5	7 45	9 2	..	..	..	..	..	..	..	..

B On Saturdays arrives Liverpool Street 5 minutes *earlier*
D Maldon (East) and Heybridge
E or E Except Saturdays
F On Saturdays departs Liverpool Street 2 15 pm
K On Saturdays departs Liverpool Street 1 36 pm
S Saturdays only

Tickets from Wickham Bishops and Langford and Ulting are issued on the train.

WEEKDAYS WITHAM AND MALDON

Mileage M	C	DOWN	K	K SUSPENDED	K SX	K SO	G SX LE After working 6.20 pm from Maldon E.
			am	am	PM	PM	PM
0	0	WITHAM .... dep	6 35	......	12X25	1 15	7‖55
2	49	Wickham Bishops	R	..	..	R	..
4	48	Langford and Ulting					
5	58	MALDON EAST arr	6X55	..	12 45	1 40	8‖ 5
0	0	.. dep	......	U	......	......	......
1	23	Maldon West .. arr	..	D	..	..	..

Mileage M	C	UP	G LE to work 6.35 am to Maldon E.	K SUSPENDED	K SX	K SO	K SX
			am	am	am	PM	PM
0	0	Maldon West .... dep	......	U	......	......	......
1	23	MALDON EAST arr	..	D	..	..	..
0	0	.. dep	6‖ 5	......	10X20	12 25	6X20
1	10	Langford and Ulting ..	..	..	..	..	..
3	9	Wickham Bishops					
5	58	WITHAM .. .. arr	6‖20	..	10 40	12X43	6 40

MALDON (Essex)
Miles 44¼. Map Sq. 24. Clos. day Wed.
Pop. Maldon, 6,559. Heybridge 2,061.
MALDON EAST AND HEYBRIDGE STATION.
From Liverpool Street via Chelmsford and Witham.
1st cl.—Single 14/7, Mth. Ret. 17/8.
3rd cl.—Single 8/9, Mth. Ret. 11/9.

Liv. St.	Mal. E.	Mal. E.	Liv. St.
a.m.		a.m.	
4 25 3	7 49	7 9	8 47
8 12r	9 48	8 19er	9 43
8 24	10 33	8 19sr	9 46
9 55	11 46	9 54	11 21
11 10	12 58	10 48	12 40
p.m.		p.m.	
1 0er	2 31	12 7r	1 38
1 0sr	2 46	1 45e	3 20
2 18e	3 56	1 45s	3 33
2 18s	4 11	3 9s 3	4 54
4 0	5 30	4 19	5 54
4 57er	6 26	5 36r	7 6
4 57s	6 26	7 24	9 4
6 44	8 26	—	—
Sunday	Trains.		
a.m.		a.m.	
8 30	10 16	9 34	11 34
10 0	11 34	10 45	12 38
p.m.		p.m.	
3 55	5 28	4 34	6 40
6 5	8 2	6 4	7 34
—	—	7 9	8 44

3 3rd. cl. only.
e Not Sat. s Sat. only.
r Refresh. Car.
Bus facilities. From Chelmsford, Bus Station, approx. half-hourly (hourly Sunday a.m.), 43 min. journey.

Above: ABC Railway Guide, December 1949. *Author's collection*

Left, top to bottom: Summer 1946 timetable. *Author's collection*

Summer 1942 timetable. *Author's collection*

September 1955-June 1956 timetable. *Author's collection*

11 June-16 September 1956 freight working timetable. *Author's collection*

Below: ABC Railway Guide, December 1962. *Author's collection*

BRAINTREE (Essex)
44¾ miles. Pop. 17,481. E.C. Thur.
From Liverpool Street via Witham.
2nd class 11/3, 1st class 16/11.

Liv. St.	Brain.	Brain.	Liv. St.
a.m.		a.m.	
4 35	6 10	6 35	7b43
7 0	8 11	6 50 e	8 1
8b 0	9 6	6 50 s	8 26
9b 0	10 10	7 29 e	8 35
10b 0	11 4	7 37 s	8b43
11b 0	12 4	8 30	9b35
12b 0	1 4	9 15	10b30
p.m.		10 15	11b25
1b 0	2 4	11 9	12b20
2b 0	3 4	p.m.	
3b 0	4 4	12 15	1b25
4b 0	5 4	1 9	2b20
4 33 e	5 41	2 15	3b25
5b 0 s	6 4	3 9	4b20
5b 0 e	6 9	4 15	5b25
5 45 e	6 58	5 9	6b20
6b 0 s	7 4	5 44 e	7 15
7b 0	7 59	6 9 s	7b25
8b30	9 45	6 12 e	7b25
—	—	7 9	8b20
—	—	9 1 e	10 25
—	—	9 1 s	10 30
—	—	—	—
—	—	—	—
—	—	—	—
—	—	—	—

No Sunday Trains.

Buses from Chelmsford Omnibus Station, approx. half-hourly (approx. hourly Sunday), 40 min. journey.

Above:
Braintree station is seen on 13 August 1956 with F6 No 67228 having arrived on the 3.53pm from Witham. It was usual for almost all trains to arrive and depart from this platform, which saved passengers having to cross the footbridge. *D. Holmes*

Below:
Class F6 242T No 67227 arrives at Braintree from Witham on 6 November 1958. *John Brodribb collection*

Above:
Braintree station had been allowed to deteriorate in quite a bad way before electrification started. Here, it has been reduced to basic railway, with all track removed except for the main platform. The line onwards to Dunmow has been lifted. Today it forms a pleasant cycle- and footpath. *J. G. Glover*

Below:
A Derby two-car diesel multiple-unit (No E79623 leading) replaces the normal railbus on the 1.14pm Maldon to Witham on 8 November 1960. The arrangement of level crossing and bridge is clear, and a good idea of the station layout can also be gained. *M.V. Edwards*

Above:
Maldon East on 23 August 1960, with railbus No 79960 forming the 10.12am to Witham.
The bay platform is on the left. *L. Sandler*

hauled by a 'J69', and which blocked Witham station almost completely because of its length. This train was later retimed to 6.20pm.

By 1955, the winter Sunday service had been withdrawn, although the basic pattern of 10 trains each way remained on weekdays, with the first from Maldon tending to become earlier to give an earlier arrival in London. It now left at 6.59am, with arrival at Liverpool Street at 8.24am. On the Braintree line the same trends were evident, there being 12 trains each way Mondays to Fridays, with one fewer on Saturdays, and an arrival in London at the same time; both branch trains arrived at the junction at the same time. Both branches had lost their winter Sunday service.

Motive power on the Maldon line was restricted by the axle loadings permitted over the trestle bridges, and thus Classes B12, E4, F4, F5, J15, J24, J67, J68 and J69 were the only ones allowed, although in practice 'B12s' were not seen at Maldon because of the lack of turning facilities. A Class D16 'Claud Hamilton' did once reach Maldon by mistake, with a Stratford crew, but special permission had to be obtained form the District Engineer before it was allowed to return to Witham. The 'F5' 2-4-2 tanks formed the backbone of the local service for many years, with 'J15s' appearing on goods or through trains off the branch, such as to Chelmsford and Liverpool Street.

British Railways made considerable efforts to promote travel by the introduction of diesel trains, scheduled for the start of the 1956 summer timetable, and service levels were increased considerably. Initially two-car units were tried, but with the summer 1958 service four-wheeled German railbuses were introduced, and operated on the Maldon line until the passenger service was withdrawn. Summer 1959 saw 18 trains each weekday from Witham to Maldon, and 17 the other way, with eight return workings on Sundays. Langford & Ulting had become a request stop in the up direction. There was no significant change to the starting time of the service, although it continued later into the evening, with the last train from Witham now at 9.35pm, connecting with the 8.30pm from London. Four years previously it had left Witham at 8.11pm and connected out of the 6.42pm from Liverpool Street. Mirroring the morning, the last train down to Braintree left at the same time and connected with the

same London service. During the rest of the day on the Braintree branch there were 17 trips each way, the earliest now being the 6.42am and giving a London arrival at 8.1am. The sole steam working of the week was provided by the 10.15am Braintree to Clacton service on Sundays, which returned from there at 5.56pm and reached Braintree at 7.8pm. There were eight other trains each way on Sundays.

The Beeching report had the usual mention for both lines, and both were proposed for closure. Frequencies had remained generally at the level noted for the start of diesel services, and despite appearing in the Winter 1964-5 timetable, withdrawal of the Maldon service came on and from Monday 7 September 1964. Since there was still a summer Sunday service, the last trains ran on the previous day, 6 September. Freight continued for a while longer, and the branch closed to all traffic from 18 April 1966.

The story of the Braintree branch was altogether different. Far from following the usual pattern of decline, the Braintree & Witham Railway Campaign Committee galvanised it into revival with a campaign of leafleting and other publicity. The railbuses were replaced in June 1963 by diesel multiple-units, and passenger loadings continued to rise. Eventually it was decided to electrify the branch, and the wires went up in the mid-1970s, with other work being done at the same time. Platforms at Cressing and White Notley were lengthened and raised, while the line was also reduced to a 'basic railway' with sidings and loops removed. Only the former up platform at Braintree remained in use when the new service started on 3 October 1977. With privatisation, ownership of the infrastructure passed to Railtrack, and the line continues to be served by trains operated by First Great Eastern. Apart from early mornings and late evenings, when it operates between Braintree and Witham, the branch now enjoys an hourly service of through trains to and from Liverpool Street on weekdays, and has a year-round Sunday service, also at an hourly frequency. It has even had a new station opened, at Braintree Freeport, three-quarters of a mile from the terminus, to serve an out-of-town shopping development. It is thus one of only two lines in this book to retain a service that is part of the national network.

Mid-Suffolk Light Railway

THE Mid-Suffolk Light Railway was one of the schemes born out of the Light Railways Act of 1896, which had been intended to provide for local lines to be built cheaply and with Treasury support in order to open up rural areas and relieve the agricultural depression then prevalent. It is certainly true that many earlier lines had to be built and operated to too high a standard, or perhaps were not built at all for that very reason, and that their costs were far higher than they need have been. The 'Middy' was one of the relatively few that did get off the ground, although the grandiose schemes of its promoters ultimately made little progress.

The initial proposals had been made as early as 1889, although the Mid-Suffolk Light Railway Company was not incorporated until 1901, the order being confirmed by the Board of Trade on 5 April 1900, and amended on 1 June 1901. The plans were for a line between Haughley Junction, on the Great Eastern's Ipswich to Norwich main line, via Kenton to Halesworth on the East Suffolk, a distance of 27¾ miles, and another from Westerfield, on the East Suffolk, through Debenham to Kenton (14¼ miles). In the early stages there was to have been a further branch from Needham Market, also on the GER main line, to Debenham. The lines were to traverse that district known as High Suffolk, sparsely populated but with rich agricultural land, and it was hoped that they would open up an area until then poorly provided with transport facilities.

Optimistic projections, as ever, were given by the promoters about the numbers of passengers likely to be carried, but the populations of local towns and villages were low. In the 1891 census Debenham had 1,219 inhabitants, Laxfield 905, Stradbroke 1,069, Wetheringsett-cum-Brockford 967 and Mendlesham 1,138. Based on Board of Trade agricultural returns for the previous 10 years, the prospects for freight traffic were also regarded as good. However, none of the villages was more than seven miles from an existing station, usually Finningham, Needham, Halesworth or Framlingham, although the MSLR main line would have provided a useful cross-country link, more so if it had joined with a regauged Southwold Railway. The authorised capital of the company consisted of 10,000 preference shares of £10 each, and 12,500 ordinary £10 shares, with the company also empowered to issue debentures up to £75,000. It was expected that the whole system could be built for between £223,000 and £227,720.

However, at an early stage the idea of two links into the Great Eastern main line had to be abandoned, and the line to Needham was not pursued. Optimism ran high about the rest of the scheme, despite the problems of raising capital, and work started on both the Haughley to Halesworth and Westerfield to Kenton sections. The Duke of Cambridge officially cut the first sod in a ceremony at Westerfield on 3 May 1902, which was followed by the usual

Below:
**A photograph which well illustrates the nature of the operation at Laxfield,
with 'J15' No 65388 standing outside the engine shed on 15 June 1952.** *R. E. Vincent*

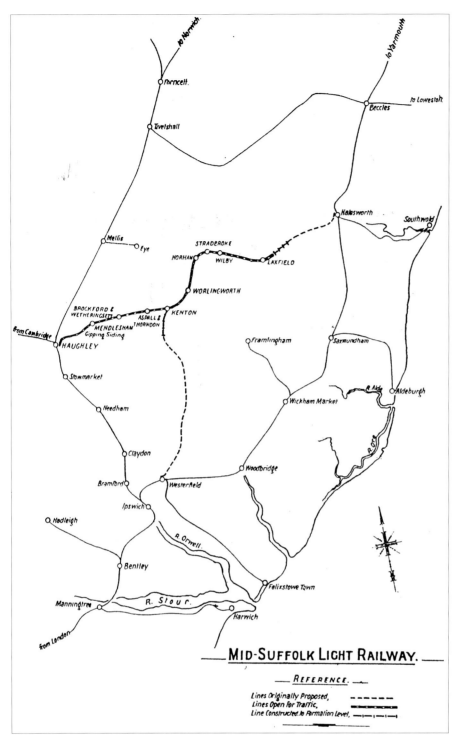

banquet for the great and the good. Unfortunately, it turned out to be almost the only sod cut on that particular section. Work had started on the 'main line' as well, and by 20 September 1904 was sufficiently advanced for it to be opened for goods traffic between Haughley and Laxfield. There remained much unfinished work, including the cutting to take the line under the Ipswich to Norwich road (now the A140), so it crossed it by a temporary level crossing. Work was also in progress at the northern end of the Kenton to Westerfield line, with track being laid from Kenton Junction towards Debenham. Some earthworks had been carried out here, notably an embankment and bridge over the Eye to Debenham road, and some further cuttings to get the line to Debenham itself. The station would probably have been in Low Road, and the area was fenced off. There would have been a level crossing at the station, which would have been very close to Derry Brook Farm. The land was certainly fenced off as far as Winston, about a further mile, and the formation possibly made up, and is likely also to have been fenced as far as Pettaugh, about 2½ miles from Debenham. The line would have been very useful to Bloomfield's agricultural engineering business in Debenham, which instead received and despatched traffic via Aspall station, about two miles to the north. Two Debenham coal merchants, List and Eagle, also received coal the same way, and bagged it up at Aspall station.

The line was inspected in early July 1905 by Lt-Col Von Donop of the Board

Left:
The Mid-Suffolk Light Railway.
The Railway Magazine

Below:
Mendlesham station site (line under construction), 1904. *Crown Copyright*

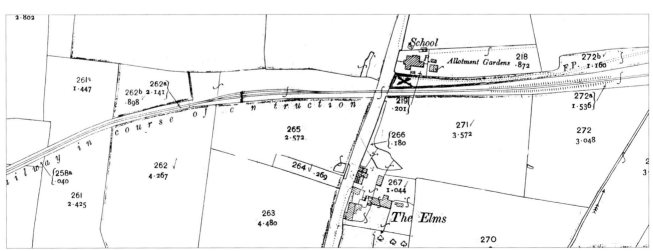

of Trade, who found a number of deficiencies and refused to sanction its opening for passengers. The platforms had been built, but the station buildings generally had not, and there were several connections in the track that required removal. An amending order, issued by the Board of Trade in 1905, provided for a deviation in the line on the section between Laxfield and Halesworth, where difficulties were being encountered in crossing the marshy ground of the Blyth Valley. The line finally opened for passenger traffic between Haughley and Laxfield on 29 September 1908, the extension between Laxfield and Cratfield having been in use for goods traffic since 1906. This closed in 1912, and the rails were taken up beyond Laxfield Mill during World War 1, together with those on the unopened section between Westerfield and Debenham.

When the Mid-Suffolk opened, the general manager was Mr H. I. Godden, the traffic manager Mr H. J. Rednal, Mr W. Warren the secretary and Mr H. R. Gillingwater the assistant manager — very soon he was the only officer on the spot, combining the posts of general and traffic managers. Mr C. D. Szlumper was briefly the engineer. Inability to meet interest on the debenture stock and other liabilities resulted in the appointment of a receiver, and on 6 October 1906 Mr Warren was given the job, being replaced in February 1907 by Maj J. F. R. Daniel. In February 1918, Mr A. P. Parker, assistant to the general manager of the Great Eastern, was appointed to the post, and remained there until the LNER absorbed the Middy in 1924.

The railway was built with 30ft Vignoles rails weighing 56lb per yard spiked directly to the sleepers, the joints being staggered. Being a light railway, speeds were limited to 25mph. The only passing place was at Kenton, intended as a junction, and the line was controlled by split staffs, an unusual arrangement for the British Isles. This allowed trains following through the section to use the Annett's keys combined with the staffs for working intermediate sidings, although a train could not pass through the section in the opposite direction unless the whole staff was present. There were many level crossings — 11 at or near stations, seven under the charge of gatekeepers, 12 protected by cattle guards and warning boards only, and 86 occupation crossings — all on a line of only 19 miles.

There were separate Great Eastern and Mid-Suffolk stations at Haughley, although the two railways were connected via exchange sidings. The Middy station was slightly higher, and had the usual 130ft long single platform with buildings constructed of corrugated iron. The line curved fairly sharply away from the main line in a northeasterly direction, and started a steep climb out of the Gipping Valley. Close to the station was one of the few underbridges, with Haugh Lane passing under the railway. Having crossed Silver Street and thus got the worst of the climb over, there was another level crossing at Old Newton, where the keeper was provided with a standard Mid-Suffolk four-roomed cottage built in the same manner as the station buildings, of corrugated iron. There was a remarkable piece of family continuity involved with this crossing. Arthur Borley moved there with his wife Florence when the railway was being built, and he was involved with its construction, having previously worked for the Great Eastern on the main line. He worked as a ganger between Haughley and Mendlesham, with his wife working the crossing gates, and their daughter Ena was born after the Middy opened. During the 1930s Mrs Borley's eyesight began to fail, and her eldest daughter Mary took over. Trains often ran out of course in the early days, and there was no warning system provided; the keeper had to rely on hearing trains approach. After Mary got married Ena took over the duties of crossing keeper, performing them until the line closed in 1952.

There was one of the few earthworks on the line on the east side of the Old Newton road, the line being carried on a substantial embankment across the valley of a small stream. It then crossed Brown Street, and started to climb again past Gipping Lane and the

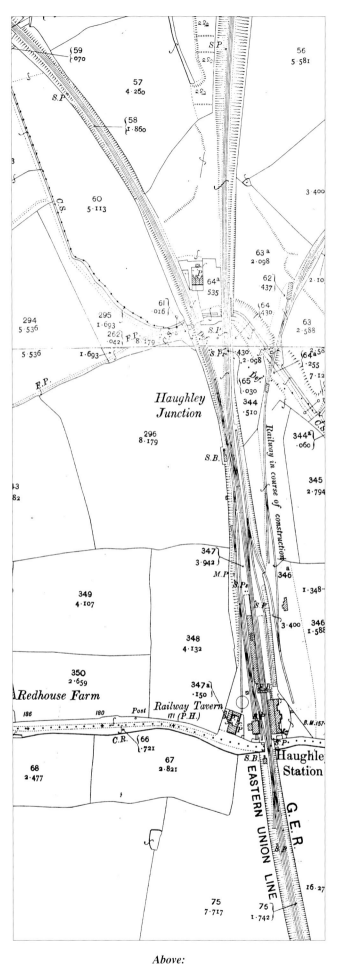

Above:
Haughley Junction station, 1904. *Crown Copyright*

Above:
Mendlesham station, first stop for passengers along the Mid-Suffolk line after the junction at Haughley. This view is looking towards Laxfield, and shows the station building, now preserved at the Mid-Suffolk Light Railway Museum at Wetheringsett. *Lens of Sutton*

double-ended siding there, 2 miles 44 chains from Haughley. It continued its course across country towards Mendlesham, a substantial village together with Mendlesham Green to the south. The station here (4 miles 37 chains) was on the west side of the road between the two, and had one of the larger pattern buildings, with an open waiting area and an office each end. There was also a double-ended siding and a loading dock at the end of the platform. The village school was on the other side of the level crossing, which was at the east end of the platform. From the station the line fell again, and then went into the deep cutting taking it under the main road, the banks of which were noted for their profusion of bee orchids as well as the ubiquitous dog daisies. It then rose on the east side to pass Brockford Green, and the two gated level crossings in quick succession that heralded the approach to Brockford & Wetheringsett station (only 'Brockford' on the station nameboard), 6 miles 4 chains from Haughley; both were operated, at least in theory, by the station staff. The porter-in-charge for many years was Fred Keeble, and very often local children would work the top gates (furthest from the station), the incentive being a halfpenny or penny thrown out by the driver. The boys would scramble for this and then go and spend it on four gobstoppers on their way to school. At Brockford there were only two small corrugated iron sheds functioning as a store and booking office; there was a siding on the north side of the line, again with a loading dock.

For a station seemingly in the middle of nowhere, it saw a fair amount of activity. There were many farms in the area, which would collect sacks from the station store and use them to send away various crops such as barley or clover seed, which would be brought to the station by tumbrel. The weight of these sacks varied according to content: for example, clover weighed 20 stone, wheat 18, barley 16 and oats only 12 stone. All were despatched in covered vans. Corn would generally arrive in four-wheeled carts drawn by two horses abreast, and because there was only one member of the railway staff — Fred Keeble — the farm workers

had to do almost all their own loading and unloading. Another source of traffic, which lasted to the very end of the railway, was schoolchildren who had passed the 11-plus examination going to Stowmarket Grammar School; most local children went to the village school until they were 14 years of age.

Seasonal traffic included the annual truckload of coal for Chappell, the thrashing contractor who would bring his engine round to the various farms. They would send tumbrels for the coal and take it back, ready for his engine to arrive. Sugar beet became increasingly important, the season lasting from September to January, and sometimes necessitated the running of extra trains, it being sent to the works at Bury St Edmunds. Farm removals provided occasional and heavy traffic, when all the equipment and stock would arrive by train.

One of the gangs of men who maintained the line was based at Brockford, and included Charlie Missen the ganger, Bob Pleasance, lineman, and Hubby Garrod and Jack Gayfer. Arthur Borley kept a trolley near his home at Old Newton gatehouse, and this was used to convey men and materials along the line, although there were occasions when it had to be taken off the line in somewhat of a hurry.

The line fell sharply away from the station for a short distance before climbing again, then heading for Aspall & Thorndon station (8 miles 41 chains). Aspall is a large and diffuse parish; Thorndon is a much larger village, but a very considerable distance from the station, with others such as Rishangles much closer. There was the obligatory level crossing, over the Debenham to Eye road to the west of the station, and a single siding. The buildings were of an unusual pattern for the line, and it is thought that they may have been reused contractors' huts.

The line onwards undulated a little more gently, eventually reaching Kenton, 10 miles 1 chain from Haughley. The station was situated on the east side of the Bedingfield to Kenton road, and about a quarter of a mile short of this was a pond that had been dug

Above:
Brockford & Wetheringsett on the final day of operation, 26 July 1952. The last train is standing at the station, far too long for the platform. Eve Keeble, daughter of Fred who was leading porter there, looks on. *Vera Goudy/John Brodribb collection*

Below:
Brockford & Wetheringsett station site (line under construction), 1904. *Crown Copyright*

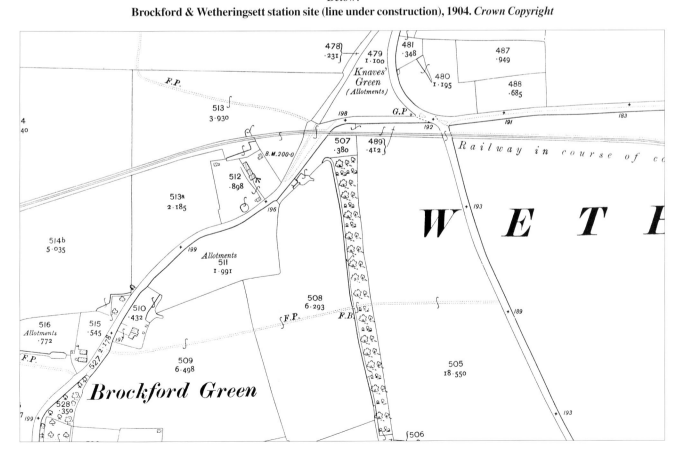

Above:
Brockford & Wetheringsett station as the last train for Laxfield pulls into the platform on 26 July 1952. Crowds of people wait to make their last journey on the 'Middy'. *Vera Goudy/John Brodribb collection*

by the railway to provide water for the locomotives, since there was originally a shed there. It was located at the point of divergence of the branch to Westerfield, the two lines running towards the station as parallel single tracks. Kenton had been planned as a junction, and there were two platforms, the up (towards Haughley) being an island. It had been the intention that the outer face of this would be for branch trains, but in the event it was used as a siding. The buildings were on the down platform, and of the larger double-ended pattern. There were sidings both sides of the line, and the East Anglian Farmers Co-operative had substantial premises adjacent to the station. The main outward traffic from Kenton was livestock, there being 281 tons shipped in 1938.

The branch diverged to the southwest, the junction facing Laxfield, and it is not certain that a station site had been selected in Debenham. The track reached as far as the bridge over the Eye

road, and the trackbed was formed as far as Little London Hill, which was approached by a cutting. It is possible that goods may have been carried unofficially to Debenham, but the branch did not survive the scrap drive of World War 1. The Eye road bridge, a brick arch, was blown up at some time during the late 1920s, and the rubble was carted away by the Davys, a local farming family, for use in their stackyard. Later, George Davy had the job of plough-ing the trackbed back into his fields, which was easy enough, since it only had hoggin as ballast, while the main line used ash. The Davys reckoned that the only way they got through the Depression of the 1930s was by their ability to reuse materials rescued from the abandoned parts of the Middy.

From Kenton, the line headed in a northeasterly direction, passing Bedingfield Hall on its right, and turning gradually north-wards. The next station was Worlingworth, 12 miles 9 chains from

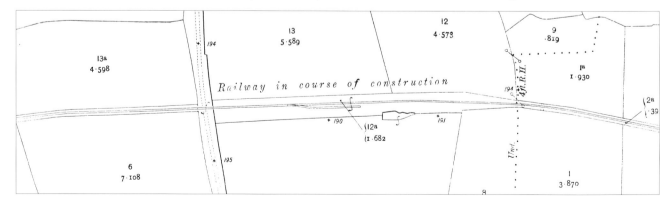

Above:
Aspall station site (line under construction), 1904. *Crown Copyright*

144

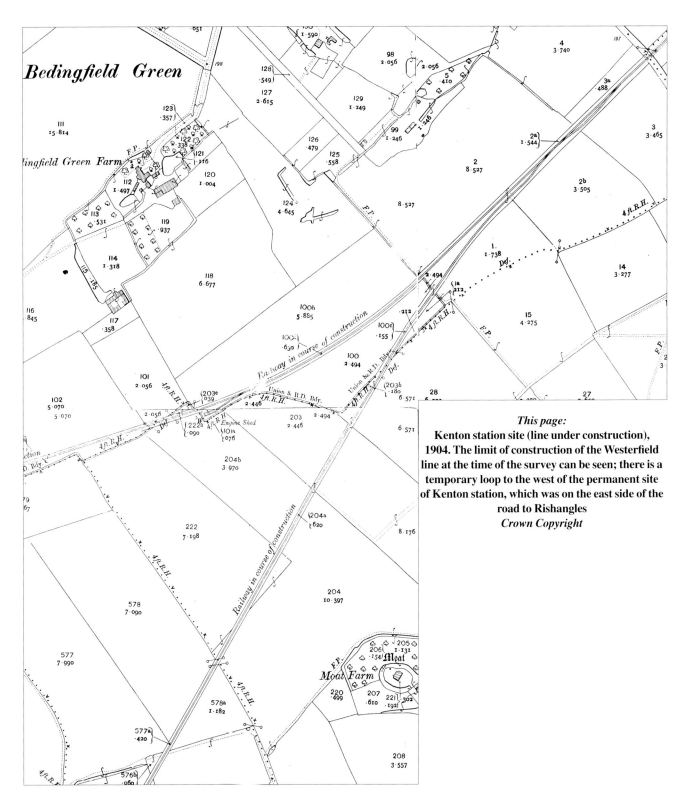

Bedingfield Green

This page:
**Kenton station site (line under construction),
1904. The limit of construction of the Westerfield
line at the time of the survey can be seen; there is a
temporary loop to the west of the permanent site
of Kenton station, which was on the east side of the
road to Rishangles**
Crown Copyright

Haughley, where there was the usual level crossing just before the station, a single platform and building with office at one end, and a siding. Horham station (13 miles 74 chains) was the only one where the platform was on a curve, and this time there were level crossings at each end of the station. It had the normal Middy style of buildings and single siding, and vegetables, especially beet, were an important outward traffic. Stradbroke (15 miles 8 chains) was the administrative headquarters of the line, and the most populous place served. Passenger accommodation was as elsewhere, with the standard platform and double-ended building, but there was greater provision for goods than at most, with two sidings. There was also a corn warehouse at the station. Outward traffic included both grain and livestock, the 1938 tonnages being respectively 1,192 and 266.

The station was a little way to the south of the village, to the west of the level crossing of the road to Wilby. A short distance beyond this was another ungated level crossing, and then an undulating section of line towards Wilby station (16 miles 33 chains), where a single small corrugated iron shed served as the booking office, together with a grounded van body as a store. This was probably the least busy station on the line for both passengers and goods, especially as Wilby was further from its station than from Stradbroke.

At last, 18 miles 71 chains from Haughley, trains reached Laxfield. The layout here was decidedly odd, since trains had to turn off the main line to run into the platform. The usual buildings — single-ended — were provided, plus others beyond the platform. The locomotive shed occupied a site on the south side of the line at the

146

Above:
Worlingworth station, showing the typical Mid-Suffolk layout of level crossing,
130ft platform, single siding and corrugated iron buildings. *Lens of Sutton*

Below:
Wilby station, almost certainly the quietest on the Mid-Suffolk, and the last before the terminus at Laxfield.
The date is 24 May 1952. The locomotive crew pose with 'J15' No 65467. *Adrian Vaughan collection*

Kenton end, and latterly was so dilapidated that it lost its roof. Water was provided by damming a stream and forming a concrete pool, but, when this ran dry in the summer, engines had to run beyond the station to Gorham's Mill and use the pond there. There were two sidings on the north side of the line, the one nearest the platform being used for carriage storage, and the other by the coal merchants Thomas Moy. Train crews were based at Laxfield, although there was also an establishment at first at Kenton. If it was necessary to send out relief men from Ipswich, this could involve lodging, since the last train terminated at Laxfield. In the summer, the men found a sleeping place in one of the coaches, but in winter took advantage of the coal fire in the hut and slept on a wooden locker there. In postwar conditions meals consisted of tinned beans and toasted cheese — bacon was too dear and was still on ration and any stray chickens or eggs soon disappeared into the pot. There was no Sunday service, so the last train down the branch often ran extremely early on Saturday afternoon, with the crew making their own way back via Halesworth to Ipswich. Richard Hardy, who was shedmaster at Ipswich, relates an occasion when he was standing on the platform at Ipswich as an East Suffolk train ran in, and watched the crew from the Mid-Suffolk train getting off at about the same time as they should have been arriving in Laxfield.

The line continued for about half a mile to Gorham's Mill, beyond Laxfield station, where there was a little-used siding. Track had been laid to Cratfield, about two miles further on, and land was bought and pegged out as far as Huntingfield, but the problems of finance and difficulties with the route on to Halesworth precluded further work. For some years various schemes to complete the line were mooted, but the rise of the motorbus and the reluctance of local councils to provide the necessary finance ensured that they came to nothing. The line escaped the closures of the 1930s by the skin of its teeth. The LNER considered the possibility of taking up the track and converting it into a road for the use of its own buses, but abandoned the idea when it realised that the formation, including bridges, would actually have to be widened to allow them to pass safely; this wiped out any possible cost savings.

The Middy retained an individuality which may have had something to do with the fact that it was far from the main centres of population and could operate as a more or less self-contained unit. The station nameboards were in a most unusual and ornate style, and operating procedures may have varied from those officially sanctioned, except when officialdom was about. The buildings had been painted in the Mid-Suffolk's crimson lake livery, with cream woodwork, but later took on a drab wartime grey. Some survived the closure period, however, in LNER green and cream. Locomotives in independent days were Hudswell, Clarke 'Canal' class 0-6-0Ts, later replaced by ex-GER types such as 'J65s', with 'J15s' almost universal in later days. Coaching stock was primitive almost to the end, and the line was the last refuge of four-wheelers anywhere in regular service. These had partitions of part-height, so that schoolchildren could easily see over them, and if necessary do things such as put orange peel round the brims of gentlemen's bowler hats. The roofs were not watertight, and in wet weather a more modern bogie coach would be sent out from Ipswich to provide relief. Again, late in the line's life the last down train was altered to start from Stowmarket for the benefit of the schoolchildren who were most of the passenger traffic, and having waited and watched the Norwich expresses thunder through with their sleek smart locomotives and shiny coaches, they felt embarrassed when the Laxfield train, with a 'J15' and rake of assorted four-wheelers, pulled in. That said, the Middy crews took a great pride in the condition of their engines, and they were kept spotlessly clean — they had the time for it.

The line had its own drivers and firemen, based at Laxfield, although they were not necessarily local men. Cliff Bloom certainly was local, and a member of a family which was very much involved with the railway. He had originally worked from Kenton, but later moved to Laxfield, living with his family in the gatehouse at White Horse Road. His wife was the gatekeeper, and after she retired train crews had to operate them. As with all the gatehouses, the railway had dug a pond to provide water when the line was built, and there was one summer when even the pond at Gorham's Mill ran dry, depriving the engines of their supply. However, the pond at White Horse Crossing retained water, and trains stopped there on their way to or from Laxfield, the portable pump having been moved for the purpose. George Rouse, on the other hand, was not local, and moved to Laxfield from Penistone, where he had driven the huge Beyer Garratt, banking coal trains.

Above:
The last train, a special to Haughley Junction, waits to return on 26 July 1952 from Laxfield.
The engine, 'J15' No 65447, is immaculate. *Vera Goudy/John Brodribb collection*

On occasion, when an Ipswich fireman or passed cleaner had to go out to Laxfield, covering for holidays or sickness, he would try to convince the rookie of the delights of Laxfield, claiming that it had all the attractions of Ipswich. Asked where the swimming pool was, his answer was that 'We've got plenty of ponds!' Another of his habits was to tie his own tobacco using tarred cord from wagon sheets.

Services on the line had never been extensive, and doubtless would have been better had it reached Halesworth. In 1937 there were three mixed trains each way on weekdays, leaving Laxfield at 7.25 and 11.3am and 3.25pm, taking about 1hr 20min to cover 19 miles; they shunted everywhere, although calling at Gipping siding only in the up (downhill) direction. From Haughley trains left at 9.33am, 1pm and 5.30pm (6.5pm Saturdays only). Goods traffic was covered by a train at 11.50am from Laxfield to Aspall, which arrived at 1.50pm and returned at 2.5pm. This might be extended to Haughley if required, arriving at 2.34pm, and so there was a conditional path at 3.15pm from Haughley to Laxfield, and if this ran, the 2.5pm from Aspall did not. Special workings for beet traffic might be run in season, and in Middy days there was a need to run an early morning cattle train on Tuesdays. During World War 2 passenger services were cut back to two (mixed) each way, still with a daily goods working, and although there was often little general goods traffic, the timetable still allowed for shunting everywhere by the mixed trains. The first part of the branch, near the junction, was relaid to a higher standard so that it could be used by heavier locomotives for shunting, and for banking on the first stretch towards Mendlesham. The branch had the benefit of traffic in connection with two airfields locally, at Horham and Mendlesham, although even there much of the material for construction was brought in by road, including sand from the pits at Weybread. Mendlesham was taken over by the Canadians, who promptly crashed three Spitfires, although one of the benefits was that there was never a shortage of certain materials — local women who did work such as washing for the officers were able to get supplies of sugar from them.

During the war a huge silo was erected at Haughley, on the site of the MSLR station, and trains were diverted into Haughley Junction station, where the up platform was modified to incorporate a bay for Laxfield trains. More or less the only passengers were the schoolchildren for Stowmarket Grammar School, and, later on, enthusiasts coming to see this eccentric rural railway. During 1951 proposals were put forward to withdraw the service, and because objections were made, statutory hearings by the local Transport Users' Consultative Committee were held. The TUCC agreed to the proposals, subject to the usual safeguards, and the date for withdrawal of all services was set for 28 July 1952. Being a Monday, this meant that the last trains would run on Saturday, 26 July. It was a fine day, and the two trains were scheduled to run at the usual times from Laxfield at 7.21am and 1.45pm, and from Haughley at 11.15am and 3.55pm. The old four-wheelers had been replaced during the previous summer by two sets of two bogie coaches — the last investment made in the line — and one set was in use on the morning working, which was heavily loaded. It proved necessary to use both for the afternoon train, the locomotive for the day

149

STRADBROKE (Suffolk)

Miles 98. Map Sq. 19.
Pop. 903. Clos. day Thur.
From Liverpool Street via Ipswich and Haughley.
1st cl.—Single 33/7, Mth. Ret. 40/11.
3rd cl.—Single 20/2, Mth. Ret. 27/3.

Liv. St.	Strad.	Strad.	Liv. St.
a.m.		a.m.	
8 12r	12 25	7 48r	11 28
p.m.		p.m.	
1 0r	4 57	2 8	6 52
—	—	—	—

No Sunday Trains.
r Refresh. Car.
Bus facilities. From Wickham Market,
White Hart, 5 journeys Weekdays,
4 Sunday, 70 min. journey.

Table 32   **HAUGHLEY and LAXFIELD (Light Railway)**

Miles from Haughley		Week Days only a.m	p.m S	p.m E	Miles		Week Days only a.m	p.m
	3 London (Liverpool St.).. dep	8 30 .. 1 30	..	1 30 ..		Laxfield........................ dep	7 21 .. 1 45	.. .. ..
	3 Colchester............... "	9 47 .. 2 47	..	2 47 ..	2½	Wilby.............................	7 33 .. 1 53	.. .. ..
	3 Ipswich................... "	1022 .. 3 16	..	3 16 ..	4	Stradbroke...................	7 38 .. 2 4	.. .. ..
	3 Norwich (Thorpe) .... "	9 55 .. 1 46	..	2 55 ..	5	Horham......................	7 43 .. 2 10	.. .. ..
	42 Bury St. Edmunds..... "	1071 .. 3 5	..	3 55 ..	7	Worlingworth	7 49 .. 2 16	.. .. ..
—	Haughley................dep	1115 .. 3 55	..	4 42 ..	9	Kenton	8 4 .. 2 35	.. .. ..
4½	Mendlesham................	1128 .. 4 - 8	..	4 55 ..	10½	Aspall and Thorndon A	8 10 .. 2 41	.. .. ..
6	Brockford and Wetheringsett..	1137 .. 4 17	..	5 4 ..	13	Brockford and Wetheringsett	8 22 .. 2 53	.. .. ..
8½	Aspall and Thorndon A......	1152 .. 4 29	..	5 16 ..	14½	Mendlesham	8 33 .. 3 4	.. .. ..
10	Kenton.......................	12 4 .. 4 41	..	5 28 ..	19	Haughley .... arr	8 48 .. 3 18	.. .. ..
12	Worlingworth...............	1216 .. 4 52	..	5 39 ..	31½ 42	Bury St. Edmunds......arr	9 35 .. 4 11	.. .. ..
14	Horham......................	1222 .. 4 58	..	5 45 ..	51	3 Norwich (Thorpe)...... "	9 43 .. 7 10	.. .. ..
15	Stradbroke...................	1223 .. 5 3	..	5 50 ..	33½	3 Ipswich................. "	9 22 .. 3 53	.. .. ..
16½	Wilby........................	1233 .. 5 8	..	5 55 ..	50½	3 Colchester............... "	10 52 .. 5 19	.. .. ..
19	Laxfield..................arr	1244 .. 5 19	..	6 6 ..	102	3 London (Liverpool St.).. "	11 23 .. 6 39	.. .. ..

A Station for Debenham.   E Except Saturdays   P Via Stowmarket.   S Saturdays only.

Above:
Above: Winter 1951-2 timetable. *Author's collection*

Top: ABC Railway Guide, December 1949. *Author's collection*

being 'J15' No 65447, which was decorated with various paper streamers and laurel wreaths. The journeys were made noisy by a great deal of whistling at the level crossings and by detonators placed on the rails at stations, and there was a festival atmosphere at times, in spite of the sadness of the occasion. Many people were dressed in period costume, including a party from East Suffolk County Council who wore Edwardian costume and travelled from Haughley to Laxfield and back. Local people had developed a great affection for the line, even though many had not travelled on it for years. During its last week parties of school-children made the journey from Haughley, some for the first time, while many travelled from London on the 1.30pm down from Liverpool Street hoping to catch the last train. However, this was seriously delayed by an engine failure earlier in the day, and in the event the last train to Laxfield left 53 minutes late awaiting its connection. The stationmaster at Haughley had made special arrangements to provide refreshments for the crowds of passengers, and this was much appreciated. The guard was Willis Keeble, who had worked on the line for many years, the driver, Joe Skinner, and the fireman, Jack Law. Many railway officials travelled on the train including Mr H. G. Rampling, area operating superintendent, Norwich, Mr R. E. Lawler, commercial superintendent, Ipswich, and Mr R. Vereker, locomotive superintendent, Ipswich. Richard Hardy was on the locomotive. Time was made up on the journey to Laxfield, where the train would normally have terminated. However, because of the large number of people wishing to get back to Haughley for their return journey, and the need to get the engine and stock back to the main line, it was worked in service back to the junction. A correspondent in the *Diss Express* wrote: '. . . back to the coaches poured the passengers, the flag was waved for the last time, the

whistle sounded, and the Mid-Suffolk pulled slowly out of her home station. We watched her slowly wind up the hill, round the bend, out of sight. Goodbye, Mid-Suffolk, we shall miss you; Laxfield is the poorer for your passing.'

There were some wagons left on the branch, and they were worked back to the main line during the following week. Lifting took place the following year, much being done by a Scottish firm of contractors which brought in a small diesel locomotive to work the trains. Ipswich crews and 'J15s' went over the line regularly to collect trains of recovered materials, often having to break through barbed wire put across the line where farmers had already fenced over crossings. Lifting was complete by early 1954, although the stations themselves were left largely intact. A surprising number survive, and at the excellent Mid-Suffolk Light Railway museum on the site of Brockford station are those from Mendlesham, Wilby and one from Brockford itself. Horham and Laxfield buildings are at the Mangapps Farm Railway Museum at Burnham-on-Crouch, and both sites also have a number of other smaller items from the railway. The MSLR museum also has a Middy building from Haughley, and some coach bodies and other rolling stock typical of the line. Worlingworth station building also survives. On the ground, a paradox is that some of the most prominent remains are the abutments of the bridge on the Debenham section which never opened; the Haugh Lane bridge abutments are also extant. A waymarked footpath has been made between Brockford station (actually in Wetheringsett) and Haughley by Mid-Suffolk District Council, although it does not use much of the trackbed. Other small sections are easy enough to find, preferably with the aid of a 1:25,000 map, bearing in mind that much is in private ownership. As with so many of these former railways, it is well worth the effort to get out and look for them on the ground.

Ramsey Branches

RAMSEY is a small town in Huntingdonshire, about five miles from the East Coast main line at Holme, and about seven from Somersham and Chatteris on the St Ives to March line. It is a typical fenland settlement on slightly higher ground, surrounded by the rich agricultural land so characteristic of this part of East Anglia. The name derives from 'Ram's Island', and generations of drainage engineers have left their mark, as did the monks who built the Abbey. The railway between St Ives and March opened for passenger traffic in August 1847, and the Great Northern main line in August 1850, also initially for passenger traffic. In both cases goods traffic started later.

One of the first proposals for a railway to Ramsey came with the scheme in 1846 to build from Somersham, with Robert Stephenson and M. A. Borthwick as engineers. The junction was shown on the plans as being with the 'Cambridge–St Ives–Wisbeach Railway as staked out', and would have been 6 miles 5 furlongs and 9 chains long, with negligible gradients. The Somersham, Ramsey & Holme Railway, with J. S. Burke as its engineer, deposited a bill for the 1859-60 session, in which the Eastern Counties and/or the Great Northern were authorised to work, manage, maintain and use the line, and the possibility of a joint committee was allowed. Either or both could subscribe. In the end, an independent concern, the Ramsey Railway Company, was authorised by an Act dated 22 July 1861, with the Great Eastern Railway subsequently contributing much of the capital cost; it was fearful of incursion into its territory by the Great Northern. The branch from Holme on the Great Northern's main line opened on 1 August 1863 with one intermediate station at St Mary's, and trains were worked from the outset by the GNR. The local company was absorbed by the GER in 1875, who then leased it to the Great Northern. The Great Eastern never ran trains independently over the line.

Meanwhile, the Great Eastern was continuing its efforts to build a line from the east to Ramsey. In the 1862-3 session a bill was deposited for the Ramsey & St Ives Railway, with Sir Charles Fox as the engineer. This would have made an end-on junction with the authorised Ramsey Railway, although it appears from the detailed drawings that the junction would actually have been just on the Holme side of Ramsey station. This line would have passed through the middle of Warboys. In 1865 the Somersham & Ramsey, with Robert Sinclair as engineer, proposed to build a line that would have passed well to the south of Somersham, but further north of Pidley than the one built. The junction at Ramsey would

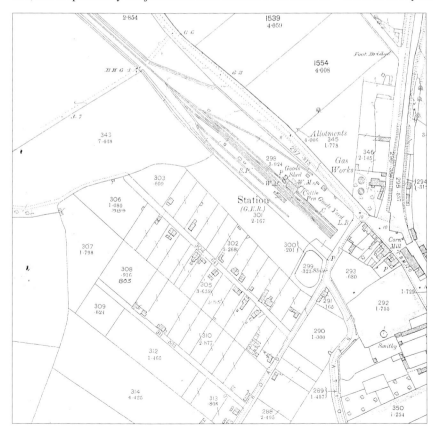

Left:
Ramsey North station, c1900. *Crown Copyright*

151

Above:
**Warboys, the only intermediate station on the branch to Ramsey from Somersham, is
seen in 1954 before the track layout was simplified.** *Stations UK*

Below:
Warboys station, c1900. *Crown Copyright*

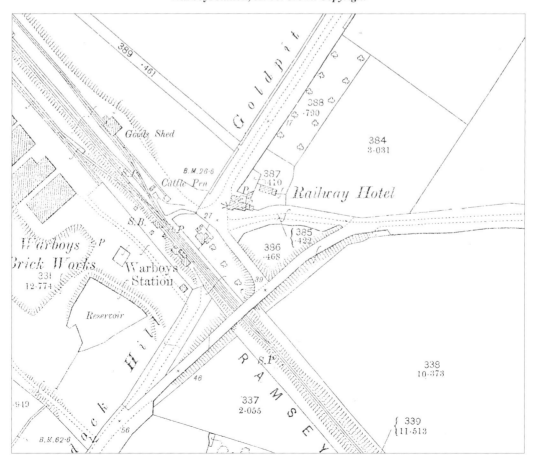

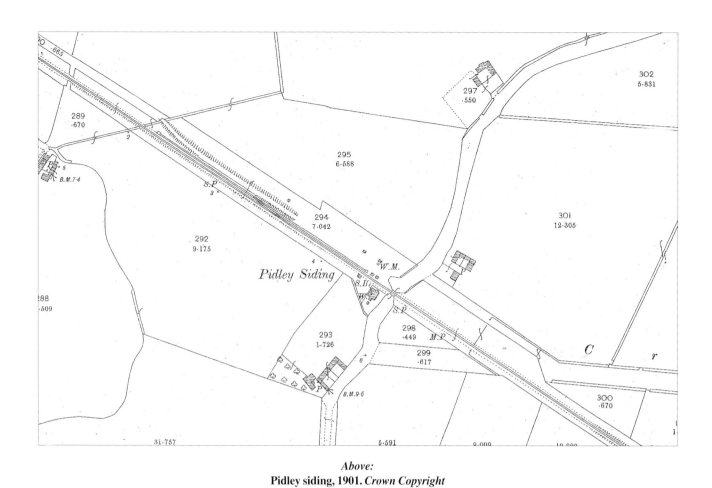

Above:
Pidley siding, 1901. *Crown Copyright*

Below:
A fine view of Somersham pre-1908, looking northwards from the level crossing. *SLS Collection*

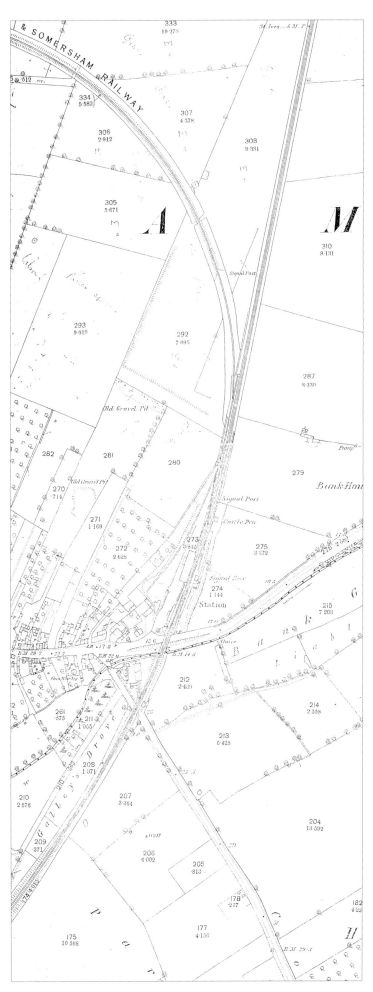

have been much as described for the previous scheme, and the total length almost eight miles. A bill proposing modifications to the scheme was deposited in the following year. Finally, on 13 August 1875 the Great Eastern obtained powers to build a branch from Somersham to Ramsey, and also authorised a link with the other line. This railway opened to Ramsey High Street station on 16 September 1889, but the connection to the other branch was never built. Yet another small town had acquired two railway stations; the link between the lines would have allowed considerable economy and probably a better and more useful service. On the new line passenger and goods services were operated by the Great Eastern, and although it was officially part of the GN&GE Joint line, the Great Northern only ever operated a few goods trains over it. The stations were renamed from 1 July 1923 by the LNER, High Street becoming Ramsey East, and the other, known simply as Ramsey, became Ramsey North. Both stations had facilities for all classes of traffic, although North had the larger crane (5 tons instead of 2 tons). St Mary's could also handle all traffic, and although Warboys also had a 2-ton crane, it could not handle some of the heavier traffic such as portable engines or wheeled machinery. However, it did have a private siding for B. J. Forder & Son Ltd, and there was a public siding at Pidley, about halfway to Somersham.

Both lines were largely devoid of visible earthworks. The GN&GE Joint line between St Ives and March was double track, and Somersham had a substantial station to the east of the village, 4 miles 30 chains from Somersham. There were goods facilities on both sides, and a very large shed with a through siding on the down (to March) side. The signalbox stood opposite this on the east side of the line, and the pointwork was concentrated here, so that the branch ran parallel to the main line to the point of divergence about 300 yards north of the station. It then curved westwards and swung round the north of the village. One of the few cuttings on the line was here, and the line then took an almost straight course to Ramsey. Pidley public siding (officially Pidley-cum-Fenton) was at 2 miles 24 chains, on the north side of the line, with cart road access from the east. There was a clay pit on the southwest side of the line at Warboys, and the London Brick Company had a private siding here. The station was about three-quarters of a mile to the north of the village and extensive in layout. There was a road bridge over the line at the Somersham end, the passing loop starting just before this was reached. There were two platforms, with the offices on the down side, consisting of a brick building with two single-storey sections at right angles to the line linked by a central section parallel to it; the roof was corrugated. There was a wooden hut at the Ramsey end of the down platform, and the two were linked by a barrow crossing. The goods yard was on the opposite side from the brick works, and had cattle pens, a goods shed with through road and two other sidings. The station could not handle furniture vans, but had a 2-ton crane. Warboys' traffic was accounted with Somersham.

Ramsey (High Street) station was 6 miles 77 chains from Somersham, and despite its name it was in Bury Road, just short of the High Street. It had generous provision, with a single platform and loop, the building being very similar to that at Warboys, except that the roof was tiled. The goods

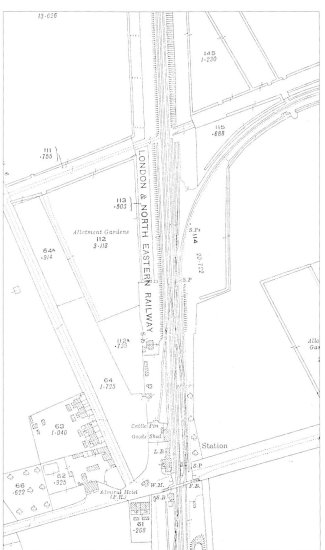

yard was on the east side of the line, with a small goods shed with
through road, and earlier another passing around it, though this was
later taken out. Two more sidings ran along the eastern edge of the
yard. The cattle pens were at the Bury Road end of the loop. A 2-ton
crane was available.

The Great Northern had initially leased the branch from Holme
to Ramsey from the Great Eastern until July 1896. In 1895 a
dispute arose between the two companies about the state of the line,
deficiencies having been alleged, and Henry Oakley of the GNR
wrote in March 1895 that his company was not prepared to spend
any money on the line in view of the imminent expiry of the lease.
It had been resignalled in 1894 to bring it up to current passenger
standards, and was inspected on 27 October by Maj Marindin. He
reported that the points and signals at St Mary's and Ramsey had
been interlocked, with signalboxes being provided. At St Mary's it
had 14 working levers, including the level crossing bolt lever, and
six spare, while there was also an outlying three-lever frame locked
by Annett's key. At Ramsey signalbox there were 17 working and
eight spare levers, again with a three-lever outlying ground frame
bolt-locked from the box. Maj Marindin commented that 'the
accommodation for passengers at both stations is very poor, and I
trust that steps may be taken to improve it'.

Trains from Holme worked from a bay platform on the up side of
the main line, and swung sharply away to head almost due east for
a short distance before the branch gradually turned more to the
south, crossing the River Nene, and then the road between Ramsey
St Mary's and Ramsey Heights about two miles from the terminus.
St Mary's station was 3¾ miles from Holme on the west side of the

Above:
St Mary's station is besieged by enthusiasts from the REC's 'Charnwood
Forester' excursion on 14 April 1957. *David Lawrence*

Below:
Ramsey North seen in about 1930, with a Great Northern 4-4-2T running round its train.
The old goods shed is still in place. *Stations UK*

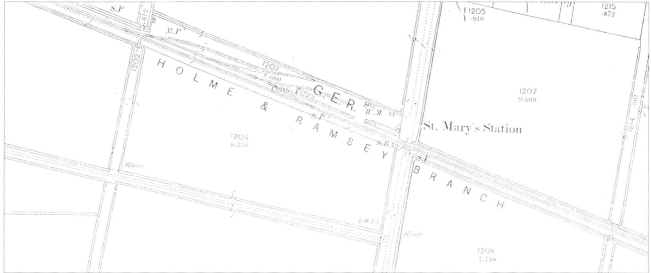

Top:
St Mary's station served Ramsey St Mary's, a relatively populous parish. The wooden station buildings are shown in this view from the level crossing, looking towards Holme. *Stations UK*

Above:
St Mary's station, 1900. *Crown Copyright*

level crossing of the Whittlesey road. The single platform was on the north side of the line, and hosted a substantial wooden building with a large number of chimneys, although shelter was restricted to two small awnings over the doors. Goods facilities were more generous and there were several sidings in the compact yard, which also had cattle pens. The station could handle all classes of traffic, but there was no crane. In 1924 E. J. Coleman & Sons and George Coleman Ltd were potato merchants at the station.

Ramsey was a further 2 miles away, and also had a generous layout, sidings fanning out from the approach to the station. There was a very wide passenger platform with an assortment of wooden buildings, and with sidings behind it on the southwest side. Opposite was the goods shed, with through road, also wooden,

together with the goods offices, cattle pens and other facilities. The goods shed was later replaced with a much more modest structure with awnings projecting form each side. Access to all parts of the station was from Station Road, which went across the end of the layout, turned sharp left and became St Mary's Road, and went to there and Whittlesey. The station had all facilities, including a 5-ton crane, and was gas-lit, probably because the gas works was just across the road. In 1924 Major Bros was a potato merchant based at the station, together with E. A. Newton & Co and James Martland Ltd. Herbert E. Cullen was the stationmaster covering both of those in the town, as well as St Mary's.

Train services were always fairly limited. The Great Northern operated seven return journeys over its line in 1922, the first from

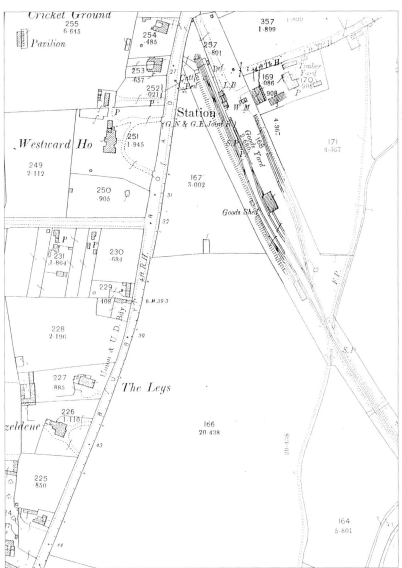

Ramsey at 6.55am, arriving at Holme at 7.14am. The last worked back at 7.50pm, arriving at Ramsey at 8.4pm. All trains called at St Mary's, which served a substantial village of some 1,600 people. From Somersham there were fewer trains, with only four each way except on Mondays when there was an extra return working in the middle of the day. The time was around 20 minutes for the seven-mile journey. This gave Ramsey 11 trains each way on weekdays, not bad for a town whose population was only 4,684 in 1891.

Passenger trains were withdrawn from Ramsey East on and from Monday 22 September 1930, the last running on the previous Saturday. Services on the line to the North station were drastically cut in 1931, all passengers trains after 10.15am being withdrawn. An Eastern Counties bus service was provided in the afternoon, and two trains in the morning. This spartan provision was withdrawn on 6 October 1947, although both lines continued to handle goods traffic. Signalling was removed after closure to passengers, and the Ramsey East line was worked by a train staff without tickets. On this branch, there were generally two goods trains Mondays to Fridays, with one on Saturdays. The morning train left Whitemoor Yard at 5.25am (6am Saturdays) and arrived at Somersham at 7.45am, not leaving until 9.10am, it shunted Warboys between 9.30 and 10.15am, when it left for Ramsey East, arriving at 10.25am. It left again at 11.10am, this time calling also at Pidley-cum-Fenton siding, finally leaving Somersham for Whitemoor at 12.50pm. It ran back somewhat later on Saturdays.

The afternoon train, which did not run on Saturdays, started at Somersham at 2.30pm and was booked to run only as far as Warboys, though it would go to Ramsey if required. It returned from Warboys at 4.15pm and was required to clear all traffic from there, called at Pidley-cum-Fenton and Owen's sidings if needed, and reached Somersham at 5pm. The engine and brake van then ran to Chatteris. On Mondays a conditional engine and brake van working started from Whitemoor at 6am and ran to Ramsey to pick up cattle for St Ives market; on its return from St Ives it worked the 9.10am goods down the branch. Ramsey North had a considerable traffic in potatoes, shipping 3,238 tons in 1938, together with 377 tons of livestock, the latter worth £486 to the LNER. In the same year, St Mary's despatched 1,972 tons of potatoes and 2,586 tons of other vegetables: this is rich fen farmland. On the Somersham line, Warboys loaded 3,395 tons of vegetables, worth only £894 to the railway, whilst the 1,326 tons of potatoes loaded at Somersham attracted a much higher revenue of £1,091.

Closure of Ramsey East came relatively early, the terminus losing its goods services from 17 September 1956. Warboys and Pidley-cum-Fenton did not close until 13 July 1964, and with them the entire branch. Somersham itself lost its goods services in December of the same year, and closed entirely from 6 March 1967.

The branch to Ramsey North survived somewhat longer. St Mary's closed for goods traffic 28 February 1972, although it had been a private siding since 1960. Ramsey North lost its trains from 2 July 1973.

Miles		Week Days only.				Miles			Week Days only		
		mrn	mrn	aft J	aft K				mrn	mrn	aft
1	London (King's Cross).. dep	..	7 23	4 50	4 50	..	—	Ramsey (North) .... dep	6 50	..	8 33	5 30	..
—	Holme .... dep	7 35	10 6	7 30	7 35	..	2	St. Mary's..................	6 57	..	8 38	..	..
3¼	St. Mary's...................	7 44	10 13	..	..	..	5¼	Holme.............. arr	7 10	..	8 45	6 7 0	..
5¼	Ramsey (North) .... arr	7 49	10 18	8 7 0	8 7 5	..	75	1 London (King's Cross).. arr	10 15	..	11 37	8 57	..

A Change at Hitchin.   **J** Except Fridays.   **K** Fridays only

7 Omnibus service provided by the Eastern Counties Omnibus Co. Ltd., Lincoln Road, Peterborough.

Above:

Ramsey North in 1961 makes an interesting contrast with the earlier period. Passengers are long gone, and the goods shed is decidedly different. There is still plenty of traffic on offer. *Stations UK*

Scole Railway

ONE of the smallest byways in East Anglia was the Scole Estate Railway, a private system from the main line station at Diss and serving the interests of William Betts, then owner of the Frenze Estate. This was devoted largely to intensive market gardening, and Betts saw the railway as the quickest and most economical way of getting his produce to market. It started from the goods yard on the up side at Diss station, where the back siding was known for very many years as Betts siding, and extended to a total of seven miles. There was a spur here giving access to his engine shed, and the administrative office for the railway was also here. The line then curved sharply to the east, with a short spur going off on the north side into brick kilns which were on the east side of the main line station. The line crossed Sandy Lane, and immediately after this was a short passing loop. It then crossed a small tributary of the River Waveney by means of a

timber bridge approached by iron caissons, which were thought to be more economical than an embankment. About a quarter of a mile further was a junction near the crossing of Dark Lane, where one branch turned northwards to go to Frenze, and the other continued in a southeasterly direction towards Scole.

Past the junction, the Scole line then passed the Great Barn, built by Betts, where there was a water storage tank, turntable and several sidings. There were maintenance sheds here, plus stores of permanent way materials such as rails, sleepers and chairs. Continuing eastwards the line passed another barn, and then two more junctions, where one branch again turned north, and another to the south which served brickfields and terminated near Scole Rectory, on the main Diss to Yarmouth road, until recently the A143. The main line continued along Miller's Lane, turning to the south about a quarter of a mile

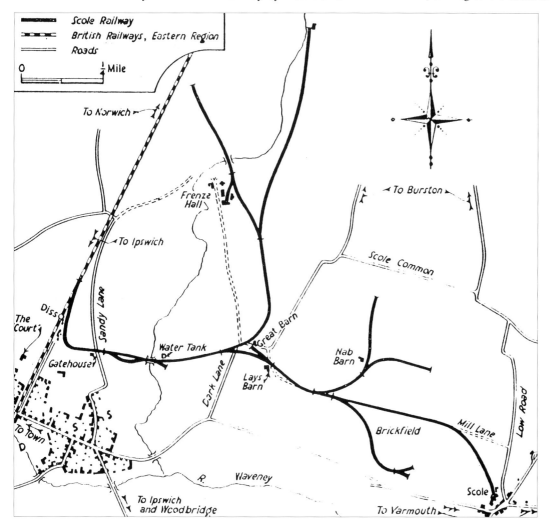

Left:
The Scole Estate Railway.
The Railway Magazine

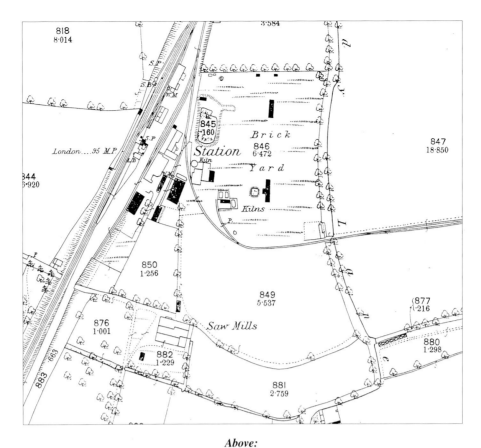

Above:
The Scole Estate Railway at Diss, 1884. *Crown Copyright*

from Scole, and terminating at Street Farm, with the buffer stops at the garden wall of the Scole Inn.

The line towards Frenze from Dark Lane junction also split into two branches. The western arm went to Frenze Hall, where there was a further siding to the hall itself, and after crossing the river by another wooden bridge, continued almost to the main line, nearly a mile north of Diss station. The other arm went further north, terminating at a pump house on the same small river.

Motive power was provided by two locomotives, one a 2-4-0 saddle tank built by Brotherhoods of Chippenham, and the other an 0-4-0T from Hughes of Loughborough. The larger was in normal use on the railway, while the smaller was kept in reserve or used for shunting. The rolling stock consisted of various wagons which were built to Betts' own design, and which were attached to Great

Eastern trains at Diss. Passengers, in the form of agricultural students, were occasionally carried by the simple expedient of putting temporary seats in open trucks. Extra wagons were hired in as required. Apart from the outward horticultural traffic and manure, coal was carried from Diss to Scole and Frenze.

William Betts died in 1885. He had intended his estate to go to his sons, but both died before him, and the estate was broken up and sold off. The sale took place on 18 and 19 July 1887 at Frenze Hall, when all the stock such as rail, machinery and plant, engines, ploughs, railway wagons and so on was auctioned off, it still being spread over the estate. The rail — which was of a lightweight section and in 18ft lengths — went for scrap to George Archer of Yarmouth, although some was stolen. Little trace of the system now remains.

Southwold Railway

THE Southwold Railway was one of the very few narrow gauge lines in East Anglia, and also one of the few passenger railways, apart from the M&GN, not to fall into the clutches of the Great Eastern Railway. It had a working life of almost exactly 50 years, and its passing was much mourned. Indeed, it is still remembered with affection in the area.

The geography of Suffolk made it inevitable that the East Suffolk Railway between Ipswich and Yarmouth took an inland course, linking Woodbridge, Saxmundham and Beccles. The coastal towns and resorts perforce had to be reached by branches off the main line, so that company also built branches to Aldeburgh, Snape and Lowestoft, while Felixstowe was served by a line built by the docks company there. Southwold was left in limbo, and it was not long before a group of prominent local landowners decided that a railway was needed to open up the area and bring visitors to the growing resort. Prior to the building of the new line the town was served only by a horse bus from Darsham station, near Yoxford on the Yarmouth turnpike, to the Swan Hotel in Southwold. Following public meetings in both Halesworth and Southwold in 1875, Ransomes & Rapier, the well-known engineering firm in Ipswich, took an interest in the project, Mr R. C. Rapier becoming chairman of the Southwold Railway Company.

The company was incorporated under its own Act on 24 July 1876, with powers to build a line from the Great Eastern at Halesworth to Southwold, with branches to the River Blyth navigation at Halesworth and to the Black Shore Quay at Southwold. It proved difficult to raise the necessary capital locally, and the local board resigned, being replaced by a new one chaired by Richard Rapier, a post he occupied until 1897. Meetings were held at his London office, and the company's registered offices remained in London for its whole existence. The authorised capital was £40,000 in £10 shares, and construction started in May 1878. It was to be built to 3ft gauge. The engineer in charge was Mr W. G. Jackson, who was also associated with the Shanghai & Woosung Railway in China. The line was inspected on 23 September 1879 and opened to the public on the following day.

The Southwold and Great Eastern stations at Halesworth were adjacent, the two being linked by an extension to the GER's footbridge which remained in existence to cross the main line long after closure of the Southwold. The Southwold station was on the east side of the East Suffolk line, and its booking office was in a small wooden building on the platform. Transhipment sidings and platforms were provided, and after closure of the railway, these tended to be used by wagons from the nearby dairy. Both railways headed south by separate bridges over the Holton Road, then briefly running side by side on the same embankment before the Southwold swung away to the east, picking up the Blyth Valley. It then continued across a small bridge over a rough track, which has now had a short length of track relaid on it by the Southwold Railway Society. Continuing on a relatively level course the line ran parallel to the river, crossing it about two miles from Halesworth, with Wenhaston station just under a mile further on, 2½ miles from Halesworth. This was situated on the east side of the road from Blyford to Wenhaston, about halfway between the two villages. As at other stations on the railway, it had a low platform only a few inches high, on the south side of the line. This was also the site of the only public level crossing on the line. There was initially a single siding on the north side, the points being at the east

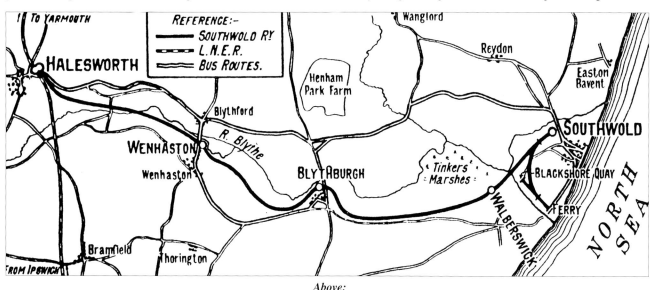

Above:
The Southwold Railway. *The Railway Magazine*

Left and below:
**Halesworth station
with a mixed train
for Southwold
about to depart.
The locomotive is
No 4 *Wenhaston*,
an 0-6-2T built by
Manning, Wardle
& Co Ltd, and
which retained its
dark green livery.**
SLS Collection

end. This was made into a loop in 1921. The station buildings were in the timber-framed style characteristic of the railway.

The line continued to run parallel with the river, which had once been navigable as far as Halesworth, but had become badly silted at an early stage. Heading southeast for about 1½ miles, it then turned east and ran alongside the river much more closely, forming the only passing loop on the line as it approached Blythburgh, passing under the Yarmouth turnpike — now the A12 — immediately beyond the station which was five miles from Halesworth. Initially just provided with a siding, this was later converted to a loop. The buildings and platform were, as usual, on the south side of the line, with a wooden goods shed on the other, which was also provided with a loading platform. Beyond this, at the Halesworth end, was another wooden shed used for coal storage and this survives at the present time. The passenger platform had a wooden surface, as at Halesworth, and could be also reached across the tracks by a board crossing.

Having left Blythburgh station, the line continued to hug the edge of the estuary, by now widened greatly with extensive mud flats and salt marshes. It continued eastwards through the woodland

of Tinker's Covert, or The Heronry, before curving slightly towards the north on its approach to Walberswick, eight miles from Halesworth. The station there was about half a mile from the village, and approached only by tracks. The platform was of the usual dimensions, with a very small wooden building containing a booking office and urinal. This station was rebuilt on a larger scale in 1902. It was only a short distance onwards to the swing bridge over the River Blyth, which was visible from the station and was very rarely opened to river traffic. The line then crossed Buss Creek marshes before going into a cutting through Southwold Common, the railway being spanned here by a bridge built from old rail and provided for the convenience of local golfers. It terminated in Station Road, 8 miles 63 chains from Halesworth, with the Station Hotel opposite. Horse buses ran from the station to various hotels in connection with the trains, and the forecourt later had to be extended to accommodate them all. There was a sizeable goods yard, and a large carriage shed was later constructed; the locomotive shed and servicing facilities were also located here. The main buildings were extended at intervals, in a similar style to the

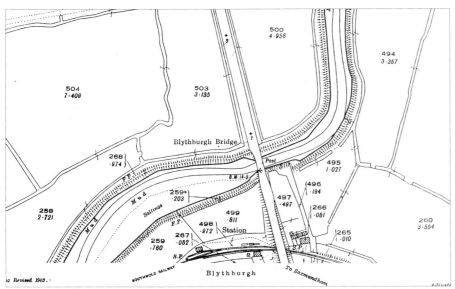

Above:
**The railway passed through some very pleasant countryside between Blythburgh and Southwold,
such as this stretch known as 'The Heronry'. The track and formation are immaculate
in this view. It is still possible to walk along parts of the trackbed here.** *SLS Collection*

original, and this can be used to date photographs. W. H. Smith had a small bookstall at the station.

The line, following the River Blyth for most of the way, was subject to flooding at intervals, and on the opening day trains could not reach Halesworth because of flooding at Wenhaston. In November 1897, flooding washed away much of the embankment between the swing bridge and Southwold Common, and passengers had to take the train as far as Walberswick and then cross by boat!

There were several locomotives which worked on the line. When it opened, the company had ordered three Sharp, Stewart 2-4-0 side tanks numbered 1, 2 and 3. However, it was decided that only two were needed, so No 1 was returned to the makers, and the others were named *Halesworth* and *Blyth* respectively. In 1893 increasing traffic justified the ordering of another locomotive, again a Sharp, Stewart similar to the others, but this time a 2-4-2T with larger coal and water capacity, which took the vacant number 1 and was named *Southwold*. Delivered in a green livery, they were later turned out in Great Eastern blue. Finally, in 1914 a Manning, Wardle 0-6-2T was bought and named *Wenhaston*, being latterly painted in a dark green livery, while the others were black. Heavy repairs were carried out at the Great Eastern's Stratford Works, the engines being carried there and back on flat wagons.

The six-wheeled coaching stock made use of the Cleminson flexible wheelbase system. They were built with longitudinal seating, provided with a carpet strip for some comfort in the second class, while first class passengers had blue cushions. The coaches originally had open verandahs giving access to the passenger accommodation via a central door, although later these were enclosed and side doors were provided. When first built the livery was cream and black, but this was later changed to all-over maroon. There were 39 wagons on the line at the end, and the coal merchants Thomas Moy had their own vehicles. Their six-wheeled trucks also used the Cleminson system, although most were four-wheeled. Operation of the line was by train staff, and some fixed signals were provided, with arms for opposite directions fixed on the same post.

Although authorised in the original Act, the branches to Southwold Harbour and the Blyth Navigation at Halesworth were not built at the outset, probably because of the difficulties with raising capital. However, just before World War 1, powers for the first were revived, and it was duly built, together with a short spur running back towards Black Shore Quay. World events prevented the hoped-for expansion of the fishing trade, and the branch saw relatively little use, although it was valuable in coastal defence construction

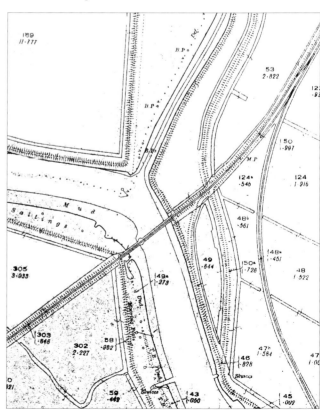

work. The poor relations between the railway company and the harbour authorities over traffic from the harbour into the town did not help. There had long been talk of converting the line to double track should the traffic warrant it, and allowance was made for this in cuttings, bridges and so on. Consideration was also given to conversion to standard gauge, and there was talk at one time that the Mid-Suffolk Light Railway, after completing its line from Haughley to Halesworth, would take it over and convert the gauge, thus gaining a useful independent access to the east coast. The swing bridge was the first structure to be rebuilt to standard gauge clearances, and there was also evidence of the standard gauge on

the Harbour branch, where the weighbridge — a second-hand structure — had had a third rail added to make it suitable for the Southwold's 3ft gauge vehicles. The bridge carrying the main road over the line at Blythburgh was rebuilt at the start of the 20th century, again to standard gauge clearances, and survived longer than most structures on the line, not being demolished until 1961.

For many years the Southwold Railway gave good service to its local community, although it was the butt of local humour, epitomised by the postcards drawn by Reg Carter, and still on sale locally. The Summer 1913 timetable showed trains from Southwold arriving at Halesworth on Mondays to Saturdays at

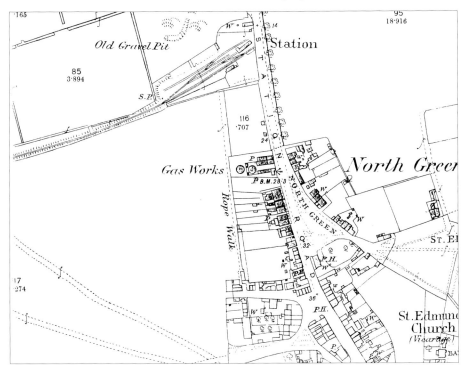

Above:
One of many postcard views of a mixed train leaving Southwold. It gives a very good impression of the terminus, showing the carriage shed and Station Hotel clearly. Note also the characteristic signal, with the glasses below the arms. *SLS Collection*

Below:
No 1 *Southwold* on a train for Southwold at Wenhaston station, about 1905. The second carriage, is painted white, and so must be either No 1 or No 5, which were composites. This particular postcard view was issued many times, and continued to be available after closure. *Ian Allan Library*

Above:
A fine view of the train, staff and luggage at Southwold. This view has also been reissued a number of times. It shows the coaches after the verandahs had been covered in and also illustrates the amount and variety of traffic carried. *SLS Collection*

Below:
No 1 *Southwold* on shed at the terminus, and looking in pristine condition. Note the details of the coupler, and the protective plate fixed to the back of the bunker. *Ian Allan Library*

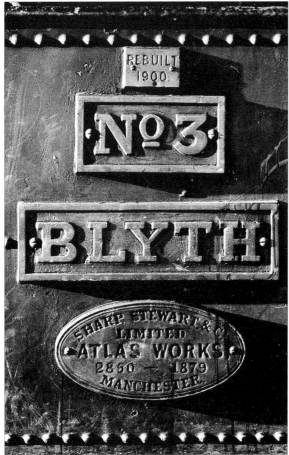

8.7 and 10.52am, and 12.53, 2.57, 6.12 and 7.47pm, returning from there at 8.40 and 11.33am, and 1.33, 3.35, 6.26 and 7.53pm. On Sundays there was one return working reaching Halesworth at 5.32pm and returning to Southwold at 7.32pm. In summer 1922 the service was similar, although with some minor changes to the timings. Later there were more trains on summer Sundays, but none in winter. End-to-end journey times were just over 40 minutes. Although primarily a passenger line, and marketing itself to visitors and tourists, it carried a useful amount of freight, but was hampered by the break of gauge. In 1913 this amounted to 7,334 tons of merchandise and 6,474 tons of minerals, while in 1927 there were 4,276 tons of merchandise and 14,144 tons of coal and other minerals. Passengers, however, had fallen from 108,677 in 1913 to 81,704 in 1927, with a reduction in net receipts from £1,803 to £751. The company had rejected earlier offers of takeover by the Great Eastern, and the LNER in 1923. At the end in 1929, the latter refused to entertain the idea.

The situation was greatly worsened by the granting of licences in April 1928 by Southwold Corporation for motorbuses to pick up fares within its boundaries. This allowed them to get much closer to the centre of trade and population than the railway station, and they were also able to go faster: legally 20mph instead of the railway's 16mph. Passenger traffic on the Southwold Railway melted away, and it cut its fares from 2s 3d to 1s 6d return in winter, with special rates of 1s 0d return from May to October during the holiday season. It was not enough; it was not a local company, and the line closed on the evening of 11 April 1929, large crowds turning out to see and travel on the last trains. The LNER then provided through bookings to Southwold via Halesworth by arrangement with the Eastern Counties Road Car Company, and instituted a road delivery service in the area, also based on Halesworth. The railway was more or less abandoned where it lay, with locomotives, coaches and wagons in the sidings and sheds left to decay gently.

Schemes were soon afoot to reopen the line. Ronald Shepherd, secretary of the Wimbledon Model Railway Club, was one of the main proponents, and by the end of 1929 was proposing to

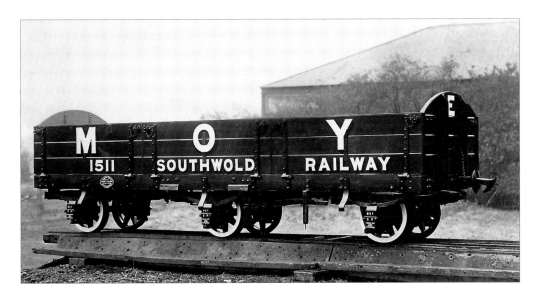

Left:
A new wagon for Thomas Moy, coal merchants, who had their own fleet on the railway. *Ian Allan Library*

inaugurate a fast and frequent passenger service with a petrol railcar, connecting with East Suffolk services at Halesworth. Freight was to be hauled by a geared steam locomotive, using transporter wagons to handle standard gauge stock. In 1939 the railway was still substantially intact, but derelict. A tramp had set fire to one of the coaches at Halesworth, and the line was very overgrown in places. The swing bridge at Southwold remained intact, but was difficult to cross on foot because of the lack of any decking. Although ticket stocks had been removed from the stations, other papers, letters and books were still there. Most of the locomotives were at Southwold: No 2 *Halesworth* and No 4 *Wenhaston* were in the shed, with the motion on No 2 partly dismantled. No 3 *Blyth* was in the remains of the shed half a mile from Halesworth, by now very dilapidated. No 1 *Southwold* was reported as nowhere to be seen. It appeared that the town clerk at Southwold, Mr E. G. Naunton, had been appointed as receiver of the railway in 1929, and had been reluctant to dispose of any property without an enabling Act of Parliament because of the arrears of rates to the Town Council. However, by 1940 the drive for scrap metal to aid the war effort was in full cry, and

Halesworth Urban District and Southwold Town Councils passed a resolution allowing the material to be used under the Emergency Powers Act.

By November of the following year, dismantling was well in hand, with the track being removed and the rolling stock broken up, although some of the bridges were not removed for a further 20 years. The company remained legally in existence, and in spite of conversion to a limited company and the issuing of a winding-up order in 1960, this had not been executed in late 1962 and the company finally ceased to exist in 1963. Today, there is a society dedicated to the Southwold Railway, and some interesting exhibits in the local museum in the town, as well as the short length of relaid track and refurbished bridge near Halesworth. It is difficult to get to most of the remains of the trackbed between Halesworth and Blythburgh, but thence to Southwold it can almost all be walked relatively easily. There is a commemorative seat on the site of Walberswick station, a modern footbridge has replaced the swing bridge destroyed by the Army during World War 2, and the station site at Southwold is occupied by the local fire station, which bears a plaque recording its former use.

Below:
Shunting in progress in the yard at Southwold. *SLS Collection*

THE SOUTHWOLD EXPRESS·

THE GUARD GOES BIRDSNESTING & THINKS AN EGG IN THE NEST IS WORTH TWO IN
THE EYE —   N B THE SPEED LIMIT IS STRICTLY OBSERVED ON THIS LINE.

Left and below:
Reg Carter drew a series of humorous cartoons of the Southwold Railway which were on sale for many years. Although not without some foundation, they were unkind to the railway and staff that worked hard and served the area well. Examples of other cards which are not as well-known can be seen in the Halesworth Museum, at the railway station, and also in the Southwold Museum. Both are well worth a visit for anyone interested in the railway. *SLS Collection*

THE SOUTHWOLD·EXPRESS·   A·SLIGHT·ENGINE·TROUBLE·CAUSES·A·DELAY — BUT·IS·SOON·REMEDIED

Stoke Ferry Branch and Wissington Light Railway

THE Stoke Ferry branch started life in much the same way as so many other rural lines: an area missed by the main lines, local towns and villages anxious to be connected to the rail network so that they did not miss out on the new trade and prosperity, and later taken over by the larger company. What made it of interest was the development of the Wissington line, built to serve the growing sugar industry and spreading out across the fens, bringing beet for the refinery. Ultimately, it survived the original branch by quite a handsome margin. In so doing it became a haven for small and ancient engines and rolling stock picking their way through overgrown tracks, and a Mecca for enthusiasts.

The Lynn & Ely Railway had to endure considerable financial problems in building the main line between the two, and it worked its way south to Downham Market in 1846 and Denver Road Gate in January 1847, not reaching Ely until the end of the year. Denver Road Gate became simply Denver in November 1847, and given its location fairly close to Downham Market, and in an area otherwise almost devoid of population, it is hardly surprising that it closed to passengers within a relatively short time, from 1 February 1870. When the Stoke Ferry branch opened Denver reopened, but was served only by branch trains.

The Downham & Stoke Ferry Railway received its Act on 24 July 1879 to build a branch east from Denver. The contract for its construction went to John Waddell & Sons of Edinburgh, and there seem to have been problems with the sub-contractor, Urquhart, who was taken on to form the trackbed. Progress was not particularly rapid, and the line was not ready to open until 1 August 1882. There were intermediate stations at Ryston and Abbey, and the branch was 7 miles 7 chains in length, with trains travelling a further 1 mile 56 chains along the main line to Downham Market. There were no significant gradients on the line, which ran close to the cut-off channel for the rivers Little Ouse and Wissey for most of its length. Populations were very limited: Stoke Ferry boasted 724 in the 1891 census, Hilgay (relatively near to Ryston station) 1,491, West Dereham (half a mile from Abbey station) 554, and Wereham, 2½ miles from Abbey, 554. Denver itself, now almost a suburb of Downham Market, then had 803 inhabitants. Abbey was renamed 'Abbey for West Dereham' on 1 January 1886, and 'Abbey and West Dereham' on 1 July 1923. The local company was formally absorbed by the Great Eastern in 1897.

Denver station, being on the main line, had two side platforms, and stood immediately to the north of the level crossing where the

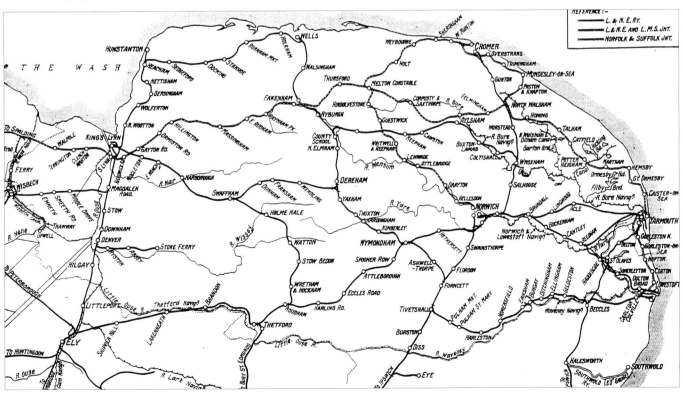

Above:
Map of the railway lines in Norfolk, including the Stoke Ferry branch and the Wissington Light Railway. *The Railway Magazine*

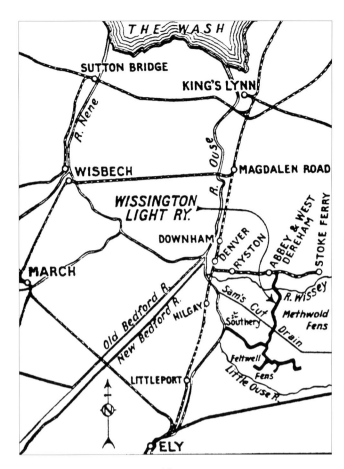

Above:
The Wissington Light Railway. *The Railway Magazine*

Right:
Denver station. *Crown Copyright*

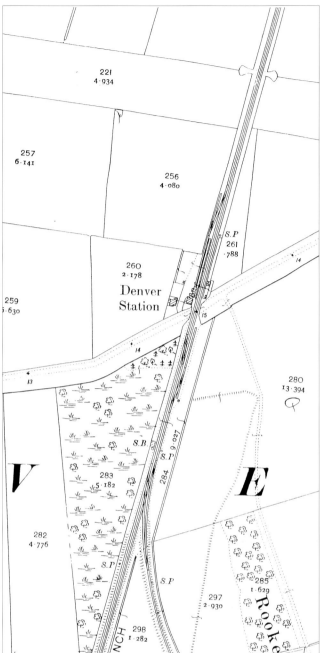

line crossed the minor road between Denver and Denver Sluice. The main buildings were on the down side, with a house of almost idyllic outward appearance, having roses around the door and windows. The platforms were short, and both had brick-built shelters. The branch curved away sharply to the east, and was limited to 30mph. Initially the stations were all staffed, and were able to issue tickets. Conductor-guard working was introduced in 1895 as an economy measure, and because it was thus necessary for him to be able to get through all coaches of the train, two coaches were transferred from the Wisbech & Upwell Tramway for this purpose. However, these had to return in 1896, and an order was placed for replacements from Stratford Works. They entered service at the end of that year, coinciding with the GER taking over the line. The low steps of the tramway were not required, since the Stoke Ferry branch had normal height platforms, and drop plates were provided to allow the guard access between the coaches. Although new, the coaches had an appearance reminiscent of an earlier era, and proved a success, since they survived until the withdrawal of the passenger service. After a period in store they were sent to the Kelvedon & Tollesbury, and were also in the last train on that line, in 1951.

Ryston station, 1 mile 35 chains from Denver, had a single platform on the south side of the line and to the east of the level crossing of the Ely to King's Lynn road, now the A10. The station building consisted of a single-storey white-brick structure, with a glazed waiting area facing the platform, a fully hipped slate roof and offices and other facilities at each end. The station house was on quite a lavish scale, in essentially the same style and materials, and stood in gardens bounded by the railway line and the station approach road, nearer to the level crossing. A siding ran back

behind the platform. Ample land had been fenced opposite the platform, which was carefully cultivated as allotments. The station handled passengers, parcels, ordinary goods and livestock, and also had a siding for E. R. M. Pratt, the family owning the entire parish. The towing of wagons by rope was permitted at Ryston.

Abbey was a further 2 miles 37 chains along the branch, and had a very obvious resemblance to Ryston, although the platform was slightly curved instead of straight. The railway had run beside the Black Drain for about $1\frac{1}{2}$ miles on reaching the station, which was approached by a minor lane from West Dereham. The station was to the east of the usual level crossing, and on the north side of the railway; the station house was again near the road. There were two sidings and a peculiar track layout whereby they crossed over, one leading to the cattle pens and the other to a loading dock at the back of the platform. The signalbox was opposite the Stoke Ferry end of the platform. The station could also handle goods, passenger and parcel traffic, and it was the home station for the Wissington Railway, officially a siding, of British Sugar Manufacturers Ltd. There was no crane or goods shed; use of a rope for towing wagons was permitted. The Wissington line branched away about half a

Above:
Class D16/3 No 62530 runs through Denver on a local train in 1957.
The Stoke Ferry branch diverged behind and to the right of the camera. *Stations UK*

Below:
Denver station photographed in about 1925, looking towards Downham Market and King's Lynn.
The station was served only by Stoke Ferry trains, having been reopened when the branch opened. *Stations UK*

Above:
**Ryston station was the first on the branch, and was located by the level crossing on the main road to King's Lynn.
At the time of this 1925 view looking east, it still had a passenger service and retained full signalling.** *Stations UK*

mile to the east of Abbey station, curving sharply to the south and crossing the Black Drain, while the branch continued along on the north side, although turning slightly away from it. There was a level crossing over the Southery to Wereham road about a mile from Abbey station, with the railway continuing in a more or less straight line, to terminate just to the south of Stoke Ferry village, on the north side of the road bridge over the River Wissey.

There was relatively generous provision at the terminus. Again, there was the single platform, but this time with the station building and house part of the same structure, and fronting the platform. In passenger days a generous awning was provided. There was a locomotive siding and shed on the north side of the layout, with a water column, and the signalbox was located on this side, off the end of the platform. On the opposite side were the main goods facilities, with a goods shed with a through road, loading docks, cattle pens and other sheds; an old coach body also provided some accommodation. The running line and loop terminated in loading docks, running right up to Bridge Road. Most classes of traffic could be handled, and there was a 1½-ton crane, although horseboxes and carriage trucks could not.

Train services always worked between Downham Market and Stoke Ferry, the branch being operated on the one-engine-in-steam principle, by train staff without tickets. The staff was kept by the signalman at Denver, and Stoke Ferry was also a staff station. The 1913 train service provision was not particularly generous, although fairly complex. It started from Stoke Ferry at 7.15am, when there was a goods working to Abbey, arriving at 7.30am and calling at Keeble siding (the then designation for the Wissington line), which returned at 7.40am. On Tuesdays this was a train to Downham, calling at all stations on the branch, but not Denver, and it returned from there as a general goods at 8.20am. On other weekdays the first train along the branch was the 8.10am goods to Abbey, which returned from there at 8.45am. On Mondays

the 8.10am was a passenger train to Downham, arriving at 8.35 and returning at 8.44am. The first working to run every weekday was the 9.18am passenger from Stoke Ferry to Downham, which worked back mixed at 10.25am, followed by the 11.17am passenger, which could convey cattle from Stoke Ferry provided Westinghouse-braked trucks were used. Other trains from Stoke Ferry were at 1.53pm (mixed), 3.20pm (goods), 5.15pm (passenger but could work two braked trucks of goods) and 6.55pm (passenger, Wednesdays, Thursdays and Saturdays only). The service in the other direction was equally complex, with the last train back from Downham being the 6.49pm passenger on Mondays and Fridays, or 7.38pm on Wednesdays, Thursdays and Saturdays. Mixed trains were generally not allowed to work trucks from intermediate stations as they were for goods traffic between Downham and Stoke Ferry only. As ever, it paid passengers to seek out bargains for rail travel, and one perk enjoyed by members of the Cambridge and Ely Angling Society was the purchase of return tickets at the single-fare price to certain stations on production of their membership cards. Stoke Ferry was one such destination, with possible departures from Cambridge on weekdays at 8.54 and 10.45am, and 1.30, 4.6 (not Mondays) 5.47 or 6.49pm (not Mondays or Tuesdays). Return from Stoke Ferry could be at 8.10am (not Mondays, and presumably only for those who had stayed overnight), 9.18 and 11.15am, and 1.58 and 5.15pm, and 6.55pm (not Mondays or Tuesdays).

By 1922, the passenger service was simpler, with four trains in each direction, from Downham at 9.22 and 11.7am, and 2.23 and 5.56pm, plus another at 4.20pm on Tuesdays only. From Stoke Ferry they ran at 8.25 and 10.15am, and 1.34 and 5.15pm. In spite of the economies that had been made with the introduction of conductor-guard working in 1895, the service continued to lose money, and it was withdrawn from Monday 22 September 1930 which meant that Denver again closed to passengers at the same

Above:
Abbey for West Dereham, taken in about 1958, and showing the exchange sidings to the east of the station. *Adrian Vaughan collection*

Below:
Abbey station on 11 November 1952, with 'J17' No 65526 shunting the Wissington exchange sidings. *SLS Collection*

Above:
Abbey for West Dereham station. *Crown Copyright*

177

Above:
A view of Stoke Ferry station from the buffer stops in about 1910, with a train for Downham at the platform.
The goods shed is out of sight, behind the coach body, left. *Stations UK*

Below:
Stoke Ferry is host to an enthusiast excursion on 24 July 1955. *T. J. Edgington/SLS Collection*

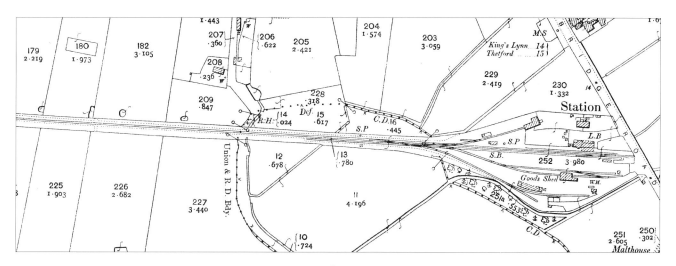

Above:
Stoke Ferry station, 1882. *Crown Copyright*

time. The line was converted to Light Railway status after it closed to passengers, following which the only gated level crossing was at Ryston station, and the speed limit was reduced to 25mph. Occasional enthusiasts' excursions ran, such as that by the Midland & Great Northern Society on 26 May 1962, which covered a number of freight-only lines as well as the Mildenhall branch. A goods service was maintained along the line, and in the 1964-5 timetable, the branch was served by the 10.30 from King's Lynn, 12.00 from Downham, calling at Ryston as required, and reaching Abbey at 12.35. It then shunted the exchange sidings, taking outward traffic on to Stoke Ferry, whence it returned at 13.45 direct to Downham. Denver closed on 13 July 1964, Ryston on 28 December 1964, and Stoke Ferry on 19 April 1965. Interestingly, the whole branch having been worked as one-engine-in-steam in passenger days, the

Denver to Abbey section later became staff-and-ticket, with only the final section confined to one-engine working. After Stoke Ferry closed the branch went back to one-engine status.

The Wissington Light Railway was a private concern constructed by Mr A. J. Keeble, without Act of Parliament, in 1905 in order to develop his estate in the Wissington, Methwold and Feltwell areas. The area had rich fenland soils and he felt that it was not cultivated as fully as possible because of poor transport facilities. The first section, from Abbey to Wissington and Methwold, was opened in 1906, with an extension to Feltwell later. The estate had several farms, and the railway had a number of loops and short sidings serving them, so that farmers had the least possible distance to cart their produce, which was mainly potatoes, celery and other root crops, and in later years sugar beet. Mr Keeble died

Left:
Downham Market on Saturday 20 September 1930, with No 7272 taking water prior to working a train to Stoke Ferry. This was the last day of regular passenger services on the branch.
Ian Allan Library/ Bucknall Collection

in 1914 and the railway was taken over by a Mr Towler. In 1924 British Sugar Manufacturers Ltd built a beet sugar factory on the south bank of the River Wissey, about 1½ miles south of Abbey station, and took over the light railway. Exchange sidings were provided at Abbey, with inward traffic being left there by the main line company for onward transit by the sugar company, and vice versa. British Sugar maintained the section of line to its factory, but the remainder was neglected, although the company carried other agricultural produce to Abbey station, as well as beet to its factory. Traffic on the line was worked by one 0-4-0 and four 0-6-0 tank engines.

The lease of the railway expired in March 1941 and the sugar corporation did not feel able to renew it. The Ministry of Agriculture therefore used emergency wartime powers to take it over and renovate it, and the line was formally reopened by the Minister on 21 July 1941, who then rode on one of the 0-6-0 saddle tanks. At this time there were about 18 miles of line, including loops, spurs and loading sidings in use, the track consisting of 60lb flat-bottom rails spiked to sleepers placed at 2ft 6in to 3ft apart, laid directly on the ground without ballast. The track was carried over waterways on 10 bridges consisting of rolled steel joists supported on timber piled abutments, with the one crossing over a county road on Methwold Fen being protected by cattle guards and warning signs on the road approaches. There was no signalling or telephones. Prior to the takeover the British Sugar Corporation worked its own traffic, continuing to work the line under contract afterwards as a haulage contractor. There were five tank locomotives in use: 1899-built 0-4-0 Hudswell, Clarke builder's No 533; 1909 0-6-0 Andrew Barclay No 1158; 1917 0-6-0 Manning, Wardle

No 1927; 1921 0-6-0 Manning, Wardle No 2006 and 1938 0-6-0 Hudswell, Clarke No 1700. The line was, however, managed by the LNER, with Mr W. McAuley Gracie appointed as Administrator by the Minister of Agriculture. The line was bought by the Ministry of Agriculture in 1947, the traffic in beet continuing to be heavy. This arrangement continued after the war, and in 1954-5 traffic on the line amounted to 19,512 tons, mainly sugar beet. However, in the middle of 1956, the Minister of Agriculture announced that his department could no longer justify the administration of the line, and that the current arrangements would end in a year's time; growers would be given first chance to take it over. At this stage, the locomotives presented a decidedly antiquated appearance, especially as they meandered along the track which could scarcely be seen for much of its length. The growers did not take up the offer to retain the line, and it was scheduled for closure on 30 June 1957, although the British Sugar Corporation considered retaining it between Abbey and its factory. This is what happened, and the line continued to operate over the remaining 1½ miles with the original locomotives, and became the last regular steam-operated service in East Anglia. Traffic continued to be heavy, to the extent that loaded trains from the factory had to be banked up to the exchange sidings. In 1964, the Norfolk Fen Drainage Scheme necessitated the provision of a brand-new bridge over one of the channels, which produced the incongruous sight of elderly saddle tanks hauling long trains of wagons over a bright, white concrete bridge. Well into the 1980s, long after Denver, Ryston and Stoke Ferry had closed, together with Abbey for public traffic, the line as far as the sugar factory continued to be the *raison d'être* for the Stoke Ferry branch.

Above:
The Wissington Light Railway served the beet sugar factory at Wissington,
having been an extensive system in the immediate area. Here, a train is crossing
the river near the factory. *W. A. Camwell/SLS Collection*

Above:
Andrew Barclay No 1158 *Ellesmere* seen at Wissington on 26 April 1953. *SLS Collection*

Stour Valley, Colne Valley and Long Melford to Bury

THE Stour Valley was an important East Anglian cross-country route that took a long time to reach its full extent, although it had been one of the earliest railway projects in the area. Despite its long stretches of single line it provided important links for goods, became busy on summer Saturdays with a variety of holiday trains to the Essex coastal resorts, and assumed strategic significance during World War 2. It made a number of connections along its length, and provided the backbone of a rural network whose absence from the present-day system is increasingly felt.

With the Eastern Counties line from London to Colchester under way, thoughts turned early on to connecting some of the many Essex and Suffolk towns to it, and the Stour Valley was an obvious line of communication. It linked a string of towns and villages, was a prosperous farming area and already had long-distance carriage of goods via the Stour Navigation. It was well known as an area of great natural beauty: it was Constable country. Colchester and the Colne ports also provided an important focus. The Colchester, Stour Valley, Sudbury & Halstead Railway, promoted in the company's bill deposited in 1845, was one of the first attempts to get rail communication going, and was quickly followed with another bill for the following session, deposited in November 1846.

The first, with Peter Bruff as its engineer, envisaged a line from Mark's Tey, where there would have been a triangular junction with the Eastern Counties main line. Interestingly, in the light of modern developments, the main line was considered to be the southern part of the triangle so that through running from London to Sudbury would have been possible, with the northern arm shown as the branch, going to Mark's Tey station. Sudbury station, just under 12 miles from Mark's Tey, would be at one apex of another triangular junction, the line from the other going on to Stowmarket and Norwich. It would have been difficult to extend the railway through the proposed terminal site in Sudbury, which turned out to be the case after the line had been built. Halstead (Halsted on the contemporary map) would have been reached by a branch about 8½ miles from Chappel. The bill also proposed an extension of 1½ miles from Colchester to the Hythe, which was the town's port, the two parts being connected by running powers over the Eastern Counties. This was the first section to be opened, on 1 April 1847, and helped stimulate development of the port and the Colne Navigation, as well as being the starting point for later lines to Walton, Brightlingsea and Clacton.

The next bill, for the 1846-7 session, proposed an extension of the original scheme to Melford, Lavenham and Clare. Schemes were being put forward for large numbers of lines. Maps showed the Ipswich & Bury's proposals to reach the latter, the same company's extension from Haughley to Norwich, with a triangular junction at Haughley, and the extension of the Eastern Union & Hadleigh Junction line to Lavenham and Bury. The lines proposed

in the new bill were one from Sudbury to Lavenham, where it would have met the line from Hadleigh, and a triangular junction at Melford, heading westwards to Cavendish and Clare. Already the problems at Sudbury were recognised, by the new line being shown as branching from the earlier proposals short of the terminus. Peter Bruff remained as engineer, with the surveyor being Mr W. H. Holland. In the event, these new powers were allowed to lapse, together with the Halstead branch. Construction of the line to Sudbury went ahead, and it opened from Mark's Tey on 2 July 1849. The Stour Valley company was then leased to the Eastern Union Railway at £5,387 per year, and was in turn worked by the Eastern Counties from 1854.

The original Stour Valley proposals for a Halstead branch had been in part to head off an Eastern Counties projection from Braintree, and neither was built. Meantime, the Colne Valley & Halstead company deposited its bill for the 1855 session for a line from Chappel & Wakes Colne to Halstead. It was to be 5 miles 5 furlongs and 3 chains in length, with a new single line running from Chappel station to the actual point of divergence just to the north. There were two bridges over the River Colne near Earls Colne and another near Halstead. Apart from a short section of 1 in 60 and ¾ mile at 1 in 80, gradients were very gentle. The engineers were Peter Bruff and N. Beardmore. Later, for the 1859 session the company deposited a further bill for an extension to Haverhill, and then on to Saffron Walden and Wenden, in other words, Audley End. The total length of line would then have been a shade over 25 miles. Work was already in progress, the first sod having been cut on 16 February 1858, but the section from Chappel to Halstead did not open until 16 April 1860. However, the extension to Haverhill was authorised on 13 August 1859, and work started the following year. Opening to (Castle) Hedingham followed on 26 May 1862 and Yeldham on 30 June, when the line onwards was said to be nearly finished. The CV&H was steadily progressing with its line to Haverhill, and at a meeting at the end of February 1863 confidently expected it to be open within eight weeks. It duly did so, on 10 May 1863, although the chairman had said that he did not expect the line to pay until it reached Cambridge! Earlier in that year the company was proposing its own extensions from Haverhill to Withersfield, west of Haverhill, to meet up with the Great Eastern, and at the same time was calling for abandonment of the GER's line to Haverhill, which had been authorised as part of its Act of Incorporation of August 1862. They also sought running powers to Cambridge.

People had been getting concerned about the lack of progress, and a public meeting to promote the railway from Sudbury and Long Melford was held in Clare Corn Exchange in July 1860, attended by over 200 people. On 12 October 1860, the *Ipswich Journal* reported that surveyors had started staking out the railway to Clare on the previous Saturday, and that it was believed that the line would be complete within the next 12 months.

Above:
**Class E4 2-4-0 No 62789 heads the 6.18pm Mark's Tey to Sudbury train on
Sunday 16 June 1957, nearing Chappel & Wakes Colne.** *G. R. Mortimer*

Little progress was being made on the Stour Valley line, and in November 1860 the Eastern Counties Railway deposited further plans for a number of associated projects. The Sudbury line was extended both to Bury St Edmunds via Lavenham, and to Shelford. At this time the only railway serving Newmarket was the branch from Six Mile Bottom to Cambridge, which was crossed at Balsham (then called Balsam). The line from Great Chesterford with its intermediate station at Bourne Bridge, which the Stour Valley was shown as crossing about there, had already been abandoned. The line from Sudbury to Shelford was to be just over 31 miles long, and the branch from Melford to Sudbury slightly over 16 miles. A further short section was proposed to connect with the Colne Valley at Haverhill.

When the line first opened to Sudbury, four passenger trains were provided from Mark's Tey on weekdays, and five from Sudbury. The 8.30am, 12.35pm, 4.10pm and 6.20pm up from Sudbury took between 27 and 35 minutes for the journey, and called at Bures and Chappel only when required, whereas the 9.10am called anyway. The best time to London was by the 4.10pm, which got its passengers there at 6.20pm, but about three hours was more usual. In the down direction there were trains at 10am, 1.25pm, 5.53pm and 7.35pm, only the first always stopping intermediately. The 4.25pm from London offered an arrival at Sudbury in just under two hours, at 6.20pm. Two years later, after the Colne Valley had opened its first section, all trains called at Chappel to provide connections with the new service to Yeldham,

although the last up did not have one. A Sunday service of two trains each way was provided, leaving Sudbury at 8.55am and 5pm, and Mark's Tey at 9.45am and 6.40pm.

Meanwhile, another railway was projected between Long Melford and Bury St Edmunds, and the Eastern Counties Railway was first authorised to build such a line in the 1861 session. Surveying was carried out during the latter part of 1860, which allowed the plans to be deposited in November of that year. Lavenham was to be the main intermediate station, the town being very keen to be linked to the rail network. Authorisation for the line was renewed for the Great Eastern in 1862, landowners already receiving preliminary notices in February that work was about to start. A particular benefit of the new line was felt to be that the distance between Bury St Edmunds and London would be substantially reduced, so that both journey times and fares could also be brought down. In 1862 the fares were first class 18s 0d, 2nd 14s 6d, 3rd 9s 8d and parliamentary 7s 1½d, and since they were calculated on a strict mileage basis, the opening of the new line would bring them down respectively to 16s 0d, 12s 9d, 8s 6d and 6s 5d.

By early 1863 construction was well under way. At Lavenham the fences were in place and a wooden house had been erected for the director of works. Earth was being dug near Bury for the contractors to make bricks, and new kilns were to be erected at the brick works at Lavenham belonging to Mr Mumford. Progress was slow on building the new lines, although the Saffron Walden Railway was projected in 1863 to make a junction with it at

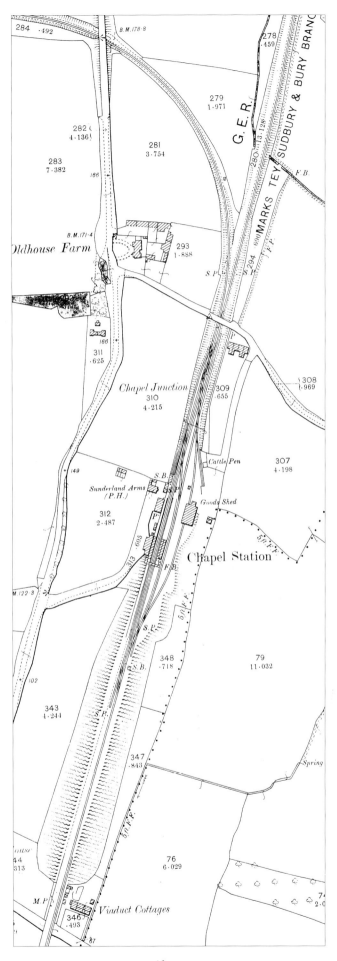

Above:
Chappel station, 1897. *Crown Copyright*

Bartlow. The Stour Valley itself at last opened between Shelford and Haverhill on 1 June 1865, but a serious accident occurred on the remaining unopened portion at Melford in mid-July. A large number of workmen employed by Thomas Brassey, the contractor for both the lines to Bury and Haverhill, were involved in bringing ballast from Clare to Sudbury with trucks and an engine, doing about eight journeys daily. The procedure was to draw the full train to Sudbury, and then propel back to Clare. On Saturdays they finished at about 4pm, but the engine driver worked later. On one Saturday, the last train from Sudbury passed Melford at between 4.10 and 4.15pm, the points being set, scotched and checked by gangman Brown. The train was being propelled back at 10-20mph, with about 20 men in the trucks. However, the points were not set correctly, and the 'guard' cried out, whereupon the engine was reversed. Too late: the trucks rode up over the points, and there was a violent collision with other stationary trucks. Some men jumped clear, but others still on the train were crushed. The locomotive was derailed, which prevented further damage. Three men were killed, and others were released by those who had jumped clear. All the men were local, from villages such as Clare, Pentlow, Wickhambrook, Belchamp and so on.

The lines between Sudbury and Haverhill, and Sudbury and Bury were finally opened on Wednesday 9 August 1865. The first train with passengers left Bury at 7.35am and reached Sudbury in time to connect with the express and parliamentary up trains. The *Bury Free Press* hoped that the inhabitants of Clare and district would not only be able to reach the market at Bury but also be able to get back the same day. At the time, the Bury branch was described as having a good road, and a pleasant journey, although the stations were not yet finished. On the opening day there were fireworks in Lavenham's market place, Mr Hitchcock entertained a very large party there, and Lavenham generally was very lively. Bury, however, seems to have shown very little interest.

From having no rail provision, Haverhill suddenly had lines to Sudbury, Cambridge and Colchester, with two stations and companies providing the services. Long Melford became a junction. The main line between Colchester and Cambridge, opened by the Eastern Union (as successors to the Ipswich & Bury) to Bury St Edmunds on 20 November 1846, and thence to Newmarket on 1 April 1854 by the Eastern Counties Railway, always provided a better route between the two in terms of engineering and possible speeds. It was largely built as a double-track main line, with the exception of Newmarket Tunnel, whereas the Stour Valley — although constructed with a double-track formation — never had the second line added.

Although following river valleys for most of their course, the lines nevertheless had to contend with some severe gradients. From Chappel the Stour Valley line crosses a ridge between the Colne and Stour Valleys — one of the most spectacular engineering feats in East Anglia carries the line across the river on Chappel Viaduct. It drops rapidly down to Bures, and then follows the Stour almost to Sturmer, where it again climbs out of a valley and crosses the watershed into the next, of the River Granta, whose company it then keeps to Shelford. In the meantime, the Colne Valley line, having followed its river as far as Yeldham, then has to reach Haverhill by again crossing the watershed between the Colne and Stour rivers.

The Stour Valley line leaves the Colchester to Liverpool Street main line at Mark's Tey, the only junction facing Colchester and thus allowing through running from that town. Branch trains at Mark's Tey use a curved platform at the back of the down main platform, the two fitting into the vee of the junction. The line curves sharply away to the north, soon going on to an embankment and quickly past a tramway and siding into a brick and tile works. The junction here was on the east side of the line, the tramway then turning sharply and crossing under the line to the works on the west

Above:
A Great Eastern view of Chappel & Wakes Colne, looking north. The junction from the Colne Valley is beyond the station to the north, and the viaduct behind the camera.
Lens of Sutton

Left:
Chappel on a cold winter's day, with an up train arriving.
David Lawrence

side. The main line crosses the Roman River before climbing in a long cutting, then after a short level section drops down towards the River Colne. The line is carried over the river and Halstead road on the 32-arch brick-built Chappel Viaduct, 75ft high at its greatest, and giving fine views of the valley. Chappel & Wakes Colne station is just to the north, 3 miles 38 chains from Mark's Tey.

The running line was on the up side of the formation, while the main station buildings were on the down. Trains for Sudbury therefore crossed over to the down side, there being a headshunt running back towards the viaduct, which was later extended to form a siding for oil tank wagons. Built of red brick, the buildings look, from platform level, as if they are single-storey when in fact they go well below because of the way the station site had been created. Approached from the south on a high embankment, both lines were in cutting beyond, while the down platform remains perched high above the approach road, and passengers reached the booking office by means of a substantial flight of steps. However, only a few yards further on, at the Sudbury end of the platform, there is an almost level exit once leading to the Sunderland Arms pub. The pub is no longer there, although the exit remains.

The goods yard was on the up side, and had a large goods shed with through road, cattle pens and loading dock. The station was able to handle all classes of traffic, and had a 1½-ton crane available. There were originally signalboxes at both ends of the layout, one just beyond the end of the down platform and controlling the junction with the Colne Valley line, and the other between the exit from the yard at the Colchester end, and the loop points. A footbridge was provided immediately to the south of the platform buildings.

The pointwork at the north end of the station was complex, so that both Stour Valley and Colne Valley trains could leave from and arrive at the appropriate platform. Trains also had to gain access to the goods yard, and there was also a refuge siding accessible from the Colne Valley line and running back to the Junction signalbox. Sudbury trains continue straight ahead and start on a climb over the watershed between the Colne and Stour rivers, at first on an embankment, but then for nearly two miles in a deep cutting. Once over the summit, it falls steeply at about 1 in 90 towards Mount Bures level crossing, and down to Bures station. This was a token station, but could not pass passenger trains because it had

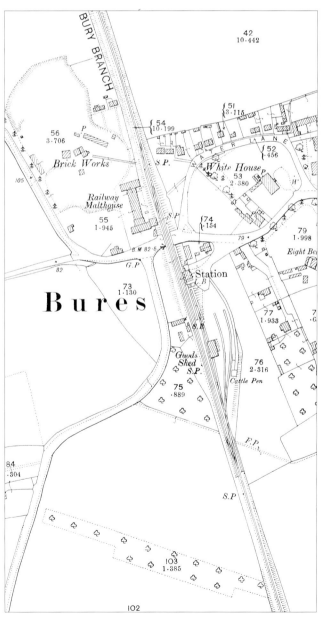

only one platform. The original CSVS&HR structure survived many years and was still standing in the 1950s. The line is still in Essex at this point, the station being in Bures Hamlet, Bures itself being on the Suffolk side of the river. The goods yard, goods shed and cattle pens were on the up side of the line, with rail access at the Colchester end of the station. In 1938 Bures forwarded 597 tons of timber.

The passenger platform and station building were on the east side of the line, reached by a steep approach which branches off the road from Bures Bridge, which then goes under the railway. The buildings were of three floors, partly because of the nature of the site, and retained the belfry which had once housed the train arrival bell. There was a large malthouse on the west side of the line at the Sudbury end, with a brickworks beyond this. The signalbox was on the down side, opposite the Colchester end of the platform. Cross & Garrods and Grimston & Co both had sidings at the station, which could handle all classes of traffic except furniture vans, carriages and portable engines; it had a 1½-ton crane. Outward goods traffic was mainly grain and livestock, 2,308 and 130 tons respectively being handled in 1938.

Having now picked up the Stour Valley, the line continues to fall beyond the station for a further mile or so, crossing the river and county border into Suffolk, about 2½ miles from Bures. It stays close to the river and its parallel road between Bures and Sudbury, passing Cornard to the east, and reaching Sudbury station just over 4¾ miles from Bures. As hinted earlier, it had been impossible to extend the railway through the original station which was turned over to goods usage, and the extension to Long Melford started from Sudbury Goods Junction. The new passenger station, built on a sharp curve on the new alignment, opened with the extension to Haverhill on 9 August 1865. The junction between the old and the new lines was controlled by Sudbury Goods Junction signalbox, with the station box at the western end of the layout. This was abolished in 1932 and all work concentrated on the former. There were two passenger platforms, linked by a covered footbridge, with the main buildings in typical Great Eastern style on the north, or up side (to Mark's Tey). Accommodation for the stationmaster and his family was in a substantial brick-built house at the Haverhill end, with the single-storey office buildings adjacent. Substantial awnings were provided on both sides. A siding ran behind the down platform which formed a loop. There was a loading dock at the up

Left:
When the line from Mark's Tey was extended to Long Melford and beyond, Sudbury's old station was turned over to goods use. Here it is many years later.
Ian Allan Library/ LGRP

Below:
Sudbury station, 1926.
Crown Copyright

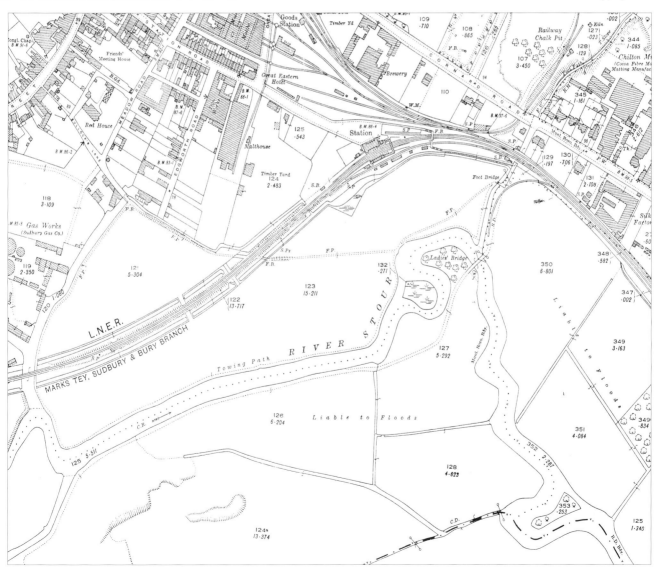

Right:
The approach to Sudbury passenger station in Great Eastern days.
Lens of Sutton

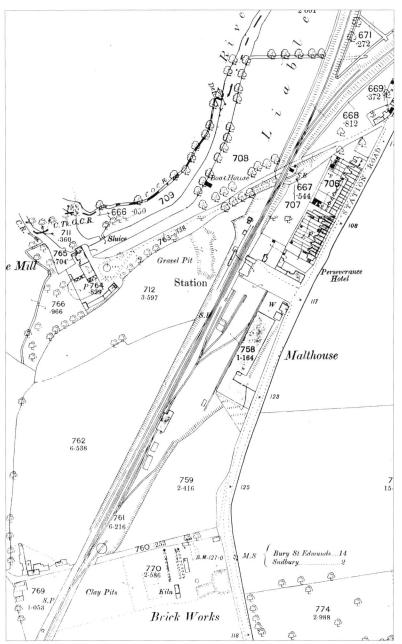

end of the up platform, and another footbridge carrying a footpath over the tracks at the east end of the passenger station. This then went down behind the Goods Junction signalbox to a small cut off the river which was also served, at least until the 1920s, by a short siding. There was much industry around the railway. Station Road had been extended from the Great Eastern Hotel towards the new station and had a timber yard on the left, looking towards the town, a malthouse straight ahead, served by a siding from the goods station which crossed the approach road, an iron works behind that, and a brewery on the right-hand side beyond the goods station. The gasworks and electricity supply station were a short distance away. The railway also served a chalk pit with a siding from the Goods Junction, and there was a coconut matting factory nearby. The goods station itself had many sidings, plus a number crossing Great Eastern Road, which ran across the end, serving various industries such as maltings. Another siding running parallel to this road connected many of the others by means of wagon turntables. As might be expected from the number of maltings, Sudbury shipped substantial amounts of grain and malt, amounting to 2,308 tons in 1938, plus 130 tons of livestock.

Having turned through well over 90° from its approach, the line now skirted the southwest corner of the town on a series of bridges or embankments, crossing the river about three-quarters of a mile west of the station and back into Essex. It then swung round sharply to the north, crossing the main Halstead road in so doing. With the river to the east, it crossed the Sudbury to Cavendish road at Rodbridge level crossing, and then over the river and back into Suffolk almost at once on a long, low iron bridge. Long Melford station, right at the southern end of the main settlement, was a further

Left:
Long Melford junction, 1886.
Crown Copyright

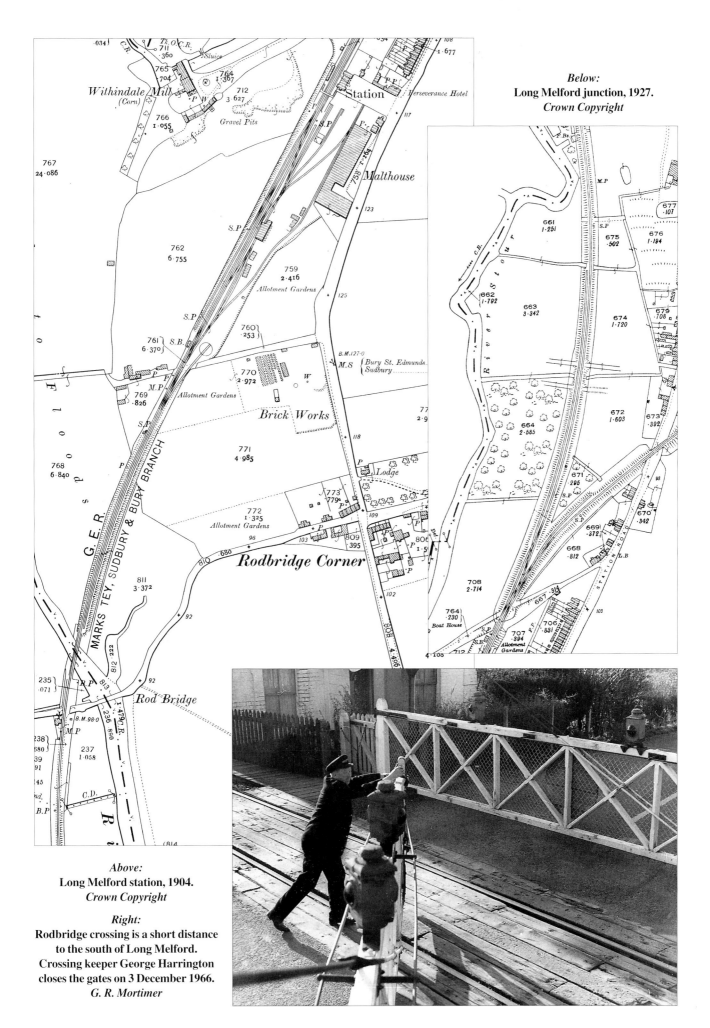

Below:
Long Melford junction, 1927.
Crown Copyright

Above:
Long Melford station, 1904.
Crown Copyright

Right:
**Rodbridge crossing is a short distance
to the south of Long Melford.
Crossing keeper George Harrington
closes the gates on 3 December 1966.**
G. R. Mortimer

Above:
Ex-Great Northern 4-4-2 No 67367 Class C12 stands at Long Melford with
a train from Bury St Edmunds in the 1950s. *Real Photographs*

Below:
An elevated view of the junction at Long Melford, which clearly shows the line to Lavenham, even though the track
has been lifted. The 10.55am Cambridge to Sudbury approaches on 21 January 1957. *G. R. Mortimer*

half a mile on. Immediately to the north was the double junction between the Haverhill and Bury St Edmunds lines, controlled by Long Melford Junction signalbox, just off the Haverhill end of the down platform, although there had also been another — Long Melford Yard — until the 1920s.

The approach to the station was from the east side, and the main buildings were on this side. A combination of red and white brick with slate roofs, the station house was towards the north end and at right-angles to the line, with a single-storey extension parallel to the platform housing the booking office and other facilities. On the down platform was a large, single-storey building, mostly a waiting room but with toilets at the end. There was a large iron water tank on a brick base behind the down platform, which supplied columns at the ends of both platforms. The yard was on the up side, and was reached from the main station approach road; a 1½-ton crane was available, and Long Melford could handle all classes of traffic. Stafford, Allen & Sons had a siding between the station and Glemsford, traffic usually being worked to and from Long Melford. The goods shed adjoined the up loop and, most unusually, the up advanced starter signal was bracketed out from the wall. There was a loading dock behind the up platform, and further sidings in the yard. There was also a refuge on the down side capable of holding 38 wagons; the main loop could hold 40.

Beyond the junction, the line started to swing gently to the west, following the curve of the River Stour. Sharford crossing, over the minor road to Liston, had a substantial house for the crossing keeper. Briefly passing back into Essex, the line was soon back in Suffolk and reached Glemsford station about 2½ miles beyond the junction. There was only a single platform here, and the signalbox was not a block post. Glemsford is rather a straggling village along the road to Stanstead and Boxted, and the station was not particularly conveniently situated. The minor road to Foxearth passed over the level crossing. Only passenger, parcels and ordinary goods traffic could be handled, but the usual 1½-ton crane was provided.

A further 1¼ miles brought the line to Cavendish, which was a block post, and had two platforms and a small goods yard. The station was very well placed near the centre of the village, with the road to Foxearth and Sudbury going over the level crossing at the west end. The main station buildings were on the up platform, on

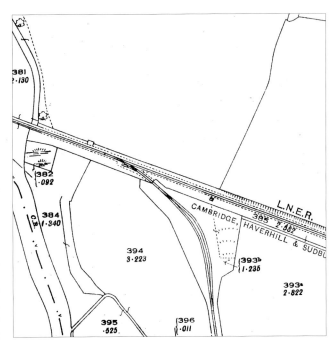

Above:
Stafford, Allen & Sons siding, 1926. *Crown Copyright*

the village side, with a shelter on the other platform similar to that at Long Melford. The station could handle all classes of traffic, but there was no fixed crane.

Clare was just under 2¾ miles further, the line having again briefly passed into Essex and back on the way. The line approached the station in a cutting, which was constructed more or less in the grounds of the castle. The station had two platforms, and was also a passing place and block post, with a number of sidings. It could also handle all classes of traffic and had the usual 1½-ton crane. There was a large goods shed on the down side, with grain being one of the main outward traffics. The main buildings were on the up side, and to a similar pattern to those at Long Melford; again, there was a similar waiting room on the other platform.

Having been almost level all the way from Sudbury, the line then had a couple of short stretches of 1 in 88 as it started to rise towards Stoke, two miles from Clare, and there was another brief incursion into Essex on this stretch. Another single-platform station, the LNER felt it necessary to designate it Stoke (Suffolk) from June 1932, although it lost the suffix in 1965 not long before it closed. It was not a block post, but had an intermediate token instrument, which allowed the sidings to be operated and a goods train shunted clear if necessary. The signalbox had been abolished in 1931. Beyond Stoke the line crossed the main road to Haverhill and ran in a mixture of cuttings and embankments past the village of Wixoe, to the south of the line, and across the River Stour for the last time, back into Essex. Here it left the

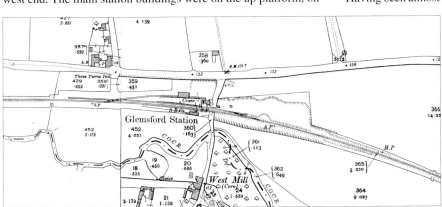

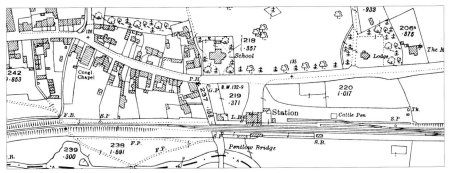

Above left:
Glemsford station, before 1927.
Crown Copyright

Left:
Cavendish station, 1927.
Crown Copyright

191

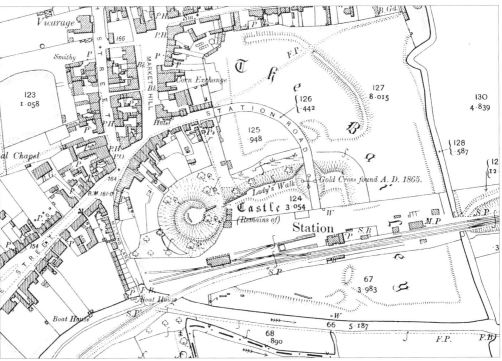

Above:
Clare station was in the grounds of the castle. Here, young passengers await a Cambridge train in October 1966.
P. Hocquard

Right:
Clare station, 1904.
Crown Copyright

Above:
**A spotless Brush Type 2 No D5524 and coaches hurry between Clare and Cavendish
on a local working in October 1966.** *P. Hocquard*

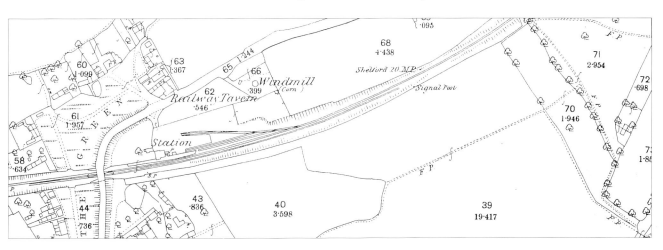

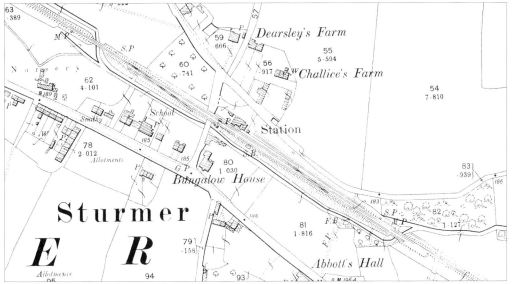

Above:
Stoke station, 1887.
Crown Copyright

Left:
Sturmer station, 1904.
Crown Copyright

Left:
The exterior of Haverhill North station from the approach road, about 1950. *Ian Allan Library/LGRP*

Below:
Haverhill North station, 1904. *Crown Copyright*

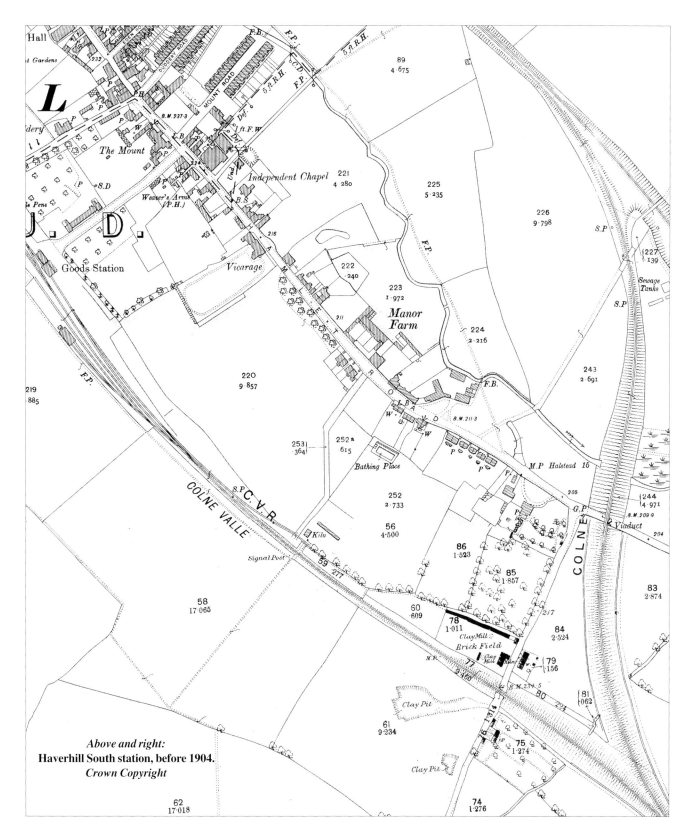

Above and right:
Haverhill South station, before 1904.
Crown Copyright

river, which turned northwards, the railway continuing in a general westerly direction and climbing out of the valley. It was close to the main road, reaching Sturmer, three miles from Stoke and two from Haverhill. Another single-platform station with an intermediate token instrument, there had once been a signalbox (abolished in 1931) opposite the platform, where there was a loop and sidings. Another siding ran behind the platform from the Sudbury end. The station could handle all traffic except livestock, but had no crane.

The line continued to climb away from Sturmer, sometimes as steeply as 1 in 82, crossing back into Suffolk just before reaching Haverhill and the junction with the Colne Valley line. The two single lines ran parallel for a short distance, before becoming the up and down roads through the station via a scissors crossover. There was a small engine shed at Haverhill, which survived at least until the 1950s.

Haverhill's Great Eastern or North station had an extensive goods yard on the down side of the line; this was on the south side, nearest the town, and at the Sudbury end of the layout. There was a large brick-built goods shed, plus a double-sided loading dock and cattle pens. There were also substantial coal sidings. There were further sidings on the Cambridge side of the station beyond the bridge taking the Bury St Edmunds road under the railway, on both sides of the running line, and also reached via a scissors crossover. The signalbox was at the Sudbury end, opposite the goods shed, although there was once another (Haverhill Station) at the Cambridge end. The train staff-and-ticket system on the sections between Bartlow, Haverhill and Clare was abolished in 1931 when it was replaced by tablet working. There was a water tank on a brick base off the end of the down platform at Haverhill, serving cranes at the ends of each platform. As might be expected, the station could deal with all classes of traffic, and had the usual 1½-ton crane. Other goods traffic was handled at the Colne Valley station, which had become Haverhill South when both were renamed by the LNER soon after its formation. One of the main outward traffics from the North station was meat, with 4,400 tons being despatched in 1938, together with much smaller amounts of livestock, hay and straw.

An unfortunate accident happened at Haverhill in the winter of 1919. A Great Eastern train for Cambridge was leaving the station in a snowstorm and was derailed, telescoping two first-class coaches. Mr Jarvis, a retired builder from Clare, was killed, although a daughter travelling in the compartment with him was extricated, badly shaken, after rescuers smashed through the wooden bodywork. Other passengers escaped with slight injuries. The train pushed the buffers of one of the sidings for about 20 yards.

Leaving Haverhill and continuing westwards, the line crossed the ridge separating the valleys of the rivers Stour and Granta. The first short stretch was level, followed by a climb for about 1½ miles to the summit, passing Withersfield public siding on the way. It was about a mile from the village of the same name and had closed on 1 January 1937, but reopened on 1 November 1943. Before the introduction of tablet working there had been a signalbox there, which was replaced by a ground frame released by the tablet. After crossing the main Cambridge road almost on the county border, the line then descended at 1 in 80 towards Bartlow, six miles from Haverhill, the station being approached through the Bartlow Hills, a group of tumuli to the south of the village. The station had two platforms and was a crossing place, the main buildings being on the down side. There was a down refuge at the Haverhill end of the station able to hold 40 wagons, plus a loading dock behind the Cambridge end of the down platform. The signalbox was at the junction with the Saffron Walden line, and in common with others, the station had had another (Bartlow Station), abolished in the cuts of the 1920s and '30s. Saffron Walden trains had their own platform linked to the main station by a footpath. The pattern of the station buildings was essentially similar to those elsewhere on the extension, with the two-storey house at right-angles to the line, a single-storey building beyond that, and linked by a section parallel to the platform and housing the booking office and waiting area, with a large glazed area facing the platform. There was a much more modest shelter on the up platform.

The line continued on gentle gradients along the Granta Valley towards Linton, two miles from Bartlow, where the station had two platforms and was a block post and passing place. The station was

Below:
Bartlow, junction for Saffron Walden. 'B17' No 61613 *Woodbastwick Hall* **passes through eastbound on 23 August 1963 carrying express headcode discs.** *Hugh Davies*

196

Above:
Haverhill North on 9 September 1961, with the departing 9.48am Colchester to Cambridge.
There were sidings on both sides of the line beyond the bridge. *M. Edwards*

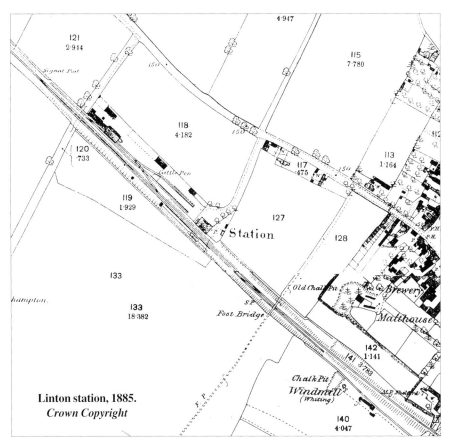

Linton station, 1885.
Crown Copyright

close to the village, a little to the south-west, with the main buildings on the north side of the line and of the usual pattern, together with cattle pens and loading docks. There was a large goods shed at the Cambridge end of the layout, also on the up side, Linton despatching substantial amounts of vegetables and some timber. The loop was long, holding 33 wagons in the down and 35 in the up direction, with a shorter down refuge. There was a pit on the down side at the Haverhill end of the layout, which produced agricultural chalk; there was also a brewery and malthouse close to the station. A further 2¾ miles on was Pampisford station — Abington until 1 May 1875 — which was situated immediately to the west of the Icknield Way, this part of which is now the A11 trunk road, the station being where the Stour Valley line crossed the abandoned Newmarket & Chesterford line near Bourne Bridge. There were two platforms with a loading dock and cattle pens behind the up, and the usual style of station buildings. The signalbox was abolished in 1946 and the down platform became disused. Shelford Junction was about four miles away, where there was a restriction of 15mph

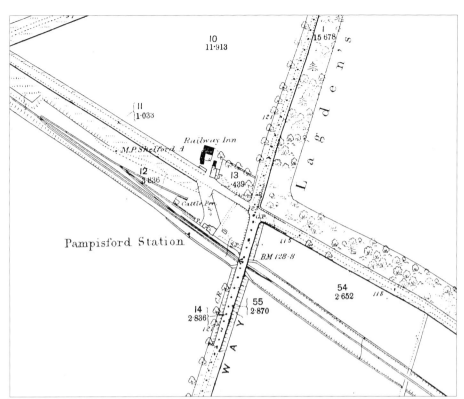

Below:
Linton on Saturday 23 July 1966, with the driver of the 14.00 Clacton to Leicester, with No D5656, about to exchange tablets, while a train for Haverhill and Colchester waits in the other platform. *G. R. Mortimer*

Above:
Class B1 No 61371 slows for the junction at Shelford with an excursion to Clacton on 25 June 1961. *Michael Fox*

through the curve to and from the main line. All trains worked through to or from Cambridge, just over three miles further.

The Colne Valley line curved sharply westwards to the north of Chappel & Wakes Colne station, following the river which the Stour Valley line had just crossed. The section to White Colne, two miles long, involved some stiff gradients, with down trains to Haverhill facing stretches at 1 in 70 and 1 in 60, and up trains about half a mile at 1 in 60 and three-quarters of a mile at 1 in 70-80. Known when it first opened as Colne, the station closed on 1 May

1889 and reopened for goods traffic in 1907, and for passengers on 1 April 1908 as White Colne. It had a single platform, a goods shed, loading docks and cattle pen. The old single-storey station building was by the level crossing, and in later years passenger facilities were housed in an old coach body on the platform.

Earls Colne was 1½ miles further on. When opened, the station was called Ford Gate, becoming Colne when the original closed, and Earls Colne in 1905, supposedly to avoid confusion with Calne in Wiltshire and Colne in Lancashire. The single platform, characteristic of all Colne Valley stations, was on the south side of the line, with a level crossing at the west end; although a block post, it had a short goods loop only, capable of taking only nine wagons. The station buildings were among the most substantial on the line, all of brick, with a large house on the platform and a single-storey booking office and other facilities adjoining it. There was a brick-built waiting room with awning nearer to the level crossing, and between these was the signalbox. The goods shed was also a substantial wooden structure, and there were sidings, loading docks and cattle pens. In addition to the usual traffic through a rural station, Earls Colne despatched

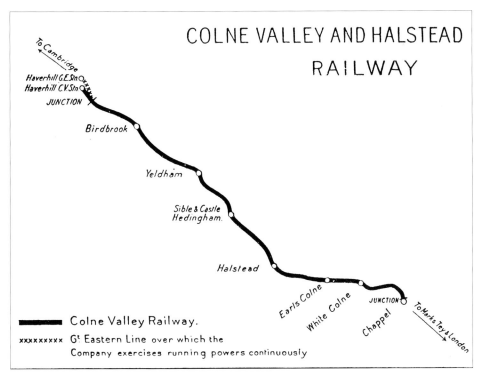

COLNE VALLEY AND HALSTEAD RAILWAY

To Cambridge
Haverhill G.E.Stn
Haverhill C.V.Stn
JUNCTION
Birdbrook
Yeldham
Sible & Castle Hedingham.
Halstead
Earls Colne
White Colne
JUNCTION
Chappel
To Marks Tey & London

——— Colne Valley Railway.
xxxxxxxx Gᵗ Eastern Line over which the Company exercises running powers continuously

Left:
Colne Valley Railway.
The Railway Magazine

Right:
White Colne, showing the original buildings and the level crossing at the east end of the station. *Stations UK*

a substantial tonnage of machinery from Messrs Hunt's works, amounting to 1,348 tons in 1938. This was valuable traffic, worth £2,904 to the LNER.

Halstead, headquarters of the independent company, was 2½ miles away. A thriving market town of some 7,000 people at the turn of the century, the station had extensive sidings, a large goods shed, cattle pens and loading docks, plus the other facilities for the upkeep of the company's stock. These included carriage, wagon and locomotive repair shops, smithy, a pumping station for the company's own water supply, general office and stores, a granary and three stables for shunting and local cartage horses. The company also had its general offices there. A long footbridge spanned the site, connecting Factory Lane West and King's Road, and crossed 10 tracks. There were originally signalboxes at both ends of the layout and a level crossing at the Haverhill end. Industries at Halstead included Courtauld's silk mills, Portway's foundry, Clover Ltd, millers, tanners Hugh Brown & Co and many other smaller concerns.

Sible & Castle Hedingham station was a further 3½ miles, and

had also undergone changes of name during its existence. It opened as Castle Hedingham, became simply Hedingham for a time, and then gained its full title in September 1867. The station had a small, single-storey building on the platform, with a narrow awning. The wooden goods shed was very much larger, and the substantial brick-built signalbox was beyond that. The crossing loop was long, holding 35 wagons, and the station was a block post, although again there was only a single platform. There were extensive brickworks at Hedingham, served by private sidings, and Ripper's steam joinery works adjacent to the station also had its own rail connection.

Yeldham was 2½ miles away, also with a level crossing, this time with the signalbox at the crossing. A collection of assorted low buildings was spread along the platform, and then the wooden-sided goods shed (with brick ends) which backed on to it. The goods loop was opposite, together with loading dock and water tank. Birdbrook had a lesser assortment of buildings, and no loop. The goods shed was off the Halstead end of the platform, with the signalbox almost opposite. The station was not a block post. There

Left:
The first station along the Colne Valley after it diverged from the Stour Valley at Chappel was White Colne, which had rather basic passenger facilities. It is seen here with a diesel-hauled freight arriving on a very wet day. *David Lawrence*

Left:
Earls Colne was a substantial station with imposing buildings. This view is looking towards Chappel in 1960. *Stations UK*

Below:
Earls Colne station, 1897. *Crown Copyright*

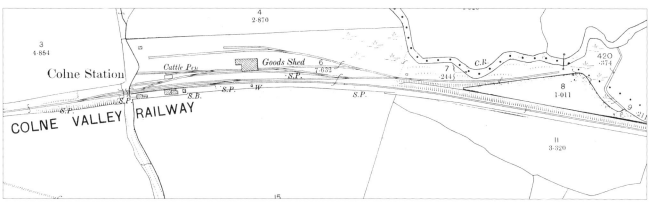

Below:
Halstead had been the headquarters of the independent Colne Valley & Halstead Railway, and it had extensive facilities for conducting most railway work. Here Class 2 No 46467 shunts at the station. *David Lawrence*

201

Above:
Halstead, looking towards Haverhill in 1955.
Stations UK

Below:
Halstead station, c1897. *Crown Copyright*

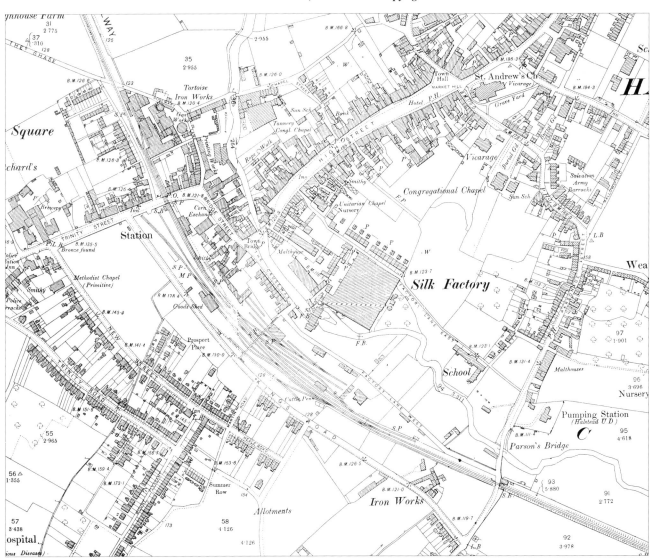

Above:
**Yeldham station, with
a fairly ramshackle
set of buildings on its
single platform.**
David Lawrence

Left:
**Sible & Castle
Hedingham station,
with the nameboard
a most prominent
feature.**
David Lawrence

was a cattle pen and loading dock, plus stores and other sidings on the north side of the line.

It was then a little over three miles to the Colne Valley station at Haverhill. At Colne Valley Junction there had originally been a signalbox, replaced later by an auxiliary token instrument. Until 1911 the junction was protected by four signal arms, two for each direction, carried on posts above the signalbox, with two double-faced lamps serving the arms. They were replaced by conventional semaphores in 1911. From the start, few passenger trains were run from the CV&H station (South from 1 February 1925), most going to or from the Great Eastern's station, later Haverhill North. It retained a passenger platform until formally closed on 14 July 1924, the last train of the day in the 1923 timetable terminating there since it had no connections with Stour Valley services. From

Colne Valley Junction a single line curved northwards to meet the Stour Valley line, crossing the main road from Sudbury on a high viaduct just before reaching it.

The Stour Valley line kept to the west of Long Melford, with the station at the southern end of the village. Beyond the junction it swung round to the west, following the valley, while the line to Lavenham and Bury continued in a northeasterly direction, passing to the southeast of the village. It very soon crossed the main road to Bury and then continued to climb, passing behind the village. It then picked up the course of the Chad Brook, a tributary of the Stour, and continued to climb through Lineage Wood and a long cutting of nearly a mile on its way to Lavenham, which lay to the south of the railway.

About 5¼ miles from Long Melford, Lavenham boasted a

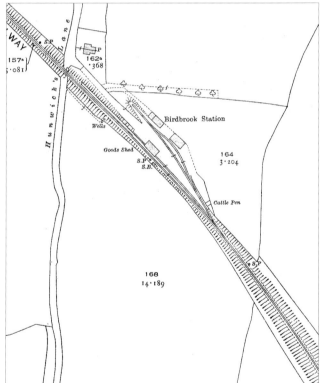

substantial station with two platforms and a sizeable goods yard.
There were loading docks behind the main up platform, together
with the substantial brick-built goods shed and stores for local feed
merchants. The station could handle all classes of traffic, and had a
1 ton 2cwt crane. The station buildings were very similar in style
and layout to others on the Stour Valley line, the stationmaster's
house being a two-storey structure, linked by the single-storey
booking office and waiting area to a further single-storey building
housing the toilets. On the down platform was a substantial brick-
built shelter with glazed front, again incorporating toilets. The
signalbox was at the Bury end of the up platform which had been
extended towards it. The station was a block post and the only one
between Long Melford and Bury able to pass passenger trains.
There were bridges taking roads over the line at both ends of the
layout. Lavenham had had the oldest works in England for the
manufacture of sugar from beet, although it had closed by 1884.
There was also a coconut matting factory at the end of the 19th
century. A serious accident happened near Lavenham on Saturday,
17 October 1891. The 4.5pm from Bury to Sudbury had left Lavenham and was near Lineage Wood, about two miles away. The train
was described as jumping and oscillating, and the engine left the
rails and turned over, landing chimney-down in a field. The five
coaches — a brake, first class, second class and two third class —
were thrown down the embankment which was about 20ft high at
this point. There were only eight passengers on the train, and all
escaped without serious injury, although the driver, Fred Harvey of
Bury, and the guard, George Rampling of Sudbury, were both badly
injured. The driver was taken by train to hospital in Sudbury, where
there were fears for his life. Breakdown trains arrived on Saturday
evening under the direction of Mr J. Flower, district superintendent,

and Mr G. H. Jones, district engineer. Work continued throughout
Sunday, and the line was cleared by Monday. The immediate cause
of the accident was not clear, the line having been relaid four
years previously with 80lb/yd steel rails. Passengers on passing
trains were treated to the spectacle of the large engine lying on its
side with two of its six wheels broken off, and the carriages lying
apparently undamaged on the other side of the line. The relative
lack of injuries was attributed to the effectiveness of the
Westinghouse automatic brake on the carriages, which had
immediately locked the wheels.

Beyond Lavenham the line curved around to the north again, and

Left:
Lavenham station is framed by the overbridge at the Long Melford end of the layout; the architecture is characteristic of this group of lines.
Ian Allan Library/LGRP

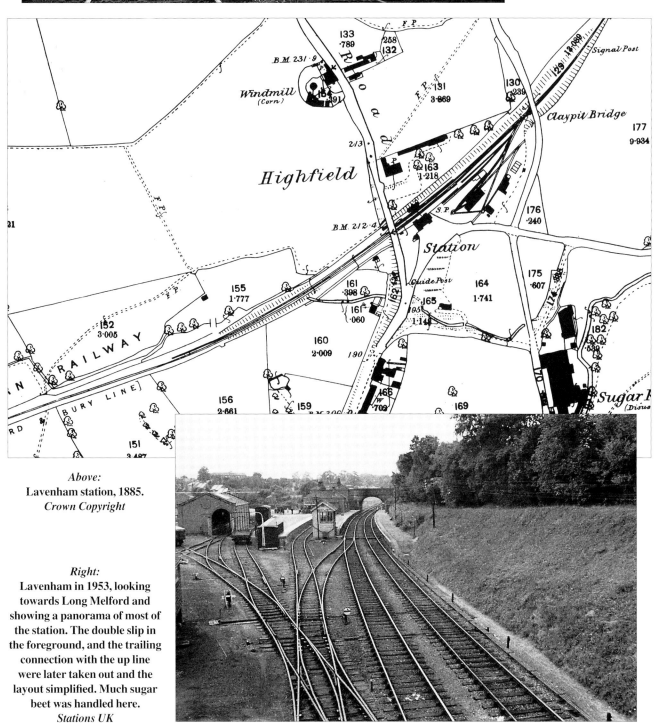

Above:
Lavenham station, 1885.
Crown Copyright

Right:
Lavenham in 1953, looking towards Long Melford and showing a panorama of most of the station. The double slip in the foreground, and the trailing connection with the up line were later taken out and the layout simplified. Much sugar beet was handled here.
Stations UK

A Long Melford to Bury train arrives at Lavenham in 1961, shortly before closure to passengers. *Stations UK*

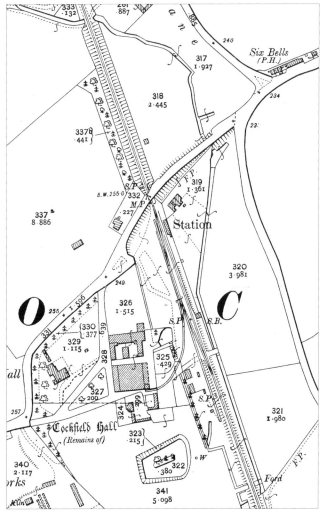

Above:
Cockfield station, 1904. *Crown Copyright*

then ran close to the main road to Bury St Edmunds, now the A1141 and A134. The railway had also been following the River Brett, another Stour tributary, to a point shortly beyond Cockfield, itself 3¼ miles from Lavenham. The station was renamed Cockfield (Suffolk) on 1 October 1927, to avoid confusion with Cockfield in County Durham, and this duly appeared on the station nameboards. Cockfield had a single platform and was unusual in that the station building was a single-storey brick structure similar to those on the secondary platforms elsewhere. Perhaps because of the pressure on space, the gents' toilet was housed in a brick-built extension, although there was also, further along the platform, a cast-iron urinal. There was a road bridge over the tracks at the north end of the station, and access for both passengers and vehicles was from the west side. This meant that passengers had to reach the booking office and platform by means of a barrow crossing over the track. A goods loop was opposite the platform at a greater distance than might have been expected, together with the loading dock, although the station could not handle livestock. A 1½-ton crane was available, and a siding ran from the south end of the station back into a brickworks in the grounds of Cockfield Hall. The signalbox was at the south end of the platform and was a block post, although passenger trains could not pass there.

Having passed the summit, the line started to fall towards Welnetham station, about equidistant between Great and Little Welnetham. Three miles from Cockfield, it had a single platform on the southwest side of the track, this time with the more typical style of buildings. Unusually, the station retained its ornate Great Eastern-style nameboard to the very end, when others had been replaced variously, ending with the Eastern Region blue enamel. This nameboard is now in the National Railway Museum. Welnetham had no crane, and could not handle livestock, but had a loading dock behind the platform with a siding extending towards Bury. It was one of the few where towing of wagons by rope was

Above:
**Cockfield (Suffolk) with a train for Colchester arriving from Bury on the last day of service in April 1961.
The station still looks smart and the gardens full of spring colour.** *Stations UK*

Below:
**Cockfield station looks very smart indeed in 1953, with colourful gardens and a fair amount
of goods to be loaded into the brake van of the approaching train. The unusual layout,
with most of the goods yard at the far end of the station, can be seen.** *Stations UK*

Above:
Welnetham in 1954, with 'J15' No 65391 at the head of a train to Long Melford. *Stations UK*

Below:
Welnetham station, with its famous nameboard which is now in the National Railway Museum.
It had only a single platform and was about equidistant from Great and Little Welnetham villages.
The goods yard is at the Bury end of the layout. *Stations UK*

permissible, since there was effectively no loop. The station was not a block post.

A short distance beyond Welnetham station the line passed into the valley of the River Lark, crossing it just north of Sicklesmere, and descended towards Bury St Edmunds. East Gate station, on the south side of Eastgate, and on the main road into the town from Diss, was about half a mile from the junction with the main line to Ipswich and served that side of the town, to the east of the River Lark. The main station was known as Northgate. East Gate had no goods facilities, although there was a siding there which was reached by points at the north end. The main hotels, such as the Suffolk, Angel and Everards, ran buses to and from both stations to meet all trains. East Gate had its own stationmaster, William Brooks, for example, serving for several years at the end of the 19th century, and the last being James Stevenson. The station closed on 1 May 1909, although the remains were visible for many years afterwards. Had proposals from the Bury & Thetford Railway been realised, the line might have crossed the Ipswich & Bury route to the east of the junction and provided a through route to Swaffham which would have avoided the main stations at both Bury and Thetford.

Passenger services were sparse at best on the Bury branch and by either the Stour or Colne Valley routes, although the latter company remained independent of the Great Eastern until both were incorporated into the LNER in 1923. The main route was regarded as being between Bury, Sudbury and Mark's Tey, and services were generally well co-ordinated between the lines. The opening

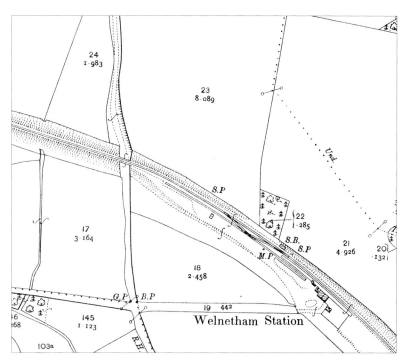

Above:
Welnetham station, 1904. *Crown Copyright*

timetable between Bury and Sudbury showed up trains (to Sudbury) at 7.35am, calling at Bury (Eastgate Street), Welnetham, Lavenham and Melford, and connecting with the 8.30am express to London, or the 8.55am Parliamentary. The 10.30am from Bury connected with the 9.45am from Cambridge at Melford, while the 3.20pm from Haverhill went through to Mark's Tey. The 5.20pm from Bury to Mark's Tey arrived there at 6.55pm, while the last (and only the second) up from Cambridge was the 6.52pm to Melford, which had no onward connections. Cockfield station was not open for passengers, the Great Eastern having had some doubt as to whether it was worth providing facilities at all. It was only thanks to a campaign by local people that a station was provided, and it finally opened in November 1870.

In the down direction there were trains from Melford to Cambridge at 7.45am, Mark's Tey at 10am, for both Bury and Cambridge, Mark's Tey to Bury at 1.25pm, Sudbury to Cambridge at 4.30pm, and Mark's Tey to Bury at 5.50pm. There were thus only two up and one down trains running the length of the Stour Valley line each weekday, and three in each direction between Long Melford and Bury. There were two trains each way between Bury and Mark's Tey on Sundays, and one between Melford and Cambridge, although they did not connect at all with each other.

In 1874 there were three trains on the Stour Valley line on weekdays, from Cambridge at 9.50am, 1.55pm and 7pm; Abington, Sturmer and Stoke were served only when required by some trains, and the 7pm went only as far as Sudbury. By 1913, things had improved and there were five up trains, from Cambridge at 8.58 and 10.40am, and 1.52, 4.47 and 7.12pm; all went through to Mark's Tey except the 4.47pm which terminated at Sudbury. In the down direction trains left Sudbury for Cambridge at 7.15am, and Mark's Tey at 9.15 and 11.15am, and 4.7 and 5.55pm. Empty stock for the 11.15am was worked out from Colchester at 10am. There were three trains each way on Sundays between Sudbury and Mark's Tey: down from Mark's Tey at 10.41am and 5.8 and 7.28pm, and up at 9.27am, and 4.30 and 5.57pm. This last was allowed to work two piped cattle wagons if required, and there were other goods trains if needed on Sundays. There was no Sunday service west of Sudbury, although Haverhill could be reached via the Colne Valley line, which had trains at 10.55am and

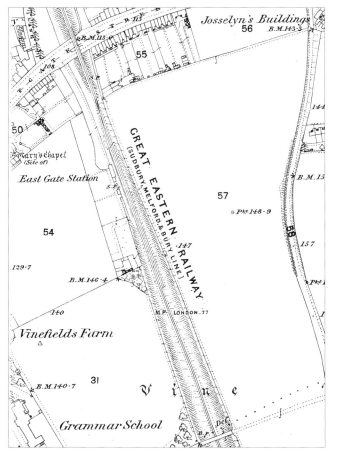

Below:
Bury East Gate station, 1886. *Crown Copyright*

209

BURY AND SUDBURY RAILWAY.

FROM	Week Days: Exp. 1 2 Class.	Parly. 1 2 3 Class.	P. 1 2 Class.	1 2 Class.	1 2 Class.	1 2 Class.	Exp. 1–2 Class.	Sundays: Parly. 1 2 3 Class.	Parly. 1 2 3 Class.	1 2 3 Class.
	morn.		morn.	morn.	even.	even.	even.			
LONDON .... dep.	...		6 27	8 0	..	..	5 0	...	1 30	...
Cambridge .... dep.	...		9 45		...	—	6 52	...	5 30	...
Shelford .... "	...		9 53		...	...	7 0	...	5 35	..
Haverhill .... arr.	...		10 27		...	...	7 35	...	6 10	...
Haverhill .... dep.	...		10 30		3 20	...	7 38	...	6 13	...
Sturmer .... dep.	...		10 38		3 28	...	7 46	...	6 21	...
Stoke .... "	...		10 47		3 37	...	7 55	...	6 30	...
Clare .... "	...		10 54		3 44	...	8 2	...	6 37	...
Cavendish .... "	...		11 2		3 52	...	8 10	...	6 45	...
Melford .... arr.	...		11 12		4 0	...	8 20	...	6 55	...
Bury .... dep.	7 35		10 30		...	5 20	...	8 0	...	4 10
Bury (Eastgate St.) "	7 38		10 33		...	5 23	...	8 3	...	4 13
Whelnetham ...... "	7 48		10 43		...	5 33	...	8 13	...	4 22
Lavenham .... "	8 3		10 58		...	5 48	...	8 28	...	4 35
Melford .... "	8 15		11 10		...	6 0	...	8 40	...	4 46
Melford .... dep.	8 18		11 14		4 2	6 8	...	8 43	...	4 48
Sudbury .... arr.	8 25		11 20		4 10	6 10	...	8 50	...	4 55
Sudbury .... dep.	8 30	8 55	11 25		4 15	6 25	...	8 55	...	5 0
Mark's Tey .... arr.	8 57	9 30	11 50		4 42	6 55	...	9 28	...	5 35
London .... "	10 30	12 10	1 40		6 30	8 45	...	12 15	...	8 0

P Parly between London and Melford and intermediate Stations.

FROM	Week Days: Exp. 1 2 Class.	Parly. 1 2 3 Class.	P. 1 2 Class.	1 2 Class.	1 2 Class.	1 2 Class.	Exp. 1–2 Class.	Sundays: Parly. 1 2 3 Class.	Parly. 1 2 3 Class.	1 2 3 Class.
	morn.		morn.	morn.	even.	even.	even.			
LONDON .... dep.	...		6 27	8 0	..	..	5 0	...	1 30	...
Cambridge .... dep.	...		9 45		...	—	6 52	...	5 30	...
Shelford .... "	...		9 53		...	...	7 0	...	5 35	..
Haverhill .... arr.	...		10 27		...	...	7 35	...	6 10	...
Haverhill .... dep.	...		10 30		3 20	...	7 38	...	6 13	...
Sturmer .... dep.	...		10 38		3 28	...	7 46	...	6 21	...
Stoke .... "	...		10 47		3 37	...	7 55	...	6 30	...
Clare .... "	...		10 54		3 44	...	8 2	...	6 37	...
Cavendish .... "	...		11 2		3 52	...	8 10	...	6 45	...
Melford .... arr.	...		11 12		4 0	...	8 20	...	6 55	...
Bury .... dep.	7 35		10 30		...	5 20	...	8 0	...	4 10
Bury (Eastgate St.) "	7 38		10 33		...	5 23	...	8 3	...	4 13
Whelnetham ...... "	7 48		10 43		...	5 33	...	8 13	...	4 22
Lavenham .... "	8 3		10 58		...	5 48	...	8 28	...	4 35
Melford .... "	8 15		11 10		...	6 0	...	8 40	...	4 46
Melford .... dep.	8 18		11 14		4 2	6 8	...	8 43	...	4 48
Sudbury .... arr.	8 25		11 20		4 10	6 10	...	8 50	...	4 55
Sudbury .... dep.	8 30	8 55	11 25		4 15	6 25	...	8 55	...	5 0
Mark's Tey .... arr.	8 57	9 30	11 50		4 42	6 55	...	9 28	...	5 35
London .... "	10 30	12 10	1 40		6 30	8 45	...	12 15	...	8 0

Parly between London and Melford and intermediate Stations.

Above:
1865 timetable, *Bury Free Press* 19 August 1865. *Author's collection*

Table 22—see pages 279 and 280

Table 23 LONG MELFORD and BURY ST. EDMUNDS

Miles		Week Days: am H	pm A (Saturdays only. Runs 25th July to 5th Sept. inc.)	pm		pm				Sundays:	pm B	
	3 London (L'pool St.) dep	..		12L38	..	4N58	..	..	..	..	6 20	..
—	Long Melford ...... dep	7 54		2 50	....	6 50	....	....	....	....	8 27	....
5½	Lavenham	8 6		2 59	..	6 59	..	..	..	..	8 37	..
8½	Cockfield (Suffolk)	8 12		3 6	....	7 6	....	....	....	....	8 44	....
11½	Welnetham	8 18		3 11	..	7 11	..	..	..	..	8 50	..
16½	Bury St. Edmunds.. arr	8 26	2 12	3 20	....	7 20	....	....	....	....	8 58	....

Miles		Week Days: am D C	am F (Saturdays only)	pm (Saturdays only)	pm (Except Saturdays)	pm G	pm		Sundays: am K		
—	Bury St. Edmunds.. dep	7 45	11 9	1 23	1 48	4 19	5 49	..	9 0	..	..
5	Welnetham	7 53	....	1 31	1 56	4 27	....	....	9 9	....	....
8	Cockfield (Suffolk)	7 59	..	1 37	2 2	4 33	6 2	..	9 15	..	..
11½	Lavenham	8 5	....	1 46	2 7	4 38	6 8	....	9 21	....	....
16½	Long Melford .. .. arr	8 14	..	1 55	2 17	4 48	6 17	..	9 30	..	..
	3 London (L'pool St.) arr	9 52	....	4L20	4L20	....	8 44	....	1129	....	....

D Diesel Train

A Through Train Clacton-on-Sea dep 12 10 pm to Sheffield (Vic.) arr 6 52 pm (Tables 24, 3, 22, 30 and 65)

B Through Train from Clacton-on-Sea dep 6 58 pm (Tables 24, 3, 22)

C Through Train to Mark's Tey arr 8 46 am (On Mons. to Fris. to Norwich (Thorpe) arr 10 48 am) (Tables 22, 3)

F Through Train Leicester (Lon. Rd.) dep 8 10 am to Clacton-on-Sea arr 1 7 pm (Tables 37, 35, 30, 22, 3, 24)

G Through Train to Sudbury arr 4 54 pm (Table 22)

H Through Train from Sudbury dep 7 48 am (Table 22)

K Through Train to Clacton-on-Sea arr 11 4 am (Tables 22, 3, 24)

L Via Colchester

N On Saturdays dep 4 36 pm via Colchester

Left:
Summer 1959 timetable.
Author's collection

Table 17

MARK'S TEY, SUDBURY, BURY ST. EDMUNDS, HAVERHILL (North), and CAMBRIDGE

Miles		Week Days mrn	mrn	mrn		mrn	aft	aft	aft	aft	aft		Sundays mrn		aft	
	3 London (L'poolSt) dep	..	..	6 55	..	10 0	1 0	2 15	4A54	..	7 30	..	8 30	..	5 0	..
	3 Colchester ..... "	..	..	8 56	..	11 2	2 0	3 50	6 16	..	8 55	..	1043	..	6 2	..
—	Mark's Tey .... dep	..	..	9 14	..	1129	2 23	4 5	6 30	6 39	9 8	..	11 0	..	6 30	..
3¼	Chappel & Wakes Colne.	..	..	9 23	..	1138	2 31	4 14	6 38	6 46	9 17	..	1110	..	6 40	..
6¾	Bures	..	..	9 32	..	1147	2 40	4 23	6 47		9 26	..	1119	..	6 49	..
11¾	Sudbury (Suffolk) arr	..	..	9 40	..	1155	2 48	4 31	6 55		9 34	..	1127	..	6 57	..
	Sudbury (Suffolk) dep	6 45	7 34	9 43	..	1157	2 53	5 5	6 58	To Haverhill (Table 18)	9 36	..	..	..	7 0	..
14¾	Long Melford .... arr	6 51	7 40	9 49	..	12 3	2 59	5 11	7 4		9 42	..	..	..	7 6	..
—	Long Melford ..... dep	..	7 41	10 3	..	1210	3 7	..	7 6		..	..	..	..	..	..
20	Lavenham	..	7 52	10 14	..	1221	3 18	..	7 19		..	..	..	..	..	..
23½	Cockfield (Suffolk)....	..	7 59	10 21	..	1228	3 25	..	7 26		..	..	..	..	..	..
26½	Welnetham	..	8 5	10 27	..	1234	3 31	..	7 34		..	..	..	..	..	..
31½	Bury St. Edmunds arr	..	8 14	10 36	..	1243	3 40	..	7 42		..	..	..	..	..	..
—	Long Melford ...... dep	6 53	..	9 53	..	12 5	3 2	5 19	..	..	..	..	..	..	..	..
17¾	Glemsford	6 58	..	9 59	..	1210	3 7	5 24	..	..	..	..	..	..	..	..
18¾	Cavendish	7 2	..	10 3	..	1214	3 11	5 28	..	..	..	..	..	..	..	..
21¾	Clare.....................	7 9	..	10 9	..	1220	3 17	5 34	..	..	..	..	..	..	..	..
23¾	Stoke (Suffolk)..........	7 14	..	10 14	..	1225	3 22	5 39	..	..	..	..	..	..	..	..
26¾	Sturmer	7 20	..	10 20	..	1231	3 28	5 45	..	..	..	..	..	..	..	..
28¾	Haverhill (North)	7 29	..	10 27	..	1238	3 35	5 56	..	..	..	..	..	..	..	..
34¼	Bartlow .... arr	7 39	..	10 37	..	1248	3 45	6 6	..	..	..	..	..	..	..	..
83¾	31 London (L'poolSt) arr	9 53	..	1 57	..	..	..	..	..	..	..	..	..	..	..	..
—	Bartlow .... dep	7 41	..	10 39	..	1250	3 47	6 9	..	..	..	..	..	..	..	..
36¾	Linton....................	7 47	..	10 44	..	1255	3 52	6 13	..	..	..	..	..	..	..	..
39	Pampisford...............	7 53	..	10 50	..	1 1	3 58	6 19	..	..	..	..	..	..	..	..
43¾	Shelford	8 2	..	10 58	..	1 9	4 8	6 27	..	..	..	..	..	..	..	..
46½	Cambridge.......... arr	8 8	..	11 8	..	1 15	4 16	6 39	..	..	..	..	..	..	..	..
99	4 London (L'poolSt) arr	9 53	..	1 57	..	5F10	6 40	8 48	..	..	..	..	..	..	..	..

Miles		Week Days mrn	mrn	mrn	mrn	mrn	aft	aft	aft	aft	aft		Sundays mrn		aft	
	4 London (L'poolSt) dep	..	..	5 50	..	8 20	..	..	..	2 25	5 49	..	..	..	..	..
—	Cambridge.......... dep	..	..	8 38	..	11 10	1 10	..	..	5 12	7 40	..	..	..	..	..
3¾	Shelford	..	..	8 45	..	11 17	1 17	..	..	5 19	7 47	..	..	..	..	..
7½	Pampisford..............	..	..	8 53	..	11 25	1 25	..	..	5 27	7 55	..	..	..	..	..
10¼	Linton....................	..	..	9 0	..	11 32	1 32	..	..	5 34	8 2	..	..	..	..	..
12¼	Bartlow .... arr	..	..	9 4	..	11 36	1 37	..	..	5 38	8 7	..	..	..	..	..
—	31 London (L'poolSt) dep	..	..	..	..	9B10	11 55	..	..	2 25	5 49	..	..	..	..	..
—	Bartlow .... dep	..	..	9 5	..	11 37	1 40	..	..	5 39	8 8	..	..	..	..	..
18¼	Haverhill (North)	..	..	9 18	..	11 50	1 55	..	..	5 51	8 20	..	..	..	..	..
20¾	Sturmer	..	..	9 22	..	11 54	2 0	..	..	5 55	8 25	..	..	..	..	..
23¼	Stoke (Suffolk).........	..	..	9 29	..	12 0	2 7	..	..	6 2	8 31	..	..	..	..	..
25¼	Clare.....................	..	..	9 34	..	12 5	2 12	..	..	6 8	8 37	..	..	..	..	..
28	Cavendish	..	..	9 40	..	12 15	2 18	..	..	6 14	8 43	..	..	..	..	..
29¼	Glemsford	..	..	9 44	..	12 20	2 24	..	..	6 19	8 48	..	..	..	..	..
31¾	Long Melford .... arr	..	..	9 50	..	12 26	2 31	..	..	6 25	8 54	..	..	..	..	..
—	Mls — Bury St. Edm'ds dep	7 28	From Haverhill (Table 18)	9 12	1125	..	1 55	4 43	From Haverhill (Table 18)	..	..	..	..	..	..	..
—	5 Welnetham	7 38		9 22	1138	..	2 5	4 53		..	..	..	..	..	..	..
—	8 Cockfield (Suffolk)..	7 45		9 28	1144	..	2 11	4 59		..	..	..	..	..	..	..
—	11¼ Lavenham	7 53		9 34	1150	..	2 17	5 8		..	..	..	..	..	..	..
—	16½ Long Melford .. arr	8 3		9 44	1159	..	2 26	5 17		..	..	..	..	..	..	..
—	Long Melford ...... dep	8 5		9 52	..	12 28	2 34	5 18		6 27	8 56	..	..	..	..	..
34¾	Sudbury (Suffolk) arr	8 11		9 58	..	12 34	2 40	5 24		6 33	9 2	..	..	..	..	..
	Sudbury (Suffolk) dep	8 13		10 6	..	12 36	2 50	5 37		6 59	..	..	9 30	..	5 36	..
39¾	Bures	8 22		10 15	..	12 45	3 0	5 46		7 8	..	..	9 40	..	5 46	..
43	Chappel & Wakes Colne.	8 30	1019	10 23	..	12 53	3 7	5 54	6 50	7 15	..	..	9 48	..	5 54	..
46½	Mark's Tey .... arr	8 42	1026	10 35	..	1 1	3 19	6 2	6 57	7 25	..	..	10 0	..	6 6	..
51½	3 Colchester .... arr	8 59	..	10 47	..	1 16	3 30	6E21	7 7	7 36	..	..	10 23	..	6 25	..
93½	3 London (L'poolSt) "	10 7	..	12 7	..	3 38	5 P0	7 47	..	9 30	..	..	11 31	..	7 30	..

NOTES

A Dep. 4 18 aft. on Saturdays.

B Third class only between Liverpool Street and Audley End

E Except Sats

F Arr 5 13 aft on Mons. and Fris.

P Via Colchester.

S Saturdays only.

For **OTHER TRAINS between Shelford and Cambridge, see Table 4**

Left:
Starting 4 May 1942 timetable.
Author's Collection

7.40pm from Chappel, leaving Haverhill at 8.48am and 5.13pm, the last being mixed.

By 1922 the Stour Valley service had expanded to four trains each way between Cambridge and Mark's Tey, with a further two from Sudbury to Cambridge at 6.45am, and back at 7.22pm. Further trains from Bury St Edmunds linked Sudbury to Mark's Tey and Colchester. Sunday services were confined to three trains each way between Mark's Tey and Sudbury. Haverhill continued to be served via the Colne Valley, with connections at Chappel. In 1923 there were only three trains each weekday making the full journey both ways on the Colne Valley & Halstead, with a further return working between Chappel and Hedingham which started at Haverhill on Mondays. The 8.3am from Hedingham to Chappel (7.38 from Haverhill, Mondays only) utilised a set of six-wheeled stock, which worked back as the 9.26am from Chappel, but other trains used a more modern pair of experimental bogie coaches plus a bogie van that had been purchased from the Metropolitan District Railway, then modified and refurbished by the CV&H.

The 1937-8 winter service showed a similar pattern, but with only three trains on weekdays from Cambridge to Mark's Tey, but four the other way. The 5.1pm from Cambridge terminated at Sudbury at 6.17pm, which meant a long wait for the 7pm for Mark's Tey, which had left Bury at 6pm. The first train westwards was the 6.54am from Sudbury to Cambridge. It was, of course, also possible to travel from Mark's Tey and stations to Long Melford to Cambridge by changing at Bury St Edmunds, for example by the 1.52pm from Mark's Tey, which gave an eventual arrival at 4.29pm as against the normal journey time of just under two hours. The guard of the last down train had to collect tickets of passengers alighting at Sturmer, and also at Pampisford, where it called to set down only. However, since he also had to lock up the station, a call was guaranteed, and the train was allowed an extra six minutes to get to Shelford in consequence.

The Bury line enjoyed a relatively good service, with up trains at 7.28am from Bury to Mark's Tey, at 9.16 and 11.14am, and 1.41pm to Long Melford, followed by the 3.43pm to Colchester and Harwich, and the 6pm to Colchester. Those terminating at Long Melford made good connections with Cambridge trains. The same was true in the down direction, with through trains from Mark's Tey at 1.52pm (1.36pm Saturdays only [SO]) and 6.46pm from Colchester, with the 7.34am starting from Sudbury, and the 10.3am, 12.5 and 4.34pm from Long Melford. The 6.46pm, the last train of the day down the branch, called at Welnetham to set down or take up passengers only, the guard having to collect tickets, advise Bury of any passengers joining, and then put out the station lights and lock up. No extra time was allowed for this!

There were four trains each way on the Colne Valley line, mostly

Table 25 MARK'S TEY, BURY ST. EDMUNDS, HAVERHILL and CAMBRIDGE

Miles	Station					Week Days														Sundays		
		am	am	am	am	am	pm	pm	pm	pm	pm	pm	pm	pm	pm	pm		pm	pm		pm
	5 London (Liverpool St.).. dep	..	..	..	6 54	1036	12L30	..	2F10	..	4 56	..	8 30	..	..	4 45	..	6R5..			
	5 Colchester .. .. "	..	..	8G48	1138	2 1	4 14	6 2	9 24	6 3	9										
—	Mark's Tey .. .. dep	..	..	9 6	9 16	1152	12 1	2 25	4 28	4 37	6 17	6 26	9 43	6 18	6 27	9 1					
3¾	Chappel & Wakes Colne	9 14	9 24	12 0	12 9	2D34	4 36	4 45	6 25	6 34	9 51	6 26	6 35	9 9							
6¾	Bures	9 32	12 9	2 42	4 44	6 33	9 59	6 44	9 22												
11¾	Sudbury (Suffolk) { arr	9 40	1217	2 50	4 52	6 41	10 7	6 52													
	{ dep	6 30	7 40	9 42	1219	2 56	4 59	6 45	6 53												
14¾	Long Melford .. arr	6 36	7 46	9 48	1226	3 2	5 5	6 51	6 59												
—	Long Melford .. dep	7 47	3 15	7 5																	
20	Lavenham	8 0	3 25	7 15																	
23¾	Cockfield (Suffolk)	8 8	3 32	7 22																	
26¾	Welnetham	8 14	3 38	7 29																	
31¾	Bury St. Edmunds .. arr	8 28	3 46	7 37																	
—	Long Melford .. dep	6 37	9 54	1228	3 6	5 13	6 53														
17¾	Glemsford	6 42	9 59	1233	3 11	5 18	6 58														
18¾	Cavendish	6 46	10 3	1237	3 15	5 22	7 3														
21¾	Clare	6 52	10 9	1244	3 21	5 28	7 13														
23¾	Stoke (Suffolk)	6 57	10 14	1249	3 26	5 33	7 19														
26¾	Sturmer	7 3	10 20	1255	3 32	5 39															
28¾	Haverhill { arr	7 8	10 8	10 25	1 2	1254	3 37	5 44	5 34	7 24	7 31	7 11									
	{ dep	7 10	10 29	1 6	3 39	5 53	7 50	7 15													
34¾	Bartlow	7 21	10 40	1 17	3 50	6 4	7 26														
83¾	34 London (Liverpool St.) arr	9 1	12J37	4 52	11 23																
—	Bartlow .. dep	7 23	10 42	1 18	3 51	6 5	7 51	7 27													
36¾	Linton	7 28	10 48	1 24	3 56	6 10	8 0	7 32													
39	Pampisford	7 34	10 54	1 30	4 2	6 16	8 7														
43¾	Shelford	7 42	11 2	1 40	4 10	6 24	8A17	7 46													
46¾	Cambridge .. arr	7 48	11 8	1 50	4 18	6 30	8A23	7 54													
99	6 London (Liverpool St.).. arr	9H47	k12S39	4 52	6 2	8 40	11 23	9 15													

(Interspersed column notes: Via Colne Valley Line (Table 26); TC Via Colchester; Via Colchester to Cambridge; TC Ipswich dep 5 20 (Table 5); TC from Colchester; Runs 15th April and October to inclusive.)

A On Saturdays dep Shelford 8 20 and arr Cambridge 8 27 am
D Arr 2 minutes *earlier*
E Except Saturdays
F On Saturdays dep Liverpool Street 2 15 pm
G Dep 8 45 am on Saturdays
H Arr 9 53 am on Saturdays
J Arr 12 39 pm on Saturdays
k Via Shelford
L Via Colchester. On Saturdays dep Liverpool Street 12 50 pm via Mark's Tey
R Via Colchester
S Saturdays only
TC Through Carriages

Table 25—continued CAMBRIDGE, HAVERHILL, BURY ST. EDMUNDS and MARK'S TEY

Miles	Station					Week Days											Sundays				
		am	am	am	am	am	pm	pm	pm	pm	pm	pm	pm	pm		pm	pm	pm			
	6 London (Liverpool St.).. dep	4 24	..	..	5 54	..	12S10	..	3k24	..	5C57	..	2 24								
—	Cambridge .. dep	6 22	8 36	11 5	1 33	5 10	7 35	4 1													
3¾	Shelford	6 31	8 43	11 12	1 41	5 17	7 42	4 8													
7¾	Pampisford	8 52	11 21	1 50	5 26	7 52															
10¾	Linton	6 45	8 59	11 28	1 57	5 33	7 59	4 22													
12¾	Bartlow .. arr	6 49	9 3	11 32	2 1	5 37	8 3	4 26													
—	34 London (Liverpool St.).. dep	9 54	12J24	3 24	5 54																
—	Bartlow .. dep	11 40	2 2	5 38	8 4	4 27															
18¾	Haverhill { arr	7 3	9 16	11 52	2 14	5 50	8 16	4 39													
	{ dep	7 11	9 22	9 18	11 54	2 20	2 16	5 56	6 5	8 18	4 43										
20¾	Sturmer	9 22	12 4	2 22	6 0	8 22															
23¾	Stoke (Suffolk)	9 28	12 9	2 26	6 6	8 30															
25¾	Clare	9 34	12 15	2 31	6 12	8 35															
28	Cavendish	9 40	12 19	2 37	6 18	8 41															
29¾	Glemsford	9 45	12 19	2 46	6 22	8 45															
31¾	Long Melford .. arr	9 50	12 24	2 46	6 27	8 50															
—	Bury St. Edmunds .. dep	7 38	2 8	4 37	5 50																
—	Welnetham	7 47	2 17	4 46	5 59																
—	Cockfield (Suffolk)	7 53	2 23	4 58	6 5																
—	Lavenham	8 1	2 29	4 58	6 11																
—	Long Melford .. arr	8 10	2 38	5 7	6 20																
—	Long Melford .. dep	8 12	9 53	12 29	2 48	5 12	6 30	8 51	7 15												
34¾	Sudbury (Suffolk) { arr	8 18	9 59	12 35	2 54	5 18	6 37	8 57	7 21												
	{ dep	8 21	10 5	12 37	2 59	5 23	6 43	5 30	7 22												
39¾	Bures	8 30	10 14	12 45	3 7	5 23	6 52	5 40	7 31												
43	Chappel & Wakes Colne	8D 4	8D40	1016	10D24	12 54	3 8	3 16	5 41	7 1	7 13	5 32	5D50	7 40							
46¾	Mark's Tey .. arr	8 11	8 47	1023	10 31	1 1	3 15	3 23	7 8	7 20	5 39	5 57	7 49								
51¾	5 Colchester .. arr	8 32	8 58	10 48	1 16	3 34	6 17	7 43	7 43	6 14	8 3										
93¾	5 London (Liverpool St.)	9 57	11 52	2A59	4B34	7 45	9 2	9 2	7 19	9 9											

(Interspersed column notes: Via Colne Valley Line (Table 26); TC to Colchester; Via Colne Valley Line; TC to Colchester.)

A Via Colchester. On Saturdays arr Liverpool Street 3 21 pm via Mark's Tey
B On Saturdays arr Liverpool Street 4 46 pm
C Via Shelford. On Saturdays, also Fridays until 28th October dep Liverpool Street 5 54 pm via Cambridge
D Arr 2 minutes *earlier*
J. On Saturdays dep Liverpool Street 12 10 pm
k Via Shelford
S Saturdays only
TC Through Carriages

Above:
Top: September 1955-June 1956 timetable. *Author's collection*

Above: September 1955-June 1956 timetable. *Author's collection*

with good connections at each end, and providing the last service to Haverhill from the east. The 7.4pm from Mark's Tey to Bury called at Chappel at 7.11pm, with the last Colne Valley following it out at 7.17pm. The same applied in the other direction, since although there was a train leaving Haverhill for Sudbury at 8pm, it offered no onward connections, whereas the 6.12pm Colne Valley gave a good connection at Chappel with the 6pm from Bury. This also avoided the long wait at Sudbury, and gave a later departure from Haverhill. The winter Sunday service showed two trains each

way via the Colne Valley line, and the summer three to Haverhill, but only two up to Chappel. An unfortunate incident occurred in December 1952 when two passenger trains collided in fog at Chappel. The 10.30am Cambridge to Colchester ran into the back of the 9.20am Haverhill to Mark's Tey, the two rear coaches of the latter being derailed. The engine of the Cambridge train was badly damaged. Between 20 and 30 passengers left the Haverhill train and walked the 100 yards to the station, the trains having collided at the junction by the bridge at the north end of the station.

Above:
The 14.00 summer Saturdays through train from Clacton to Leicester eases through Haverhill in the charge of Brush Type 2 D5550, on 5 September 1964. There was a short double-track section between the junction with the Colne Valley spur and the west end of the station. *G. R. Mortimer*

Replacement bus services had to be introduced between Mark's Tey and Earls Colne, and Mark's Tey and Sudbury.

The lines were dieselised in the late 1950s, and with multiple-units taking over most services, the level of service was improved dramatically on the Colne and Stour Valley lines. Through trains now ran from Mark's Tey to Haverhill via the Colne Valley, some extending all the way to Cambridge. Some even ran through from Clacton or Walton. Stour Valley services started at Colchester, with some trains originating at Haverhill and running through to Audley End. In summer 1958, the first down train still started from Sudbury at 6.33am and called at all stations to Cambridge, with the best London connection offered via Saffron Walden. The 9.6am went from Mark's Tey to Haverhill via the Colne Valley, followed by the 9.16am to Cambridge via Sudbury. The 11.31am Saturdays-only was a Clacton to Cambridge through train which did not stop after Mark's Tey, but the 11.43am all-stations from Colchester via Sudbury did not run on Saturdays. The 12.4pm Mark's Tey to Haverhill was followed by the 12.13pm (SO) via Sudbury, the 2.1pm and 4.5pm Colchester-Cambridge workings, and the 4.38pm from Mark's Tey to Haverhill via Halstead. Next through was the 5.20pm Ipswich to Haverhill via Sudbury, and then the 5.25pm Clacton to Cambridge via the Colne Valley, whose timings differed on Saturdays. There were corresponding

workings in the other direction, and two trains each way between Cambridge and Mark's Tey via the Colne Valley, one of which went through to Clacton and Walton. The Bury line had not fared as well, and still only saw four local trains each way, although there was a Manchester to Clacton service routed that way on summer Saturdays.

The three branches had been selected for the big traffic survey in 1955. The service described above represented a serious attempt to increase the facilities on offer and tempt people back on to the local trains by increasing the frequency and variety of destinations. The survey found that in the week in March, Stour Valley services ran 3,270 miles with a load factor of 17%, while Colne Valley trains covered 1,345 miles with a load factor of 9%, giving respective movement costs to revenue ratios of 415% and 772%. Bury to Long Melford trains covered 900 miles with a load factor of 15% and a costs to revenue ratio of 594%. When the whole year's results were analysed and the summer traffic had been assessed, the average throughout loads were 23, 14 and 18, giving load factors of 17%, 11% and 12%, with movement to costs ratios of 341%, 545% and 496% respectively. None of the routes had been dieselised by the end of 1956, which was usually reckoned to show substantial benefits.

The Summer 1959 timetable showed even more improvements,

with a wider range of destinations. For example, the 8.39am from Halstead ran fast to Mark's Tey, and was one of five up trains via the Colne Valley. Another innovation was a return working between Norwich and Haverhill, and there was even a 7.34am Mildenhall to Mark's Tey working, although nothing direct in the reverse direction. On the other hand, the Long Melford to Bury St Edmunds line, long regarded as the more important through route in both working and public timetables, was now downgraded and appeared as a separate table with fewer trains, there being only three down and four up local services. There was, however, a train to and from Clacton on Sundays, which called at all stations.

Goods traffic was always relatively healthy on the lines, much of that on the section between Mark's Tey and Long Melford being to and from Bury St Edmunds, especially the Wednesday cattle market. The 1913 timetable showed an early train from Colchester to Mark's Tey at 4.30am, which then worked to Chappel at 5.35am, and back to Mark's Tey at 6.18am. It then went to Long Melford at 9.25am, and did not call at Bures. On Wednesdays it was followed by a Class B express cattle from Colchester to Bury, leaving the former at 6.40am, and which was allowed to call at Chappel, Bures and Cockfield to attach cattle trucks for Bury. The Cambridge line was then served by the 6.10am (5.40am Mondays) from

HALSTEAD (Essex)

Map Sq. 19.
Pop. 5,878.   Clos. day Wed.
From Liverpool Street via Marks Tey and Chappel 56¼ miles.
1st cl.—Single 19/6, Mth. Ret. 23/11.
3rd cl.—Single 11/9, Mth. Ret. 15/11.

Liv. St.	Halst.	Halst.	Liv. St.
a.m.		**a.m.**	
6 50	9 52	8 10	10 8
9 55	12 4	9 58	12 7
p.m.		**p.m.**	
2 18	5 2	2 41s🅱	4 54
4 57er	7 5	2 41r	5 8
4 57s	7 5	6 30	9 4
—	—	—	—
—	—	—	—
—	—	—	—

Sunday Trains.

a.m.		**a.m.**	
8 30	11 3	9 20	11 34
p.m.		**p.m.**	
5 0	6 56	5 12🅱	7 20
—	—	5 12	7 34
—	—	—	—

🅱 3rd cl. only. r Refresh. Car.
e Not Sat. s Sat. only.

Another Route

From Liverpool Street via Haverhill 68 miles.   Same fares.

Liv. St.	Halst.	Halst.	Liv. St.
a.m.		**a.m.**	
4 20	8 10	9 52	1 55
5 50	9 58	**p.m.**	
11 50r	2 41	12 4e	5 0
p.m.		12 4s	5 3
3 35e	6 30	5 2	8 45
3 42s	6 30	7 5	11 19
—	—	—	—

Sunday Trains.

p.m.		**p.m.**	
1 0	5 12	6 56	10 34
—	—	—	—

e Not Sat.
r Refresh. Car.
s Sat. only.
" Bus facilities. From Colchester, Bus Park, approx. hourly 55 min. journey.

Colchester, which was shunted at Chappel to let the 9.15am passenger from Mark's Tey to Cambridge pass, and also so that the express cattle could overtake it. The train conveyed newspaper traffic for Chappel and Bures. There was a stopping goods at 11.45am from Mark's Tey to Long Melford, and then the 1.16pm Colchester to Peterborough via the Stour Valley and Cambridge followed by a 4.50pm Mark's Tey to Sudbury, and a 7.25pm (9.15pm on Saturdays) to Chappel. On Sundays there were two down workings from Mark's Tey, at 12.15pm to Sudbury, and 6pm to Chappel, the latter allowed only to work traffic for the Colne Valley beyond Chappel.

In the up direction workings were generally balanced, but started later in the day. The 6.40am from Cambridge called at all stations (Withersfield siding on request) to Long Melford, arriving at 11am. The 11.30am from Long Melford called at all stations to Mark's Tey, and was allowed to call at Cornard siding (32 chains from Sudbury), in which case it could not call at Bures. It was followed by the 10.45am from Cambridge, which had called at all stations, but had to shunt at Sudbury to let both the 2.25pm from Bury and the 1.52pm from Cambridge pass. The 2.7pm goods from Cambridge had started from Peterborough on Saturdays at 11.40am, called at Stoke and Glemsford on request, shunted at Cavendish, allowing the 4.47pm passenger from Cambridge

Above:
ABC Railway Guide, December 1949. *Author's Collection*

Below:
Illustrating the strategic importance of the route, 'J17' No 65523 heads a Whitemoor to Colchester goods on 17 May 1952 between Chappel & Wakes Colne and Mark's Tey. *G. R. Mortimer*

Right:
'J15' No 65477 heads the
2.8pm Bury to Long
Melford train near
Lavenham on
26 September 1953.
G. R. Mortimer

Below:
Long Melford station,
junction for the
Haverhill and Bury
lines, looking north. The
multiple-unit has just
arrived off the Stour
Valley line.
David Lawrence

Above:

The 11.23am Saturdays only train from Cambridge to Colchester leaves Sudbury in the charge of 'E4' No 62789 on 3 August 1957. *G. R. Mortimer*

Above:
**An idyllic scene on a rural branch line. The 07.52 from Colchester to Sudbury is reflected
in the River Stour near Bures on Sunday 22 June 1969.** *G. R. Mortimer*

to overtake, and finally reached Mark's Tey at 8.15pm and Colchester at 9pm. The 9.15pm from Chappel took traffic forward from the Colne Valley, Chappel having to advise Mark's Tey of the number of trucks going forward to Spitalfields and Bishopsgate.

The 1937 timetable showed the 11.35am from Colchester calling at all stations except Glemsford, Stoke, Sturmer and Withersfield siding to Cambridge, continuing to Whitemoor on weekdays, and March on Saturdays. On Mondays to Fridays the engine off the 1.41pm from Bury worked a trip from Long Melford to Cavendish, the main purpose of which was to carry traffic for Stafford, Allen's siding, and also to clear Glemsford and Cavendish of traffic, all of which was then worked back to Long Melford, arriving at 3.55pm. On Saturdays only, the 2.40pm from Sudbury performed the same duties, but then continued on to Cambridge. It had to call at Glemsford to leave the key to Stafford, Allen's siding. On Mondays to Fridays the 2.10pm from Earls Colne

worked via the Colne Valley line, calling at all stations except White Colne, reaching Haverhill North at 5.30pm and leaving for Cambridge an hour later, using the same path as the 2.40pm (SO) from Sudbury. On Saturdays it started from Chappel at 2.5pm. Another Saturdays-only working was the 4pm Sudbury to Cambridge, reached at 9.34pm.

The Bury line no longer saw quite the same emphasis on cattle traffic to and from Bury market, although there continued to be several workings daily over the line. In the down direction there was a Class B goods from Colchester to Whitemoor at 4.18am, followed by an ordinary goods at 5.50am, calling all stations except Welnetham, and carrying newspaper traffic as far as Long Melford. However, the station was served by a trip out from Bury at 11.35am, returning at 12.5pm. Another Class B left Colchester for Whitemoor at 4.15pm, running via Lavenham, while the 11.35am Class A goods ran via the Stour Valley line. In the up direction there was only the 4pm from Bury to Colchester calling at all stations (Welnetham as required), which picked up Whitemoor traffic at Bury, and carried a vacuum-braked box van for Bishopsgate traffic. The 9.16am passenger from Bury was allowed to work one piped wagon of pigs from Lavenham or Cockfield to Haverhill North. This would be taken forward by the

CLARE (Suffolk)
Map Sq. 19.
Pop. 1,252. Clos. day Wed.
From Liverpool Street via Saffron
Walden and Bartlow 62 miles.
1st cl.—Single 21/5, Mth. Ret. 26/2.
3rd cl.—Single 12/11, Mth. Ret. 17/5.

Liv. St.	Clare	Clare	Liv. St.
a.m.		a.m.	
5 50‡	9 33	6 57	9 54
10 0	12 24	10 13‡	1 55
11 50r	2 15	p.m.	
p.m.		12 25e	5 0
3 35e	6 6	12 25s	5 3
3 42s	6 6	3 22r	6 48
5 54r	8 27	5 31	8 45
—	—	7 10	11 19

No Sunday Trains.
‡ Via Cambridge or Shelford.
e Not Sat.   s Sat. only.
r Refresh. Car.

Another Route
From Liverpool Street via Marks Tey
68 miles. Same fares.

Liv. St.	Clare	Clare	Liv. St.
a.m.		a.m.	
6 50	10 13	9 33	12 7
9 55	12 25	p.m.	
p.m.		12 24s	3 1
1 0r	3 22	12 24e	3 20
2 18	5 31	2 15s🅱	4 54
4 57er	7 10	2 15r	5 8
4 57s	7 10	6 6	9 4
—	—	—	—
—	—	—	—

No Sunday Trains.
🅱 3rd cl. only.   r Refresh. Car.
e Not Sat.   s Sat. only.

Above:
**ABC Railway Guide,
December 1949.**
Author's collection

LAVENHAM (Suffolk)
Map Sq. 19. Pop. 1,451. Clos. day Wed.
From Liverpool Street via Marks Tey
and Long Melford 66¾ miles.
1st cl.—Single 22/10, Mth. Ret. 28/2.
3rd cl.—Single 13/10, Mth. Ret. 18/9.

Liv. St.	Laven.	Laven.	Liv. St.
a.m.		a.m.	
6 50	10 19	7 50	10 8
9 55	12 31	9 35	12 7
p.m.		11 52s	3 1
1 0r	3 28	11 52e	3 20
4 57er	7 16	p.m.	
4 57s	7 16	2 17s🅱	4 54
—	—	2 17r	5 8
—	—	5 1	8 11
—	—	6 7	9 4
—	—	—	—

No Sunday Trains.
🅱 3rd cl. only.
e Not Sat.   s Sat. only.
r Refresh. Car.

Above:
**ABC Railway Guide,
December 1949.**
Author's collection

Above:
Colne Valley No 2 *Halstead*, an 1887 Hawthorn, Leslie 2-4-2T. It is seen
here as rebuilt by the Great Eastern in 1896. *Ian Allan Library/Bucknall Collection*

Below:
Colne Valley No 2 *Halstead*, before rebuilding. *Bucknall Collection*

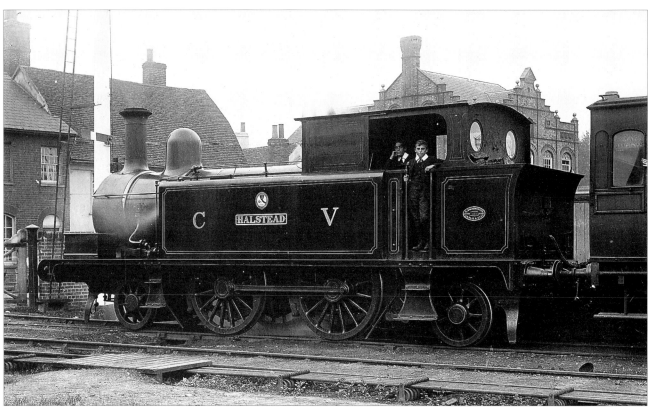

Above:
CV&HR No 1, built by Neilson in 1887, and seen here as rebuilt in 1894. *Ian Allan library/Bucknall Collection*

9.13am from Mark's Tey and called at Long Melford between 9.47 and 9.54am, crossing the 8.38am from Cambridge there; some smart working would have been needed at the junction.

Colne Valley goods workings included the 4.40am from Colchester, which left Chappel at 5.47am and reached Haverhill North at 8.35am. The corresponding up working was the 6.30am from Cambridge, which left Haverhill North at 8.45am, and went to Earls Colne on Mondays to Fridays, and Chappel on Saturdays. There was also the 3.30pm Haverhill North to Colchester, which attached at Halstead, Earls Colne, White Colne and Chappel, all having to be marshalled in the right place. There were also numbers of trips between Haverhill North and South either for light engines or for tripping goods. Some Colne Valley passenger trains were also allowed to carry freight, such as the 6.10pm Sundays-only Haverhill North to Colchester via Halstead, which could work fitted vans of Sainsbury's meat for London. This had to be attached next to the engine with an extra brake; Chappel then had to arrange to have it specially forwarded to Mark's Tey.

Locomotives working over the lines were very varied, and in the 1950s many ex-Great Eastern classes were represented. They included Class D16 4-4-0 'Claud Hamiltons', 'Intermediate' Class E4 2-4-0s, various 'F' class 2-4-2 tanks and the ubiquitous Class J15 0-6-0s on both goods and passenger trains. The larger 0-6-0s — Classes J17, J19 and J20 — also appeared on the Whitemoor trains, although later displaced by 'Austerity' 2-8-0s. The summer Saturday through trains often saw 'B12' haulage. The 'Intermediates' were the last class of 2-4-0 locomotives in service on British Railways, and No 62785, then station pilot at Cambridge, was working the Bury-Long Melford service on 31 October 1959, the last day before dieselisation. Ex-Great

Northern Class C12 4-4-2 tanks were also used.

The Colne Valley line had been rather more lightly built, and so the larger classes were prohibited, mainly because of the weaker bridges. The company had had five locomotives at the time of Grouping in 1923, numbered 1, 2, 3, 4 and 5. Nos 2, 3 and 4 had once been named *Halstead, Colne* and *Hedingham* respectively. No 1 was an 0-4-2T built by Neilsen in 1877, and rebuilt in 1888 by Hawthorn, Leslie. Further rebuilding was undertaken at Stratford in 1894, and at Halstead in 1911, the last involving the removal of supplementary water tanks fitted alongside the smokebox. This restored it to a more conventional appearance. Nos 2, 3 and 4 were 2-4-2 tanks built by Hawthorn, Leslie, in 1887 and 1894, with 5ft 3in coupled wheels and 16 x 24in cylinders. No 5 was a 1908 Hudswell, Clarke engine, which was more powerful than the others and was used mainly on the goods trains. Halstead Works carried out most normal repairs to engines, carriages and wagons, but heavy locomotive repair work was undertaken at GER's Stratford Works. At the time of Grouping, the company employed 119 staff.

As the steam era drew to a close, local services were turned over to operation by the new diesel railcars, and other locomotive classes appeared on the lines, notably the Brush Type 2s, later to become Class 31. Although helping slightly to stem the flood of people moving away from the lines and on to alternative forms of transport, the extra railcars did not attract sufficient extra passengers. The Long Melford to Bury service was the first to succumb, closing on and from Monday 10 April 1961, although Lavenham and Cockfield continued to handle parcels and goods, while Welnetham became an unstaffed public delivery siding. Passenger services were withdrawn from the Colne Valley line from 1 January 1962, and as there were no Sunday services the last trains ran on Saturday 30 December 1961. The line north of Yeldham went completely, including Birdbrook station, although Haverhill South did not close officially until 19 April 1965. Parcels and freight facilities were maintained at all the other stations. The lifting of the section between Lavenham and Long Melford took place during the first half of 1962, the remainder of the line then being served from the Bury end.

Sturmer was the first on the Stour Valley line to lose its goods facilities, on 25 June 1962. Welnetham followed on 13 July 1964, Sudbury losing its public facilities on the same day. After the Colne Valley closed to passengers, goods traffic was worked out and back between Colchester and Yeldham. In the autumn of 1964 the 11.28 (Saturdays excepted [SX]) from Colchester and 14.55 return called at all stations except White Colne, while the 6.28am from Colchester went to Halstead, and called at White Colne and Earls Colne as required. The 11.39 from Chappel went through to Cambridge on Saturdays, arriving at 17.07, calling at Bures, Sudbury, Glemsford and Cavendish as required, Haverhill North and Linton. It terminated at Cavendish on weekdays. A working at 13.20 from Haverhill called at Bartlow, and Linton on Mondays to Fridays. The 14.55 from Long Melford called at all the stations which remained open for goods, including Stafford, Allen's siding, and that was that for the day. The only trip to Haverhill South left North at 11.40 and returned from there at 12.22. This was withdrawn from 2 November 1964 when the workings were reorganised. The early morning return to Halstead was withdrawn, and Stour Valley trains then ran between Cambridge and Sudbury only, with one trip from Sudbury to Bures as required. However, the latter closed on 28 December, together with Cavendish and Bartlow. At the same time, White Colne, Earls Colne, Hedingham and Yeldham closed, with Halstead following on 19 April 1965. On

this date Pampisford, Haverhill South and Stoke also went, together with Lavenham and Cockfield, which finished that line completely. Linton, Clare, Glemsford and Long Melford closed on 12 September; Sudbury and Haverhill North followed on 31 October, and with them, freight traffic through the Stour and Colne Valleys.

The Stour Valley's remaining passenger trains did not escape the eagle eye of Dr Beeching, and his report recommended final closure between Shelford and Mark's Tey. In the event, Mark's Tey to Sudbury was one of the few lines to survive his axe, although this fell on the remainder of the line on 6 March 1967 when passenger services were withdrawn between Sudbury and Shelford. Long Melford had ceased to be a junction for passengers in April 1961 when the service to Bury was withdrawn, and Bartlow on 7 September 1964, when the Saffron Walden line closed to passengers. There were no booked freight trains between Saffron Walden and Bartlow after this date.

Since the line closed, Haverhill has become a London overspill town, and with the growth of the so-called 'Silicon Fen' has become part of the Cambridge 'travel to work' area. Together with the complete inadequacy of the local road network, this has led to increasing pressure for reinstatement of the line. Haverhill's railway may yet rise from the dead. Chappel & Wakes Colne station has become the home of the East Anglian Railway Museum, and can still be reached by train from Mark's Tey. Sudbury station has been demolished and replaced by a basic platform. The Colne Valley, although lifted completely following closure, has risen from the dead in the form of the Colne Valley Railway museum, situated on a site next to the A1017 Halstead to Haverhill road, and between the sites of Yeldham and Sible & Castle Hedingham stations. Former CVR buildings have been re-erected, and about a mile of track laid.

Below:
The Colne valley had its own fleet of locomotives in independent days. This is No 5, a Hudswell, Clarke 0-6-2T. *Ian Allan library/Bucknall Collection*

Above:

The last through train to Colchester via the Stour Valley, the 19.58 from Cambridge, waits at Sudbury on Saturday 4 March 1967. It had been strengthened to two units, and a group of undertakers dressed in period costume attended, and fireworks were let off. *G. R. Mortimer*

Table 22 MARK'S TEY, HALSTEAD, SUDBURY, HAVERHILL and CAMBRIDGE

Miles	Miles		Week Days														
			am	am	am	am	am	am	am	pm	pm	pm	am	pm	pm	pm	pm
				To Bury St. Edmunds arr 8 26 am (Table 23)	Through Train Ipswich dep 9 12 am (Table 3)		Saturdays only. Through Train Clacton-on-Sea dp 9 39 am to Leicester (Lon. Rd.) arr 2 55 pm (Tables 24, 3, 33 and 37)	Saturdays only. Through Train from Ipswich dep 11 12 am (Table 3)	Except Saturdays. Through Train from Ipswich dep 11 15 am (Table 3)	Except Saturdays	Saturdays only	Saturdays only		Through Train Clacton-on-Sea dep 12 10 pm to Sheffield (Vic.) arr 6 52 pm (Tables 24, 3, 23, 30 and 65). Saturdays only. Runs 25th July to 5th September inclusive			Through Train Colchester to Cambridge
		3 London (L'pool St) dep	..	..	8Q 5	8Y33	8C53	10C30	10C30	..	..	..	11E33	..	..	..	12C38
		3 Colchester .... „			9 40	9 40	10 8	11 41	11 45					12 44	1 9		1 49
			D		D	D		D	D	D	D		D		[D]	[D]	
—	—	**Mark's Tey** .. .. dep	..	..	9 48	9 55	1019	11 49	11 53	..	..	..	12K52	1 0	1 22	..	2 2
3¼	3¼	Chappel & Wakes Colne			9 54	10 1							12 58		1 28		2 10
2	5½	White Colne			10 0										1 34		
3¾	7	Earls Colne			10 3										1 37		
6	9½	**Halstead**			10 9							12 19			1 43	2 32	
9¾	13	Sible & Castle Hedingham			10 15							12 26				2 38	
12	15½	Yeldham			10 21							12 31				2 44	
15¾	19¾	Birdbrook			10 28							12 39				2 51	
6¾	—	Bures				10 8							1 5				2 18
11¾	—	**Sudbury** (Suffolk) arr				10 15		12 21	12 10				1 12				2 26
		dep	6 38	7 48		10 15			12 11				1 13				2 29
—	—	Long Melford	6 45	7 54		10 22			12 17				1 20				2 37
17¼	—	Glemsford	6 50			10 27							1 25				2 42
18¾	—	Cavendish	6 54			10 30							1 28				2 45
21¼	—	Clare	6 59			10 35							1 33				2 51
23¼	—	Stoke (Suffolk)	7 3			10 40							1 38				2 55
26¼	—	Sturmer	7 9			10 45							1 43				3 1
28¼	23	**Haverhill** arr	7 13		10 36	10 50						12 47	1 48			2 59	3 6
		dep	7 14			10 50				12 17	12 32						3 12
34¼	29	Bartlow arr	7 24			11 0				12 27	12 42						
83¼	78	**29 London** (L'pool St) arr	9 5			12S39											
—	—	Bartlow dep	7 24			11 0				12 27	12 42						
36¼	31	Linton	7 29			11 5				12 32	12 47						
39	33¾	Pampisford	7 34			11 10				12 37	12 52						
43¼	38	Shelford } A	7 42							12 45	1 0						
46½	41¼	**Cambridge** } A arr	7 48			11 26	12 7			12 51	1 6						3 45
	96	**8 London** (King's C.) arr	9 58														
99	93¾	4 „ (L'pool St) „	9H48			1Y42				2 42	2 41						6Z 9

	Week Days—continued											Sundays						
	pm	pm	pm	pm	pm		pm	pm	pm			pm	pm	pm	pm	pm	pm	pm
	Through Train from Norwich (Thorpe) dep 12E53, 12S18 pm			Through Train Colchester to Cambridge			Through Train Ipswich dep 5 20 pm to Cambridge (Table 3)		Through Train from Colchester			Through Train from Colchester			Through Train Clacton-on-Sea dep 5 34 pm to Cambridge (Table 24)		Through Train Clacton-on-Sea dep 6 55 pm to Bury St. Edmunds arr 8 58 pm (Tables 24, 3 and 23)	
3 London (L'pool St) dep	1C30	..	..	2 33	..	..	4F58	5B45	8C30	..	..	2 21	..	4 45	4 45	6 2J	6 20	8 30
3 Colchester .... „	2 45			4N26			5 49	6P19	9 50			3 39		6 2	6 12		7 39	8 53
	D	[D]	D	D	D		D	D	D			D	D	D		D		D
Mark's Tey .. .. dep	2 53	..	3 46	4 35	..	..	6 5	7 7	9 58	..	..	3 47	5 17	6 17	6 25	7 35	7 53	9 45
Chappel & Wakes Colne	2L59		3 52	4 41	4 46		6 11	7 14	10 4						6 33		8 1	
White Colne					4 51										6 38			
Earls Colne					4 55			7 21							6 42	7 47		
Halstead					5 0			7 27				4 3			6 49	7 53		
Sible & Castle Hedingham					5 7			7 33							6 56	7 59		
Yeldham					5 12			7 39							7 2	8 5		
Birdbrook					5 20			7 46							7 10			
Bures			3 59	4 48			6 18		10 11				5 28	6 28			8 10	9 56
Sudbury (Suffolk) arr	3L12		4 6	4 55			6 25		10 18				5 36	6 36			8 18	10 4
dep			4 7	4 58			6 26										8 23	
Long Melford			4G13	5 5			6 32										8 27	
Glemsford				5 10			6 37											
Cavendish				5 13			6 41											
Clare				5 18			6 46											
Stoke (Suffolk)				5 23			6 50											
Sturmer				5 28			6 56											
Haverhill arr				5 33	5 27		7 0	7 54				4 26			7 18	8 18		
dep		3 23		5 33			7 0	7 54							7 20			
Bartlow arr		3 33		5 44			7 11	8 5							7 31			
29 London (L'pool St) arr		..		..	..	..	..	11 28				..	..	..	..	..	..	..
Bartlow dep		3 37		5 44			7 11	8 5							7 32			
Linton		3 42		5 48			7 15	8 10							7 37			
Pampisford		3 47		5 54			7 21											
Shelford } A		3 55		6 1			..	8 24							7 48			
Cambridge } A arr		4 2		6 8			7 33	8 31							7 54			
8 London (King's C.) arr		6S24	..	7S47	..	..	9h59	10E53	..	..	..	..	..	..	..	..	..	..
4 „ (L'pool St) „		b6R 9		8T41				11U28							9 59			

D Diesel Train
[D] Diesel Train. Second class only

A For other trains between Shelford and Cambridge, see Table 4
B On Saturdays dep Liverpool Street 5 33 pm
b First and Second class
C Via Colchester
E Except Saturdays
F On Saturdays dep Liverpool Street 4 36 pm via Colchester
G Arrival time
H Via Shelford. On Sats. arr 9 50 am
h Second class only Cambridge to Baldock (on Saturdays to King's Cross)
J Via Shelford
K On Saturdays dep 12 49 pm
L On Saturdays runs 3 minutes later
N On Saturdays dep Colchester 4 17 pm
P On Saturdays dep Colchester 6 15 pm
Q Via Colchester. On Sats. dep 8 30 am
R On Fridays 10th July to 28th August arr 6 3 pm
S Saturdays only
T On Fridays arr 8 31 pm
U On Saturdays arr 9 56 and on Mondays to Fridays 20th July to 28th August 10 3 pm
V On Saturdays dep 8 30 am via Colchester
Y On Fridays 26th June to 4th Sept. arr 1 29 and on Sats. arr 1 39 pm
Z From 10th July to 29th August arr 6 3 on Fridays and 5 18 pm on Saturdays

Table 23—see page 278

Table 22— *continued*

CAMBRIDGE, HAVERHILL, SUDBURY, HALSTEAD and MARK'S TEY

Miles	Miles	Week Days																
			am	am	am	am	am	am	am	am	am	am	am	pm	pm	pm	pm	am
					Through Train Bury St. Edmunds dep 7 45 am to Mark's Tey (on Mondays to Fridays to Norwich (Thorpe) arr 10 49 am (Tables 23 and 3)		Through Train from Mildenhall dep 7 34 am (Table 31)		Through Train from Audley End dep 9 34 am (Table 29)	Through Train to Norwich (Thorpe) arr 1 50 pm (Table 3) Except Saturdays	Through Train to Norwich (Thorpe) arr 1 54 pm (Table 3) Saturdays only	Except Saturdays	Saturdays only	Saturdays only Through Train Leicester (London Rd.) dep 8 10 am to Clacton-on-Sea arr 1 7 pm (Tables 37, 35, 30, 3 and 24)	Saturdays only	Except Saturdays		Through Train to Norwich (Thorpe) arr 4 50 pm (Table 3)
		4 London (L'pool St) dep	4J20				5 54					9J 2	10P20					11N24
		8 " (King's C.) "										9 7	9 18					10E30
			D	D	D	D	[D]		[D]	D	D	D	D		D	D	D	D
—	—	Cambridge A dep	6 35				8 21					1137	11 50					1 19
3¼	3¼	Shelford A	6 42				8 27					1143	11 59					1 25
7¼	7¼	Pampisford	6 50				8 34					1150	12 6					1 32
10¼	10¼	Linton	6 56				8 40					1156	12 12					1 38
12¼	12¼	Bartlow arr	7 0				8 44					12 0	12 16					1 42
—	—	29 London (L'pool St) dep							8b24			1024	10 24					
—	—	Bartlow dep	7 0				8 44		9 51			12 0	12 16					1 42
18½	18½	Haverhill arr	7 11				8 55		10 5			1211	12 27					1 53
		Haverhill dep		7 27			8 56	9 4		1051	10 51						1 57	1 53
20¾	—	Sturmer						9 7		1055	10 55							1 57
23¼	—	Stoke (Suffolk)						9 13		11 1	11 1							2 3
25¼	—	Clare						9 18		11 5	11n10							2 7
28	—	Cavendish						9 24		1111	11 15							2 13
29¾	—	Glemsford						9 27		1114	11 19							2 16
31¾	—	Long Melford			8 18			9 33		1119	11 24					1222		2 21
34¾	—	Sudbury (Suffolk) arr			8 24			9 40		1126	11 30					1228		2 28
		Sudbury (Suffolk) dep			8 25			9 40		1126	11 31				1226	1229		2 28
39¾	—	Bures			8 32			9 49		1133	11 38							2 36
—	22	Birdbrook		7 34			9 3										2 4	
—	25¼	Yeldham		7 41			9 10										2 11	
—	28¼	Sible & Castle Hedingham		7 46			9 15										2 16	
—	31¼	Halstead		7 53		8 39	9 22										2 23	
—	34	Earls Colne		7 58			9 27										2 28	
—	35¼	White Colne					9 30										2 31	
43	37¾	Chappel & Wakes Colne		8 4	8 40		9 35	10h 3		1141	11k56						2 36	2 43
46½	41½	Mark's Tey arr		8 11	8 46	8 54	9S41	10 10		1147	12 3			1214	1244	1247	2 42	2 50
51¾	46½	3 Colchester arr		8 24	8L55	9R59	10S 8	11E 2		1155	12 10			1232				2 57
93¾	88	3 London (L'pool St) "			9 52	9 52	C11S29	11E28		1C20	1C20					2 28		4C20

	Week Days—continued										Sundays							
	pm	pm	pm	pm	pm	pm	pm	pm	pm	pm	am	am		pm	pm	pm	pm	pm
	Through Train Sheffield (Vic.) dep 8 55 am to Clacton-on-Sea arr 3 47 pm (Tables 65, 33, 32, 3 and 24) Saturdays only. Runs 18th July to 29th August inclusive		Through Train Cambridge to Colchester	From Bury St. Edmunds dep 4 19 pm (Table 23)	Saturdays only	Except Saturdays		Through Train to Colchester (Table 3)	Through Train from Audley End dep 7 0 pm (Table 29)	Through Train Cambridge to Colchester	Through Train Cambridge to Clacton-on-Sea arr 10 25 am (Tables 3 and 24)	Through Train Bury St. Edmunds dep 9 0 am to Clacton-on-Sea arr 11 4 am (Tables 23, 3 and 24)						Through Train to Ipswich arr 11 0 pm (Table 3)
4 London (L'pool St) dep			12G24		3J24	3J24				5F57								
8 " (King's C.) "			1E25															
		D	D				D		[D]	D				D	D	D	D	D
Cambridge A dep	1 31		3 1		5 15	5 17				7 38	7 55							
Shelford A			3 7		5 21	5 23				7 44	8 2							
Pampisford			3 14		5 30	5 32				7 53								
Linton			3f27		5 36	5 38				7 58	8 16							
Bartlow arr			3 31		5 41	5 43				8 3	8 20							
29 London (L'pool St) dep			12E24		3 24				5b54	5 54								
Bartlow dep			3 41		5 45	5 45			7 16	8 10	8 21							
Haverhill arr			3 51		5 57	5 57			7 33	8 20	8 33							
Haverhill dep			3 51		5 58	5 58	6 2			8 22	8 36			4 30			8 23	
Sturmer					6 1	6 1				8e29								
Stoke (Suffolk)					6 7	6 7				8e37								
Clare					6 12	6 12				8 41								
Cavendish					6 18	6 18				8 47								
Glemsford					6 21	6 21				8 50								
Long Melford				4 48	6t35	6t35				8 56		9 31						
Sudbury (Suffolk) arr				4 54	6 41	6 41				9 2		9 38						
Sudbury (Suffolk) dep		3 20						7 6		9 3		9 40			5 40	7 9		10 9
Bures								7 14		9 10		9 50			5 48	7 16		
Birdbrook			3 59				6 9				8 46						8 30	
Yeldham			4 6				6 16				8 55			4 43				
Sible & Castle Hedingham			4 11				6 21				9 2			4 48				
Halstead			4 17				6 28				9e11			4 55			8 46	
Earls Colne			4 22				6 33				9 17			5 0				
White Colne			4 26								9 22							
Chappel & Wakes Colne		3 33	4g42				6 40	7 23		9d22	9 28							
Mark's Tey arr		3 40	4 49				6 46	7 30		9 28	9 35	10 5		5 12	6 0	7 29	9 1	1027
3 Colchester arr	3 14	3 55	4 59				6B59	7 54		9 42	9 47			6 14	6 14	7 42	9 48	1035
3 London (L'pool St) "		5T31	6C24				8 44	8 44		12a1	1119	1129		7 19	7 29	9 3	1025	1157

D Diesel Train
[D] Diesel Train. Second class only

A For other trains between Cambridge and Shelford, see Table 4
a am
B On Saturdays arr Colchester 7 54 pm
b First and Second class
C Via Colchester
d Arr 4 minutes earlier
E Except Saturdays
e Arr 3 minutes earlier
F Via Shelford. On Saturdays dep Liverpool Street 5 54 pm via Cambridge
f Arr 7 minutes earlier
G On Saturdays dep 1J24 pm
g Arr 12 minutes earlier
h Arr 6 minutes earlier
J Via Shelford
k Arr 10 minutes earlier
L On Saturdays arr 9 3 am
N Runs on Mondays to Fridays 20th July to 28th August incl. and every Saturday
n Arr 5 minutes earlier
P On 20th June and from 29th August dep 9J0 am; on 27th June and 4th July 8J54 am
R On Saturdays arr 10 8 am
S Saturdays only
T On Saturdays arr 5C28 pm
t Arr 8 minutes earlier

Table 23—see page 278

Above and left:
Summer 1959 timetable. *Author's collection*

K56 WEEKDAYS — COLCHESTER AND CAMBRIDGE

DOWN

Mileage M C	M C	Station	No	8-69	8-69 SX	8-00 SO	8-69 SO	8-69 SX		8-69 SO	8-69 SX			8-69 SX
0 0		COLCHESTER ...... arr	1	.....	.....	..	..	..		..	..			
5 3		Mark's Tey .. dep	2	6 28	11 28	..	..	..		..	..			
		Mark's Tey .. arr	3	.....	.....	..	..	..		..	..			Stafford Allen's Siding—R
8 41	0 0	Chappel .. dep	4	6R44	11 46	..	..	..		..	..			
		Chappel .. arr	5	6 58	11X57	..	..	..		..	..			
		Chappel .. dep	6	7 15	12 20	..	..	..		11 39	11 39			
	2 10	White Colne .. arr	7	..	..	..	..	..		..	..			
		White Colne .. dep	8	R	..	..	..	..		..	..			
	3 48	Earls Colne .. arr	9		12 33	..	..	..		..	..			Glemsford arr. 15.56
		Earls Colne .. dep	10	R	12 43	..	..	..		..	..			
	6 6	Halstead .. arr	11	7 50	12 53	..	..	..		..	..			
		Halstead .. dep	12		13 45	..	..	..		..	..			
	9 30	Sible and Castle .. arr	13		13 57	..	..	..		..	..			
		Hedingham .. dep	14		14 17	..	..	..		..	..			
	11 72	Yeldham .. arr	15		14 28	..	..	..		..	..			
11 67		Bures .. arr	16	..	..	..	..	..		11X50	11X50			..
		Bures .. dep	17	..	..	..	..	..		12 05	12 05			..
16 56		Sudbury .. arr	18	..	..	..	..	..		12 20	12 20			..
		Sudbury .. dep	19	..	..	..	..	..		12 42	12 42			14X55
19 63		LONG MELFORD .. arr	20	..	..	..	Cambridge South Jn. 14 54	Cambridge South Jn. 15 13		12 55	12 55			15 08
		LONG MELFORD .. dep	21	..	..	..				13 25	13 25			15 46
22 27		Glemsford	22	..	..	..				R	R			16 15
23 47		Cavendish .. arr	23	..	..	..					13 50			16 22
		Cavendish .. dep	24	..	..	..				R	..			16X33
26 15		Clare .. arr	25	..	..	..					..			16 43
		Clare .. dep	26	..	..	..				13 58	..			16 57
28 26		Stoke	27	..	..	..				..	..			..
31 21		Sturmer	28	..	..	..				..	..			..
	0 0	Haverhill South .. dep	29	..	..	12 22	..	..		..	..			..
	0 53	Colne Valley Jn. .. arr	30	..	..	12 26	..	..		..	..			..
		.. dep	31	..	..	12 31	..	..		..	..			..
33 21	1 63	HAVERHILL .. arr	32	..	..	12 35	..	..		14X15	..			17 17
		.. dep	33	..	..	..	13 20	13 20		14 40	..			18X13
39 24		Bartlow .. arr	34	..	..	..	13 41	13 41		..	..			..
		.. dep	35	..	..	..	14X05	14X05		15R04	..			18 30
41 26		Linton .. arr	36	..	..	..		14 15		15R14	..			18 37
		.. dep	37	..	..	..	14 13	14 25		16X37	..			18 49
44 5		Pampisford	38	..	..	..	[6]	..		..	..			..
48 16		Shelford .. arr	39	..	..	..	..	..		..	..			..
		.. dep	40	..	..	..	14 35	14*53		16 55	..			19 07
50 41		Trumpington ..	41	..	..	..	14X42	15X02		..	..			..
51 32		CAMBRIDGE .. arr	42	..	..	..	14 59	15 18		17 07	..			19 19

Code					8-69 SO	8-69 SX	8-69 SX Q
Cambridge	..	..	..	.. dep.	6 05	11 20	11 30
Shelford	..	..	..	.. arr.	6 15	11 30	11 40
Pampisford	..	..	..	.. arr.		11 42	11 52
	..	..	..	.. dep.		11 52	12 02
Linton	..	..	..	.. arr.		12 04	12 14
	..	..	..	.. dep.	6 32	12 23	12 34
Bartlow	..	..	..	.. arr.	6 37	12 30	12 41
Haverhill	..	..	..	.. arr.	6 54	12 47	12 58
	..	..	..	.. dep.	7 14	13 12	13 12
Stoke ..	..	..	..			R	R
Clare ..	..	..	..	.. arr.	7 33	13 37	13 37
	..	..	..	.. dep.	7 43	13 47	13 47
Cavendish	..	..	..	.. arr.	7 53		
	..	..	..	.. dep.	8 03	13 55	13 55
Glemsford	..	..	..	.. arr.	8 11		
	..	..	..	.. dep.	8 21	13 58	13 58
Long Melford	..	..	..	.. arr.	8 31		
	..	..	..	.. dep.	8 41	14 03	14 03
Sudbury	..	..	..	.. arr.	8 54	14 13	14 13
	..	..	..	.. dep.			14 22
Bures ..	..	..	..	.. arr.			14 38

Code					8-69 SO	8-69 SX	8-69 SX Q	8-69
Bures ..	..	..	..	.. dep.	..	..	14 48	..
Sudbury	..	..	..	arr.			15 03	..
	..	..	..	.. dep.	10 00	10 15	..	15 15
Long Melford	..	..	..	.. arr.				15 28
	..	..	..	.. dep.	10 11	10 26	..	15 45
Stafford Allen's Siding	..	..			R	R		
Glemsford	..	..	..	.. arr.	10 28			15 55
	..	..	..	.. dep.	10 38	10 42		16 10
Cavendish	..	..	..	arr.				16 17
	..	..	..	.. dep.	10 43	10 45		16 32
Clare ..	..	..	..	.. arr.	10 50	10 52		16 41
	..	..	..	.. dep.	11 05	11 02		16 50
Haverhill	..	..	..	.. arr.	11 25	11 22		17 10
	..	..	..	.. dep.	11 42	12 15		17 18
Bartlow	..	..	..	arr.	12 01	12 34		
	..	..	..	.. dep.	12 11	12 45		17 35
Linton	..	..	..	.. arr.	12 21			17 42
	..	..	..	.. dep.	12 42	12 53		18 12
Shelford	..	..	..	.. arr.	13 00	13 08		18 30
Cambridge	..	..	..	.. arr.	13 10	13 18		18 40

Above:
Monday, 7 December 1964 working timetable. *Author's collection*

K56 WEEKDAYS

COLCHESTER AND CAMBRIDGE

DOWN

Mileage M	C	M	C	Station	Ln	8-69 SX	8-69	8-00 SX	8-69 SO	8-69 SX		8-69 SO	8-69 SX			8-69 SX	
0	0			COLCHESTER ...... arr	1												
				.. .. dep	2	6 28	11 28										
5	3			Mark's Tey .... arr	3										Stafford Allen's Siding—R		
				.. .. dep	4	6R44	11 46										
8	41	0	0	Chappel ...... arr	5	6 58	11X57										
				.. .. dep	6	7 15	12 20					11 39	11 39				
		2	10	White Colne ..... arr	7												
				.. .. dep	8	R											
		3	48	Earls Colne .. arr	9		12 33										
				.. dep	10	R	12 43										
		6	6	Halstead .... arr	11	7 50	12 53								Glemsford arr. 15.56		
				.. dep	12		13 45										
		9	30	Sible and Castle arr	13		13 57										
				Hedingham .. dep	14		14 17										
		11	72	Yeldham .. .. arr	15		14 28										
11	67			Bures .. arr	16							11X50	11X50				
				.... dep	17							12 05	12 05				
16	56			Sudbury .. arr	18							12 20	12 20				
19	63			...... dep	19							12 42	12 42			14X55	
				LONG MELFORD .. arr	20				Cambridge South Jn. 14*54	Cambridge South Jn. 15*13		12 55	12 55			15 08	
				.... dep	21							13 25	13 25			15 46	
22	27			Glemsford	22							R	R			16 15	
23	47			Cavendish ...... arr	23								13 50			16 22	
				.. dep	24							R				16X33	
26	15			Clare .... arr	25											16 43	
				.. dep	26							13 58				16 57	
28	26			Stoke	27												
31	21			Sturmer	28												
		0	0	Haverhill South .... dep	29			12 22									
		0	53	Colne Valley Jn. .. arr	30			12 26									
				...... dep	31			12 31									
33	21	1	63	HAVERHILL .. .. arr	32			12 35				14X15				17 17	
				.... dep	33				13 20	13 20		14 40				18X13	
39	24			Bartlow .. .. .. arr	34				13 41	13 41							
				.... dep	35				14X05	14X05		15R04				18 30	
41	26			Linton .. .. arr	36					14 15		15R14				18 37	
				.... dep	37				14 13	14 25		16X37				18 49	
44	5			Pampisford	38				[6]								
48	16			Shelford .... arr	39												
				.. dep	40				14 35	14*53		16 55				19 07	
50	41			Trumpington	41				14X42	15X02							
51	32			CAMBRIDGE .. .. arr	42				14 59	15 18		17 07				19 19	

Above and above left:
September 1964-13 June 1965 working timetable. *Author's collection*

Waveney Valley Railway

THE Waveney Valley line had a protracted gestation, and has always been fertile ground for students of 'what if . . .' It took many years to plan and build, had many alternative routes, and sported some of the earliest closed stations in the country, largely because they had been provided at extremely close intervals. The architecture was outstanding, and many buildings survive to this day, but the traffic potential was not because, although it linked a series of small towns, it was orientated the wrong way for the predominant flows.

An 1847 scheme would have involved the Norfolk Railway in building a line from Reedham to the Eastern Union near Diss, which would have crossed the River Waveney by a swing bridge 1½ miles below Beccles, and which would have needed over 40 level crossings, each with a station or lodge, and would have had to be completed within five years.

In 1850 the Eastern Union deposited plans for a line from Tivetshall to Bungay, Beccles, Reedham and Halesworth, with Peter Bruff as the engineer. There would have been a triangular junction at Tivetshall, then more or less as built to Bungay, where it would have passed to the south of the town. A junction between the Beccles and Halesworth sections was proposed just east of the station there.

The Waveney Valley line proper was first mooted in 1851. The Eastern Union line between Haughley Junction and Norwich was open for traffic, and the businessmen of Harlestone, as it was then spelt, saw that their market town would be passed by. The Waveney Valley Railway Company was formed, and in plans deposited in 1852 proposed a line from Tivetshall, on the EU main line, to Beccles, on the proposed Halesworth, Beccles & Haddiscoe line. This would have run between Bungay and Beccles almost exclusively within Suffolk, required two bridges over the River Waveney, and formed a triangular junction with the HB&H.

Progress on the line was slow, and severely limited by lack of funds. By 1855, construction had advanced eastwards as far as Harleston, and the line was opened thence from Tivetshall on 1 December. The Waveney Valley Railway Act of 1856 applied for an extension of time on the Extension Act of 1853, which had already been extended by the 1855 Act. The line was now shown going only as far as Bungay, again passing to the south of the town. Construction continued to be slow, and the route changed yet again before Bungay was finally reached.

Local feelings had run high about the course of the line and the position of the proposed station in the town. Just to the north of Bungay, in the loop of the river, is Outney Common, of which it was said in the *Ipswich Journal* that there was '. . . nothing more salubrious or beautiful than this remarkable peninsula'. Townspeople wanted the railway to skirt the common to the south, thus bringing it and the station nearer the town, but the WVR wanted to go across the common. Fears were expressed that there would be no station at all, goods and passengers having to go to Earsham or Ditchingham on either side.

Peter Bruff, engineer to the local company as well as the Eastern Union, assured the town that its conditions would be met. The owners of Outney Common, not above a little strong-arming, intimated in late March of 1860 that if this were so, they would settle with the railway on favourable terms; if not, the price would be much higher. The directors decided in April that they would not put the station where the town wanted it, and claimed to be responding to a letter from Mr Scott saying that they should not cross land occupied by the National School Room. By 16 June the railway had reached nearly as far as the west edge of the common and had paid a deposit for land there, although few shares had been taken up locally.

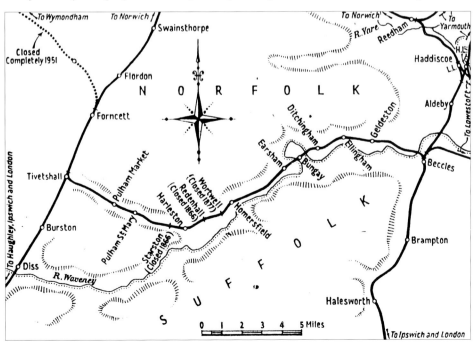

Left:
The Waveney Valley Railway.
The Railway Magazine

Above:
**Beccles station, with Beccles North Junction signalbox prominent. The engine shed is in the distance.
The Waveney Valley branch curves round past the box, while the Yarmouth and
Lowestoft lines sweep away to the right.** *Adrian Vaughan collection*

Meanwhile, the Waveney Valley had been in dispute with the Eastern Counties Railway, which had taken over working of the former Eastern Union lines on 1 January 1854, and also worked the WVR for 75%. The local company wanted it worked for 50% of gross receipts, as was the Sudbury-Clare line, and decided to take over the operation itself from 15 September. The directors expressed the desire to do so in harmony with the ECR, and would take on the men now working their line on the same terms. The ECR responded with an offer to work the line for 50% when it opened to Beccles, but negotiations seem to have foundered on the question of maintenance, the Waveney Valley contending that it had deteriorated under ECR operation. The WVR duly obtained its own rolling stock and operated the line itself.

The line opened on 2 November 1860 to a temporary wooden station at Bungay described as 'comfortable and convenient'. This was just as well, as it had to last for over 70 years before replacement! The *Ipswich Journal* reported that work was to start immediately on the line to Beccles. The bill for the purchase of the necessary land had received the Royal Assent on 23 July of that year. In December, the town gas supply was extended to the station, and on Monday 10th, one of the first accidents on the newly opened line happened when a train went through the Five Acre Lane gates at Earsham, the crossing keeper having failed to open them.

A succession of bills continued to be sought for the extension of the line, which now passed to the north of Bungay. Construction towards Ditchingham was in progress when the company submitted its bill in November 1859 for extension to Beccles, the proposed line now being almost entirely within Norfolk. It was envisaged that the Waveney would be crossed by a bridge with three openings of 50ft span, 8ft 6in high, and that there would be level crossings at both Northgate and Ravensmere in Beccles, but not at Pound Lane, which was to be diverted. Construction

continued slowly, but by November 1862 was almost complete. Traders were concerned at the potential disruption to traffic along Ravensmere and Northgate, two important roads into the town, and by the low clearance of bridges. They called for a level crossing instead of the low arch at the former.

On Friday, 20 February 1863 the line was ready for inspection by Col Yolland, who arrived by special train at Beccles at 12.45pm and went immediately to Bungay, accompanied by Peter Bruff and William Bruff, the engineers, Mr Boys the agent to the contractor, Mr Fenn the company's land valuer, and others. Lunch was taken at Bungay station, and the line was then inspected on the journey back to Beccles. Every bridge and culvert was tested by running an engine over it several times. When they reached the bridge over the Waveney just outside Beccles, a second engine was attached and the pair was run over several times at high and low speeds. Col Yolland pronounced that the 'entire works appear to have been done in a most substantial manner'. The local company was taken over by the Great Eastern Railway on 1 March 1863, when a special train was run from Ipswich to bring staff to the line, including Mr H. Wilkes who was left in charge of Ellingham for a few days. The line opened to the public on the following day and the *Ipswich Journal* expressed the hope that the timetable was only temporary. The Waveney Valley, unfortunately, arrived a little too late for the towns along its route, and did not then connect them with a direct line to Norwich, or provide an obvious outlet to the west. Beccles was also on the main lines between Lowestoft, Yarmouth and London, and grew vigorously.

Waveney Valley trains had their own bay platform (No 1), known as the Waveney dock, on the down side of Beccles station. There were very extensive livestock pens here, Beccles having an important market. The line passed Beccles North Junction signalbox, which had 84 levers and controlled all of the north end of the

Above:
A view of Beccles station looking south in about 1924, with a Waveney Valley train waiting in the bay. Cattle pens are to the right of the engine, and the main down and up Yarmouth platforms to the left. *Stations UK*

Below:
Beccles station. *Crown Copyright*

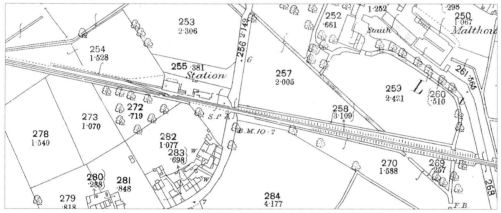

station, including the junction of the Lowestoft and Yarmouth lines. The small turntable was in the angle between the Yarmouth and Waveney Valley lines, the latter swinging away to the west almost immediately, passing through coal sidings and over Pound Road level crossing. The bridge over Ravensmere was one of very low headroom, and liable to flood, whereas Northgate had a level crossing with a pedestrian subway, one of the first in East Anglia. Almost immediately the line crossed the River Waveney, this bridge being rebuilt in the 1930s, and headed over the marshes on a low embankment. The speed limit was 50mph throughout, except for the curve at Tivetshall to join the main line, which was restricted to 20mph.

The first stop was at Geldeston where there was a spacious red-brick goods shed and single siding running through it, plus a single platform on the north side of the line and station building, to the west of the level crossing. The station was closed completely on 22 May 1916, but reopened unstaffed on 14 September, and was restored to full status on 2 October 1922. In any case, although not a block post, it had a small signalbox on the platform, by the gates, and in the later years of the passenger service was run by a porter-signalman. George Beckett had this job when the passenger service closed, and then went to Barnby, near Oulton Broad. It was one of the stations on the Waveney Valley where towing of wagons by rope was authorised, the others being Ellingham, Homersfield and both Pulhams. It was not wholly unknown for this to go wrong. It was the responsibility of the porter-signalman to open the goods shed doors prior to detaching wagons, but on one occasion when a mineral wagon was being knocked off this was not done, and although it did not need to go into the shed it rolled through the doors and demolished them. Both guard and porter-signalman received a 'Form 1' (a serious reprimand) for this escapade.

In later years the shed at Geldeston was let to Lever Bros, who used it to store animal feed — pig meal, cattle cake, chicken feed, etc. The agent would get orders, which would then be delivered by a Scammell lorry. This came out from Lowestoft with parcels, and was then loaded with feedstuffs from the goods shed which it then spent the rest of the day delivering. The feed arrived in 9-ton covered goods vans, at least one per week. Another particularly delightful traffic was human manure, or 'sludge', from London. This had been dug from the settlement beds at a treatment works, and farmers would shovel the clay-like material out of the wagons, being charged demurrage if not done within three days. The station was able to handle most traffic except livestock and horseboxes, and had a 1½-ton crane.

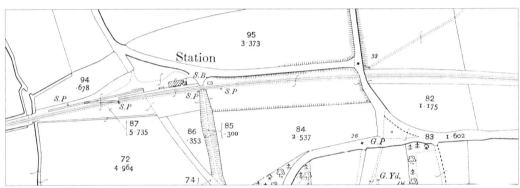

Ellingham station was only 1½ miles further on, and had a rather more imposing building in the same Italianate style as others on the line, but only a single platform and siding, which handled brick traffic. It had no goods shed but there was a loading dock behind the platform. During World War 2 sidings between these two stations had been used in connection with petrol supplies to nearby airfields, and trains of tank wagons would be held under cover of darkness at Beccles prior to forwarding. After the war, sugar beet was also handled here. Ellingham had fairly limited facilities, handling only passengers and parcels, general goods and furniture vans, etc. There was no crane, and it could not handle livestock.

Ditchingham was a further 1½ miles on. For the Waveney Valley, these seemingly close spacings represented a reduction in the number of original stations! It could handle all types of traffic, and had yet another level crossing, this time over the main road to Norwich, and again controlled from a signalbox, although it was not a staff station. The passenger platform was on the north side of the line, with the goods shed backing on to it, and there was a loading dock opposite. It did have a small yard on the north side, with storage sheds. Ditchingham brewery was a short distance away on the Norwich road, and there was a silk works close by to the west, which later became a maltings. Not surprisingly, a great deal of malt was loaded at the station, which was put in sacks and then in covered vans; in 1938, this amounted to 1,374 tons worth £1,538 to the railway. Latterly the roofs of these vans were so poor that they had to be sheeted over. Silcocks had the goods shed, and arrangements for delivery of feed were similar to those at Geldeston. There were always bantams roaming around the goods yard, because of the abundance of grain, and their descendants can be seen to this day by the roundabout on the A143, on the old trackbed.

All the while the railway followed the gradually narrowing river valley, usually on the Norfolk side, making a brief foray back into Suffolk in reaching Bungay, only a mile further on. The River Waveney forms a large loop around the north of the town, and the railway cut across this at the Beccles end by means of an iron girder bridge on concrete supports. Bungay was one of the three block posts and passing places on the line, but not from the start. It appears that this was not done until 1893, when Maj-Gen Hutchinson inspected alterations at the station, which included the provision of a new down loop line and new platform, and a new signalbox off the Beccles end of the new platform. Located on the northern edge of the town and with Outney Common further to the north, the station was a busy place with a sizeable goods yard. It could handle all types of traffic, having a 1½-ton crane. The temporary wooden buildings survived until the mid-1930s — much longer than their permanent replacements! The station was particularly noted for the high quality of its floral displays in the summer. The main buildings and goods yard were on the south (town) side of the line, with access to the latter from Broad Street, which led directly to the town centre. Broad Street crossed the railway on the level, leading to the common and marshes on the other side of the line. Passengers arrived via Outney Road, and a brick arch bridge led from this over the railway to the common. There were a number of goods sidings, cattle pens, a large goods shed with through road, and loading docks. The Chaucer Press was a prominent local company whose printing works was close to the station, and for some years they attached one or two vans to the 6.10pm from Beccles for forwarding to London via Tivetshall, Mondays to Fridays. Bungay saw special traffic in connection with the steeplechases held on the common every spring and autumn

Above:
Ditchingham station and level crossing, where the main Yarmouth to Diss road crossed the line. The maltings were about a quarter of a mile on the left. The date is around 1910. *John Brodribb collection*

Right:
Ditchingham station in about 1950, with a good crowd of people for the Beccles train. *Stations UK*

Below:
Ditchingham station. *Crown Copyright*

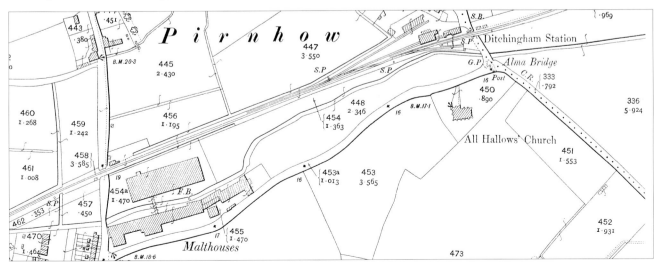

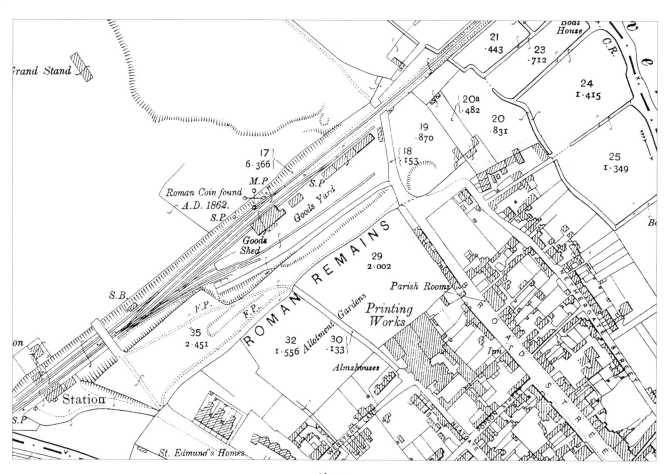

Above:
Bungay station. *Crown Copyright*

Below:
**An interesting view of the signalbox at Bungay, probably taken about 1900,
and with a long rake of wagons standing on the up line.** *John Brodribb collection*

Above:
Bungay station about 1950, looking west. *Stations UK*

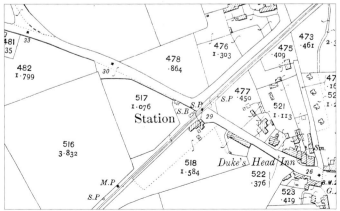

Above:
Earsham station and level crossing, with the signalman standing on the verandah of his box just visible. The station itself is to the right of the picture, probably taken about 1900.
John Brodribb collection

Left:
Earsham station, 1905.
Crown Copyright

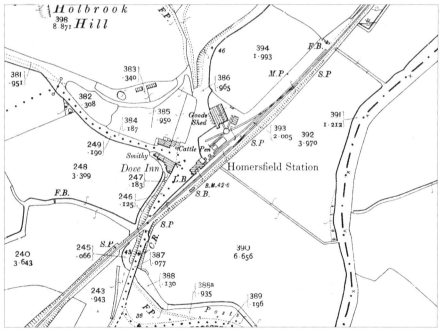

Above:
Homersfield suffered seriously in the 1912 floods, when much of the line was washed away. This poor quality postcard view shows the station, signalbox and the Dove Inn, from the south side of the line. The extent of the devastation can be judged by the fact that the signal post has been scoured out of the ground by the force of the water. *John Brodribb collection*

Left:
Homersfield station. *Crown Copyright*

until 1924, after which they were confined to the spring, Whit Monday 1937 being the last. These trains for racegoers started from far afield, including Yarmouth and Lowestoft. Many special trains were needed on the only occasion that the Suffolk Agricultural Show was held on Bungay Common, on Thursday 6 and Friday 7 June 1929.

Earsham was a mere ¾ mile west of Bungay, and had a station building of distinct character quite unlike the general style for the line. It closed during World War 1 at the same time as Geldeston, and reopened as a halt on 1 August 1919; the only member of staff was a porter in charge. Entrance to the platform was via a wooden gate or through double doors in the building. There was a small waiting room with booking and parcels office. There were no sidings or signals here, except in connection with the level crossing, having been taken out of use when the station closed. A long loop between Earsham and Homersfield, installed during World War 2, served the nearby RAF station and remained in use in the early 1950s for the loading of ammunition from USAF airfields in the area.

The line continued to follow the valley towards Homersfield, with a level crossing over the main road, about halfway from Earsham. The next station was three miles further on, where there

Left:
For many years there were several stations on the Waveney Valley which had closed very early on, but which remained more or less intact. This is Wortwell, just to the west of Homersfield; all it lacks is a complete platform. This view dates from about 1924. *Stations UK*

Right:
The station at Harleston, as befitted the original objective of the line, was built on a large scale, although very much in the same style as elsewhere. This 1921 view shows a number of horse-drawn carriages outside the entrance. *Stations UK*

was a large goods shed set at an angle to the railway line, and reached by wagon turntable. All facilities were on the north side of the line; the station could handle all types of traffic, and had a 1½-ton crane. The railway crossed the main road at the west end of the station, the level crossing being controlled by the signalbox, and then passed immediately over a small stream. This bridge had to be replaced after the 1912 floods. The goods shed here was let to Woods, Sadd & Moore, who were Norwich-based corn merchants, and sugar beet — as with all stations on the line — was an important traffic. The last stationmaster, Jack Mayhew, was made redundant when the passenger service finished on Saturday, 3 January 1953.

This section was particularly prone to flooding, which happened with devastating effect after the exceptional conditions of August 1912. Torrential rain over the Bank Holiday — some things never change — caused havoc over much of Norfolk and north Suffolk, and in the Waveney Valley four inches fell within 36 hours.

Railways out of Beccles to Lowestoft, Yarmouth and Bungay were all under water, with the swing bridge there being the only visible part of the line. Much of the platform at Homersfield was washed away, and a great deal of track was left suspended in mid-air. The Great Eastern put on a bus service between Harleston and Bungay for about a week while the track was reinstated. A similar situation arose between 29 January and 1 February 1939 when the line was flooded between Bungay and Geldeston.

Less than half a mile distant was Wortwell, which never had goods facilities and closed from 1 January 1878, and only slightly beyond that Redenhall, which lost its service in August 1866, seeing less than six years of active use. When open, all trains had called at both on an 'as required' basis. Harleston, the original impetus for the line, lay only 2¾ miles from Homersfield, the station being reached by an iron girder bridge over the main Bury St Edmunds to Lowestoft road, later the A143 and long since bypassed. The formation was double-track width for some distance

Above:
Harleston, in about 1950, looks like a main line station in this view towards Tivetshall. *Stations UK*

Below:
Harleston station *Crown Copyright*

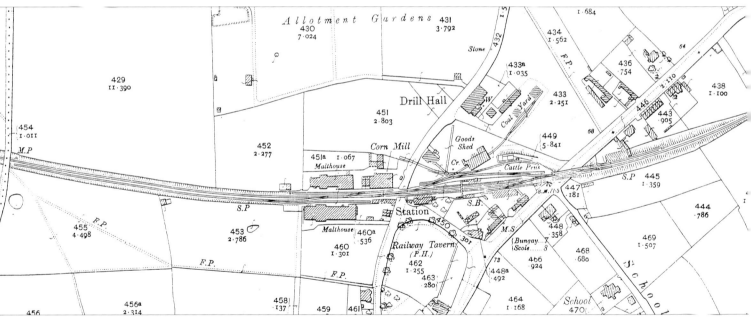

either side of the station, occupied by headshunts as well as the running line. There were two platforms linked by a footbridge, the main buildings being on the up (to Tivetshall) side. The passenger loop was not particularly long, the lines converging at the west end just beyond the level crossing. Watney's maltings had their own sidings. The goods yard, on the north side of the line, had an interesting and compact layout. The goods shed had a through road which then gave access to the coal yard behind the Drill Hall, Kerrison's and Thomas Moy operating from there. A loop ran round the back of the down platform and gave access to some short sidings via a wagon turntable, including one which crossed the road to a corn mill opposite. There were cattle pens at the other end of

the yard. This was possibly the most imposing station on the line, and was also a block post and passing place. In goods terms, Harleston handled considerable tonnages of sugar beet, flour, grain, malt and livestock.

The line now started to climb gently — albeit with a short section at 1 in 99 — out of the Waveney Valley, although it remains wide and the river meanders at this point. Yet another station at Starston, under a mile west of Harleston, closed at the same time as Redenhall; Pulham St Mary was only 2½ miles onward. It changed to 'Pulham Mary' in 1866, and although it reverted to its original title in June 1894, the change did not appear in the timetables until 1946, and railway staff knew it by this name ever after. The station

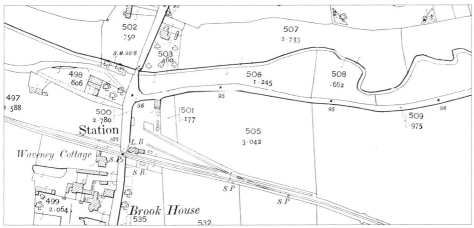

was on the east side of the level crossing, on a minor road from the village. Goods facilities ran to two sidings and a headshunt, with the station only able to handle ordinary goods, passengers and parcels. Pulham Market was only a mile further and, as with many on the line, underwent a name change (in March 1856), opening as Pulham St Magdalene. It was a staff station or block post able to pass goods, but not passenger trains, and did not have a loop. Between the two the spur to Pulham airfield, officially the Air Ministry Siding, branched to the south; this was the home of the airships known as the 'Pulham Pigs', the mile-long branch being built in 1915 by the Great Eastern Railway. During World War 2 a loop was installed on the branch, but later became disused. The RAF base at Pulham closed in February 1958, and the branch was abandoned soon afterwards. The line, gently graded on this section, crossed the main Ipswich to Norwich road, built originally by the Romans, on the level (the only such crossing between the two on what is now the A140), and continued on to Tivetshall Junction, a total distance of 19½ miles from Beccles. The junction faced Norwich, with Waveney Valley trains running into the outer face of the up platform, which was an island, and unable to cross on to the main line until they reached the points beyond the down end of the

station. There was a trailing connection at the other end with the up main. Some trains originally continued to Norwich Victoria station, later transferring to Thorpe.

Train services were never particularly extensive. When the line first opened between Tivetshall and Harleston there were six up trains on Mondays to Saturdays, with the first, at 6am from Harleston, running on Mondays only. Subsequent services left at 7.55am, 11.5am, 12.25pm, 3.30pm and 6.25pm. The down service was similar, with the 6.40am Mondays only and the 5.40pm Saturdays only. All the intermediate stations — Pulham Market, Pulham St Mary and Starston — were request stops, and there were no trains on Sundays.

In 1862, when the line had opened to Bungay, the service was essentially similar, consisting of five trains each way, with Earsham, Wortwell and Redenhall also being request stops and all trains calling intermediately at Homersfield. There was a Saturdays-only train for Norwich Market which left Bungay at 9.35am and arrived at Norwich Victoria at 11.10am, but the 11am from Bungay did not run on Saturdays. On the other hand, there was an 'engine and light carriages' which worked nonstop from Bungay to Tivetshall in connection with the Norwich Market

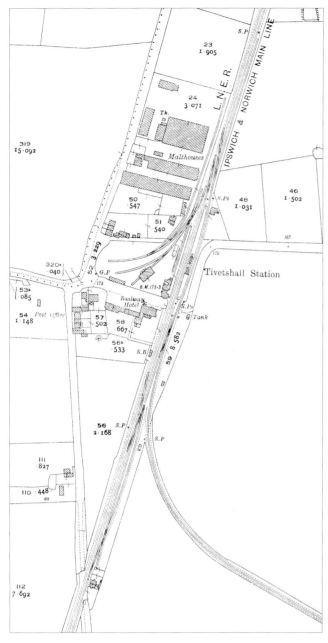

traffic. Once the Waveney Valley route opened throughout to the public on 2 March 1863, the passenger weekday service pattern was set for many years to come, and looked like this:

Beccles dep.	8.35am	12.15pm	2.50pm	7.10pm
Geldeston				
Ellingham				
Ditchingham				
Bungay	8.52am	12.35pm	3.10pm	7.30pm
Earsham				
Homersfield	9.0am	12.45pm	3.20pm	7.40pm
Wortwell				
Redenhall				
Harleston	9.10am	12.55pm	3.30pm	7.50pm
Starston				
Pulham St Mary				
Pulham Market				
Tivetshall arr.	9.30am	1.15pm	3.50pm	8.8pm
Tivetshall dep.	10.35am	1.30pm	4.10pm	8.25pm
Pulham Market				
Pulham St Mary				
Starston				
Harleston	10.55am	1.50pm	4.30pm	8.45pm
Redenhall				
Wortwell				
Homersfield	11.3am	2.0pm	4.40pm	8.55pm
Earsham				
Bungay	11.10am	2.10pm	4.50pm	9.5pm
Ditchingham				
Ellingham				
Geldeston				
Beccles arr.	11.30am	2.30pm	5.10pm	9.25pm

Other stations were served on an 'as required' basis. In the Summer 1913 weekday timetable an up train left Beccles for Tivetshall at 6.22am, calling only at Bungay, Earsham on request by passengers for London, and then all stations. The 6.56 and 9.2am trains called at all stations and went to Norwich Thorpe, except that the 6.56am went to Victoria on Saturdays only. The 11.40am was a Thorpe train, while the 2pm called at all stations to Forncett, being extended to Victoria on Saturdays. The 6.12pm from Beccles was actually a through train from Yarmouth South Town, where it started at 5.10pm and called at Belton, St Olaves, Haddiscoe High Level and Aldeby, a reversal being needed at Beccles. There was another Beccles to Norwich train at 7pm, and then an excursion from Yarmouth at 6.50pm on Mondays and Thursdays calling at all stations on the branch. The last up train was a Saturdays-only

Above:
Tivetshall junction, 1924. *Crown Copyright*

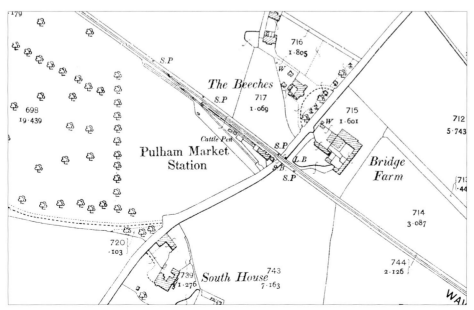

Left:
Pulham Market station.
Crown Copyright

Above:
Tivetshall Junction was served by a number of main line trains so as to give connections to and from
the Waveney Valley line. After closure of the latter to passengers, the occasional excursion was organised,
such as this one by the M&GN Preservation Society in October 1960. Class B12 No 61572 handled
the main line sections, being replaced on the Waveney Valley by 'J15' No 65469. *John C. Baker*

Above:
Pulham Market station in about 1950, looking westwards. *Stations UK*

Left and right:
ABC Railway Guide, December 1949. *Author's collection*

HARLESTON (Norfolk)
Map Sq. 19. Clos. day Thur.
From Liverpool Street via Ipswich and
Tivetshall 106¼ miles (122½ via Beccles).
1st cl.—Single 36/8, Mth. Ret. 44/-.
3rd cl.—Single 22/-, Mth. Ret. 29/4.

Liv. St.	Harlest.	Harlest.	Liv. St.
a.m.		a.m.	
4 25	8 56	7 35r	11 28
8 12r	11 41	7 36†r	11 28
10 25r	2 17	9 35r	1 38
p.m.		11 41†r	3 37
12 25s†	3 54	p.m.	
1 0r	5 51	1 10r	5 8
3 44†r	7 29	2 17†	6 52
5 8r	8 36	3 54r	7 6
—	—	5 51†	10 22
--	—	7 29	12 22
—	—	8 40§	2 30
—	—	—	—
—	—	—	—
—	—	—	—

No Sunday Trains.
† Via Ipswich and Beccles.
§ Via Tivetshall and Norwich.
e Not Sat.   s Sat. only.
r Refresh. Car.

TIVETSHALL (Norfolk)
Miles 100¾. Map Sq. 19
Pop. 543. Clos. day Wed.
From Liverpool Street via Ipswich.
1st cl.—Single 34/6, Mth. Ret. 41/6.
3rd cl.—Single 20/10, Mth. Ret. 27/8.

Liv. St.	Tivet.	Tivet.	Liv. St.
a.m.		a.m.	
4 25	7 58	7 4r	10 48
8 12r	11 0	8 26r	11 28
10 25r	1 48	9 58r	1 38
p.m.		p.m.	
1 0r	4 9	1 43r	5 8
3 44r	6 45	4 16r	7 6
5 8r	7 56	5 49r	9 15
8 8	11 11	7 56	12 22
—	—	9 0§	2 30
—	—	11 35e	3 56
—	—	—	—
	Sunday Trains.		
a.m.		a.m.	
10 0	1 38	10 4	1 48
p.m.		p.m.	
5 0	8 40	3 7	6 11
—	—	7 55	12 37
—	—	—	—

§ Via Norwich.   r Refresh. Car.
e Not Sat.   s Sat. only.

passenger to Harleston at 10.10pm. Goods traffic was covered by the 10.30am from Beccles, calling at Bungay, Harleston and Tivetshall, with different timings on Saturdays, and then running through to Wymondham via Ashwellthorpe. Cattle traffic could be attached at Pulham Market. There was an 11.53am goods from Beccles to Bungay, and another from Harleston to Norwich at 3.42pm. A brake goods left Beccles for Norwich at 2.40pm and called at all stations, to attach traffic if required. Tail traffic, in the form of braked trucks, could be worked between Beccles and Tivetshall only, provided that the trains actually started there, although the 8.40am from Forncett to Yarmouth was allowed one Westinghouse-piped truck of cattle from Tivetshall or Harleston to Beccles.

In the down direction there was a comparable service level. Trains left Norwich for Beccles via the Waveney Valley at 8.5 and 9.48am, and 12.10, 2.53 and 7.50pm, from Forncett at 3.57pm, and Tivetshall at 7.15am. There was also the Monday and Thursday Forncett to Yarmouth excursion, which worked out empty stock from Norwich at 7.55am, and left Forncett at 8.40am, a Saturdays-only market train from Norwich at 5.22pm, and the empty stock off the last Saturdays-only up train which returned from Harleston at 10.55pm. Goods services were the 5.40am Norwich to Beccles,

calling at all stations, the 8.25am Norwich to Harleston, the 4.1pm Bungay to Beccles, and the 4.40pm from Wymondham (5.20pm Saturdays-only). Victoria finally closed to passengers from 22 May 1916, and all trains went to Thorpe after that.

The Summer 1922 timetable showed six trains each way on weekdays, the journey time being around 50 minutes, which was a little quicker. A Sentinel steam railcar was tried out on the line for about a year in 1933, as well as on a number of other local services. The number of trains was reduced to five down and six up in 1942, although it had been restored to six each way by 1951, a year before the line closed. In the Winter 1951-2 timetable, the 6.55 and 10.54am, and 5.3pm from Norwich were through trains to Beccles, while the 8.35am, and 1.55 and 8.15pm started from Tivetshall. In the other direction, the 7am, and 12.35 and 6.55pm from Beccles called at all stations to Tivetshall, while the 9am, 3.25 and 8.2pm continued through to Norwich. Goods traffic was handled from each end of the line by the 10am Beccles to Harleston all-stations, returning at 4.5pm, and the 8am Wensum Junction to Harleston, returning at 1.20pm.

The Waveney Valley line was relatively lightly constructed, and the weakness of the bridge over the river at Beccles was often cited as the reason that larger locomotives could not be used. Regular motive power tended to be 'F4' 2-4-2 tanks for the

TIVETSHALL AND BECCLES — WEEKDAYS

				K	K							K	K
DOWN				8.4 am from Wensum Jn.			**UP**						To Trowse
Mileage					SX		Mileage				SX		
M	C			am	am		M	C			am		PM
0	0	TIVETSHALL ...... arr	8 56				0	0	BECCLES .... dep	10 30			
		...... dep	9 16	..	..	..	2	50	Geldeston .. .. .. arr	10 40	..	..	..
									dep	10 50			
2	53	Pulham Market .... arr	9 36	..	..	..	4	12	Ellingham .. .. .. arr	10 57	..	..	..
		...... dep	9 46	..	..	..			dep	11 15			
3	55	Pulham St. Mary ...... arr	9 51	..	..	..	5	53	Ditchingham .. .. .. arr	11 22	..	..	..
		...... dep	10 4	..	..	..			dep				
6	22	Harleston .... arr	10 24	..	..	..	6	48	Bungay .. .. .. arr		..	..	..
		...... dep	10 54	..	..	..			dep	.....	.....	12 30	
8	73	Homersfield .... arr	R	..	..	..	10	33	Homersfield .. .. .. arr	..	..	..	..
		...... dep		..	..	..			dep				
12	65	Bungay .... arr	11 49	..	..	..	13	14	Harleston .. .. .. arr	..	..	1 20	..
		...... dep		..	..	..			dep		..	2 0	..
13	63	Ditchingham .... arr		..	..	..	15	61	Pulham St. Mary .. .. arr	..	..	R	..
		...... dep		..	11 45	..			dep				
15	24	Ellingham .... arr		..	R	..	16	63	Pulham Market .. .. arr	..	..	2 35	..
		...... dep		..		..			dep			2 55	
16	66	Geldeston .... arr		..	R	..	19	36	TIVETSHALL .. .. arr	..	..	3 15	..
		...... dep	..	..	..								
19	36	BECCLES .... arr	..	..	12 10	..			dep	.....	.....	3 17	..

Above:
11 June-16 September 1956 timetable. *Author's collection*

passenger services, with 'J15' 0-6-0s on goods trains. Yarmouth excursions would often be double-headed, since they loaded very heavily, and had been known to stall with a single locomotive. A pair of 'J15s', or a 'J15' and an 'E4' were likely combinations. It is certainly known that a 'Claud Hamilton' worked over the line, an occasion being the 12.35pm Beccles to Tivetshall and 1.55pm return one day in June 1951. In April 1950 a Class B12 4-6-0 ran from Tivetshall to Bungay and back to work a goods train loaded with oak trees felled from a local park and being sent to the North of England.

The Waveney Valley passenger service was one of the earlier postwar casualties, although British Railways continued to promote travel until the last. In the summer of 1952 cheap excursions were advertised on Sundays to Great Yarmouth; on 29 June passengers could go from Tivetshall at 11am for 4s 6d return, Pulham Market 4s 3d, Pulham St Mary 4s 0d, Harleston 3s 9d and Homersfield 3s 6d, reaching South Town at 12.25pm and leaving there at 8.15pm. Day returns were available any day; for example, Harleston to Yarmouth was 4s 9d, or Lowestoft 4s 1d. However, the last regular passenger trains ran on Saturday, 3 January 1953 amid much controversy and a determination not to let the line pass without notice. There were intermittent snowstorms during the evening, but platforms at the various stations were crowded with residents and visitors. At Harleston, representatives of the parish council, chamber of trade, Divisional Police and the Harleston Bench of Magistrates, together with many other local organisations, were present. Residents living near the station had prepared a mock coffin with a plate inscribed 'Waveney Valley Line, Aged 97 Years, Taken Away 3rd January 1953'. A cortège bore the coffin and its 'corpse' — Mr J. Ashworth, who frequently lifted the lid to see what was going on — from the Railway Tavern to the station, the pallbearers wearing traditional top hats and followed by a crowd of weeping mourners. The train from Beccles arrived at 7.30pm carrying many travellers in fancy dress and early Victorian costume, and the coffin was carried into the guard's van where a hymn was sung and photographs taken. The coffin was transferred to the last down train at Tivetshall and returned to Harleston at 8.35pm, where all concerned retired to the Railway Tavern.

Harleston stationmaster Mr W. G. Elsey, there since March 1947, took over responsibility for the Pulhams and Homersfield after passenger closure. The other staff on duty that evening were Mr F. Coleman, clerk, Mr George Frost, signalman and Mr E. Francis, porter. The final bags of mail were loaded on to the up train — they had to be taken by road to Diss from Harleston thereafter. Meanwhile, the last down train had continued along the line relatively peacefully until reaching Bungay, where the whole town

seemed to have turned out. Those present included the Town Reeve, Mr D. L. Hewitt and his wife, Mr W. H. Sutton, chairman of Bungay Urban District Council, and members of the council and other civic leaders. The Beccles Crazy Gang had arrived by bus in assorted fancy dress, together with a model engine which was drawn through the streets until the train arrived. The Mayor and Mayoress of Beccles, Alderman and Mrs A. E. Pye, had travelled to Bungay to make the final trip. The last train was somewhat delayed getting back to Beccles because of the large number of detonators on the line, and the frequent pulling of the communication cord, and it did not arrive until nearly 10pm, although due at 9.9pm. At Beccles the station approach had been floodlit, and music was played over loudspeakers while the train was awaited. When it arrived a 'guard of honour' was provided for the model engine, which was paraded around the streets before being returned to the station where it was 'buried' with full rites. In spite of the sadness of the occasion it passed as more of a celebration than mourning, and the two pubs at the station had even been granted extensions so that passengers off the final trains were able to refresh themselves after their historic journey.

Goods services continued for some time. Costs were cut by converting the line to light railway status, this being the first such move since Nationalisation in 1948. The orders were first published in January 1954, and came into force on 15 November 1954. It meant that most level crossings no longer needed gates and could be protected only by cattle guards, and that the signalling could be simplified. A 25mph speed limit was imposed. As before, the branch was served from each end, the 1956 timetable showing the 8.4am from Wensum Junction leaving Tivetshall at 9.16am and calling at all stations (Homersfield as required) to Bungay, arriving there at 11.49am, and leaving again at 12.30pm. This train ran Mondays to Saturdays; the 10.30am Beccles to Ditchingham all-stations did not run on Saturdays. The line was, in theory, still open throughout at the time. As was often the case, closure came in stages, with Homersfield the first to go on 1 February 1960. Geldeston and Ellingham closed for public traffic on 13 July 1964, but Ditchingham hung on until 19 April 1965, which finished the section from Beccles. The Pulhams closed together on 13 July 1964, followed by Bungay on 3 August; Clay's printers bought much of the station site to extend its works. Finally, Harleston closed on 18 April 1966, Tivetshall losing its goods service at the same time, thus ending train services along the Waveney Valley. It is still possible to follow a great deal of the line; by the end of the 20th century, the A143 had taken over the section between Ditchingham and Redenhall, and was poised to extend even further eastwards towards Ellingham. Many of the station buildings exist and are visible, but are in private hands.

Round the World

FOR much of its recorded history, Norfolk was one of the most densely populated and prosperous parts of England, good agricultural land and sheep forming the basis of much of its wealth. By the time the railway era arrived, this prosperity had moved elsewhere, and the county's lack of mineral resources meant that it had become one of the more remote areas. Railways arrived early in Norwich, and had soon spread to connect it with Lowestoft and Yarmouth, Ipswich and Cambridge. The other towns, villages and ports realised that they needed connection to this lifeline, while London needed the produce from the countryside. The newly emerging fashion for holidays also prompted development of lines to the coast.

Norwich to London trains were running by mid-1845, while Yarmouth had been connected to its county town a year earlier. Routes to the north were much slower in coming, with Wells-on-

Sea presenting a complex situation; it was the target for a number of schemes, including direct lines from Norwich. The Norfolk Railway had opened its line between Wymondham and East Dereham as early as 7 December 1846 for goods, and 15 February 1847 for passengers. An extension to Wells and Blakeney was soon sanctioned, but was completed only as far as Fakenham, which opened in March 1849. The line onwards was completed by the Wells & Fakenham Railway, and opened on 1 December 1857. A start was finally made by the East Norfolk Railway on the line from Whitlingham to North Walsham as late as 1865, but there were many problems and construction was slow. An extension to Cromer was projected, and North Walsham was reached in 1874 and — at long last — Cromer in 1877.

This left a considerable tract of land between the two lines without rail communication, and there were several towns and

Below:
**Coltishall station from the road bridge on 7 September 1958, looking towards Aylsham.
The sidings still look busy, although passenger traffic has been gone for nearly six years.** *SLS Collection*

villages such as Aylsham and Reepham which were left out in the cold. Plans were soon afoot to fill the void. Long before the Cromer line came to fruition the East Norfolk Railway proposed to build extensions westwards. With its line from Whitlingham to North Walsham already authorised, it sought powers in the 1864-5 session to build a branch westwards from its main line just south of Wroxham, quickly crossing the River Bure twice and then going via Horstead to Aylsham, where the station site was not as eventually built. Nothing came of this proposal, but it deposited plans again in 1865-6, for a line between Salhouse and Aylsham. This would not have crossed the River Bure, and would have terminated in Aylsham also on a different site from that eventually used, if a little nearer the town centre. The engineer for both of these projects was Robert Sinclair, but this scheme again came to nothing.

The company came back yet again in the 1875-6 session, when there was far more progress to show on its original railway to Cromer. This time the proposal was for a branch from Wroxham to Aylsham, on an alignment more or less as built, but also with proposals for a spur to a quay by the River Bure at Wroxham. This would have faced the opposite direction to the Aylsham line, and have been on the east side of the main line, but was not built. The Aylsham Extension Railway was duly authorised, but still with the station at Aylsham in a relatively central location from which it would have been almost impossible to extend. Accordingly, a further Act was sought for the 1879 session which took the line westwards via Cawston, Reepham and Foulsham to a triangular junction with the Dereham and Wells line immediately north of Broom Green. In order to achieve this it branched from the authorised line at a point about 1½ miles to the east of Aylsham, necessitating a new station site there.

Construction had at last been put in hand, and on Tuesday, 8 July 1879 the first section of the new line — 5½ miles in length — opened from Wroxham, with stations at Coltishall and Buxton, while at the same time some very positive comments were being made by the Norwich Mercury about the Great Eastern's arrangements for extra holiday trains, and in particular its district superintendent, Mr T. Stevenson. The section onwards to Aylsham opened on 1 January 1880, adding 3¼ miles. There were problems with the onward extension, with Robert J. Woods-Purdy Esq, of Woodgate House, Aylsham, claiming against the company for damage done to his estate by the railway going through it. The jury decided that the value of the land taken, including timber and crops, was £730, and that damage caused by severance was £900. Purdy had claimed £2,008 16s, so the railway escaped the full burden. The extension to Cawston, 13 miles 16 chains from Wroxham, opened on 1 September 1880, and the Norwich Mercury reported that this

piece of line had been built rapidly, a start having been made on 13 March of that year. Mr J. E. Wilson was the East Norfolk's engineer, and the contractor, Mr J. Waddell of Edinburgh. Mr Jones was the resident engineer, and the signalling contractors were Mackenzie & Holland. From Aylsham the line passed under the turnpike from Norwich in a deep cutting, under a second bridge and then on a considerable embankment not far from the workhouse. The official inspection had been made on Monday 30 August by Maj-Gen Hutchinson of the Board of Trade, who had had one of the heaviest GER engines, at 43 tons, to test the bridges. He made a minute inspection of the points and signals at Aylsham, and then made stops at all the bridges and other structures. The line had been built with a single track, but sufficient land had been taken and fenced for a second. Halfway between Aylsham and Cawston there was a splendid straight piece of line nearly level with the surrounding countryside for more than a mile. Cawston station was exactly similar in design to those at Coltishall, Buxton and Aylsham, with spacious platforms and ample public accommodation for both passengers and goods. The inspection took two hours, after which an elegant lunch was laid on by Mr Stapleton of the Black Boys, Aylsham, in the station waiting room at Cawston. The special train then returned to Aylsham at 40mph. Maj-Gen Hutchinson duly gave the company his certificate allowing the line to open.

The new lines were rapidly filling in the railway map of Norfolk, and concerns were beginning to be expressed about their continued construction. In June 1880, when the Aylsham extension had been open for six months, an article in the Norwich Mercury pointed out that Norfolk had an area of some 2,000 square miles, or 1,300,000 acres. The population in 1871 was 438,656, and it had a circumference of 180 miles, of which 90 miles were seaboard. Of its 13 towns, Fakenham was the smallest, and if their populations were deducted the rural total was 263,576. At the time, 330 miles of railway were open, the Great Eastern having most of them. When the lines to Broom Green and Stoke Ferry, and from Brundall to Yarmouth and Stalham to North Walsham were completed, a further 50 miles would be added, with a total of £4 million capital expended. Only 2,000 people would be left more than five miles from a railway station. The writer argued that no more lines were needed, and in particular that the Lynn & Fakenham should not go ahead.

The East Norfolk pressed ahead with its line, and it opened to Reepham on 2 May 1881, and County School on 1 May 1882, finally linking the two routes to the coast, and giving Aylsham and Reepham, the two towns served, a choice of connections to Norwich and the outside world. For obvious reasons, it was always known to local railwaymen as the 'Round the World' line. Unfortunately for the company, the Eastern & Midlands had

Below:
Coltishall station. *Crown Copyright*

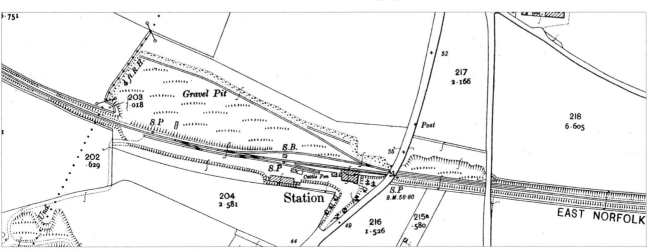

opened through Aylsham within a year, and so a town whose 1891 population was only 2,533 had two stations, neither of them well placed for travel to Norwich or London. Reepham (population 447) was similarly situated, although Whitwell & Reepham was at least convenient for Norwich City.

Wroxham station, being on the main Cromer line, had two side platforms with no terminal provision for Aylsham trains: they ran to and from Norwich. The main line had bridged the River Bure just to the south of the station, and then recommenced its climb northwards. The lines diverged a short distance to the north of the station, with the Aylsham route, which had an overall speed limit of 50mph, initially rising towards a level crossing at Belaugh Green, but then curving westwards to pass north of Coltishall, and pick up the valley of the Bure again. This necessitated a number of cuttings, some quite deep, to cut through the higher ground, and several roads crossed the line on bridges. At 2 miles 66 chains Coltishall station was on the west side of the bridge carrying the North Walsham road over the line, and a little to the north of the village centre. There were a number of gravel pits in the area, which the line was able to serve, and also, at one time, glasshouses near the station. The approach road was on the south side of the line, as were the main buildings and goods yard. There was a single platform, with a loading dock and cattle pen behind at the west end, with further storage sheds on the south side of the yard. On the north side, a long siding in the facing direction for up (to Norwich) trains diverged well beyond the platform, and ran behind the signalbox, extending under both road bridges, which had been built for double track. Opposite the platform another long siding diverged on the north side, running back to serve the gravel pit there.

The station buildings were characteristic of the line. The station-master's house was a two-storey structure of white brick, with red relief, gable-ended slate roof with ornate bargeboards, the roof ridge being at right-angles to the platform. A feature of the design was the raised portion of roof partway along the long side at the end of the building, below which was a narrow window, and on the ground floor a small porch; this was the entrance for the family,

through a small yard. Adjoining this house was a single-storey office section, parallel to the platform, incorporating the booking office and other facilities. Beyond this again were further assorted buildings, including oil stores, toilets and so on. Some of the stations were provided with awnings, and it appears from marks on the buildings that Coltishall was one of them. In spite of having a signalbox, it was not a block post.

After leaving Coltishall the line dropped down to follow the river closely. In later years the RAF airfield was near to the line on the north side, about a mile from the station, and provided traffic during World War 2. Finally coming very close to the River Bure, the railway crossed it near Buxton Mill, then passed under the road between Buxton and Lamas, reaching the station at 5 miles 46 chains from Wroxham. This was very similar in many ways to Coltishall — single platform, similar buildings and track layout except that there was no long siding and headshunt. The signalbox was a block post, and although two passenger trains could not pass here, goods and passenger trains were scheduled to do so.

Aylsham (Aylsham South from 27 September 1948) was 8 miles 68 chains from Wroxham, about three miles on from Buxton, and although the station started out to the south of the town, the latter grew towards it. This was easily the most important intermediate place on the line, and had facilities to match this status. There were two platforms, with the goods yard, station buildings and all facilities on the north side of the line. The platforms were connected by a barrow crossing at the west end, and there was a shelter on the down platform, together with oil lamps and well-tended gardens. By the crossing on the up side was a water tank on a tall brick base. The station buildings were of the same style as elsewhere, although provision was more generous, and there was a long awning supported by both the buildings and stanchions. There was what might have been termed a bay platform facing Wroxham which functioned as a loading dock, and beyond this was the goods shed and office, with through road. The shed had a trailing connection with the up line. At the east end another trailing connection gave access to long sidings running around the north side of the

Above:
**Buxton Lamas, showing the station buildings in the characteristic style for the line; was there ever a canopy here?
A Class 31 diesel heads for Norwich with a freight train.** *Stations UK*

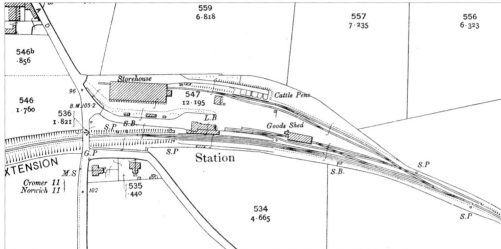

Above:
Aylsham South in about 1950, looking eastwards from the Norwich Road bridge. A train for County School stands in the platform. This station and its buildings have been completely replaced by those of the 15in gauge Bure Valley Railway. *Stations UK*

Above:
Cawston station, 10 years after closure to passengers, and looking towards Reepham.
The station remains more or less intact; the goods yard is behind the platform. *Stations UK*

yard where the cattle pens and a very large storehouse were located. At one time there were signalboxes at each end of the layout. The station was located exactly halfway between Norwich and Cromer, there being a milestone on the road by the bridge; it was 11 miles to each place. Unfortunately it was 17½ miles by rail to Norwich via Wroxham, and 42 via Dereham, which put it at a great disadvantage. Nevertheless, the station generated considerable goods traffic, which in 1938 amounted to 2,329 tons of vegetables, 2,131 tons of grain and 103 tons of livestock, worth £3,338 to the railway

in total. It could handle all classes of traffic and had a 1½-ton crane. At that time, R. Coller & Son were corn and coal merchants at the station, as were Cross & Co, which also dealt in animal feeds, and there were other firms based at Aylsham Town station on the M&GN system. Despite the generous rail provision, the town's population had risen only to 2,646 at the 1931 census.

Cawston station was about 4½ miles onward from Aylsham, a much smaller affair with a single platform on the south side of the line, goods loop opposite and a fair-sized goods yard. It was

Right:
An elevated view of Reepham, looking towards County School, in about 1925. The large shed to the left of the view was rail served, and there was considerable goods traffic there. The station is now on the Marriotts Way, and is open as a café and shop. *Stations UK*

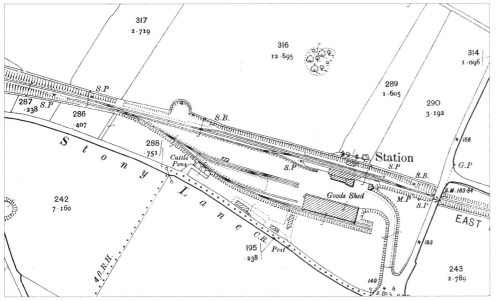

approached over a level crossing, the village being to the south, and the general layout and style were much the same as elsewhere. The line crossed under the Norwich to Holt road about a mile short of the station, and entered a deep cutting at the west end of the station to pass under the Reepham road. Few & Son were grain merchants at the station in the 1930s, and Barclay, Pallett & Co Ltd were corn and coal merchants there. The line to Reepham had some embankments necessitated by the need to cross some small streams, and the station was just over two miles away. The railway crossed under the road between North Elmham and Aylsham, the station — Reepham (Norfolk) from November 1927 — being on the west side of this. Reepham was a small but busy town to the south of the line, and had fairly extensive rail facilities. It was the only other intermediate stop where passenger trains could pass, and

so had two platforms, and originally two signalboxes. There was a shelter on the up platform, which was connected to the other by a barrow crossing at the east end. The buildings took the usual form and were on the down side, and a large awning similar to that at Aylsham was provided. There was a loading dock behind the west end of the down platform, and a large goods yard with five sidings, two running through the large goods shed on the south side. There were also cattle pens some way west of the shed, and these had their own road access from Stony Lane. The main outward traffic was in livestock, and in 1938 177 tons were forwarded. Businesses based at the station included R. Coller & Sons, coal merchants, and E. Stimpson & Son, coal, corn, cake and fertilizer merchants, who were also agents for ICI fertilizers. The station could handle all classes of traffic, and had a 1½-ton crane.

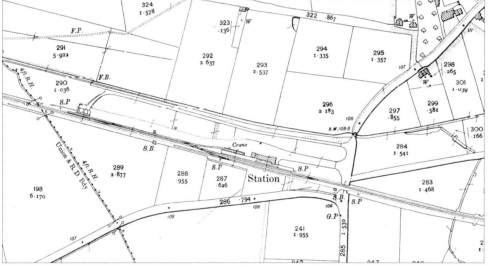

The line undulated somewhat beyond Reepham, and about three miles west of the station, near the hamlet of Themelthorpe, it passed under the M&GN route between Melton Constable and Norwich City; there was no connection between the two. Foulsham, another important village, was about 4½ miles from Reepham and had the usual East Norfolk Extension station and facilities. The railway here ran to the south of the village, where the road to Bintree and Bawdeswell crossed the line. The platform and most facilities were on the north side, with only the goods loop and a headshunt opposite, although in later years a new signalbox to replace the earlier two was erected opposite the platform. There was the usual loading dock at the back of the platform, also with a crane, and the cattle pens were far away at the west end of the yard. The station loaded large quantities of vegetables, such as the 1,634 tons in 1938. Continuing west from Foulsham there were few earthworks of note, except that the line crossed the River Wensum about three miles onwards, shortly before reaching the junction with the Wells to Dereham line at Broom Green, where the curve was limited to 35mph. Trains then headed south on a falling gradient for about another mile before reaching County School

station. The single lines from Wroxham and Wells ran parallel from Broom Green, although in 1882 the Great Eastern had installed a signalbox and junction, abolished at an early stage. The earthworks had been made so that a triangular junction could be built there, which would have enabled trains to run from Aylsham to Fakenham without reversal, but it seems unlikely that track was ever laid.

County School, six miles north of Dereham, had three platform faces, the up being an island, with trains from Wroxham able to terminate at the easternmost or outer face. Before about 1913 most did so, but after that trains ran through to or from Dereham along the single-line section via North Elmham. County School station was built to serve the nearby Norfolk County School, which opened in 1874, closed in 1895 and reopened in 1901 as the Watts Naval Training School for Dr Barnardo's boys. The station had modest brick buildings, with a generous awning on the down side, and a waiting room, again with very generous awnings, on the up. As was often the case, it started with two signalboxes, one at the level crossing to the south of the station and the other to the north of the platforms, on the west side of the line. Staffing at the station in

Above:
**County School in August 1955, with Class D16/3 No 62610 heading a train for Dereham. The Wroxham
platform is the other face of the one from which the train is leaving. The signalbox can just be seen beyond the down
platform, and the Wroxham and Wells single lines ran parallel from there to Broom Green, where they diverged.**
W. A. Camwell/SLS Collection

later years consisted of two signalmen and two leading porters, the latter collecting tickets and collecting or delivering the train staff to or from drivers. The signalbox was situated at the north end of the layout so that all points came within the 350-yard limit for manual operation. Facilities were very limited, and the station could handle only passengers and parcels, and ordinary goods.

Services on the line, which was operated on the staff-and-ticket system, were limited throughout its life. In summer 1913, there were weekday trains at 7.42am, and 2.9, 7.12 (7.16 from 11 July to 13 September) and 9.35pm, calling at all stations and taking 50-60 minutes for the journey. There were others at 11.40am and 4.21pm from Norwich Thorpe, the latter terminating at Foulsham, while the 7.12pm finished at Reepham. Goods services operated in the down direction at 6.45am from Thorpe to County School, while the 7.42am from Wroxham and 11.40am from Norwich could work Westinghouse-piped vans of goods from London and the last down could collect up to two piped cattle vans off the 9.10pm from Norwich. There was also a 5.32pm Foulsham to Dereham train, which was the return working of the 5.5pm from Dereham.

In the other direction, the first train of the day was the 7.20am from Foulsham to Wroxham, due in at 8.11am, and was followed by the 9.25 and 11.55am, and 2.20pm trains, the first and last of these going to Norwich. Goods traffic was covered by the 12.5pm from Wymondham (1pm on Saturdays) which called at all stations except Whitlingham Junction to Norwich Thorpe, where it finally arrived at 9.25pm. There was then the 5.34pm from Foulsham to Wroxham, connecting with the 5.26pm arrival from Dereham, and the 8pm Reepham to Wroxham completed the day's services.

The summer 1937 times reflected the changed destination at the western end, and nothing terminated at County School, the service being between Norwich Thorpe and Dereham. There were ordinary passenger trains from Norwich at 6.25 and 9.45am, and 2.17, 4.49 and 8.34pm (9.7pm Saturdays only), with steam railcars additionally at 9.12am to Aylsham, and 11.46am and 6.17pm to Dereham. In the other direction, services left Dereham at 6.55, 8.37 and 11.50am, and 4.50 and 7.10pm; the steam railcar formed the 10.30am back from Aylsham, plus a Thursdays-excepted 2.12pm from Dereham. There was a conditional path on Saturdays only for

Above:
County School in 1937 looking towards Dereham from the up platform, with a train clearly due. This station is now open to the public on some weekends in summer, under the auspices of the Mid-Norfolk Railway. It is hoped to relay the track missing between here and Dereham, and to restore train services to County School in the future. *Stations UK*

Left:
County School station. *Crown Copyright*

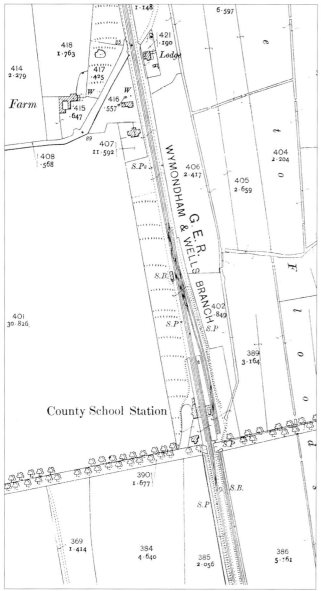

horseboxes from Cawston to Norwich at 8.5am, which had worked out if needed from Norwich at 6.5am, reaching Cawston at 6.48am. The up goods working was the 8am from Norwich via Wymondham, which left Dereham at 2.25pm and reached Wroxham at 6.35pm. On Wednesdays there was provision for an engine to be attached to this as far as Foulsham, where it would be detached and run ahead to Reepham to haul a special cattle train to Dereham in connection with the market, if required. On Sundays there was a train from Dereham at 9.22am which called at all stations to Wroxham, then Norwich Thorpe, and which then continued to Yarmouth Vauxhall. The return left there at 7.55pm and reached Dereham at 9.58pm. From Dereham it was quicker to get the 9.55am all-stations to Wymondham, which then ran direct to Yarmouth via the Wensum curve, thus avoiding the need for reversal at Norwich. There was, however, no return through working in the evening via this route. Dr Ian Allen related how the 'Round the World' line could be travelled at leisure many times on one ticket. One booked a 3s 6d day return from Norwich to Foulsham, and caught a train out via County School. On arrival at Norwich, one stayed on the train, not passing through a barrier, and another 'E4' backed on, taking the train back via Wroxham. Dr Allen was restricted by having to get to and from his afternoon surgery at Framlingham, but once met a man who claimed to be on his third return trip that day!

Wartime meant the inevitable cuts, and the May 1942 timetable showed an unbalanced service of four trains from Norwich to Dereham, and only three the other way. This was little changed in 1946, and there were concerns about the future of the line. The inevitable happened, and the axe fell on and from Monday,

15 September 1952, the start of the winter timetable. The last train was hauled by 'D16/3' No 62593, the crew being driver Herbert Bishop, fireman Cyril Baker and guard Eric Baines, all Dereham men. Goods traffic continued to be handled at all stations, but the line was severed between Reepham and Foulsham, and worked from each end. The Reepham line was converted to a light railway, and the Summer 1956 timetable showed a Class K goods from Wensum Junction sidings on weekdays at 9.37am, calling at Coltishall and then all stations to Reepham, arriving at 12.31pm. It then returned to Wroxham, calling at all stations, and then forming the Class H to Wensum Junction. Foulsham continued to be served until 1964, the winter timetable showing a train at 12 noon from Dereham on Mondays and Thursdays until 1 October, and Wednesdays and Saturdays from 7 October. However, these trains were withdrawn from 2 November 1964, which effectively meant the closure of the branch.

It had been a different matter on the Reepham section. The closure of the Midland & Great Northern system to passengers on the last day of February 1959 is well documented, and it is difficult to avoid the conclusion that not all the consequences had been thought through. Freight traffic continued to be worthwhile from stations on the Norwich City line, but the route west of Melton Constable had been closed completely. It thus became necessary to route traffic from Norwich City to Thorpe, a distance of about a mile as the crow flies, via Melton Constable and Sheringham, a total distance of about 60 miles. This was clearly a considerable waste of resources, and the short-term solution adopted was to build a connection between the East Norfolk Extension Railway and the M&GN lines at Themelthorpe. This necessitated re-laying the line from Reepham, and the provision of key token working between Aylsham and Whitwell, with an intermediate instrument and ground frames at Reepham, which had been converted to operation by hand-points. The new line was brought into use in September 1960, and the M&GN between the curve and Melton Constable was closed completely. The rail distance from Norwich Thorpe to City had been reduced to a mere 30 miles.

There was still coal traffic at Norwich, and considerable business in precast concrete sections form the factory at Lenwade. However, Norwich City and Drayton closed on 3 February 1969, and the line was cut back to Lenwade, serving the factory there. Facilities were withdrawn from Buxton and Coltishall on 19 April 1965 (although a private siding remained at the latter), from Cawston on 31 October 1966 and from Aylsham on 1 March 1977. Reepham hung on until 6 June 1981, but the line remained open to Lenwade until the middle of the decade. After the track was lifted much of it became a long-distance footpath, and can be walked, ridden or cycled between Norwich, Themelthorpe and Aylsham. The 15in gauge Bure Valley Railway took over the formation between Wroxham and Aylsham, when the station at the latter was demolished and replaced with new buildings and facilities. A footpath was constructed alongside the line, and this has now also been opened to cyclists. This section is thus one of the very few in this book over which it is still possible to travel by train, albeit in a rather different form from that envisaged by its original promoters.

AYLSHAM (Norfolk)
Map Sq. 19.
Pop. 2,646. Clos. day Wed.
SOUTH STATION.
From Liverpool Street via Norwich and Wroxham 132¼ miles.
1st cl.—Single 44/5. Mth. Ret. 53/8.
3rd cl.—Single 26/9. Mth. Ret. 35/9.

Liv. St.	Aylsh.	Aylsh.	Liv. St.
a.m.		a.m.	
4 25	10 1	7 26r	11 32
5 50*	12 44	9 17r	1 38
10 25r	2 55	p.m.	
p.m.		12 44r	5 8
1 0r	6 23	2 56r	7 6
3 40r	7 40	7 40*	2 30
5 8r	9 39	—	—
10 25e	6 51	—	—
—	—	—	—
Sunday Trains.			
p.m.			
11 25	6 51	—	—

* Via Wymondham.
e Not Sat. s Sat. only.
r Refresh. Car.

Another Route
NORTH STATION.
From King's Cross via Peterborough and South Lynn 157 miles.
From Liverpool Street via King's Lynn and South Lynn 142¼ miles.
Same fares.

King's X	Aylsh.	Aylsh.	King's X
a.m.		a.m.	
4 10	9 57	8 5r	1 15
8 50r	1 52	9 58r	2§40
10 15r	4 9	11 16m	4 45
p.m.		11 16e	5§ 0
1 30r	6 46	11 16s	5§ 3
2*25r	7 37	11 16qr	5 23
—	—	p.m.	
—	—	1 53r	7 7
—	—	7 33	2§30
—	—	—	—
—	—	—	—

No Sunday Trains.

* Departs Liv. St., not King's X.
§ Arrives Liv. St., not King's X.
e Not Sat.
m Mon., Fri. & Sat.
q Tues., Wed. & Thur.
r Refresh. Car.
s Sat only.

Bus facilities. From Norwich, Surrey Street, approx. hourly Weekdays, two-hourly Sunday, 49 min. journey.

Above:
ABC Railway Guide, December 1949. *Author's collection*

Table 57 NORWICH (Thorpe), WROXHAM, AYLSHAM (South), COUNTY SCHOOL, and DEREHAM

Miles	Week Days only		p.m	a.m	a.m	p.m	p.m E	p.m S	p.m
	3 London (L. St.) 4	dep	10Z30	4 30	1030	1 30	3 30	3 30	5 30
—	Norwich (Thorpe)	dep	6a 5	9 18	1 35	5 35	6 55	6 55	8 [illegible]
1¾	Whitlingham A		6 10	9 23	1 40	..	7 0	7 0	..
6	Salhouse		6 20	9 33	1 50	5 47	7 10	7 10	..
8¾	Wroxham	arr	6 26	9 40	1 57	5 52	7 15	7 15	8 21
		dep	6 29	9 45	2 33	5 53	7 20	7 25	8 30
11¼	Coltishall		6 36	9 51	2 40	6 0	7 26	7 31	8 37
14¼	Buxton Lamas		6 42	9 57	2 46	6 6	7 32	7 37	8 4[illegible]
17¼	Aylsham (South)		6 51	10 6	2 55	6 16	7 41	7 46	8 52
22	Cawston		7 0	1015	3 4	6 25	7 50	7 55	9 1
24	Reepham (Norfolk)		7 7	1020	3 9	6 36	7 55	8 0	9 6
28¾	Foulsham		7 16	1029	3 18	6 45	8 4	8 9	9 15
32½	County School	arr	7 23	1036	3 25	6 52	8 11	8 16	9 22
		dep	7 24	1037	3 26	6 53	8 12	8 17	9 23
34	North Elmham		7 30	1047	3 31	6 58	8 18	8 23	9 29
38½	Dereham	arr	7 38	1055	3 39	7 6	8 27	8 32	9 37
163½	54 London (L St.)	arr	12 37	3Y 0	7§55	2a28	..	..	..

Miles	Week Days only		a.m	a.m	a.m S	p.m S	a.m E	a.m	p.m
	54 London (L. St.)	dep	..	..	5 50	..	5 50	9‖30	12[30
—	Dereham	dep	6 36	8 25	1155	..	12 0	2p10	6 5
4½	North Elmham		6 45	8 33	12 3	..	12 8	2 18	6 14
6	County School	arr	6 50	8 37	12 8	..	1213	2 23	6 20
		dep	6 50	8 41	12 8	..	1213	2 23	6 20
9¾	Foulsham		6 58	8 49	1216	..	1221	2 31	6 28
14¼	Reepham (Norfolk)		7 9	8 57	1224	..	1229	2 39	6 38
16¼	Cawston		7 15	9 2	1229	..	1234	2 44	6 43
21	Aylsham (South)		7 26	9 12	1239	..	1244	2 56	6 54
24¼	Buxton Lamas		7 34	9 20	1247	..	1252	3 4	7 4
27	Coltishall		7 40	9 26	1253	..	1258	3 10	7 10
29¾	Wroxham	arr	7 47	9 31	1258	..	1 3	3 15	7 15
		dep	8 0	9 32	1 0	1 16	1 16	3 18	7 23
32½	Salhouse		8 7	9 39	..	1 23	1 23	3 25	7 30
36¼	Whitlingham A		8 16	9S48	..	1 32	1 32	3 34	7 39
38¾	Norwich (Thorpe)	arr	8 21	9‖51	1 19	1 37	1 37	3 40	7 44
153¾	3 London (L. St.)	arr	11 23	1 29	..	4 40	4 34	6 39	2a28

A Station for Thorpe St. Andrew
a a.m.
E Except Saturdays
[Via Norwich (Thorpe). Dep. 1 30 p.m. on Saturdays
‖ Via Norwich (Thorpe)
p p.m.
S or S Saturdays only
‖ 2 minutes later on Saturdays
Y Saturdays only. Via Norwich (Thorpe)
Z Dep. 11 25 p.m. on Sundays
§ Via Norwich (Thorpe). Arr. 8 6 p.m. on Saturdays

For OTHER TRAINS between Norwich and Whitlingham, Tables 55 and 58—Norwich and Wroxham, Table 55—Norwich and County School, Table 54—County School and Dereham, Table 54.

Above:
Winter 1951-2 timetable. *Author's collection*

WEEKDAYS — SWAFFHAM AND WATTON, WELLS-NEXT-THE-SEA, FOULSHAM AND KING'S LYNN TO NORWICH

TO NORWICH

	0-16	8-04	8-04	8-04	8-04	8-04		0-04	8-04	8-04	8-00	8-00	8-00	5-16§	8-16	8-16	7*16	0-04
	LE							LE										LE
(Mileage M C / M C / M C)	SO	SO	TThS	TThO	MWF						MThO	WSX	WSO		SX	SX	SX	SX
WELLS-NEXT-THE-SEA ... dep															13 30	13 30		
Walsingham ... arr															13 47	14 20		
FAKENHAM EAST arr															14 02	14 20		
... dep															16 01	15 15		
Ryburgh															R	R		
Foulsham dep										13 18		13 45						
County School arr															16X20			
... dep															16 131	15 55		
North Elmham arr										13 54		14 24			16 41			
... dep										14 00	14 15	14 38			17 21	16 03		
KING'S LYNN dep		6 15	8 15	8 15	8 15	9 21			12 28	12 56								18∥52
King's Lynn Jn.		6 17	8 17	8 17	8 17	9 23			12 30	12 58								18 54
Middleton Towers arr						9 33			12 40	13 08								19∥01
... dep								9∥39	12 55									
East Winch arr		6 31	8 31	8 31	8 31			9∥44	13 05									
... dep		7X24	9 49	9 49	9 49													
Narboro' & Pentney arr		R	R	R	R													
... dep																		
SWAFFHAM arr		8 04	10 21	10 21	10 21													
... dep		9 52	11 03	11X12	12 10													
Holme Hale ...						12 51												
Watton ... arr						13 12												
Dunham ... arr		R	R	R														
... dep																		
DEREHAM arr		10 34	11 56	12 05					14 16	14 48	15 11			17 37	16 31		18 15
... dep	7∥46													15 25			18∥31
Hardingham arr														15 35			18X38
... dep	7 57													15 45			18 56
WYMONDHAM arr														16∥00			19 56
... dep	8 06													16 19			20 19
Trowse	8 18													16∥23			20 24
NORWICH T. arr	8∥22																

K55

WEEKDAYS — NORWICH TO KINGS LYNN, FOULSHAM AND WELL-NEXT-THE-SEA, WATTON AND SWAFFHAM

FROM NORWICH

	7*15	0-04	8-16	8-16		8-04	8-04	8-15	8-16	8-16	8-16	8-04	8-04	8-04	8-04	8-04	8-04	8-04
		LE																
(Mileage)			SX	SX			SO		MThO	WSO	WSX	SX	SO	TThS	TThO	MWF	SX	SX
NORWICH T. dep	4 45								9 13									
Trowse	4 51								9 19									
WYMONDHAM arr	5 12								9 44									
dep	5 57								10 25									
Hardingham dep	6 13								11 14									
DEREHAM arr	6 27								11 38									
Dunham dep			9 05	9 00			11 08			12 00	12 00	12 40			12 58	13 12		
arr															13 29	13 39		
dep															13 40	13 50		
Watton dep																14 00		
Holme Hale																R		
SWAFFHAM arr							11 45								13 55	14 05	14 47	
dep							13 30								15 18	15 18	15 18	
Narboro' & Pentney dep							13∥47									R	R	
East Winch dep							14X02								15 40	15 40	15 40	
arr							14 16								15 54	15 54	15 54	
Middleton Towers dep			9∥15				14 23				13∥50	13∥50			16 37	16 37	16 37	
arr			9∥20								14∥00	14∥00						
King's Lynn Jn. dep								10 25			15 04	15 58					19 21	19 30
KING'S LYNN arr								10 35	14 38		15 14	16 08	16 52	16 52	16 52		19 31	19 41
								10 37	14 40		15 16	16 10	16 54	16 54	16 54		19 33	19 43
North Elmham arr			9 22								12 33	13 13						
dep			9 32	9 31							12 43							
County School dep			9 40	9 37							12X20	12 53						
Foulsham arr											12 49	13 22						
Ryburgh			9 57	R														
FAKENHAM EAST arr			10X09	10 13														
dep			11 20	11 10														
Walsingham arr			11 37	11 50														
WELLS-NEXT-THE-SEA arr			11X51	12 05														

Above:
7 September 1964-13 June 1965 timetable. *Author's collection*

Index